The Social Net
Understanding human behavior in cyberspace

Edited by

Yair Amichai–Hamburger

Department of Psychology,
Bar–Ilan University,
Ramat Gan,
Israel

OXFORD
UNIVERSITY PRESS

OXFORD

UNIVERSITY PRESS

Great Clarendon Street, Oxford OX2 6DP

Oxford University Press is a department of the University of Oxford.
It furthers the University's objective of excellence in research, scholarship,
and education by publishing worldwide in

Oxford New York

Auckland Cape Town Dar es Salaam Hong Kong Karachi
Kuala Lumpur Madrid Melbourne Mexico City Nairobi
New Delhi Shanghai Taipei Toronto

With offices in

Argentina Austria Brazil Chile Czech Republic France Greece
Guatemala Hungary Italy Japan South Korea Poland Portugal
Singapore Switzerland Thailand Turkey Ukraine Vietnam

Oxford is a registered trade mark of Oxford University Press
in the UK and in certain other countries

Published in the United States
by Oxford University Press Inc., New York

A catalogue record for this title is available from the British Library

Library of Congress Cataloging in Publication Data

(Data available)

ISBN-10: 0–19–852875–2 (Hbk)   ISBN-13: 978–0–19–852875–3 (Hbk)
ISBN-10: 0–19–852876–0 (Pbk)   ISBN-13: 978–0–19–852876–0 (Pbk)

10 9 8 7 6 5 4 3 2

Typeset by Newgen Imaging Systems (P) Ltd., Chennai, India
Printed in Great Britain
on acid-free paper by
Biddles Ltd., King's Lynn, Norfolk

Preface

The Internet has become one of the most influential factors in our lives. It was first developed as a decentralized computer network for the U.S. army, moved on to become an academic worldwide information communication system, and eventually came to encompass almost every aspect of our daily existence, and became the host to hundreds of millions of users (Gackenbach and Ellerman, 1998).

Starting from a small network of computers, the net has become a global interactive medium. The speed of its growth was such that a 1998 Information Infrastructure Task Force (IITP) report suggested that in the four years since the Internet was opened up to the general public, it had acquired fifty million users—an achievement that took radio thirty years and television, thirteen (Slater, 2002). It is estimated that nearly 950 million people around the world are net users, and the projected figure for 2006 is 1.28 billion (*www.c-i-a.com*).

The profile of the Internet user is broadening: a growing number of women are using the net (*http://www.nielsen-netrating.com/pr/pr_040318.pdf.*) and the number of senior citizens entering cyberspace is also rising. Greg Bloom, a senior analyst from Nielsen//NetRating argued that the profile of the typical user is becoming increasingly representative of the general population (*http://www.nielsen-netrating.com/pr/pr_031120*).

One of the major turning points in the Internet's growth has been its emergence as a social arena. The contemporary Internet has many social components, such as e-mail chatrooms, instant message newsgroups, forums, and community and support groups. It has been suggested that many people fulfill their most important social needs (those of affiliation, support, and affirmation) over the net (Spoull and Faraj, 1997).

From its earliest beginnings, the Internet has aroused strong reactions, both from its proponents and its critics. The net has been negatively regarded for what was once seen as its promotion of questionable social outcomes. The initial criticism, before the advent of the Internet in its current form, was of computers as communication mediators. The 'filter model' (Sproull and Kiesler, 1986) held that, since communicative cues such as facial expression, voice tone, and the physical bearing of those conversing are filtered out, computer-mediated communications are of limited value as compared with face-to-face interaction. It followed, therefore, that communication through the computer was seen as impersonal and lacking depth and emotion (Daft and Lengel, 1986; Sproull and Kiesler, 1986); and as formal and task-oriented (Hiltz and Turoff, 1993). Siegal *et al.* (1986) reported greater hostility and a greater number of aggressive responses during group processes in computer-mediated communication as compared with face-to-face interactions. Brenner (1997), basing his ideas on an Internet usage survey, claimed that most surfers report that their use of the Internet interferes with their other activities. A percentage of users even reported usage-related problems similar to those found in addictions. It was also suggested that the use of the Internet is likely to result in social isolation (Stoll, 1995; Turkle, 1995). A comprehensive longitudinal study examined the effects of the Internet on social involvement and psychological well-being (Kraut *et al.*, 1998). The authors found that Internet use is related to a decline in communication with family members, a reduction in the size of the social circle, and an increase in instances of depression and loneliness (see also Nie and Erbrng, 2000).

Conversely, other scholars have linked the positive aspects of Internet use with an increase in the user's well-being. Sproull and Faraj (1997) emphasized the social role played by the Internet in the provision of communication channels, which permit people with common interests to find like-minded others and thus build up a network of support, affiliation, and a sense of community. McKenna and Bargh (1998) suggest that the virtual groups found on the Internet may be a source of assistance to individuals from stigmatized groups (e.g. people who hold marginal political views and ideology) who, on the net, are able to socialize and receive support from similar others while retaining their anonymity. Hamburger and Ben–Artzi (2000) argued that the Internet as a protected environment may be utilized to help those with social inhibitions (e.g. introverts and neurotics) to interact with others.

It is clear that the issue is complex. Not only do scholars differ in their views as to whether the use of the Internet as a social tool is a positive or a negative development; but in some cases they have actually reached contrasting results after researching the same issues. The outcome of the study by Kraut *et al.* (1998) that Internet use leads to loneliness and depression has proved to be controversial. For example, Howard *et al.* (2001) showed that the Internet may actually increase connections with family members. Moreover, another study found that the more time people spend on the net, the more likely they are to become involved in group activities offline (Katz *et al.*, 2001). It seems that the Internet is neither entirely good nor entirely bad, and it is only by accepting its complexity that we can start to understand its implications for society. It is the challenge of this book to demonstrate the wealth of the Internet as a multi-faceted medium in the social arena.

Chapter 1 discusses social psychological research on the Internet. The authors Skitka and Sargis suggest that many of the methods used in the experimental laboratory may be transferred for use on the web. They also point out that the Internet provides opportunities for developing new ways to test social psychological hypotheses. They pay special attention to the new area of social psychological research that has developed since the Internet became a forum for social interaction for significant sections of society. The authors review the advantages and disadvantages of web-based research, particularly in relation to sampling and data quality.

In Chapter 2, Amichai–Hamburger examines the interaction between the personality of the surfer and the Internet. He discusses the impact of security and control afforded to users on the net and their influence on the effectiveness of the communication and the consequent ability of the user to express his 'real me'. This, he argues, may be especially relevant to people who are socially inhibited. In addition, the Internet has created an identity laboratory where people may explore different aspects of their identity in ways that they are unable to do offline. The complex consequences of this are discussed in the chapter. The author also deals with the relevance of personality to social problems attributed to the net and how the net may be utilized to improve well-being.

In Chapter 3, Rafaeli, Raban, and Kalman examine the complex interaction between human beings and computers, focusing on the issue of social cognition online. They discuss the ways in which the online environment influences our self-perception, and our perception of other individuals and social groups. They also assess how far the computer itself is seen as a social being, and the technological network as a social environment. The authors discuss two important related issues: the first, the validity of the use of the 'face-to-face' environment as the ultimate benchmark against which online activity is measured; the second, the contrast between the deterministic view of technology as the creator of cognitive states, and the social constructivist view that perceives technology as an enabler and a presenter of opportunities, which leaves the individual and society free to mold it according to their needs and wishes.

Surfers on the net are frequently bombarded with different images and messages attempting to persuade them to adopt certain behaviors or buy certain products. In Chapter 4, Guadagno and Cialdini discuss the foremost methods of persuasion and compliance on the net. They assess their success and the consequent effects on users' behavior. Their chapter examines Internet influence using the 'dual process' models of persuasion (Petty and Cacioppo, 1984). They suggest that surfers are usually persuaded by the central part of the message, and they point out that the impact of social influence on the net is variable, depending on the gender of the recipient. Furthermore, the authors show how traditional influence techniques, such as emphasis on status differences and the 'foot in the door', are effective online.

In Chapter 5, Ben–Ze'ev examines romantic attachments on the net. He suggests that these are paradoxical in nature, since they feature aspects found both in relationships involving close proximity and those where the physical distance is greater. He terms these net relationships 'detached attachment', and suggests that on the net there is a particular phenomenon known as the 'halo effect'. This occurs when an individual experiences a psychological liking for the person with whom he\she is interacting; from here, the user moves on to visualize the person, complete with the desired physical characteristics. The author goes on to analyze two basic evaluative patterns of romantic love—praiseworthiness and attractiveness—which he compares and contrasts in online and offline romantic relationships.

Sproull, Conley, and Moon, in Chapter 6, discuss prosocial behavior on the net. They suggest that the Internet encourages prosocial behavior since opportunities to seek help or come to the aid of another are highly visible, easy to access, and organized. The authors deal with the challenge of discovering how social behavior is learned on the net and understanding the tremendous degree of prosocial activity found over time among core group members. They discuss widely the benefits of this prosocial behavior, focusing on the consequences for the beneficiaries, as well as for the help-givers and for society as whole.

Chapter 7 focuses on the phenomenon of aggression on the net. Malamuth, Linz, and Yao suggest that the unique components of the net prompt displays of violent behavior that are not exhibited in other communication channels. They suggest that Internet aggression may be explained by a general framework suggested by social learning theory (Bandura, 1977), which focuses on the causes of aggressive behaviors—motivational, disinhibitory, and opportunity aspects. Using this model, the special characteristics of the Internet are analyzed, among them perpetual availability, low cost, interactivity, decentralization, lack of regulation, and the ability of surfers to retain their anonymity. The authors demonstrate how these, and other characteristics, encourage aggressive behavior on the net.

In Chapter 8, McKenna and Seidman examine Internet groups, as compared to offline groups. They suggest that Internet groupings have the same dynamics and follow many of the same rules that govern socializing in offline groups. Close similarities exist, for example, in norm development and the importance of group identity to its members. The authors point out that online interaction has some distinctive characteristics that create an environment unique to cyberspace: surfing is often anonymous, and on the net many typical gating features do not exist. In addition, the degree of control over the interaction is very high, and it is easy to find similar others. These special characteristics can be very helpful for people whose identity contains aspects that are socially stigmatizing. The authors point out that there is a growing tendency for the borders dividing online and offline groups to become blurred.

The plethora of groups on the Internet leads to an exploration of leadership in cyberspace, which focuses on how it is established and maintained. Related to this is the issue of how decisions are taken in an Internet environment, and the advantages and disadvantages of the methods chosen. In Chapter 9, Coovert and Burke discuss the topic of leadership and decision making on the net. They assess the attributes, tasks, and challenges of the e-leader, and focus on the interaction between the e-leader and the advanced information technology the Internet provides. They suggest that evaluating different styles of e-leadership is a complex issue and point out, for example, that groups working with transformational leaders were more effective when the input was anonymous, while transactional leaders were more successful when the individual input was identified. The authors review the prominent models in the field of decision making and their relevance to the Internet. They examine the research comparing the process of decision making in a face-to-face context with computer-mediated decision making, emphasizing issues such as anonymity and critical thinking.

In the final chapter, Glaser and Kahn suggest that the special characteristics of the Internet have a complex impact on stereotyping, prejudice, and discrimination. For example, people are more likely to express bias in the anonymous, impersonal conditions existing on the Internet. Conversely, a program promoting tolerance will capitalize on the ability of the net to reach a vast audience. Contact between different group members is likely to have some short-term positive impact, but prejudice reduction over the long term poses a less propitious scenario. Nevertheless, the authors point out that net automation and the lack of status cues may reduce the discrimination frequently found in face-to-face contacts. However, many of those most frequently discriminated against (e.g. racial and ethnic minority group members) have significantly lower levels of access to the Internet. Glazer and Kahn suggest that through careful study of the Internet's potential and pitfalls, society has an opportunity to reduce discrimination and its consequent inequities.

The topics presented in this book demonstrate, I believe, the power, wealth, and complexity of the social world of cyberspace. The continuous examination of these issues is becoming increasingly vital as more and more parts of our lives are influenced by the world of the Internet. It is important to bear in mind that while the adults among us can still remember the world before the advent of Internet, the younger generation know no other world.

This book represents a significant contribution towards a greater understanding of human behavior in cyberspace. I hope this will lead to future developments of Internet use that will enrich our lives.

References

Bandura, A. (1977). *Social learning theory*. Englewood Cliffs, NJ: Prentice Hall.

Brenner, V. (1997). Psychology of computer use: parameters of internet use, abuse and addiction: the first 90 days of the internet usage survey. *Psychological Reports*, **80**, 879–82.

Daft, R.L. and Lengel, R.H. (1986). Organizational information requirements, media richness and structural design. *Management Science*, **32**, 554–71.

Gackenbach, J. and Ellerman, E. (1998). Introduction to psychological aspects of Internet use. In J. Gackenbach (ed), Psychology and the Internet (pp. 1–25). San Diego, CA: Academic Press.

Hamburger, Y.A. and Ben–Artzi, E. (2000). The relationship between extraversion and neuroticism and the different uses of the Internet. *Computers in Human Behavior*, **16**, 441–9.

Hiltz, S.R., Johnson, K., and Turoff, M. (1986). Experiments in group decision making: communication process and outcome in face-to-face versus computerized conferences. *Human Communication Research*, **13**, 225–52.

Hiltz, S.R. and Turoff, M. (1993). *The network nation: human communication via computer*. MA Cambridge: MIT press.

Katz, J., Rice, R., and Aspden, P. (2001). The Internet, 1995–2000. Access, civic involvement and social interaction. *American Behavioral Scientist*, **45**, 405–17.

Kraut, P., Patterson, M., Lundmark, V., Kiesler, S., Mukopadhyay, T., and Scherlis, W. (1998). Internet paradox: a social technology that reduces social involvement and psychological well-being? *American Psychologist*, **53**, 65–77.

McKenna, K.Y.A. and Bargh, J.A. (1998). Coming out in the age of the Internet: identity 'de-marginalization' through virtual group participation. *Journal of Personality and Social Psychology*, **75**, 681–94.

Nie, N.H. and Erbing, L. (2000). *Internet and society: a preliminary report*. Stanford, CA: Stanford Institute for the Quantitative Study of Society (SIQSS).

Petty, R.E. and Cacioppo, J.T. (1984). The effects of involvement on responses to argument quantity and quality: central and peripheral approaches to persuasion. *Journal of Personality and Social Psychology*, **46**, 69–81.

Slater, W.F. (2002). *Internet: history and growth. Chicago chapter of the Internet society*. Available: *http://www.isoc.org/internet/history*.

Sproull, L. and Faraj, S. (1997). Atheism, sex, and databases: the net as asocial technology. In S. Kiesler (ed), *Culture of the Internet* (pp. 35–51). New York: Erlbaum.

Sproull, L. and Kiesler, S. (1986). Reducing social context cues: electronic mail in organizational communication. *Management Science*, **32**, 1492–513.

Stoll, C. (1995). *Silicon snake oil*. New York: Doubleday.

Turkle, S. (1995). *Life on the screen: identity in the age of the Internet*. New York: Simon & Schuster.

Dedicated to Debbie—my wife, my partner, my friend and for our children—Michael, Talia, Keren, and Yaron.

Acknowledgments

Without the help of a number of people this book could not have come into being. First, I thank the authors for their contributions. I would also like to express my gratitude to those whose comments and encouragement helped me with this project: Rachel Ben–Ari, Aaron Bizman, Shaul Fox, Itamar Gati, Ehud Kogut, Meni Koslowski, Israel Orbach, Joseph Schwarzwald, Louise Sylvester, Arik Tayeb, Dror Walk, and Yoel Yinon. Last, but not least, I would like to thank Martin Baum at Oxford University Press who helped me materialize my ideas into a book.

Contents

Contributors

Yair Amichai–Hamburger
Bar-Ilan University, Department of
Psychology, Ramat–Gan, 52900,
Israel

Aaron Ben–Ze'ev
University of Haifa, Department of
Philosophy, Haifa, 31905, Israel

Jennifer L. Burke
University of South Florida,
Department of Psychology,
Tampa, FL 33620–7200, USA

Robert B. Cialdini
Arizona State University,
Department of Psychology, Tempe,
AZ 85287–1104, USA

Caryn A. Conley
New York University, Stern School
of Business, New York, NY 10012,
USA

Michael D. Coovert
University of South Florida,
Psychology Department, Tampa,
FL 33620–7200, USA

Jack Glaser
Goldman School of Public Policy,
University of California, Berkeley,
CA 94720–7320, USA

Rosanna E. Guadagno
University of California, Research
Center for Virtual Environments and
Behavior, Santa Barbara,
CA 93106–9660, USA

Kimberly B. Kahn
University of California, Department
of Psychology, Los Angeles,
CA 90095–1563, USA

Daniel Linz
University of California,
Department of Communication,
Santa Barbara, CA 93106, USA

Yoram M. Kalman
The Centre for the Study of the
Information Society, University of
Haifa, School of Business, Haifa,
31905, Israel

Neil M. Malamuth
University of California,
Communication Studies,
Los Angeles, CA 90095–1538,
USA

Katelyn Y. A. McKenna
New York University, Department of
Psychology, New York, NY 10003,
USA

Jae Yun Moon
The Hong Kong University of
Science and Technology Business
School, Hong Kong

Daphne R. Raban
The Centre for the Study of the
Information Society,
University of Haifa,
School of Business, Haifa, 31905,
Israel

Sheizaf Rafaeli
The Centre for the Study of
Information Society,
University of Haifa, School of
Business, Haifa, 31905, Israel

Edward G. Sargis
University of Illinois at Chicago,
Department of Psychology, Illinois
60607–7137, USA

Gwendolyn Seidman
New York University, Department of
Psychology, New York, NY 10003,
USA

Linda J. Skitka
University of Illinois at Chicago,
Department of Psychology, Illinois
60607–7137, USA

Lee Sproull
New York University, Stern School
of Business, New York, NY 10012,
USA

Mike Z. Yao
University of California,
Department of Communication,
Santa Barbara, CA 93106,
USA

Chapter 1

Social psychological research and the Internet: the promise and peril of a new methodological frontier

Linda Skitka and Edward Sargis

The Internet has expanded people's ability to connect with others. People can connect to those with whom they have existing social ties, as well as make new connections with others who may share similar interests and ideologies. These connections can be achieved through a variety of means and with varying levels of social involvement, such as viewing or creating personal web pages, posting to online discussion forums, and communicating via e-mail or instant messaging. These unprecedented advances in communication and the proliferation of Internet-based technologies have led many social psychologists to take advantage of the power of the Internet in their research.

In a similar vein, access to large numbers of potential research participants as well as increased access to special populations have lured many to explore the potential of collecting data to test social psychological hypotheses using web-based samples. The Internet allows for generalization beyond the college student subject pool, with the benefits of experimental manipulation, audio and visual presentation of stimuli, live and spontaneous interaction between participants, and higher degrees of complexity than is possible with other methods of data collection typically used outside of the traditional social psychological laboratory. There are many reasons to be excited about the methodological possibilities of using the Internet as a medium for social psychological research.

The range of possibilities for conducting research is expanding at approximately the same rate as information technology is expanding. Just as there are increasingly more ways to obtain information and data in general, there is also a growing number of ways to obtain social psychological data. The goal of this chapter is to provide a review of how social psychologists are currently using the web and to present some specific examples of translational, novel, and phenomenological Internet research. We also review the advantages and disadvantages of web-based research, with special attention to issues of sampling and data quality that need to be taken into account when one leaves the familiarity of collecting admittedly biased data from college student subject pools, and turns instead to the less familiar but potentially richer frontier of web-based research.

How the web is used as a methodological tool

To gain a better understanding of the web as a methodological tool, we reviewed a sample of studies that used the Internet to test social psychological hypotheses. To this end, we invited subscribers to the Society for Personality and Social Psychology Listserv to send us references or copies of papers that reported on research that used the Internet as a data collection tool. From this initial request, we received a total pool of 106 papers that dealt broadly with information technology and psychology. From this pool we obtained a sample of 60 studies (taken from 43 papers) that met our review criteria that the study reported on original research and used the Internet for data collection. Although this sample undoubtedly represents only a portion of the number of social psychological studies that have used the web, like any other study that uses sampling rather than examining every member of a given population, this approach provided a basis for making estimates and inferences about the population of social psychological studies that have used the Internet.

Based on this sample of studies, we found that most web-based social psychological research, like the field overall, uses experimental designs (62%). Correlational field designs or studies were the next most frequent form of web-based social psychological research (33%). The remaining studies in our sample (5%) were qualitative in approach.

Despite turning to the Internet for data collection, a large number of these studies nonetheless relied on college student samples (38%), typically using e-mail to invite students to participate. A similarly large percentage of studies (30%) used opt-in samples (i.e. people who self-selected to participate in the study). These participants may have stumbled across the study when searching the web for information about personality or psychology in general, or they responded to web postings that invited people to come to the study website. Some researchers (20%) made use of the capacity of the web to identify groups of people with specific characteristics, and recruited participants from within these specialized groups (e.g. members of a women-only chat room). Twelve percent of the studies in our sample accessed a true random sample of participants.

No single substantive area of inquiry within social psychology appears to have 'led the charge' in turning to the Internet for data collection. Instead, researchers interested in a broad array of substantive questions (including research on personality, person perception, persuasion, leadership, and much more) have tested hypotheses using web-based methods, However, virtually all of the studies we reviewed could be classified as taking either a translational, novel, or phenomenological approach to their research. Each of these approaches, along with concrete examples, is described in more detail below.

Translational web use

Many researchers adapt materials developed for offline use for use on the Internet; in other words, they take a translational approach to using the web for social psychological research. Forty-five percent of the studies we reviewed took a translational approach. For example, Srivastava and colleagues (2003) used the Internet to test the respective predictions of biological and context-ualist models of personality development. According to the biological model, personality should become relatively stable by adulthood (i.e. age 30 and over). The contextualist model, in contrast, predicts that people's life circum-stances will continue to influence their personality throughout their life and, therefore, changes should be observed in personality regardless of age.

To test these competing hypotheses, Srivastava *et al.* (2003) adapted a version of the Big Five Inventory for use on the Internet. Potential respondents found the website where the inventory was posted (e.g. through Internet search engines using search terms like 'personality tests'), and this website was listed on a popular search engine as a 'Pick of the week'. In total, 132,515 people completed the inventory, with a range in age from 21 to 60. Although cross-sectional rather than longitudinal in design, the results revealed that there is considerable variability over different age cohorts, including those well past the age of 30, rather than a relatively common and stable distribution of people across characteristics on the Big Five from age 30 and upward. Therefore, the results were more consistent with the contextualist than the biological view of personality development.

Other researchers have taken similar translational approaches to how they use the Internet to facilitate research. For example, various other 'paper and pencil' personality inventories have been converted to web-based forms (e.g. Foster *et al.*, 2003), and Milgram's (1977) 'lost letter' technique has been successfully adapted for use on the Internet using 'lost' e-mails (Stern & Faber, 1997). The lost letter technique allows researchers to assess general atti-tudes toward various issues or issue stands by sending messages ostensibly meant for political organizations to naïve subjects instead. How many of these 'lost' e-mails are subsequently forwarded to the presumed correct address can be used as a measure of the degree of implicit support for the issue addressed in the e-mail (e.g. Stern & Faber, 1997). Other researchers have converted experiments or experimental stimulus materials that were originally designed for computer presentation in the laboratory for online use (e.g. Guèguen & Jacob, 2001; Nosek *et al.*, 2002).

In short, personality and social psychologists have found it relatively easy to translate pre-existing methods of research for use on the Internet. Other researchers, however, have found that the Internet affords some unique opportunities to study social psychological phenomena and have developed more novel approaches to data collection.

Novel web use

Approximately 8% of the studies we reviewed reported on research that used novel methods of data collection. For example, Rentfrow and Gosling (2003, Study 4) made creative use of information freely available on the Internet to inform social psychological theory. Specifically, they explored the underlying dimensions of music preferences by coding people's web-based music libraries. Many people post their music libraries on specific websites set up for the purpose of sharing and downloading of music (e.g. Audiogalaxy.com, Morpheus.com, Napster.com). Rentfrow and Gosling (2003) obtained a random sample of 500 users' music libraries, selecting 10 from each state in the U.S. Each user's music preferences were classified as a function of the number of songs they had within different music genres. These data were then used to confirm, with considerable success, the underlying pattern of dimensionality in music preferences that they had developed based on college students' responses to questionnaires (Rentfrow & Gosling, 2003, Study 2).

Other researchers have made serendipitous use of spontaneous behavior on web discussion boards to study questions of social psychological interest. For example, most, if not all, previous work on rumor transmission involved studying how participants passed along experimenter-created rumors in the lab, a method frequently criticized for being low in realism (Bordia, 1996). Bordia and Rosnow (1998), in contrast, examined rumor transmission by studying postings on an electronic bulletin board after a rumor surfaced that a specific Internet provider was tapping into the hard drives of its subscribers. The researchers coded the content of these postings using categories developed from theories of rumor transmission (e.g. statements of apprehension, disbelief, or interrogation) and examined the prevalence of these statements over time and across postings on the bulletin board. The Internet discussion, over several days, of this real rumor (of genuine concern to the participants on the discussion board) provided Bordia and Rosnow with a novel and unobtrusive way to gain insight into the dynamics of rumor transmission. The results of their analysis indicated that patterns of rumor transmission in this field setting were consistent with existing theories of rumor transmission, and that patterns of rumor transmission in this computer-mediated context were quite similar to those found in face-to-face rumor transmission. These results suggest that existing models of social interaction developed in face-to-face and in-person encounters were replicated on the web, and therefore provided some validation of the web as a methodological platform for social psychological research.

Other novel uses of the Internet to study social psychological questions included a study that used German online auctions to study ethnic discrimination. Sellers with Turkish names (a minority group in Germany) reportedly took longer to receive winning bids than did those with German names (Shohat & Musch, 2003). Another novel approach involved posting different 'problems' on hate-group discussion lists to examine whether participants advocated different levels of violence as a function of problem content (Glaser *et al.*, 2002). Both studies found ways to use the web as a novel solution to the problem that demand characteristics can introduce into the study of phenomena like ethnic discrimination.

The examples of novel uses of the web discussed here only scratch the surface of the creative potential of the web for future research on social psychological questions. Translational and novel uses of the web for research, however, tend to use the Internet more as a means to an end, rather than as an end in itself. Research that takes a phenomenological approach focuses instead on the social dynamics of interaction on the web as an interesting focus of research in itself.

Phenomenological approaches

The largest percentage of articles we reviewed (47%) took a phenomenological perspective in their research. Unlike translational and novel approaches that use the web as a method to study questions that are not substantively web-bound (e.g. people had music preferences before web-sharing of music became available), phenomenological studies extend social psychological theory and research by exploring the potentially unique impact of web-based social interaction on people's thoughts, feelings, and behavior.

The Internet offers individuals unprecedented access to a wide array of information and new channels of communication. People can connect with friends and family as well as strangers with similar interests. On the Internet, individuals are able to explore aspects of themselves they might otherwise be reluctant to share with others, and can do so in relative anonymity and in the safety of their own homes (McKenna & Bargh, 1998, 2000). They are able to meet and interact on a regular basis with others whom they may have never met in person. Moreover, this communication can take place instantaneously (e.g. via instant messaging) or over more protracted periods of time (e.g. via posts to online message boards or newsgroups). As tenuous as some of these social relationships may seem, they are often very real and of great importance to those involved in them (McKenna & Green, 2002; McKenna et al., 2002).

The unique features of the Internet as a communication medium can affect psychological functioning in any number of complex ways (McKenna & Bargh, 2000; Tyler, 2002). Phenomenological research strives to make sense of this complexity by examining the interface between web technology and psychology. Many of the general areas of inquiry of web-based research are those that have always interested social psychologists, such as persuasion (e.g. Guandagno & Cialdini, 2002), relationship formation (McKenna et al., 2002), and group dynamics (McKenna & Green, 2002; Williams et al., 2002). Researchers in each of these disciplinary areas are exploring the degree to which web-based persuasive appeals, relationships, and group dynamics differ from face-to-face and in-person social interaction.

Work by Kraut and colleagues on the relationship between Internet use and psychological well-being (Kraut et al., 1998, 2002) is one example of the phenomenological approach. Because the Internet is a social medium, it might be expected that Internet use enhances connections with others and therefore increases psychological well-being. However, because time spent on the Internet is time that could otherwise be used for face-to-face and in-person social encounters, it may increase people's sense of social isolation rather than promote a sense of social connection. In an initial study of Internet use and psychological well-being (Kraut et al., 1998), Internet-use habits were tracked in 93 households (participants were provided internet access as part of the study). This initial study revealed that higher levels of Internet use (based on server logs of hours spent online, volume of e-mails, and number of websites visited per week) were related to decreased social involvement, increased loneliness, and increased reported depressive symptoms relative to pre-trial levels. In a subsequent follow-up of the same people about two years later (Kraut et al., 2002, Study 1), many of the negative effects people experienced on initial Internet access had dissipated. This follow-up survey revealed that higher levels of Internet use were associated with a significant decrease in depressive symptoms and no longer had any effect on reported loneliness. In short, these results suggest that even if there are short-term negative effects of gaining access to the web, over time, increased Internet use facilitates better social support and therefore mental health.

Another example of the phenomenological approach to Internet-based research is McKenna and Bargh's (1998) program of research designed to explore what seems to be the relatively unique capacity of the web to allow people to try out or develop new or less well-accepted aspects of their identity. The Internet provides a non-threatening forum for people to explore aspects of themselves that others in their social circle might find objectionable. People can form social networks in cyberspace with those who share these same attributes. Participation in these online groups can help individuals come to terms with aspects of themselves that they are reluctant to share with others in their current social environment. For example, McKenna and Bargh (1998) contacted samples of people who were frequent posters on forums for those with stigmatized sexual identities (e.g. alt.homosexual, alt.bondage; Study 2) or political ideologies (e.g. alt.skinheads, misc.activism.militia; Study 3). Lurkers (i.e. individuals who read but do not post messages to newsgroups) were recruited by posting invitations for participation in the study in these same forums. Consistent with predictions, participation in these 'virtual' groups facilitated people's coming to terms with their marginalized identities. Participation led to an increased sense of the importance of the person's marginal identity, and this increased importance led to increased self-acceptance and greater likelihood of revealing the concealed identity to friends and family.

Cyberostracism (i.e. being ignored or excluded from various forms of online interaction) is another example of a web-based phenomenon that is of interest to researchers. In one study of cyberostracism (Williams *et al.*, 2002, Study 1), participants were recruited through posting notices around the campus of the University of New South Whales, by sending notices about the experiment to social psychology instructors at universities, and by posting links to the experiment on various social psychology websites. After responding to a preliminary questionnaire, participants were led to believe that they were playing a game of 'virtual' catch with two other online research participants. In actuality, participants interacted with computer-generated 'players' who were programmed to vary how often they gave the 'ball' to the research participant (five times in the inclusion condition and only once in the ostracism condition). Higher levels of exclusion from the game led participants to report lower levels of mood, self-esteem, and feelings of belongingness.

Similar results were found when cyberostracism was studied in the context of Internet chat rooms in which confederates either included or excluded targeted participants during computer-mediated communication (Williams *et al.*, 2002, Studies 2–4). Other results indicated that people are more likely to react aggressively when ostracized online than in face-to-face encounters (Williams *et al.*, 2002, Study 4).

In summary, the Internet is used by an increasing number of social psychologists to expand our understanding of existing social psychological phenomena and to begin to explore the potentially unique impact of computer-mediated social interaction on people's thoughts, feelings, and behavior. As a methodological approach, it is probably already apparent that the Internet has advantages and disadvantages, the specifics of which we turn our attention to next.

Advantages of web-based research

There are a number of advantages of turning to the Internet to conduct social psychological research. Quite simply, Internet-based research has the capacity to compensate for many of the disadvantages of lab-based experimentation with college student samples, as well as to compensate for some of the disadvantages of some of the other methods for obtaining more representative samples, such as telephone surveys. Relative to these other approaches, advantages of Internet-based research generally include:

- increased efficiency
- increased access to people with special characteristics
- larger and more diverse samples (usually at a lower cost than a telephone survey)
- increased data quality (compared to both telephone and paper modes of data collection).

Efficiency

Internet research has a number of features that can save time and money. With only a modest investment in learning some basic programming, collecting data can be as simple as designing a form and copying it to a server. It is also relatively easy to program a study so that data are automatically entered into a spreadsheet or data file, avoiding manual data entry (see Birnbaum, 2000, 2001; Fraley, 2003, for excellent 'how to' resources). Collecting data on the web is a paperless process and, therefore, avoids costs associated with paper and copying of paper questionnaires. A variety of mail merge programs allows one to field a survey to thousands of potential participants with no more than a keystroke. Therefore, labor costs in the form of either time or research assistant funding are clearly minimal, and the time required for data collection is relatively independent of sample size.

Access to underrepresented groups

In addition to the benefit of increased efficiency, the web also facilitates access to people who have characteristics that are relatively low in incidence in the general population. Social psychologists are sometimes interested in studying specific groups of people who are inadequately represented in college student subject pools; turning to the Internet can solve the problem of both finding and accessing these kinds of specialized samples. For example, social psychologists have long been interested in trying to account for the psychology of evil, or the psychological factors that are likely to lead to actions of violence toward other groups (e.g. Newman & Erber, 2002; Staub, 1989). However, the typical college undergraduate is unlikely to be so ethnocentric as to be a member of a hate group, much less admit to being so. Similarly, most people are unlikely to feel comfortable advocating intergroup violence either in a psychology lab or in a telephone interview even if it is something they were to otherwise advocate (cf. Evans *et al.*, 2003). In short, studying intergroup hatred and related phenomena in the lab is plagued with problems associated with demand characteristics, social desirability pressures, and possible psychological reactance, each of which can undermine the validity of results.

Given that hundreds of hate group-sponsored chat rooms, archives, websites, and more have popped up on the Internet (Franklin, 2000; Klanwatch, 1998), and people seem to feel relatively free to express their racist views using this medium, new avenues for studying overt racist beliefs and support for intergroup violence have emerged. In one study, an interviewer acted as a newcomer to a White supremacist online group and posed a problem, such as 'my sister is talking about getting married to a Black man' or 'I found out this Black couple is moving next door to me' (prompts varied as a function of threat and threat type in a 3 × 3 factorial design; Glaser *et al.*, 2002). Of interest was the degree of advocated violence that different prompts elicited. Results supported the notion that extremists are more likely to advocate violence in response to threats to a group identity than to material or economic interests.

Other researchers have similarly used the Internet to obtain access to difficult to reach and empirically underrepresented populations such as gays, lesbians, and bisexuals (e.g. Mathy *et al.*, 2002), people with hearing loss (Cummings *et al.*, 2002), and pet owners of a wide range of different animals (Gosling & Bonnenburg, 1998). Given the huge number of special interest, news, support, and chat groups that have emerged online, any number of heretofore difficult to find populations are suddenly more accessible.

Access to larger and more diverse samples

The Internet also has the advantage of providing social psychological researchers with access to large, diverse, and affordable samples of potential research participants, more generally. Even if the practice of sampling from university subject pools is widely accepted, building a science on the foundation of so narrow a database is less than ideal (see Sears, 1986 for a review). Subject pool participants are disproportionately White, female, young, and financially secure relative to the population at large (Birnbaum, in press). Not only do participant characteristics correspond poorly to typical populations of interest to researchers (e.g. people in general), but not even college students have an equal probability of being in university subject pools.

Although it can be argued that social psychological research is the study of general social processes that are unlikely to vary as a function of demographic characteristics like age, income, or education, there has not been sufficient research to empirically establish the credibility of this claim. Therefore, the large numbers of 'real people' that can be accessed on the web potentially allows social psychologists to better address and assess the generalizability of their research findings.

There are, of course, other ways to get more representative samples to test social psychological hypotheses. For example, social psychologists have turned to secondary analysis of archived large-scale telephone surveys or in-person interviews, such as the National Election Study or General Social Survey data (e.g. Crandall, 1995; Skitka et al., 2002), or contracted independent telephone surveys that use random digit dialing to get probability samples (e.g. Lind et al., 1997; Skitka, 1999, 2002a). Just as the web has advantages over lab-based research on college undergraduates, it also has advantages over these alternative strategies as well. For example, unlike telephone surveys that are limited to audio stimulus presentation and response, one can use text, pictures, and movies to present stimuli via the web. Studies conducted on the web are also likely to be lower in cognitive load and respondent burden than those conducted over the phone. Responding to questions over the phone requires participants to:

1 understand and interpret the question
2 search memory for relevant thoughts or feelings
3 integrate different thoughts and feelings into a coherent judgment
4 recall the response alternatives
5 and, finally, map their response unto one of the provided response alternatives (Tourangeau & Rasinski, 1988; see also Zaller, 1992).

Not surprisingly, given the number of steps involved and the burden on people's working memory, telephone survey responses are vulnerable to a number of different biases based on question framing, wording, and order effects (e.g. Schuman *et al.*, 1981; Strack *et al.*, 1991; for a review see Schwarz *et al.*, 1998). Recent research indicates that collecting data on the web avoids some of these data quality problems. Specifically, web-based surveys are lower in measurement error, survey satisficing, and social desirability bias than surveys conducted over the phone or via intercom (Chang & Krosnick, 2003*a*, 2003*b*). Other research reveals that computerized data presentation and response has similar advantages relative to either paper questionnaires or face-to-face interviewing (Richman *et al.*, 1999).

People might also be more likely to persist rather than abandon participation in studies that involve a lot of 'if then' branching when conducted on the web rather than via paper questionnaires, because branching can be programmed to occur entirely outside of the awareness of research participants. Moreover, participants are generally volunteers, so data quality may be improved because their motivation for participating may be better than that of college students who mindlessly participate as a means to other ends. People might also respond more naturally when they participate in studies in familiar contexts (e.g. their homes) rather than the unfamiliar and often sterile environment of the social psychology laboratory.

Disadvantages of web-based research

Although using the Internet for research has many advantages, it also has some limitations. Potential disadvantages of the Internet for social psychological research include:

- Web users differ from non-users in a number of ways that may be important.
- Participants are often recruited using non-probability sampling and, therefore, most web samples are not particularly representative of even web users.
- People are less likely to positively respond to invitations to participate in web than other kinds of research.
- The high anonymity and low accountability of the web, relative to other methods of data collection, may introduce a number of problems.
- There are various technical constraints on both stimulus presentation and response.
- There may be increased error due to uncontrolled features of participants' context.

- There are some ethical considerations and constraints that limit the methodological options for research on the web.

Non-representative samples

One serious limitation of Internet data collection, at least for researchers who take either a novel or translational, rather than phenomenological approach to using the web for research, is sample representativeness. Although many are likely to feel that Internet samples represent a leap forward over the heavy reliance of social psychologists on college student samples, social psychologists may be simply replacing one flawed sampling approach with another when they turn to convenient samples of web users. People who use the Internet are not representative of the general population, nor are online special interest groups representative of their specific groups (e.g. disabled people who are online differ in important ways from disabled people who are not online; Lenhart *et al.*, 2003). Even if web users were representative of either the general or a given specific population, or if one is only interested in studying web-based phenomena, there is no database from which one can draw probability samples of potential participants.

To date, there has been relatively little research that has directly examined just how well social psychological findings generalize with more representative samples of the mass public. However, very recent research has found that a number of presumed social psychological truisms in fact have limited generalizability outside of the lab. For example, Skitka (2002*b*) tested whether the classic Ross *et al.* (1977) 'quiz game' study replicated with a large representative national sample, as well as large oversamples of Blacks, Hispanics, and Asians. Participants were given a description of a game that involved two volunteers, one of whom was randomly assigned the role of a 'quizmaster' and another who was assigned the role of a 'contestant'. The quizmaster was asked to pose five questions to the contestant, with the only condition being that the quizmaster had to know the correct answer to all five questions. The contestant subsequently performed relatively poorly (he answered only one question correctly). Research participants were then asked to evaluate both the quizmaster's and contestant's intelligence. People demonstrate evidence of making the fundamental attribution error (i.e. the tendency to neglect to take into account possible situational explanations for behavior, in favor of dispositional causes) if they fail to take into account the contestant's relative disadvantage because of the random assignment to roles, and evaluate him (or her) as less intelligent than the quizmaster.

Blacks, Hispanics, and Asian Americans showed virtually no evidence of making the fundamental attribution error. Moreover, all differences between

Whites and the other groups of participants were fully explained by differences in income and political orientation. All groups rated the contestant as about average in intelligence (a rational response); however, the White, wealthy, and conservative tended to rate the quizmaster as above average in intelligence. Although more research will be needed to see if similar limits are revealed on other tests of the generalizability of the tendency to make the fundamental attribution error, these results are at least suggestive that social psychologists should be cautious about assuming that their findings will in fact generalize well to populations besides college students.

Many researchers, however, are likely to believe that getting larger samples of more diverse people is better than the alternative of using college student samples, and that the problem of lack of representativeness of those with web access is likely to resolve itself. It is therefore important to explore these assumptions.

Sampling from a biased portion of the population yields a biased sample, no matter how large the sample. Because web users are different in a number of ways from non-web users, any sample drawn from only those who use the Internet will yield biased estimates and inferences about populations generally of greater interest (e.g. people in general). Moreover, because there is not a good sampling frame from which one can take a random draw of web users, most web samples do not even allow one to make accurate estimates or statistical inferences about web users. Even web users do not have an equal probability of being included in any given web sample given the methods most researchers currently use to sample this population. Confidence intervals and inferential statistics will therefore all be misleading estimates because they inevitably are based on a non-probability sample of web users (see Couper, 2000 for a detailed review).

Are web samples in fact non-representative of the general population? Based on national representative telephone surveys that explored differences between web users and non-users, web users are younger, wealthier, and higher in education than non-users (Lenhart *et al.*, 2003). Web users also have greater trust in others, have broader social networks, and generally believe that people are more fair than are non-users (Lenhart *et al.*, 2003). Opt-in samples of web users are also more politically knowledgeable and engaged than are random samples of the population (Chang & Krosnick, 2003*a*). Other research reveals that, although college students and Internet samples are both prone to certain decision-making biases, there are nonetheless differences between them in degree (Birnbaum, 1999). Both college student and Internet samples deviated from normative models of decision making, but student samples were generally more biased than Internet samples (Birnbaum, 1999).

One source of information about potential psychological differences between people who have web access versus those who do not, is data collected using the Knowledge Networks (KN) panel. KN has blended the advantages of the web as a vehicle for research with the benefits of using random digit dialing (RDD) to obtain a representative probability sample of the U.S. public. They contact potential panelists using RDD telephone survey methods. Those who agree to participate on the panel receive a free device to access the web (e.g. a web TV) and a free web connection in exchange for their household members' participation in occasional surveys. Each household member aged 13 and above gets his or her own password-protected e-mail account. Panelists receive e-mails with embedded links to surveys about once every week or two. Panel characteristics closely match those from the U.S. census, and because it is a true probability sample, sample weights can be calculated to correct for sampling error. About 50% of KN's panelists had no prior access to the web before joining the panel (see *http://www.knowledgenetworks.com/ganp* for more details).

A number of social psychological researchers have conducted studies using the KN panel (e.g. Chang & Krosnick, 2003*a*; Lerner *et al.*, 2003; Silver *et al.*, 2002, Skitka, 2002*a*, 2002*b*; Skitka & Mullen, 2002; Skitka *et al.*, 2002, Study 4). Analysis of some of the data revealed potentially important social psychological differences between people who were web users versus non-web users before they were asked to join the KN panel. For example, people without home computers and independent web access had different reactions than those with independent web access to the September 11, 2001 terrorist attacks on the World Trade Center and the Pentagon. Panelists who had been non-users were higher in perceived threat; less supportive of civil liberties for Arab Americans, Muslims, and first-generation immigrants; higher in immediate post-attack anger, as well as anger about the attacks four months later; and were more authoritarian than those with home computers and previous access to the Internet. Interestingly, non-users were nonetheless more likely to feel that to some degree, the U.S. brought the attacks upon itself, and that the perpetrators of the attacks were caught up in circumstances that were beyond their personal control (Skitka, 2003*a*; for more substantive results see Skitka *et al.*, 2004).

Other data revealed differences between KN members who had been web users versus those who were non-users before joining the panel in reactions to the Iraq War as well. Non-users reported that they felt higher levels of fear, anger, and sadness than users when thinking about the war with Iraq; they were also less likely to report that the war brought to mind thoughts about their own death (self-reported mortality salience). Although non-users were less tolerant of dissent and more authoritarian than web users, they were nonetheless also more opposed to the war than were users (Skitka, 2003*b*).

Taken together, these results indicate that there are affective, attitudinal, and attributional differences between people who have web access and those who do not. Although some differences between web users and non-users disappear when variations in education, income, and age are controlled in both our data and others', some do not (see also Flemming & Sonner, 1999; Taylor, 2000).

Many researchers are likely to believe that the problem of non-representativeness of web users is one that will solve itself, and that it will not be long before the penetration of the Internet into people's lives across all strata of society will be as complete as the penetration of the telephone. However, recent research indicates that the non-coverage area of the Internet may be expanding, rather than retreating. Unlike other technological advances (e.g. telephone, television), some people have been opting out of the web after they have access to it. Forty-two percent of Americans report that they do not use the Internet at all; 17% of these are net drop-outs (i.e. former users who have abandoned using the web) (Lenhart *et al.*, 2003). The number of net drop-outs increased substantially between 2000 and 2002, suggesting that the growth of web use has not only slowed, but may be reversing (Lenhart *et al.*, 2003). Therefore, the Internet may not increase in use to the point that one can obtain truly representative samples of the population on the web without using something like KN or their strategies to get representative samples.

It is interesting to note that similar trends to 'drop out' have not existed with most other forms of communication technology. Once people get radios, televisions, or telephones, they rarely then decide to no longer use them. Why people drop out from the Internet is a question that might be of interest to explore in future phenomenological research.

Non-response

Non-coverage error refers to the sampling error introduced because not everyone has access to the web; non-response error refers to the fact that not everyone recruited to participate in a given study will choose to do so. Non-response error increases as the number of non-respondents increases, and as the differences between respondents and non-respondents grows, even if response rate is held constant (Couper, 2000). Non-response can be difficult to calculate for web studies that post with an open invitation for participation, because the number of people who could potentially participate but chose not to is unknown. Estimates of response rates of web users to e-mail solicitation is about 10%, and between 20–25% in response to specifically targeted banner ads (see Couper, 2000 for a review).

Comparisons of traditional versus e-mail methods of recruitment indicate that response rates are lower in response to e-mail solicitations (27%) than traditional mail (42%) for the same study (Kwak & Radler, 2000; see also Couper *et al.*, 1999 and Schafer & Dillman, 1998 for reviews). Although a number of explanations might account for these differences in response rates (e.g. technical difficulties accessing web surveys, concerns about confidentiality on the web), it seems likely that people are already overwhelmed with requests for their attention on the web. SPAM, or unsolicited e-mails, accounted for 30% of all e-mails in 2002 and more than 50% of all e-mails in 2003 (Legard, 2002). It seems likely that unsolicited e-mails will have the same negative impact on willingness to participate in web surveys as the increase in unsolicited phone calls has had on telephone survey research.

Technical constraints

Although the Internet affords greater flexibility in presentation of stimuli than, for example, paper questionnaires or telephone surveys, one nonetheless cannot deliver stimuli that can be touched, tasted, or smelled via the web. Moreover, although one can deliver audio or visual stimuli, without special equipment one cannot receive audio or visual responses from research participants. Although virtual interaction is possible in real time (e.g. in chat rooms or with instant messaging), face-to-face social interaction, with all its non-verbal cues and nuances, is not currently possible on the web without adding specialized equipment.

There are also potential concerns about both precision and control. People's ability to load web pages, and how quickly they do so, vary dramatically as a function of:

◆ whether they access the Internet via modem, cable, or a wireless connection

◆ the browser they use

◆ features of the device used to connect to the web (e.g. RAM, processing speed)

◆ monitor refresh rates.

That said, some researchers have found that they can easily replicate previously established laboratory effects, and in particular effects related to cognitive or visual processing, on the web. For example, when using relatively homogeneous populations of college students as subjects, McGraw and Wong (1992) replicated the lab finding of a right visual field advantage on the web. Other researchers have also had very good success replicating a number of cognitive effects such as Stroop task interference (Krantz & Dalal, 2000; McGraw *et al.*, 2000; Musch & Reips, 2000). However, because monitor refresh rates are often slower or similar in speed to the response latencies researchers are trying to detect, the Internet may not be optimal for research that is dependent on detecting reactions to small differences in exposure or detecting small differences in response time.

Context

In addition to error variance introduced through software and hardware variation across respondents, the experimental context is also free to vary in most Internet research, whereas it is generally kept constant in laboratory studies. Some people may participate in a given web study in the presence of others, whereas others will participate while alone; some participants may be highly distracted by other features of the environment that compete for their attention, whereas others will have little in the way of distraction; and so on. How big a potential problem this might be probably depends on the phenomena being studied.

Anonymity

A related issue is that social interaction and communication on the web are often highly, if not completely, anonymous. People can and do take on alternative identities or make efforts to explicitly protect their offline from their online identity. People can easily set up free e-mail accounts with false identities and, therefore, there is often no way to establish the veracity of any given web identity. For example, Mathy *et al.* (2002) report that it is not unusual for males to pose as lesbians interested in 'cybersex' (i.e. sexual gratification via role play in cyberspace) in chat rooms for gay and bisexual women. Although phenomenological researchers are likely to see this as an interesting feature of web-based communication and one worthy of study, the tendency to take on false identities on the web poses a problem for those whose research is either taking a translational or novel approach. Mathy *et al.* (2002) have developed some interesting methods for outing these kinds of imposters, but the apparent frequency of adopting different identities on the web may present a problem for these latter forms of research.

Higher levels of anonymity are also likely to lead to diminished levels of self-awareness and individuality (i.e. deindividuation), that in turn can lead to reduced self-regulation of behavior (e.g. Deiner, 1980; Zimbardo, 1970). Consistent with this notion, a considerable amount of research has revealed that people are more likely to respond with hostile and aggressive responses in computer-mediated rather than face-to-face interactions (Culnan & Markus, 1987; Dubrovsky *et al.*, 1991; Kiesler *et al.*, 1984; Siegal *et al.*, 1986; Williams *et al.*, 2002).

Increased anonymity is also associated with lower levels of accountability (see Lerner & Tetlock, 1999 for a review) that in turn is likely to have implications for the degree of integrative complexity people bring to bear to anything they do on the web. Considerable research has found that people exhibit more bias when they are low rather than high in social accountability for their judgments, decisions, or behaviors. Low levels of accountability are associated with stronger primacy effects in impression formation (Tetlock, 1983), an increased tendency to make the fundamental attribution error (Tetlock, 1985), stronger over-confidence effects (Tetlock & Kim, 1987), as well as greater persistence due to 'sunk costs' (Simonson & Nye, 1992). Whether positive or negative, the anonymity and low accountability of Internet communication are distinctive and important differences between it and other forms of social interaction, issues that researchers need to take into account when designing and interpreting Internet-based research.

Ethical constraints

There is considerable debate about whether behavior on the web is part of the public domain, and therefore whether researchers need to get informed consent before using web postings for research (see Frankel & Siang, 1999 for a review). For example, if one uses content on the web for analysis, such as music libraries (e.g. Rentfrow & Gosling, 2003), chat room postings (e.g. Bordia & Rosnow, 1998), or reactions to prompts planted in online discussions (e.g. Glaser et al., 2002), should one first obtain the consent of those involved? Although one can argue that information posted on the web is public, one can also argue that exploiting this material for research purposes is a violation of privacy. In fact, there are a number of documented examples where people have felt quite violated when they have learned that researchers have studied their online participation in discussion groups or chat rooms without obtaining consent (e.g. Finn & Lavitt, 1994; King, 1996).

The anonymity of Internet communication also makes it difficult to implement the informed consent process. Researchers cannot verify age and mental competency, and the lack of direct contact between researchers and participants makes it difficult for researchers to assess participants' comprehension of risks that may be involved.

Deception is another particularly problematic issue. Deception is considered by many to be ethical if the risks to participants are small, the hypothesis cannot be tested in non-deceptive ways, and participants can be effectively debriefed (Smith & Richardson, 1983). Debriefing, however, is a difficult thing to accomplish online. People are one mouse-click away from closing their participation in a chat room never to return, or similarly may leave an online experiment before reaching the debriefing. Even when researchers have e-mail addresses for participants to whom they could mail a debriefing, there is no way to be sure that they read debriefings sent to them (Azar, 2000).

Moreover, there has been considerable concern that deception may spoil the pond when conducting research with college student subject pools. People may become more distrustful and change their behavior and attitudes about research after learning that they have been deceived (Kelman, 1967). The risk of spoiling the online pond seems even greater and potentially more disastrous in the impact it could have on public perception of psychological research and those who do it. At a minimum, researchers have a responsibility to consider the potential vulnerability of the populations they study online, the level of intrusiveness of their research, and how best to protect the confidentiality of those they study.

Conclusions

Social psychologists have already found many useful ways to employ the Internet to facilitate research. Many of the methods we use in the lab can be easily translated for use on the web, and the Internet also provides opportunities for developing new ways to test social psychological hypotheses. Moreover, because the Internet is a forum for social interaction and one that is increasingly being used by significant portions of society, it is becoming the focus of social psychological study in and of itself.

Our review suggests that the Internet has some potential major benefits, for example, access to larger numbers of people or more specialized populations, than has heretofore been available to most social psychological researchers. However, it also reveals a number of potential areas for concern about the responsible use and interpretation of what we learn from Internet-based social psychological research. For example, 27% of the studies we reviewed involved deception of people on the Internet; of these studies, only slightly more than half reported that they fully debriefed their participants. Although the question of the ethicality of deception on the web for research purposes remains an issue that will have to be worked out both as a field and through the Institutional Review Boards that evaluate our research, it is our opinion that deception and the Internet are not a responsible combination. Not only do deceptive research practices on the web have the potential of creating increased distrust of research and those who do it, it also has the potential consequence of poisoning what for some has become a safe way to seek out social support and connections with others.

Similarly, turning to the Internet for more diverse or specialized samples of research participants brings into sharper relief the fact that social psychology as a field does not give enough serious attention to the potential limitations of the samples we use for research (see Sears, 1986 for an excellent discussion of this problem). Although there is likely to be more diversity with web than college student samples, replacing one biased sample with another does not fully address the fact that social psychological studies are too rarely conducted with representative samples. At a minimum, we should be training both ourselves and our students to think more carefully about questions of sampling, response rates, and related methodological issues and concerns. Clearly, cost has always been a major barrier to doing work with more representative samples. There are, however, creative ways to overcome these kinds of problems, including writing grant proposals to either foundations or federal agencies for support for one's research, or by making use of a new program that is designed to provide broader opportunities for original data collection with nationally representative samples. Specifically, the National Science Foundation has funded an interesting pilot program for data collection with representative samples using either telephone surveys or KN's web panel. Researchers can apply for free access to these means of data collection through the Time-sharing Experiments for the Social Sciences (TESS) program (see *http://www.experimentcentral.org/tess* for more information).

Taken together, the Internet provides greater flexibility for conducting research in social psychology than we had before. Future changes in communication and information technology are likely to continue to expand the ways that we can collect data to test social psychological hypotheses. Our task will be to try to use these advances in ways that allow us to not only expand the ways that we collect data, but to also advance the methodological rigor and quality of social psychological research. Technological changes in communication also may fundamentally change interpersonal interaction, and the consequences of these changes are an important new arena for social psychologists to explore. The other chapters included in this book are an important step in exploring exactly these questions; each delves into different aspects of the new frontier of web-based social interaction and the consequences of Internet use on people's subsequent thoughts, feelings, and behavior.

References

Azar, B. (2000). Online experiments: ethically fair or foul? *Monitor on Psychology*, **31**, 42–7.

Birnbaum, M.H. (1999). Testing critical properties of decision making on the Internet. *Psychological Science*, **10**, 399–407.

Birnbaum, M.H. (2000). Surveywiz and Factorwiz: JavaScript web pages that make HTML forms for research on the Internet. *Behavior Research Methods, Instruments, and Computers*, **32**, 339–46.

Birnbaum, M.H. (2001). *Introduction to behavioral research on the Internet.* Upper Saddle River, NJ: Prentice-Hall.

Birnbaum, M.H. (in press). Methodological and ethical issues in conducting social psychological research via the Internet. In C. Morf, A. Panter, and C. Sansone (eds), *Handbook of methods in social psychology,* Sage. Retrieved June 2, 2003 from *http://psych.fullerton.edu/mbirnbaum/Birnbaum.HTM*

Bordia, P. (1996). Studying verbal interaction on the Internet: the case of rumor transmission research. *Behavior Research Methods, Instruments, and Computers,* **28**, 149–51.

Bordia, P. and Rosnow, R.L. (1998). Rumor rest stops on the information highway: a naturalistic study of transmission patterns in a computer-mediated rumor chain. *Human Communication Research,* **25**, 163–79.

Chang, L. and Krosnick, J.A. (2003a). National surveys via RDD telephone interviewing vs. the Internet: comparing sample representativeness and response quality. *Under review.*

Chang, L. and Krosnick, J.A. (2003b). Comparing oral interviewing with self-administered computerized questionnaires: an experiment. *Under review.*

Couper, M.P. (2000). Web surveys: a review of issues and approaches. *Public Opinion Quarterly,* **64**, 464–94.

Couper, M.P., Blair, J., and Triplett, T. (1999). A comparison of mail and e-mail for a survey of employees in federal statistical agencies. *Journal of Official Statistics,* **15**, 39–56.

Crandall, C.S. (1995). Do parents discriminate against their heavyweight daughters? *Personality and Social Psychology Bulletin,* **21**, 724–35.

Culnan, M.J. and Markus, M.L. (1987). Information technologies. In F. Jablin, L.L. Putnam, K. Roberts, and L. Porter (eds), *Handbook of organizational communication* (pp. 420–43). Newbury Park, CA: Sage.

Cummings, J.N., Sproull, L., and Kiesler, S.B. (2002). Beyond hearing: where real-world and online support meet. *Group Dynamics: Theory, Research, and Practice,* **6**, 78–88.

Deiner, E. (1980). De-individuation: the absence of self-awareness and self-regulation in group members. In P. Paulus (ed), *The psychology of group influence* (pp. 1160–71). Hillsdale, NJ: Lawrence Erlbaum.

Dubrovsky, V.J., Kielser, S.B., and Sethna, B.N. (1991). The equalization phenomenon: status effects in computer-mediated and face-to-face decision-making groups. *Human-Computer Interaction,* **6**, 119–46.

Evans, D.C., Garcia, D.J., Garcia, D.M., and Baron, R.S. (2003). In the privacy of their own homes: using the Internet to assess racial bias. *Personality and Social Psychology Bulletin,* **29**, 273–84.

Finn, J. and Lavitt, M. (1994). Computer based self-help groups for sexual abuse survivors. *Social Work with Groups,* **17**, 21–46.

Flemming, G. and Sonner, M. (1999). *Can Internet polling work? Strategies for conducting public opinion surveys online.* Paper presented at the annual meeting of the American Association for Public Opinion Research, St. Petersburg Beach, FL.

Foster, J.D., Campbell, W.K., and Twenge, J.M. (2003). Individual differences in narcissism: inflated self-views across the lifespan and around the world. *Journal of Research in Personality,* **37**, 469–86.

Fraley, R.C. (2003). *How to conduct psychological research over the Internet: a beginner's guide to HTML and CGI/Perl.* New York: Guilford.

Frankel, M.S. and Siang, S. (1999). *Ethical and legal aspects of human subjects research on the Internet: a report of a workshop June 10–11, 1999.* Retrieved May 20, 2003 from *http://www.aaas.org/spp/dspp/sfrl/projects/intres/report.pdf.*

Franklin, R.A. (2000). *The hate directory* [Internet website]. Available: *http://www.hatedirectory.com.*

Glaser, J., Dixit, J., and Green, D.P. (2002). Studying hate crime with the Internet: what makes racists advocate racial violence? *Journal of Social Issues,* **58,** 177–93.

Gosling, S.D. and Bonnenburg, A.V. (1998). An integrative approach to personality research in anthrozoology: ratings of six species of pets and their owners. *Anthrozoös,* **11,** 148–56.

Guadagno, R.E. and Cialdini, R.B. (2002). Online persuasion: an examination of gender differences in computer-mediated interpersonal influence. *Group Dynamics: Theory, Research, and Practice,* **6,** 38–51.

Guéguen, N. and Jacob, C. (2001). Fund-raising on the web: the effect of an electronic foot-in-the-door on donation. *CyberPsychology and Behavior,* **4,** 705–9.

Hitlin, S. (2003). Values as the core of personal identity: drawing links between two theories of self. *Social Psychology Quarterly,* **66,** 118–37.

Kelman, H.C. (1967). Human use of human subjects: the problem of deception in social psychological experiments. *Psychological Bulletin,* **67,** 1–10.

Kiesler, S., Siegal, J., and McGuire, T. (1984). Social psychological aspects of computer-mediated communication. *American Psychologist,* **39,** 1123–34.

King, S.A. (1996). Researching Internet communities: proposed ethical guidelines for the reporting of results. *The Information Society,* **12,** 119–27.

Klanwatch. (1998). 474 hate groups blanket America: God, rock 'n' roll and the Net fuel the rage. *Intelligence Report Special Issue: 1997, the Year in Hate, Winter 1998,* 89.

Krantz, J.H. and Dalal, R. (2000). Validity of web-based psychological research. In M. Birnbaum (ed), *Psychological experiments on the Internet* (pp. 35–60). Orlando, FL: Academic Press.

Kraut, R., Kiesler, S., Boneva, B., Cummings, J., Helgeson, V., and Crawford, A. (2002). The Internet paradox revisited. *Journal of Social Issues,* **58,** 49–74.

Kraut, R., Patterson, M., Lundmark, V., Kiesler, S., Mukopadhyay, T., and Scherlis, W. (1998). Internet paradox: a social technology that reduces social involvement and psychological well-being? *American Psychologist,* **53,** 1017–31.

Kwak, N. and Radler, B.T. (2000). *Using the web for public opinion research: a comparative analysis between data collected via mail and the web.* Paper presented at the annual meeting of the American Association of Public Opinion Research, Portland, OR.

Legard, D. (2002). E-mail threats increase sharply. *PCWorld.com.* Retrieved May 20, 2003, from *http://www.pcworld.com/news/article/0,aid,107930,00.asp*

Lenhart, A., Horrigan, J., Rainie, L., *et al.* (2003). The ever-shifting Internet population: a new look at Internet access and the digital divide. *The Pew Internet and American Life Project.*

Lerner, J.S., Gonzalez, R.M., Small, D.A., and Fischhoff, B. (2003). Effects of fear and anger on perceived risks of terrorism: a national field experiment. *Psychological Science,* **14,** 144–50.

Lerner, J.S. and Tetlock, P.E. (1999). Accounting for the effects of accountability. *Psychological Bulletin*, **125**, 255–75.

Lind, E.A., Tyler, T.R., and Huo, Y.J. (1997). Procedural context and culture: variation in the antecedents of procedural justice judgments. *Journal of Personality and Social Psychology*, **73**, 767–80.

Mathy, R.M., Schillace, M., Coleman, S.M., and Berquist, B.E. (2002). Methodological rigor with Internet samples: new ways to reach underrepresented populations. *Cyber Psychology and Behavior*, **5**, 253–66.

McGraw, K.O., Tew, M.D., and Williams, J.E. (2000). The integrity of Web-delivered experiments: can you trust the data? *Psychological Science*, **11**, 502–6.

McGraw, K.O. and Wong, S.P. (1992). A common language effect size statistic. *Psychological Bulletin*, **111**, 361–5.

McKenna, K.Y.A. and Bargh, J.A. (1998). Coming out in the age of the Internet: identity 'demarginalization' through virtual group participation. *Journal of Personality and Social Psychology*, **75**, 681–94.

McKenna, K.Y.A. and Bargh, J.A. (2000). Plan 9 from cyberspace: the implications of the Internet for personality and social psychology. *Personality and Social Psychology Review*, **4**, 57– 75.

McKenna, K.Y.A. and Green, A.S. (2002). Virtual group dynamics. *Group Dynamics: Theory, Research, and Practice*, **6**, 116–27.

McKenna, K.Y.A., Green, A.S., and Gleason, M.E.J. (2002). Relationship formation on the Internet: what's the big attraction? *Journal of Social Issues*, **58**, 659–71.

Milgram, S. (1977). *The individual in the social world*. New York: McGraw-Hill.

Musch, J. and Reips, U. (2000). A brief history of Web experimenting. In M. Birnbaum (ed), *Psychological experiments on the Internet* (pp. 61–87). Orlando, FL: Academic Press.

Newman, L. and Erber, R. (2002). *Understanding genocide: the social psychology of the holocaust*. New York: Oxford University Press.

Nosek, B.A., Banaji, M.R., and Greenwald, A.G. (2002). Harvesting implicit group attitudes and beliefs from a demonstration web site. *Group Dynamics: Theory, Research, and Practice*, **6**, 101–15.

Rentfrow, P.J. and Gosling S.D. (2003). The do re mi's of everyday life: examining the structure and personality correlates of music preferences. *Journal of Personality and Social Psychology*, **84**, 1236–56.

Richman, W., Kiesler, S., Weisband, S., and Drasgow, F. (1999). A meta-analytic study of social desirability distortion in computer-administered questionnaires, traditional questionnaires, and interviews. *Journal of Applied Psychology*, **84**, 754–75.

Ross, L., Amabile, T. M. and Steinmetz, J. L. (1977). Social roles, social control, and biases on social perception processes. *Journal of Personality and Social Psychology*, **35**, 485–94.

Schafer, D.R. and Dillman, D.A. (1998). Development of a standard e-mail methodology: results of an experiment. *Public Opinion Quarterly*, **62**, 378–97.

Schuman, H., Presser, S., and Ludwig, J. (1981). Context effects on survey responses to questions about abortion. *Public Opinion Quarterly*, **45**, 216–23.

Schwarz, N., Groves, R.M., and Schuman, H. (1998). Survey methods. In D. T. Gilbert, S. T. Fiske, and G. Lindzey (eds), *The handbook of social psychology* (4th ed., pp. 143–79). New York: McGraw–Hill.

Sears, D.O. (1986). College sophomores in the lab: influences of a narrow data base on social psychology's view of human nature. *Journal of Personality and Social Psychology*, **51**, 515–30.

Siegal, J., Dubrovsky, V., Kiesler, S., and McGuire, T.W. (1986). Group processes in computer-mediated communication. *Organizational Behavior and Human Decision Processes*, **37**, 157–87.

Shohat, M. and Musch, J. (2003). Online auctions as a research tool: a field experiment on ethnic discrimination. *Swiss Journal of Psychology*, **62**, 139–45.

Skitka, L.J. (1999). Ideological and attributional boundaries on public compassion: reactions to individuals and communities affected by a natural disaster. *Personality and Social Psychology Bulletin*, **25**, 793–808.

Skitka, L.J. (2002*a*). Do the means always justify the ends or do the ends sometimes justify the means? A value protection model of justice reasoning. *Personality and Social Psychology Bulletin*, **28**, 588–97.

Skitka, L.J. (2002*b*). The fundamental attribution error: fact or artifact? In W.C. McCready (Chair), *Social psychology under the microscope: do classic experiments replicate when participants are representative of the general public rather than convenience samples of college students?* Symposium conducted at the meeting of the Society for Experimental Social Psychology, Columbus, OH.

Skitka, L.J. (2003*a*). [Reactions to the September 11, 2001 terrorist attacks]. Unpublished raw data.

Skitka, L.J. (2003*b*). [Reactions to the Iraq War]. Unpublished raw data.

Skitka, L.J., Bauman, C.W., and Mullen, E. (2004). Political tolerance and coming to psychological closure following September 11, 2001: an integrative approach. *Personality and Social Psychology Bulletin*, **30**, 743–56.

Skitka, L. J. & Mullen, E. (2002). Understanding judgments of fairness in a real-world political context: A test of the value protection model of justice reasoning. *Personality and Social Psychology Bulletin*, **28**, 1419–1429.

Skitka, L.J., Mullen, E., Griffin, T., Hutchinson, S., and Chamberlin, B. (2002). Dispositions, ideological scripts, or motivated correction? Understanding ideological differences in attributions for social problems. *Journal of Personality and Social Psychology*, **83**, 470–87.

Silver, R.C., Holman, E.A., McIntosh, D.N., Poulin, M., and Gil–Rivas, V. (2002). Nationwide longitudinal study of psychological responses to September 11. *Journal of the American Medical Association*, **288**, 1235–44.

Simonson, I., & Nye, P. (1992). The effect of accountability on susceptibility to decision errors. *Organizational Behavior and Human Decision Processes*, **51**, 416–446.

Smith, S. and Richardson, D. (1983). Amelioration of deception and harm in psychological research: the important role of debriefing. *Journal of Personality and Social Psychology*, **44**, 1075–82.

Srivastava S., John O.P., Gosling S.D., and Potter, J. (2003). Development of personality in adulthood: set like plaster or persistent change? *Journal of Personality and Social Psychology*, **84**, 1041–53.

Staub, E. (1989). *The roots of evil: the psychological and cultural origins of genocide*. New York: Cambridge University Press.

Stern, S.E. and Faber, J.E. (1997). The lost e-mail method: Milgram's lost letter technique in the age of the Internet. *Behavior Research Methods, Instruments, & Computers*, **29**, 260–3.

Strack, F., Schwarz, F., and Wanke, M. (1991). Semantic and pragmatic aspects of context effects in social and psychological research. *Social Cognition*, **9**, 111–25.

Taylor, H. (2000). Does Internet research work? Comparing online survey results with telephone survey. *International Journal of Market Research*, **42**, 51–63.

Tetlock, P.E. (1983). Accountability and perseverance of first impressions. *Social Psychology Quarterly*, **46**, 285–92.

Tetlock, P.E. (1985). Accountability: a social check on the fundamental attribution error. *Social Psychology Quarterly*, **48**, 227–36.

Tetlock, P.E. and Kim, J.I. (1987). Accountability and judgment processes in a personality prediction task. *Journal of Personality and Social Psychology*, **52**, 700–9.

Tourangeau, R. and Rasinski, K. (1988). Cognitive processes underlying context effects in attitude measurement. *Psychological Bulletin*, **103**, 299–314.

Tyler, T.R. (2002). Is the Internet changing social life? It seems the more things change, the more they stay the same. *Journal of Social Issues*, **58**, 195–205.

Williams, K.D., Govan, C.L., Croker, V., Tynan, D., Cruickshank, M., and Lam, A. (2002). Investigations into differences between social and cyber ostracism. *Group Dynamics: Theory, Research, and Practice*, **6**, 65–77.

Zaller, J.R. (1992). *The nature and origins of mass opinion*. New York: Cambridge University Press.

Zimbardo, P. (1970). The human choice: individuation, reason, and order versus deindividuation, impulse, and chaos. In W. J. Arnold and D. Levine (eds), *Nebraska symposium on motivation* (Vol. 17, pp. 237–307). Lincoln: University of Nebraska Press.

Chapter 2

Personality and the Internet

Yair Amichai–Hamburger

The Internet is a modern communication technology which is able to create a comprehensive environment. Here, surfers may carry out a variety of social activities, for example, joining a support group or interacting with friends or with people chosen at random. Although millions of people around the world communicate with one another every day, surfing is an individual experience and, therefore, any attempt to understand behavior on the net must involve an examination of the personality of the surfer.

Our personality is the source of our emotions, cognition, and behavior. Its structure has been compared to that of an enormous iceberg, of which only the tip is visible above the water level and the rest of its huge mass is hidden beneath. In a similar way, we know and understand only a small part of our personality; most of it remains unrevealed. Interaction over the Internet, with its anonymity, high degree of control, and the ability to find similar others, creates a unique protective environment that encourages people to express themselves more freely than they would in a regular interaction. This may be especially relevant to people who are socially inhibited and so find difficulty in expressing themselves. They may feel that it is only via the Internet that they can communicate effectively. In some cases, this may lead them to give their life in cyberspace precedence over their 'real life'. Thus, the secure Internet environment may have a direct impact on their personality, and it is on this that our chapter will focus.

This chapter is divided into four main parts. The first focuses on the issue of interaction between personality and Internet use. The second will discuss the expression of identity over the Internet. In the third part, we move on to discuss two negative social phenomena that are associated with Internet use—loneliness and addiction; and the closing section focuses on new directions in which the Internet can be utilized as a tool for the improvement of human well-being.

The interaction between personality and Internet use

People's behavior and choices on the net are, to a great extent, governed by their individual characteristics. Research into this interaction between personality and net choices is in its infancy, but it would seem that many personality theories are pertinent to any discussion of this topic. In addition, any study of this kind must include scrutiny of the unique self-expression which bursts forth all over cyberspace, and an investigation of the different components contained in the Internet environment that encourage people to express themselves with a freedom that does not exist in their normal (earthbound) connections.

Personality and differential behavior on the net

Amichai–Hamburger (2002) suggests that the Internet is an interactive medium that does not fulfill its potential. This, he believes, is a result of the lack of communication, exchange, or sharing of knowledge between Internet designers and psychologists. Internet designers perceive surfers as a homogeneous group and take no account of personality differences, while psychologists tend to see the Internet as a single entity, ignoring its richness and variety of services. As a result, studies of the Internet tend to deal in stereotypes and the Internet develops in ways that ignore the individual needs of the user. This is particularly regrettable since the Internet's unique interactive abilities mean that services may be tailored to fit the personality type of the individual surfer. Amichai–Hamburger argued that research should focus on the interaction between the different personalities of the net users and the diverse components of Internet technology. An important result of this line of research would be a bank of knowledge that would facilitate the design of a more user-friendly Internet.

There are several personality theories relevant to the Internet, among them are need for closure (Amichai–Hamburger *et al.*, 2004*a*), need for cognition (Amichai–Hamburger *et al.*, 2004*b*), and risk taking, sensation seeking, attachment, and locus of control (Amichai–Hamburger, 2002). The personality theory considered by many to have the most relevance to the social aspects of the Internet is the extroversion and neuroticism personality theory (Eysenck & Eysenck, 1975). The main reason for this is its focus on social aspects and its connection to loneliness (Hamburger & Ben–Artzi, 2000).

The extrovert is a friendly person who seeks company, desires excitement, takes risks, and acts on impulse, whereas the introvert is a quiet, reflective person who prefers his or her own company, does not enjoy large social events, does not crave excitement, and may be seen by some as distant and remote. The neurotic person is an anxious individual who is overly emotional and reacts too strongly to all types of stimuli (Eysenck & Eysenck, 1975; Jung, 1939).

In his personality typology, Jung framed two life orientations: extroversion and introversion (Campbell, 1971; Jung, 1939). Most scholars have considered these personality components to be two extremes of the same continuum (see for example, Eysenck & Eysenck, 1975). Jung himself, however, believed that they coexist simultaneously within the same personality; while one may dominate, the other is also present, although it may be unconscious and undeveloped.

Eysenck and Eysenck's (1975) extroversion and neuroticism personality theory is one of the developments of Jung's extroversion-introversion personality typology. Two models have been suggested to explain the relationship between extroversion and neuroticism and loneliness (Levin & Stokes, 1986; Stokes, 1985; Watson & Clark, 1984). The social network model states that the relationship between personality variables and loneliness is mediated by social network variables (Stokes, 1985). Specifically, the model suggests that individual characteristics may reduce one's motivation to initiate social interactions or may affect one's behavior during social contacts, resulting in unsuccessful interactions. The cognitive bias model emphasizes interpersonal cognitive processes as being responsible for feelings of loneliness. According to this model, some people tend to hold a negative view of themselves and the world and, as a result, perceive themselves as depressed, worthless, and lonely, regardless of their actual social network (Watson & Clark, 1984).

In a series of studies, Levin and Stokes (1986) provide evidence that the social network model explains the loneliness experienced by introverts, whereas the cognitive bias model explains the loneliness of neurotics. Stokes (1985) found that only the correlation between extroversion and loneliness, and not that between neuroticism and loneliness, is mediated by the size of the individual's social network. People high in neuroticism seem to be lonely not because of their difficulty in forming and maintaining social relationships, but rather as a manifestation of their negative affectivity, that is, their general negative bias.

These continua of extroversion—introversion, neurotic—non-neurotic are particularly relevant to Internet use. This is because the user is anonymous, has no physical proximity or contact with the person with whom he/she interacts, and has complete control over the interaction, so that he/she feels him/herself to be in a protected environment (Hamburger & Ben–Artzi, 2000). These factors may assist introverted and neurotic individuals to express themselves more freely on the net than they feel able to in an offline relationship. For women, introversion and neuroticism were found to be positively related to the use of Internet social sites (Hamburger & Ben–Artzi, 2000).

These results are particularly interesting because they confirm earlier studies showing that women have higher self-awareness and are more likely to use the social network for support (Leana & Feldman, 1991; Ptacek *et al.*, 1994). It is, however, suggested that, in time, introverted and neurotic males also come to realize that the Internet social services may answer their social needs, since the protected net environment allows them to express themselves freely. This preference for using Internet social services is not likely to be found among male and female extroverts and non-neurotic net users, since they do not suffer from inhibitions in their social interactions.

Maldonado *et al.* (2001) evaluated computer-mediated messages and found that introverted subjects send messages with an extroverted tone. Their messages contained more information than those sent by extroverted subjects. It seems that on the net introverts do not behave in accordance with their usual behavior pattern, but due to the secure environment conduct themselves in ways associated with extroverts in offline relationships (see also Amichai–Hamburger *et al.*, 2002). It is interesting to note that this uncharacteristic online behavior by introverts actually accords with the teachings of Jung. Jung believed that human beings are made up of opposing sets of characteristics; thus, an extroverted person will also be an unexpressed introvert, the introversion lying mainly in the unconscious. The opposite is true for the introvert. Well- being is the result of a successful creation of a balance between these opposing forces. The Internet may be able to assist in the construction of such an equilibrium, by allowing individuals to express the undeveloped part of their personalities. Thus, introverts may express their extroversion in online relationships.

A different opinion was given by Kraut *et al.* (2002) who pointed out that Internet users who are extroverts, with many friends in their offline relationships, showed a higher involvement in their communities as compared with introverts who are also net users. In addition, it was found that, although both extroverts and introverts benefit from their increased Internet use by enlarging their social circles, introverts report a higher loneliness level. They explained their results by 'The rich get richer' phenomenon. Namely, people who have many friends anyway make more friends on the net, whereas people who suffer from social problems are those who are likely to gain less from Internet interaction. However, most scholars hold that the Internet creates opportunities for the 'poor to get rich'. That is, the protected environment created by the Internet produces a situation in which people who cannot express themselves through the more traditional channels of communication find themselves able to do so on the net (Hamburger & Ben–Artzi, 2000; Maldonado *et al.*, 2001; McKenna *et al.*, 2002).

New directions on personality–Internet interaction

This chapter seeks to extend our understanding of the Internet-personality interaction. To do so, it is necessary to examine other relevant personality theories.

Need for closure

People who have a high need for closure are motivated to avoid uncertainties. They tend to 'freeze' the epistemic process (Kruglanski & Freund, 1983) and to reach conclusions speedily. They often get locked in conceptions and ignore contradicting information. People with a low need for closure are predisposed to 'unfreeze' many alternative hypotheses and to test as many implications of their own hypothesis as possible. It was found that preference of websites was in accordance with our predictions when there was no time pressure on the participants (Amichai–Hamburger *et al.*, 2004a). When it comes to the social aspect of the Internet, it seems likely that people with a low need for closure will be willing to explore their identity on the net and are open to new relationships there, while people with a high need for closure will be more inhibited about exploring their identity or starting new Internet relationships.

Locus of control

People with an external locus of control believe that life events are the result of external factors, like chance or luck. People with an internal locus of control believe in their own ability to control their life events (Rotter, 1966, 1982). These personality characteristics may explain the differences between surfers who carefully control their time on the net as opposed to other surfers who 'disappear' into the net's social/romantic relationships with little thought of time. It might also explain the differences between people's willingness or otherwise to give out personal information on the net. Individuals with an external locus of control will not have difficulty in releasing information about themselves, whereas for others, with an internal locus of control, the giving out of information will lead to feelings of loss of control.

Attachment

The signficance of attachment for infants was first studied by Bowlby (1958). Ainsworth *et al.* (1978) showed the importance of attachment beyond infancy and formulated the attachment personality typology. Hazan and Shaver (1987) examined attachment theory in terms of the adult love relationship. They suggested three types of personalities: secure, avoidant, and anxious–ambivalent. The secure style is defined by confidence in the availability of attachment figures in times of need and by comfort with closeness and interdependence. It was found to be related to happy, intimate, and friendly love relationships. The avoidant style is characterized by insecurity concerning others' intentions and preference for emotional distance. It was also found to be associated with fear of intimacy and difficulty in depending on partners. The anxious–ambivalent style is also defined by insecurity concerning others' responses and with a strong desire for intimacy. It is also associated with passionate love and with a strong fear of rejection.

A different way to understand the attachment theory is that rather than assessing attachment types, attachment can be seen as two continua of the personality dimension: avoidance and anxiety. Every individual can be located at a point on these two dimensions (Brennan *et al.*, 1998). The attachment theory may well be relevant in explaining the seeming contradiction between the very shallow relationships and the deep serious relationships that develop on the net. It seems that those surfers who are high on the avoidant continuum have a tendency towards forming relationships with no commitment to the other side. This is because they do not want to rely on others and are likely to experience tension should the relationship show signs of becoming serious. However, the surfer who would be placed in a high position on the 'anxious' continuum has a need for stable relationships and will need to spend time 'getting to know' their potential friend. They are the ones who will most probably heighten the level of intimacy between themselves and their Internet partners, and are also those who have a greater tendency to become addicted to their net relationships.

Sensation seeking and risk taking

These are two highly related personality dimensions. Sensation seeking focuses on the need for new and varied experiences through disinherited behavior. These include dangerous activities, a non-conventional lifestyle, and a rejection of monotony (Zuckerman, 1971). Risk taking is a personality dimension; people vary as to the degree to which they are ready to take an action that involves a significant degree of risk (Levenson, 1990). These personality theories appear to be particularly relevant when assessing user behavior on the Internet. People who are high in sensation seeking and risk taking will be more open to new experiences on the net. They will, therefore, be more likely to use the Internet to explore different aspects of their personality and may also be interested in exploring the extremes of the net. Should their net relationship develop, it is this type of person who is most likely to take the initiative and suggest a meeting. People who are low on sensation seeking and risk taking will conversely behave more cautiously on the net and will be less open to identity experiments. Although their relationships in cyberspace will, in all probability, develop faster than those in the offline world, they will still follow a prudent, steady course.

The personality theories described above represent an example of an effective method to explore ways in which personality and Internet interaction should make progress. Other personality theories may also be found to have relevance. One concept which is pivotal to any discussion of personality is that of the self. This refers to our subjective perception, how we perceive ourselves. One of the most important contributors to the understanding of the self is the psychologist Carl Rogers.

The Rogerian self-concept and the Internet

Rogers was one of the leaders of the Human Potential Movement, which saw itself as an alternative power to psychoanalysis and behaviorism. Rogers (1980) argued that, in modern life, people had deserted their own innate personalities and replaced them with a set of characteristics they believed would guarantee them the love of others. However, whatever façade they adopted and as hard as they tried to please others, their actions were felt to be unsatisfactory by their recipients who clearly perceived their needs differently. Rogers explains it thus: 'Hence, to a degree probably unknown before, modern man experiences his loneliness, his cut-off-ness, his isolation both from his own deeper being and from others' (Rogers, 1980, pp. 166–7).

Rogers suggested that healthy people live in congruence between themselves and their experience; they are open to experiences in life, and lack the defensiveness that creates tension between the self and the experience. He maintains that people achieve this state when they are brought up by parents who gave them unconditional love that enabled them to experience the world through their own eyes. Conversely, unhealthy people received conditional love that created a barrier, causing them to be unable to express their real self out of fear of losing the affection of their caregivers. Pathology is a disturbed relationship between the self-concept and actual experience.

The structure of the Rogerian personality (1961) contains three different selves:

- The self-concept (the phenomenological self)—the subjective perception of the self. This includes both the parts that are expressed and conscious beliefs about the self, as influenced by culture and education.
- The true self (or the organismic valuing process) represents the real self, for most people as yet unfulfilled. It is the deepest part of our personality which senses what is good or bad for the individual.

- ♦ The ideal self—what the person would like to be. This is not necessarily the same as the true self, since the person can have an ideal self that is totally at odds with that to which he/she should aspire. It is important that the gaps between the ideal self and the true self, the self-concept and the ideal self, and the self-concept and the true self should be as small as possible; should these gaps widen, the psychological well-being of the individual is liable to deteriorate.

Rogers (1980) suggested that the most important component of successful therapeutic outcomes is an environment that promotes the growth of the patient. Three conditions are required to create such a climate:

1 Genuineness, realness, or congruence—the therapist makes himself or herself open to the patient. Therefore, the patient feels that the therapist can be trusted.

2 Unconditional positive regard—whatever the patient says, the therapist accepts positively. In addition, the therapist showes the patient that his/her welfare is a matter of genuine concern.

3 Empathic understanding—listening in a way that gives the therapist entry into the private world of the client so that he/she can understand what is below the awareness level.

Although Rogers stresses that these three conditions are necessary for a climate of growth—which is the case in any significant relationship (therapist–client, father–child, teacher–student)—he emphasizes that these conditions are very rare in our regular lives.

McKenna and Bargh (2000) suggested that four major differences exist between Internet interaction and face-to-face interaction:

1 greater anonymity

2 the diminution of the importance of physical appearance

3 physical distance

4 greater control over the time and pace of interactions.

McKenna et al. (2002) believe that the secure protective environment found on the Internet is likely to have a positive effect on net relationships. They argue that the unique qualities of communicating in cyberspace are the reason that people are willing to share self-relevant information. They use the concept 'real me' to refer to a version of the self that someone believes is the truth, but that he/she find difficulty in expressing. They derive their concept from the 'true self' concept used by Rogers (1951) for the feelings of patients after successful therapy, when she/he manages to become more truly her/himself.

McKenna *et al.* (2002) differentiate between people who locate their real me on the Internet (namely, reveal their real self over the net) and those who locate their real me in offline relationships (namely, who prefer to reveal their real self in traditional offline relationships). They suggest that the location of the real me will define where people will have their more significant relationships—online or offline. When a person locates his/her real me on the Internet, it is expected that he/she will have a more significant relationship over the net than when a person locates his/her real me in offline relationships. In addition, they suggest that these people will strive to move those significant relationships outside the net, so as to make them a 'social reality' (Gollwitzer, 1986).

In a series of three experiments, they demonstrated that people who found it easier to express their true self over the net reported a rapid formation of cyberspace relationships and that those relationships endured over time. They also found that people who are socially anxious and lonely can better express themselves on the Internet than in offline relationships. Social anxiety and loneliness are linked to relationship intimacy by mediation of the location of the self. There is no direct relationship between social anxiety and loneliness to intimacy and closeness. In addition, they found that people strive to move their significant Internet relationships to their non-Internet social life to make it a social reality. More specifically, they found that Internet newsgroup participants reported bringing their Internet friends into everyday life. As many as 63% had spoken on the phone with someone they had contacted over the Internet; 56% exchanged a photograph of themselves; 54% had written and sent a letter through the mail; and 54% had met their Internet friend face-to-face. Also, they found that people who had created their first impression over the net liked the other partner more when they met face to face as compared to when the beginning of interaction had been face-to-face. According to them, this is proof that a relationship established on the basis of mutual self-disclosure is stronger than one based on physical attractiveness.

Bargh *et al.* (2002) examined the impact of the protected Internet environment on the expression of the self. They focused on response time to actual self-characteristics (which participants declared earlier, as one expresses in social interaction) in comparison to true self-characteristics (which they declared earlier as one's reflecting his/her true self) after an interaction. Experiment 1 showed that response times for actual self were faster after face-to-face interaction as compared to Internet interaction, meaning that the actual self was more accessible after face-to-face interaction. In contrast, the opposite occurred for true self, such that response times were faster after Internet interaction as compared to face-to-face interaction, meaning that the true self was more activated during Internet interaction. Experiment 3 showed that people who interacted on the net were more successful in representing their true self to their communication partner as compared with people who interacted face to face. The degree of matching between the characteristics people used when they described their real me and the way in which they were described by their partner was found to be high, as compared with the match to their actual self. In addition, a significant correlation was found between liking and the degree of suitability, in the description that the individual gave to ideal close friends when describing his/her communication partner's characteristics.

The rapid feeling of intimacy with the other side should be treated with caution. It is important that people differentiate between what is actually taking place during an Internet relationship and their feelings about that relationship that may well have been induced by the channel through which they are communicating. In addition, Internet communication is especially attractive to people who find difficulty in making friends and, therefore, have strong social needs that are unfulfilled. These people are particularly vulnerable to the possible deception induced by this form of contact.

Amichai–Hamburger et al. (2002) attempted to relate the Internet real me concept (see McKenna et al., 2002) to the extroversion and neuroticism personality theory (Eysenck & Eysenck, 1975). Subjects who were regular users of 'chat' completed questionnaires. These revealed that introverted and neurotic people locate their real me on the Internet, while extroverts and non-neurotic people locate their real me through traditional social interaction. It would appear that the social services provided on the Internet, with their anonymity, lack of need to reveal physical appearance, ability to control the degree of information revealed in the interaction, together with the ease with which it is possible to find like-minded people, provide an excellent solution to people who experience great difficulty in forming social contacts due to their introverted neurotic personality. These results are reinforced by the fact that the social anxiety and loneliness variables that McKenna et al. (2002) found as relating to the location of the real me on the Internet are highly related to introversion and neuroticism. As Norton et al. (1997) reported, there is a positive relationship between social anxiety and neuroticism and a negative one between loneliness and extroversion.

Some further ideas on the real me concept

The concept of the real me enables us to understand the importance of the Internet for certain types of people; for example, those people who find it better to express themselves on the Internet than through the more traditional channels of communication. This implies that for a significant number of people such as introverts, neurotics, lonely people, and people with social anxiety, the Internet may become a very significant part of their lives and perhaps the only one in which they truly express themselves. It would seem that the perception of the Internet as just some kind of a replacement for the 'real world' is, for these people, inaccurate. The Internet plays a pivotal role in their lives for, as Rogers points out, people who cannot express their 'true self' are prone to serious psychological disorders (Rogers, 1951). However, the Rogerian concept of the 'real self' should be treated with caution. This concept refers to the existence of a self that is largely unknown to its host, while the phenomenon found on the Internet relates more closely to that referred to by Bargh *et al.* (2002) as the 'strangers on the train phenomenon' (Rubin, 1975) (i.e. where people feel safe to tell a stranger their intimate secrets).

It is possible that, when the well-protected Internet environment is utilized by surfers who are sensitive and warm, the resulting interaction will create the optimal conditions as specified by Rogers for the building of a therapeutic environment. However, the general concept that surfers will discover their true self through the Interent should be treated with caution. The true self is unknown to most people and may be revealed through therapy. It is necessary to ask, however, whether behavior on the net is ever a revelation of the true self or simply a sharing of intimate information in what appears to be a safe environment. Nevertheless, given the safe environment of the net and the ease with which it is possible to find similar others, a setting may be created in which individuals do, in fact, strengthen their self-concept and feel at ease to express themselves.

The expression of identity over the Internet

Identity is our uniqueness, the sense of being separate from the environment. A sense of identity stems from consistency over time; it is the ability of the individual to provide a satisfactory answer to the question 'who am I?' (Erikson, 1968). It is during adolescence that our identity is formed, but shaping it is a lifelong process, a life–longitudinal challenge (Mussen *et al.*, 1979). Adolescents who have not achieved a sense of identity at this stage in their development have a lower self-esteem as compared to those who have achieved it (see Campbell *et al.*, 1984).

Eric Erikson (1968) viewed early stages of childhood similarly to Freud but, in addition to focusing on libidinal tension, also emphasized the rational or ego processes involved. As a result, his theory places a greater emphasis on societal and cultural influences. Erikson argued that our personality develops from earliest infancy and continues throughout our lives. His work was found to be relevant by many modern readers because of its emphasis on the development of the identity. This issue of self-identity has emerged as one of the most consuming topics in modern western society. According to Erikson, the ability to give and receive mature adult love is based on intimacy, the ability to reflect your identity on your partner. To be able to do so, an individual needs a sense of coherent identity. Those who fail to develop a sense of identity are likely to experience isolation.

It is significant that both Erikson and Rogers emphasized the impact of social reality. According to both scholars, social rejection significantly damages the ability of the adolescent to build a coherent sense of self or identity.

The unique protection afforded by the Internet encourages people to use it as a haven in which to explore their identity. The ability to adopt different identities on the net leads to an examination of the issue of identity structure and whether a single identity is preferable to a multiple identity structure. An analysis of the role that the Internet may play in the construction or deconstruction of identity may lead to an understanding of how it may be utilized as a tool to help in the rehabilitation of members of a negatively stigmatized group. Each of these issues is described in more detail below.

Exploring our identity on the net

Turkle (1995) studied identity swapping on the Internet through multiuser dimension (MUD). On MUD, surfers build the roles for social interaction as they go along and construct their self through the interaction with others using text only. She found that people playing frequently take on the persona of the individual they are impersonating (see also Bechar–Israeli, 1995). This is consistent with Fine (1983) who argued that in fantasy games, when a person plays a character for a long time, she/he becomes more and more identified with that character and begins to experience the emotions and feelings of that character.

Many users participate simultaneously in several different MUD sessions and so experience several identities at the same time. The anonymity allows people a unique opportunity for self-expression.

Turkle (1995) argues that the participation in Internet identity games is similar to participation in psychodrama. This ties in with the idea of the game as a means through which experience is formulated (Erikson, 1968). In 'real life', individuals experiment with different identities, until they adopt one. According to Turkle, the identity game helps to bring about psychological maturity. This is achieved by being able to discover different aspects of the self and experiencing flexible transitions between different identities. Turkle believes that the Internet supplies warmth, safety, understanding, and space (an experience similar to that of undergoing psychotherapy), which may also create an safe environment in which to rework elements from the past. However, she points out that this is not always the case. While the surfer might feel protected on the net, there is no guarantee that s/he will go through any therapeutic process and indeed might actually make things worse for her/himself. Some people use the net to 'act out' (i.e. put an old conflict in the new setting) instead of 'working through'. Turkle suggests that the Internet can help people transform themselves by using the self-fulfilling prophecy in a positive way. By building a strong identity on the net, people can eventually affect their 'real life'.

However, it is important to stress that even according to Freudian theory, the MUD game cannot be perceived as a total uninhibited fantasy on the part of the user. As Fine (1983) explains, what happens in fantasy games is not wholly autistic or egocentric, because gaming fantasy is based on shared experience, and the player must construct this experience through communication with others taking part in the fantasy game. During this process, the borders of the fantasy are determined by roles and norms that are part of the game. Therefore, there is a great need for the ego as a mediator. As Fine pointed out, when they take on fantasy roles, few people tend to create a persona which is wholly different from their own.

Gender identity games (e.g. pretending to be a woman on the Internet) may teach men something of what women may feel, at least in cyberspace. Silberman (1995), a writer for *Wired* magazine, pretended to be a woman using the pseudonym, Rose. He was surprised by the amount of attention he received as a woman and by the degree of harassment (see also Curtis, 1997). Gender swapping on the net is seen by many to be very controversial (Wallace, 1999). An interaction on the net will almost invariably start with a question referring to the gender of the other side, which indicates the importance of gender identification. This may account for the perception of Internet sex changes as perverted and unethical.

Identity swapping may be associated with the deception of other participants. This should be borne in mind by Turkle (1995) and others, who recommend the Internet as an identity lab. In some cases, this can be of no serious consequence and may be tacitly understood by all those entering the site. In other cases, the consequences can be very serious, and even fatal. If an elderly married man takes on the identity of a young single man in his twenties and subsequently becomes romantically involved with a young woman who is using her true identity of being young, single, and in her twenties, the results may be heart breaking. A recent story reported in the newspapers (Goldman, 2003) was that of a 'handsome man' called Tyrone. He was an object of admiration by hundreds of female Internet users and he even sent his photograph to any admirer who requested it. He was sent money and presents by those who thought that only they had a serious relationship with him. This continued until one of his admirers tracked him down and discovered that Tyrone was a married woman. The police were called and Tyrone was later hospitalized following a nervous breakdown. There have also been stories of abduction and abuse by pedophiles who pretend to be contemporaries of children using the net and then arrange to meet them. The long-term effects of such incidents are as yet unknown. However, as more of these stories of deception become known, perhaps people will lose their trust in the information supplied by the other side in an Internet interaction. Should this happen, the ability to use the net as an identity lab will be more limited. An individual may change his/her identity, but the other side will not necessarily buy into that persona. It may be worth recomending limiting identity games to the Interent areas where identity swapping is part of the game.

Identity and multiplicity

Turkle (1995) argues that without coherence, the self spins off in all directions, and that multiplicity can exist only between personalities that can communicate among themselves. Thus, multiplicity is unacceptable when it leads to confusion to the point of immobility. Turkle goes on to suggest that the 'many manifestations of multiplicity in our culture, including the adoption of online personae, are contributing to a general reconsideration of traditional, unitary notions of identity' (Turkle, 1995, p. 260).

However, it should be pointed out that, although there are many scholars who have advocated the idea of integrity, unity, and internal consistency of the self (Epstein, 1973; Kelly, 1955; Lecky, 1945), the concept of multiple selves is also well known. William James (1981/1890) was one of the first to suggest the multi-selves concept. He argued: 'A man has as many social selves as there are individuals who recognize him and carry an image of him in their mind' (James, 1981, p. 190). In comparison to the classical Freudian personality model, where the ego plays a more intermediary role between libidinal energy and the environment, modern psychologists see the ego as having the overall organizing role of the personality. This enables the individual to live through conflict and contradictions and still create a coherent personality (Blanck & Blanck, 1974; Hartman, 1964; Horner, 1984).

Even within the psychoanalytical approach, there are a number of scholars who took this idea further than the classic understanding of the ego. Klein (1961) suggested that, in addition to the traditional understanding of ego's role of letting the id be expressed in a socially accepted manner, the ego also initiates stimulating situations to be experienced and mastered. A feeling of mastery is achieved by improving the control and synthesis functions. Kohut (1977) refers to the cohesive self as a successful integration of the presentation of the human organized experience. In this cohesive self, contradictions can live together, but still create a cohesive experience.

It was also argued that individuals who perceive themselves as having a multi-faceted self (a man who perceives himself as a wonderful husband, a great father, and an excellent lawyer) are better equipped to face changes and stress in life than those who have a more limited aspect of self (Sarbin & Allen, 1968; Linville, 1987).

Linville suggested that individuals differ as to the complexity of their self-representation. This complexity refers to (1) the number of cognitive self-aspects, and (2) the level of distinction among the self-aspects in terms of features and propositions. According to Linville, people with high self-complexity have a greater number of aspects of the self and a greater distinction among them, and so cope better with stressful events as compared to those people with low self-complexity. When people with a low number of undifferentiated self-aspects experience stressful events that harm one aspect of the self, the effect will spill over and color their perception of the whole situation and their whole self-image negatively. However, when people have a multiple number of self-aspects that are highly differentiated, the stressful event will hurt only a specific self-aspect; its impact will not be generalized to the whole self, but will remain an isolated part of the self.

Linville (1987) did not examine what determines the number of cognitive self-aspects, but believed that as a people serve more social roles, their number of self-aspects will rise. For example, a student of physics who, in addition to studying, plays jazz in a band, plays basketball on a team, and is a member of the Green Peace movement, is likely to have more cognitive self-aspects as compared to a student devoting all of his/her time to studies.

It seems, therefore, that Turkle's (1995) multiplicity concept is heavily rooted in the literature dealing with personality structure. It would seem, however, that the protected environment created by the Internet creates opportunities to explore our identity and enables people to hold varying identities simultaneously. In some cases, this may create elements of a therapeutic process, resulting in a more coherent and comprehensive self-identity. However, it is important to stress that while MUD may contain elements of therapy, it is not a therapy. Therefore, a lack of ability to master and integrate the multi-self Internet identities may, in some cases, lead to a collapse of identity.

Personal website and identity

The creation of a personal website may be seen as a visual construction of identity, since it contains the different roles in the life of the creator. A personal website typically includes sections on family, work, leisure activities, and other interests. The more numerous and varied the sections on the personal website, the more likely it is believed to reflect a more significant construction of our identitiy.

Wallace (1999) suggested that the construction of a personal website can be seen as an expression of the ideal self. While in many cases, this is true, the personal website may also reflect an expression of the ought self (i.e. the self that the creator of the website believes is required by his/her social group). This would appear to contrast with the MUD phenomenon, described by Turkle (1995), as an identity lab in which people try out various, sometimes contradictory personae simultaneously. One way to understand this seeming contraction is simply that one type of person expresses him/herself by creating a personal website, while another is interested in exploring different aspects of his/her personality by trying out different personae. These two phenomena may also be seen as complementing one another. In the earlier discussion of chat sessions on the Internet, it was suggested that a chat session may be interpreted as awakening the objective self-awareness, whereby the individual refers to him/herself as an object (see the Self-awareness concept Duval & Wicklund, 1972). Building a personal website can also be part of seeing oneself as an object described on the website. The act of deciding which parts of one's identity to display, together with the viewing of that identity on the screen, gives the creator the opportunity to consider its form and perhaps decide to try and shape it differently, and in so doing is actually experimening with his/her identity.

Group identity on the net

Our identity is affected by both the groups that we belong to and those that we do not. This is termed group identity. When they identify as part of a group, people behave differently than when they are acting as individuals. LeBon (1903) pointed out that when people are part of a crowd, they revert to a 'group mind'. This group mind creates a situation where the individual appears not to be aware of his/her behavior and may act in extreme ways that he/she would not as an individual. It is important to people to have a positive identity. They will, therefore, be strongly motivated to perceive their group positively in comparison with other groups since this will reflect directly on their own self-concept. It is, therefore, the case that even a random categorization of people into groups (according to their supposed preference of pictures by different artists) will be sufficient to promote a group identity and for people to perceive their own group as superior to other groups (Tajfel *et al.*, 1971).

Lea *et al.* (2001) demonstrated that when interacting with strangers on the net, people become depersonalized and their group identity becomes more salient and attractive. This is expressed by their categorization of themselves in terms of their group identity. The group identity leads to a tendency to stereotype the other people on the basis of the groups to which they belong. This is an interesting result, since one could have predicted that the anonymity of the Internet would prevent the use of group categorization (see also Spears *et al.*, 2002).

Negatively stigmatized groups on the net

Belonging to a group that is perceived negatively in our society may create difficulties for members (Frable, 1993). Individuals belonging to certain stigmatized groups are able to hide their membership in these groups. However, people belonging to such groups are likely to experience two major psychological implications of their membership:

1   They will be able to hide their group identity, but may experience difficulties in detecting similar others in our society, creating a feeling of loneliness.

2   Because they are not identified as belonging to one of these stigmatized groups, other people are likely to express their negative stereotypes about the group they actually belong to in front of them. This is likely to lower their self-esteem (Frable, 1993).

Thousands of different groups exist on the Internet and it is fairly easy to find a group of similar others without having to risk being identified by society as belonging to a stigmatized sector. In addition, visiting websites of similar others may make people feel that their group of similar others is much larger than they had imagined. This may lead to feelings of happiness and confidence.

In a series of pioneering studies, McKenna and Bargh (1998) tested the implications of belonging to a newsgroup of similar others, concentrating on hidden stigmatized groups (i.e. where members attempt to conceal their stigma in daily life) with marginalized sexual interests and marginal political views and ideology. They found that people belonging to a stigmatized identity group were more likely to be involved in a newsgroup of similar others and considered their belonging to the group more important to their identity as compared to those who identified with a non-stigmatized interest newsgroup. Those people who were involved in the newsgroup (posters) reported elevated self-esteem, self-acceptance, and a reduced feeling of social loneliness. In addition, they were highly motivated to make their identity a social reality by telling their close circle of family and friends that they belonged to a stigmatized group; this, in comparison to those people who did not become deeply involved in the newsgroup (lurkers). The fact that 37% of sexually stigmatized people and 63% of politically stigmatized people who were involved in a newsgroup revealed their secret to close others is significant. It demonstrates that belonging to a newsgroup of similar others can have a powerful influence on the transformation of a negative group identity into a positive one, and that the unique protected environment of the Internet can assist people in the transformation of their self-identity.

These results confirm the self-completion theory (Wicklund & Gollwitzer, 1982) which suggests that people are highly motivated to express their significant identity in the offline world. McKenna and Bargh's (1998) results are consistent with those of Rogers (1961) who claimed that people who receive unconditional love from their parents are more likely to open up to their real selves. People are motivated to eliminate a false self-identity before opening up to close others; this then enables them to create a healthy whole self. This type of positive experience found in the newsgroup was pivotal in helping to solve the conflict between the self and everyday experiences, something that Rogers saw as the target of his therapy.

McKenna and Bargh's (1998) findings strengthen those of Pennebaker (1990) that revealing shameful aspects reduced negative health symptoms in the long term. Pennebaker (1995) argued that there is common agreement among psychotherapists that for a person to talk about traumatic and emotional experiences is beneficial to his/her physiological and psychological health. Talking about a stressful event accomplishes two 'main goals':

1 Talking about the event helps to reduce and reflect anxiety.

2 Repeated disclosure over time gradually promotes the assimilation of the upsetting event.

The Internet may be seen as a modern tool, which may be utilized by an individual to reveal him/herself to others in a protected environment.

The personality–Internet interaction may prove relevant to the understanding of social issues that have arisen, reportedly, as a result of Internet use. Two of the most prominent concerns will be discussed below.

Negative social consequences associated with net use

Internet use has been widely associated with a number of harmful results. The following section will examine the two most frequently cited—loneliness and addiction.

Loneliness

Kraut *et al.* (1998) carried out a longitudinal study to examine the effects of the Internet on social involvement and psychological well-being. One of their main findings was that heavy use of the Internet is related to the experience of loneliness among users. These results are in keeping with those of other scholars who also found that Internet use caused a negative reaction among users (Nie & Erbring, 2000).

However, other scholars disagreed with Kraut *et al.*'s (1998) conclusion (Hamburger & Ben–Artzi, 2000; Rierdan, 1999; Shapiro, 1999; Silverman, 1999). They based their objections on both conceptual and methodological grounds. Shapiro (1999) heavily criticized Kraut *et al.* (1998) over their choice of subjects for the study. She pointed out that the researchers had selected participants whose life-stage meant that social contact was likely to decline as a matter of course, regardless of their Internet use. Hamburger and Ben–Artzi (2000) raised two major objections to Kraut *et al.*'s (1998) study. The first was that Kraut *et al.* failed to take into account that there is a wide diversity of services on offer on the Internet. The second was that in their study, Kraut *et al.* regarded Internet users as a single entity, claiming that they all have the same motives and needs. Hamburger and Ben–Artzi (2000) argue that these issues lead them to reject the implications drawn by Kraut *et al.* (1998) as to surfers' well-being.

Kraut *et al.* (2002) carried out a follow-up study of the one researched in 1998. They reported that the negative effects of the Internet reported previously were no longer apparent, an exception being the association of the Internet use with increased stress. In addition, they reported that their new longitudinal survey had found many positive effects resulting from use of the Internet; for example, increase in social involvement and psychological well-being (but again with increased stress). However, they emphasized that the positive results were in keeping with the pattern of the 'rich get richer' (namely, it was the extroverts and people with more social support who showed the greatest benefits from Internet use). According to their explanation, people who are effective at using social resources are more qualified to use the Internet's social channels in a more effective way and therefore gain more out of it.

This conclusion runs counter to the finding of McKenna *et al.* (2002) that it is the less able population, for example, those with social anxiety and loneliness, who are likely to benefit from the Internet. Hamburger and Ben–Artzi's (2000) findings were similar to those of McKenna *et al.* (2002). They too found that it is the introverts and the neurotics who are likely to benefit more from the protected environment of the Internet. Amichai–Hamburger and Ben–Artzi (2003) compared two models dealing with the relationship between loneliness and Internet use: Kraut *et al.*'s (1998) model that the Internet leads to loneliness; and an alternative model that the use of the Internet by lonely people is the result of their situation and not the cause of it. They found that the use of Internet services was related to loneliness and neuroticism only in the case of women. Therefore, they then examined the goodness of the two contrasting models, as they related to women. They compared goodness of fit to the data using LISREL 8 (Jöreskog & Sörbom, 1993). A satisfactory goodness of fit was found for the second model. That is, according to this model, the increased use of the Internet social services by highly neurotic women is a result of their loneliness and is seen as a means to counter it. The case of neurotic women was the only one in which a link was found to loneliness, and even in this case the results ran counter to those of Kraut *et al.* (1998).

Addiction

Traditionally, addiction was related to chemical dependence, for example, on alcohol and drugs. Later, other behaviors were included, for example, teleshopping and Internet addiction. Griffith (1995) was the first to define technological addiction as a behavioral addiction involving human-machine interaction. Young (1997) suggested that it is not the Internet itself that is addictive, but rather specific Internet interactive services.

Overall, it seems that there are two main profiles of people who have a tendency to become addicted to the net: people with social inhibitions and sensation seekers. The first scholar to indicate this was Shotton (1991) who suggested that the two main personality characteristics found in addicts were introversion and sensation seeking. Most studies reinforced the relationship between socially inhibited surfers and addiction. Loytsker and Aiello (1997) found that proneness to boredom, private self-consciousness, loneliness, and social anxiety were related to Internet addiction. Young and Rodgers (1998) suggested that individuals who closely guard their privacy and non-conformists are those who are likely to perceive the Internet as answering their needs, and so may become addicted to its unique qualities.

Armstrong *et al.* (2000) argue that poor self-esteem is a good predictor of Internet addictive behavior. The question remains, however, as to whether low self-esteem leads to Internet addiction or, conversely, that it is in fact Internet addiction that leads to low self-esteem.

The relationship between addiction and personality is still an unsolved puzzle. To better understand the relationship, it is important to avoid falling into generalizations about Internet addiction, but rather to talk about specific addictions (e.g. chat addicts, information addicts, sex addicts). It seems that people with low self-esteem and non-conformists will not necessarily suffer from Internet addiction in the same way. It is only by understanding the relationship between addiction to specific services and specific personality characteristics that we will be able to tackle this topic and provide appropriate treatment for addicts.

Having discussed the relevance of personality to some negative phenomena like loneliness and addiction, we will now deal with how the net may be utilized to enhance our lives.

More on positive consequences of Internet use

Earlier, some of the positive abilities of the Internet to help people to express themselves were discussed. Now, we examine how the Internet can be used to help people come to terms with an existential human conflict (i.e. the need to belong to a group and at the same time the need to be an individual). In addition, we will explore how the Internet can supply tools for people to transfer the sense of effective self-efficacy they feel during a net interaction to the more traditional face-to-face communication.

Relatedness vs. autonomy

Erich Fromm (1941), the romantic humanistic psychologist, argued that human beings strive for freedom and autonomy, but at the same time have a need to relate to significant others. The way that this tension is resolved will depend on the particular society. In a capitalist system that values individual freedom and power, people are more likely to feel loneliness and isolation, whereas in a collectivist society which stresses the human need to belong to a group, members of that society may have to make sacrifices in terms of their individuality and personal fulfillment.

According to Fromm, the human conflict between the striving for freedom and the striving for security is a result of five basic human needs:

1 A need to relate to others—to have someone to care for, share with, and be responsible for.

2 A need for transcendence—to rise above our animal nature, to be creative.

3 A need for rootedness—to replace our separation from nature with feelings of kinship with others.

4 A need for identity—to achieve distinctiveness through one's efforts or through identification with another person or group.

5 A need for a frame of reference—to have a stable structure or framework that will aid in the organizing and understanding of one's experience.

When these needs are considered in terms of constituents of the Internet, it is clear that the net has the ability to answer the high need to belong and relate to others. This is achieved, for example, through the ease with which it is possible to find similar others and groups of interest. In this way, the Internet can compensate for the isolation and loneliness found in our culture. Fromm's basic human needs, especially those for relatedness, identity, and frame of reference, may be answered by the various services offered on the net.

A similar hypothesis dealing with the contradictions in human instincts was offered by the optimal distinctiveness theory of Brewer (1991). According to this theory, people are motivated by two contradicting motives: the need to express individuality and the need to belong to a large, significant group. Brewer differentiated between collective identity (the belonging to large groups) and the interpersonal identity (the relating to others on an individual basis). In both, the individual defines him/herself as an identity related to others either as part of a large group or as individuals. These needs contradict each other; satisfying one means evoking the need for satisfying the other. People strive to belong to a group that satisfies both needs in the most optimal way (see also Brewer & Gardner, 1996).

Bettencourt and Sheldon (2001) attempted to resolve the dichotomy of Brewer's (1991) motive contradiction by introducing the social role. According to Biddle (1979), the social role refers to 'a behavioral repertoire, characteristic of a person or a position; a set of standards, descriptions, norms, or concepts held for the behaviors of a person or social position' (Biddle, 1979, p. 9). Bettencourt and Sheldon (2001) suggested that social roles, by definition, involve an interaction with group members. As role holders contribute to group goals through the fulfillment of their role, they become more connected to the group. This is especially true when they fit their role well. When a social role is consistent with the individual's self-concept and his/her core skills, he/she is likely to feel autonomy and self-expression as well. It means that the seemingly contradicting motives of autonomy and relatedness can be mutually achieved when the individual performs social roles that fit his/her ability and characteristics. This argument was proved in a series of studies.

Despite the seemingly optimistic approach of Bettencourt and Sheldon (2001), it is important to stress that, in many cases, groups demand that individuals take on social roles not of their choosing. Those responsible for allocating these roles will not necessarily take into account the skills, abilities, and motives of the individual, but will rather look to the needs of the group. In addition, roles are frequently allocated according to the social role to which the group is aspiring. In such a case, an individual may be chosen to perform a certain role according to the general perception that is held of him/her. This perception may not be in keeping with whom he/she really is, or may be outdated and, therefore, the fit between personality and social roles in many cases will not be accurate. This may be the case even when the group attempts to choose the best person for the role.

In the Internet arena, it may be easier to find social roles that allow individuals their self-expression and even their self-actualization, since the net gives individuals more freedom to choose the groups and the social roles that suit them. The act of compelling someone to take on a role barely exists on the Internet, since any attempt to do this will lead the surfer to disagree, to express alternatives, and, should this not be acceptable, to leave. It seems that the Internet creates an environment where the contrast between the need to relate and the need for autonomy is very limited and, in fact, the Internet is able to sustain situations in which both needs are mutually fulfilled. In this case, there are positive implications to be considered that pertain to individual well-being.

Generalizing from positive Internet experience

Self-efficacy is closely related to self-confidence. It is a person's evaluation of his or her ability or competency to perform a task, reach a goal, or overcome an obstacle (Bandura, 1977). People who develop a high self-efficacy in a certain area believe in their ability to be agents of change in that area.

The Internet has a unique potential to assist people who have social difficulties (e.g. introverts, neurotics, or the socially anxious) to develop the ability to build and maintain relationships. In some cases, as McKenna *et al.* (2002) suggested, there may be a natural transition from an online relationship to an offline association. However, for some people, this social self-efficacy, newly acquired through the net, may be confined there and will not be generalized beyond the borders of cyberspace—this despite the fact that some of these surfers may wish to extend this ability to the offline world as well. Particularly among people suffering from an extreme form of social anxiety, the transition from an Internet connection to a 'real-life' association might be too great a leap.

However, it is my belief that as well as providing a medium through which socially inhibited people acquire social skills and the confidence that goes with them, the Internet also supplies a learning environment that may be structured to enable people to learn how to transfer their new communication skills from the net to a face-to-face interaction. This model may also serve the population of extremely socially anxious individuals who are particularly prone to generalize their Internet interpersonal skills inwards to be used widely and exclusively in virtual communication. This model advocates an exceptionally gradual process to help the individual to begin to loosen the total control he/she feels on the Internet and so equip him/herself to cope with the relative loss of control in a 'real-life' situation. The main steps in this graded contact are as follows:

1 Communicating by text only: this text-only interaction is the most common form of communication over the net. This stage will continue until the participant feels secure in this form of contact and his/her anxiety levels are negligible.

2 Text + image: participants will continue to use the text method with which they feel secure, but will simultaneously view a live video image of the person with whom they are interacting. When low-level social anxiety has been established, participants will transfer to the next stage.

3 Communicating by video + audio: at this stage, people will still interact from their secure environment and still without physical proximity to their conversation partner. However, use of text messages by the subject will be reduced; instead he/she will communicate orally. In addition, a live image of the subject will be transferred to the other participant. Again, when a satisfactory level of comfort has been achieved, participants may progress to the next stage.

4 Face-to-face interaction: this is the stage of regular face-to-face interaction. It is predicted that by this stage people will be able to bridge the gap between text-only Internet contact and total exposure through a face-to-face encounter, and do so in a way that continually preserves low levels of anxiety among participants.

By creating a very gradual process, moving slowly from a totally protected environment to one which is significantly less protected, through several stages in which the protection is gradually lifted, extremely socially anxious people may be particularly helped. This process demonstrates the power of the Internet, not only as a supplier of a protective environment, but as one providing the tools to create a process of change from social anxiety to secure social relationships.

Conclusions

This chapter has examined the ways in which the net may be used to help rehabilitate certain disadvantaged individuals, for example, those suffering from social anxiety, the lonely, introverts and neurotics, or people suffering from a stigmatized identity. These types of people may feel comfortable in the highly protected world of the Internet and will, therefore, adopt it as their chosen environment. For them, the ability to express the 'real me' on the net is not a minor aspect of life, but a very crucial one. It is important to remember that people who cannot express their 'true self' are prone to serious psychological disorders (Rogers, 1951). The chapter also showed how the Interent can serve as an identity lab for its users, both in terms of its positive potential and its hazards.

The chapter went on to demonstrate the relevance of personality to two of the main social problems attributed to the net—addiction and loneliness. The complexity of these issues was exposed and further research is recommended. The chapter concludes with a discussion of two potentially effective ways in which well-being may be improved through the Internet : first, the ability to solve the conflict between the need to express individuality and the need to belong to a large, significant group; and second, the potential to create a generalization between successful online interaction and the offline world.

This chapter has brought together the personality theories from schools such as those of Jung, Erikson, Rogers, and Fromm, one of the most modern of inventions, the Internet. It has been fascinating to discover how relevant the theories of these scholars are to the human behaviors found in cyberspace. Jung's assertion that introversion and extroversion can coexist as complementary personality aspects, rather than polar opposites, is applicable to the Internet, where introverts have been shown to behave as extroverts. Rogers' humanistic approach proved useful in explaining the significance of the Internet to people who have difficulties in expressing their real self in the more traditional world. The Internet identity experiments played out through intrigues of the MUD games were explained by Erikson, with his general emphasis on identity and more specific emphasis on the importance of games in the creation of identity. The Internet was found to have a useful role in the resolution of the existential conflict as defined by Fromm as relatedness vs. autonomy.

The Internet has been described as a virtual world; the implication being that on some level, cyberspace is a poor second to the 'real world'. This chapter has demonstrated clearly that the Internet is a powerful reality, where the most basic components of our personality are touched by others and expressed to others. However, despite our positive approach, it is important to remember that the Interent also has a negative potential. Enhancing our knowledge in this field will enable us to create a net that will enhance users' well-being.

References

Ainsworth, M.D.S., Blehar, M.C., Waters, E., and Wall, S. (1978). *Patterns of attachment: a psychological study of the strange situation.* Hillsdale, N.J.: Erlbaum.

Amichai–Hamburger, Y. (2002). Internet and personality. *Computers in Human Behavior,* **18**, 1–10.

Amichai–Hamburger, Y. and Ben–Artzi, E. (2003). Loneliness and Internet use. *Computers in Human Behavior*, **19**, 71–80

Amichai–Hamburger, Y., Fine, A., and Goldstein, A. (2004*a*). The impact of Internetinteractivity and need for closure on consumer preference. *Computers in Human Behavior*, **20**, 103–17.

Amichai–Hamburger, Y., Kaynar, O., and Fine, A (2004*b*) *The effects of need for cognition on Internet use.* Unpublished manuscript.

Amichai–Hamburger, Y., Wainapel, G., and Fox, S. (2002). 'On the internet no one knows I'm an introvert': extroversion, neuroticism, and internet interaction. *Cyberpsychology and Behavior*, **2**, 125–28.

Armstrong, L., Phillips, J.G., and Saling, L.L. (2000). Potential determinants of heavier Internet usage. *International Journal of Human Computer Studies*, **53**, 537–50.

Bandura, A. (1977). *Social Learning Theory.* New York: General Learning Press.

Bargh, J.A., McKenna, K.Y.A., and Fitzsimons, G.J. (2002). Can you see the real me? The activation and expression of the 'true self' on the Internet. *Journal of Social Issues*, **58**, 33–48.

Bechar–Israeli, H. (1995). 'FROM <Bonehead> TO <cLoNehEAd>: nicknames, play, and identity on internet relay chat.' *Journal of Computer-Mediated Communication*, **1(2)**: *http://www.ascusc.org/jcmc/vo11/issue2/bechar.html.*

Bettencourt, B.A. and Sheldon, K. (2001). Social roles as a vehicles for psychological need satisfaction within groups. *Journal of Personality and Social Psychology*, **81**, 1131–43.

Biddle, B.J. (1979). *Role theory: expectations, identities, and behaviors.* New York: Academic Press.

Blanck, R. and Blanck, G. (1974). *Beyond ego psychology.* New York: Columbia University Press.

Bowlby, J. (1958). The nature of the child's tie to his mother. *International Journal of Psycho-Analysis*, **39**, 350–73.

Brennan, K.A., Clark, C.L., and Shaver, P. (1998). Self-report measures of adult romantic attachment. In J. A. Simpson and W. S. Rholes (eds), *Attachment theory and close relationships* (pp. 46–76). New York: Guilford.

Brewer, M.B. (1991). The social self: on being the same and different at the same time. *Personality and Social Psychology Bulletin*, **17**, 475–82.

Brewer, M.B. and Gardner W.L. (1996). Who is this 'we'? Levels of collective identity and self-representations. *Journal of Personality and Social Psychology*, **71**, 83–93.

Campbell, J. (1971). *The portable Jung.* New York: Viking.

Campbell, E., Adams, G.R., and Dobson, W.R. (1984). Familial correlates of identity formation in late adolescence. *Journal of Youth and Adolescence*, **13**, 509–25.

Curtis, P. (1997). Mudding: social phenomena in text-based realities. In S. Kiesler (ed), *Culture of the Internet* (pp. 121–42). New York: Erlbaum.

Duval, S. and Wicklund, R. (1972). *A theory of objective self-awareness.* NewYork: Academic Press.

Epstein, S. (1973). The self-concept revisited: or a theory of a theory. *American Psychologist*, **28**, 404–16.

Erikson, E.H. (1968). *Identity: youth and crisis.* New York: Norton.

Eysenck, H.J. and Eysenck, S.E.G. (1975). *Manual: Eysenck Personality Inventory.* San Diego: Educational and Industrial Testing Service.

Fine, G.A. (1983). *Shared fantasy: role-playing games as social worlds.* Chicago: University of Chicago Press.

Frable, D. (1993). Being and feeling unique: statistical deviance and psychological marginality. *Journal of Personality*, **61**, 85–110.

Fromm, E. (1941). *Escape from freedom.* New York: Rinehart.

Goldman, D. (2003). *Sex, lies and the Internet.* Yediot, 10.1.03.

Gollwitzer, P.M. (1986). Striving for specific identities: the social reality of self-symbolizing. In R. Baumeister (ed), *Public self and private self* (pp. 143–59). New York: Springer-Verlag.

Griffith, M.D. (1995). *Adolescent gambling.* London: Routledge.

Hamburger, Y.A. and Ben–Artzi, E. (2000). The relationship between extraversion and neuroticism and the different uses of the Internet. *Computers in Human Behavior*, **16**, 441–9.

Hartman, H. (1964). *Essays in ego psychology.* New York: International Universities Press.

Hazan, C. and Shaver, P. (1987). Romantic love conceptualized as an attachment process. *Journal of Personality and Social Psychology*, **52**, 511–24.

Horner, A.J. (1984). *Object relations and the developing ego in therapy.* New Jersey: Jason Aronson.

James, W. (1981). *The principles of psychology*, Cambridge, MA: Harvard University Press. (Originally published in 1890).

Jöreskog, K.G. and Sörbom, D. (1993). *LISREL 8: user's reference guide.* Chicago: Scientific Software.

Jung, C.G. (1939). *The integration of the personality.* New York: Farrar & Rinehart.

Kelly, E.L. (1955). Consistency of the adult personality. *American Psychologist*, **10**, 659–81.

Klein, M. (1961). *Narrative of a child analysis.* London: Hogarth Press.

Kohut, H. (1977). *The restoration of the self.* New York: International Universities Press.

Kraut, R., Kiesler, S., Boneva, B., Cummings, J.N., Helgeson, V., and Crawford, A.M. (2002). Internet paradox revisited. *Journal of Social Issues*, **58**, 49–74.

Kraut, P., Patterson, M., Lundmark, V., Kiesler, S., Mukopadhyay, T., and Scherlis, W. (1998). Internet paradox: A social technology that reduces social involvement and psychological well-being? *American Psychologist*, **53**, 65–77.

Kruglanski, A.W. and Freund, T. (1983) The freezing and unfreezing of lay-inferences: effects on impressional primacy, ethnic stereotyping, and numerical anchoring. *Journal of Experimental Social Psychology*, **19**, 448–68.

Lea, M., Spears, R., and de Groot, D. (2001). Knowing me, knowing you: anonymity effects on social identity processes within groups. *Personality and Social Psychology Bulletin*, **27**, 526–37.

Leana, C.R. and Feldman, D.C. (1991). Gender differences in responses to unemployment. *Journal of Vocational Behavior*, **38**, 65–77.

LeBon, G. (1903). *The crowd.* London: Unwin.

Lecky, P. (1945). *Self-consistency: a theory of personality.* New York: Island Press.

Linville, P.W. (1987). Self-complexity as a cognitive buffer against stress-related illness and depression. *Journal of Personality and Social Psychology*, **52**, 663–76.

Levenson, M.R. (1990). Risk taking and personality. *Journal of Personality and Social Psychology*, **58**, 1073–80.

Levin, I. and Stokes, J.P. (1986). An examination of the relation of individual difference variables to loneliness. *Journal of Personality*, **54**, 717–33.

Loytsker, J. and Aiello, J.R. (1997, August). *Internet addiction and its personality correlates.* Paper presented at the annual meeting of the American Psychological Association, Chicago, IL.

Maldonado, G.J., Mora, M., Garcia, S., and Edipo, P. (2001). Personality, sex and computer communication mediated through the Internet. *Anuario de Psicologia*, **32**, 51–62.

McKenna, K.Y.A. and Bargh, J.A. (1998). Coming out in the age of the Internet: identity 'de-marginalization' from virtual group participation. *Journal of Personality and Social Psychology*, **75**, 681–94.

McKenna, K.Y.A. and Bargh, J.A. (2000). Plan 9 from cyberspace: the implications of the Internet for personality and social psychology. *Personality and Social Psychology Review*, **4**, 57–75.

McKenna, K.Y.A., Green, A.S., and Gleason, M.J. (2002). Relationship formation on the Internet: what's the big attraction? *Journal of Social Issues*, **58**, 9–32.

Mussen, P., Conger, J., and Kagan, J. (1979). *Child development and personality.* New York: Harper & Row.

Nie, N.H. and Erbring, L. (2000) *Internet and society: a preliminary report* [On-line]. Stanford CA: Institute for the Quantitative Study of Society. Available: *www.stanford.edu/group/siqss.*

Norton, G.R., Hewitt, P.L., McLeod, L., and Cox, B.J. (1997). Personality factors associated with generalized and circumscribed social anxiety. *Personality and Individual Differences*, **21**, 655–700.

Pennebaker, J.W. (1990). *Opening up: the healing power of confiding in others.* New York: Morrow.

Pennebaker, J.W. (1995). Emotion, disclosure, and health: an overview. In J.W. Pennebaker (ed), *Emotion, discourse, and health* (pp. 3–10). Washington, DC: American Psychological Association.

Ptacek, J.T., Smith, R.E., and Dodge, K.L. (1994). Gender differences in coping with stress: when stressor and appraisals do not differ. *Personality and Social Psychology Bulletin*, **20**, 421–30.

Rierdan, J. (1999). Internet-depression link? *American Psychologist*, **54**, 781–2.

Rogers, C. (1951). *Client-centered therapy.* Boston: Houghton–Mifflin.

Rogers, C. (1961). *On becoming a person.* Boston: Houghton–Mifflin.

Rogers, C. (1980). *A way of being.* Boston: Houghton–Mifflin.

Rotter, J.B. (1966). Generalized expectancies for internal versus external control of reinforcement. *Psychological Monographs*, **80** (No. 609).

Rotter, J.B. (1982). *The development and application of social learning theory.* New York: Praeger.

Rubin, Z. (1975). Disclosing oneself to a stranger: reciprocity and its limits. *Journal of Experimental Social Psychology*, **11**, 233–60.

Sarbin, T.R. and Allen, V.L. (1968). Increasing participation in a natural group setting: a preliminary report. *Psychological Record*, **18**, 1–7.

Shapiro, J.S. (1999). Loneliness: paradox or artifact? *American Psychologist*, **54**, 782–3.

Shotton, M. (1991). The costs and benefits of 'computer addiction'. *Behaviour and Information Technology*, **10**, 219–30.

Silberman, S. (1995). *A rose is not always a rose*. Available: *http://www/packet/com/packet/silberman/nc_todat.html* [1998, May 20].

Silverman, T. (1999). Loneliness: paradox or artifact. *American Psychologist*, **54**, 780–1.

Spears, R., Postmes, T., Lea, M., and Wolbert, A. (2002). When are net effects gross products? The power of influence and the influence of power in computer-mediated communication. *Journal of Social Issues*, **58**, 91–107.

Stokes, J.P. (1985). The relation of social network and individual difference variables to loneliness. *Journal of Personality and Social Psychology*, **48**, 981–90.

Tajfel, H., Flament, C., Billig, M.G., and Bundy, R.P. (1971). Social categorization and intergroup behavior. *European Journal of Social Psychology*, **1**, 149–78.

Turkle, S. (1995). *Life on the screen: identity in the age of the internet*. New York: Simon and Schuster.

Wallace, P. (1999). *The psychology of the Internet*. New York: Cambridge University Press.

Watson, D. and Clark, L.A. (1984). Negative affectivity: the predisposition to experience aversive emotional states. *Psychological Bulletin*, **96**, 465–90.

Young, K.S. (1997, August). *What makes online usage stimulating? Potential explanations for pathological Internet use*. Paper presented at the 105th annual meeting of the American Psychological Association, Chicago, IL.

Young, K.S. and Rodgers, R.C. (1998). The relationships between depression and Internet addiction. *CyberPsychology and Behavior*, **1**, 25–8.

Wicklund, R.A. and Gollwitzer, P.M. (1982). *Symbolic self-completion*. Hillsdale, NJ: Erlbaum.

Zuckerman, M. (1971). Dimensions of sensation-seeking. *Journal of Consulting and Clinical Psychology*, **36**, 45–52.

Chapter 3

Social cognition online

Sheizaf Rafaeli, Daphne Raban,
and Yoram Kalman

Introduction

Computers are cognitive. Humans are calculating devices. Networks are connecting devices, not just fishing instruments. More people spend more time facing computer screens, connected to each other by means of networks. Via the computer and through the network people view their world, their social, professional, romantic, and familial connections. What are the social cognition implications of humans using networked computers? How does the online environment affect the way people perceive themselves and others? Moreover, how does this influence the way they perceive the computer and the network? We look at the issue of social cognition online in progressively increasing and wider contexts: how does the online environment influence the way we perceive ourselves, other individuals, social groups, and even the computer itself as a social being, as well as the whole network as a social environment. In these expanding concentric circles, we ask how social cognition has been affected by the move into the virtual, and try to outline the main directions current research is taking in these areas.

We discuss two recurring and interrelated issues. One issue is the validity of the use of the 'face-to-face' environment as an ultimate benchmark against which online activity is measured (Rogers & Chaffee, 1983). The second issue is the contrast between the deterministic view of technology as the creator of cognitive states, versus the social constructivist view which perceives technology as an enabler, a presenter of opportunities, leaving the individual and society the freedom to mold it according to their needs and wishes (Williams & Edge, 1996).

The interplay of social and cognitive elements of computers and their use have been salient since the very early days of computing. Mazlish (1993) in his classic *The Fourth Discontinuity* refers to the 'co-evolution of humans and machines' in very dramatic terms. The ability to think with and communicate through machines is likened to only three other progress upheavals in humankind's history: the Copernican, Darwinian, and Freudian paradigm shifts. Realization of this new ability, says Mazlish, is no less than revolutionary for human emotion and social life.

Another dramatic account of computers, communication, and social life, perhaps somewhat less enthralled, is in the tale of woe told about computers by Joseph Weizenbaum. The story of Eliza, the captivating but fake computer psychiatrist program, is central to Weizenbaum's seminal *Computer Power and Human Reason* (Weizenbaum, 1966). In this cautionary account, Weizenbaum tells of the computer as both fake confidant and ostensibly failed confessor. Through Eliza, Weizenbaum placed on the agenda of computer uses many of the social cognition components with which we are still contending: persuasiveness, attitude, impression, efficacy, captivation, deception, perception, human vs. machine, augmentation of cognition vs. supplementation, thought and deindividuation, etc. Eliza has turned into a symbol of high aspirations for the technology, matched by just as high critiques and concerns.

In this chapter, we will attempt to examine the impacts on and of social cognition in computer-mediated communication environments. Our aim will be to search for middle ground between Mazlish and Weizenbaum's respective awe and fury. The fundamental thesis may be seen as soothing: the online environment has great potential, it is very interesting, but it is not as threatening to the ways we interact with self, other and one's own groups as might have been construed from some of the early theories proposed in the field.

Background

In the following we provide a definition for social cognition (SC) as the sum of our perceptions of ourselves and others. We examine social cognition online against two dilemmas. The first is the contrast between the technological deterministic and the social constructivist views of cognition. The second issue is whether face-to-face is the standard against which computer-mediated communication (CMC) should be compared. We argue that SC is a promising and interesting point of view for examining online behavior, but the face-to-face standard is not necessarily the appropriate yardstick for assessing CMC. We conclude by highlighting the importance of understanding SC online.

Social cognition offline

Social cognition (SC) deals with the mutual influences of cognition on social life, and of social environments and processes on cognition. Cognition is fundamentally influenced by the social environment (Levine & Resnick, 1993).

Research on social facilitation, social loafing, social roles, and mental representations has shown distinct social influences on cognitive abilities and task performance.

SC is about the cognitive underpinnings of social behavior (Devine *et al.*, 1994). SC studies how social structures and social processes are mentally represented, and how social interaction is important for the development and practice of cognition. Individuals are viewed as being engaged most of the time in information processing. Information is encoded from a social context, is interpreted, elaborated, evaluated, inferred, and attributed. Processed information, or knowledge, is later used in judgment processes and for guiding behavior. Judgment and behavior need not be the result of a thorough mental process. Instead, judgment and behavior can be the result of short-cuts known as heuristics. SC draws from both social and cognitive psychology. It deals with how people make sense of themselves and of others. Some refer to social structures as concepts or schema (Kunda, 1999).

The basic social structures mentioned in the literature describe person traits or perception (Fiske, 1993). These include attitudes, beliefs, stereotypes, implicit personality theory, and salience. The main social processes in SC research have been attribution, attitude change, impression formation, social comparison, decision making, social construction of reality or joint sense making (Fulk, 1993). It should be interesting to survey which of these concepts have found their way into research on social cognition online and, further, to latch on to the remaining concepts on these lists as targets for future research.

Social cognition is not limited to the study of individual cognition and how it is affected by the social environment. SC impacts the way in which individuals and cultures perceive, define, and interpret media in general, and in our special case, the Internet.

Determinism versus constructivism

Technology is powerful, or at least perceived as such. In any case, the salience of technology is undisputed. It is very tempting to ascribe all sorts of outcomes and effects directly to technology. Surely, much of the marketing narrative that surrounds the introduction of computers and networks attempts to do just that. However, although networks are complex technological structures, a network is, by definition, *socially* constructed. It grows out of the need of people to interact with others for work or leisure purposes (Fulk *et al.*, 1995). In fact, the value of the network lies in the number of users and intensity of use and is not mandated by the hardware or protocol (Metcalfe, 1995; Reed, 1998). The network infrastructure is essential but may be useless if people choose not to use it. This is in contrast to technological determinism claims that networks are used because they were constructed. Just as very few people, much less than a critical mass, would climb a mountain 'just because it's there', so would very few people use a network 'just because it's there'.

SC research has illuminated the area of social effects on shared cognitive activities. In fact, personal success depends to a large part on coordinated cognitive interactions with others (Levine & Resnick, 1993). Overdoing cognitive coordination may have negative consequences such as 'groupthink', which is said to produce poor group decisions (Janis & Mann, 1977).

If technology accounted for human behavior, people would behave much more uniformly. The plurality of needs and preferences, combined with varying social perceptions, influences our personal and collaborative computer and network usage.

McLuhan's assertions regarding media messages are probably prescient at a macro level of analysis. Technology does bring about social changes. However, change cannot occur without prior processes on micro, individual, group, and community levels. The micro level change is determined to a large part by the social perception and cognition of technology, the interactions it brings about, as well as its adoption patterns. The medium *carries* the message, it does not determine it.

In search of a benchmark

Research on SC among individuals, dyads, and groups has focused on behavior and perception in physical environments (Fiske, 1993; Fiske & Taylor, 1991). When turning to the virtual, we are naturally tempted to set up a contrast with the 'natural' way that people interact (i.e. face to face). The implied comparison pits SC against research findings from traditional research (Chapanis, 1975; Lantz, 2001). Is face to face really *an* ideal or *the* ideal—or just an ordeal? Should face-to-face processes be hoisted as the standard or human behavior optimum against which all innovations and new contexts need be judged?

One prime example of elevating face-to-face, traditional set-ups to ideal/standard status is the media richness approach (Daft & Lengel, 1986). Media richness theory argues that task performance will be improved when capabilities of the media (cues, feedback, personal focus, and language variety) are matched to task ambivalence and uncertainty. In this approach, face-to-face communication is considered the richest communication medium in a hierarchy followed by the telephone, electronic mail, letter, note, memo, special report, and finally, flier and bulletin. Some observations and predictions are made regarding the propriety and efficiency of different media. Specifically, this theory suggests that performance in equivocal tasks would be better when using 'rich' media. According to this theory, in the case of unequivocal tasks, performance would be better if leaner media are used. Unfortunately, empirical data to support media richness theory fall somewhat short (Dennis *et al.*, 1999; Dennis & Valacich, 1999; El–Shinnawy & Markus, 1997; Morris & Ogan, 1996).

Our approach critiques the line of thought that focuses on face-to-face arrangements as an ideal and ultimate standard. We take the position that SC develops in a variety of loci/media. Previous research has already contested the standard of face to face, asserting that interpersonal interactions and social influences affect media choice (Fulk *et al.*, 1990). With the Internet there is the possibility that face to face be demoted from its ostensibly classic preordained position/status as ultimate yardstick. The Internet itself is a plurality of media operated by diverse technologies which constitute a culture or a social space in its own right. In fact, the 'richness' of CMC is a variable, not a characteristic. Computer-mediated contexts, we submit, deserve treatment on their own terms, coming out from under the shadow of what used to be called 'real life' or 'meat space'. CMC is real enough.

In lieu of a backward-facing standard, we propose that the technology of computers and networks be examined against the affordances it makes. In other words, the proposed benchmark for research about social cognition is in the new possibilities opened up by the network, and the degree and manner to which these possibilities are indeed used.

The CMC social space

The CMC social space is characterized variously. Slater (2002) proposes four properties which describe the online environment as a space in its own right:

1 **Virtuality**—a computerized representation of reality.

2 **Spatiality**—the network is a space in its own right, not parallel to real-life space, and cannot be mapped on to offline spaces.

3 **Disembedding**—a community can be spatially dispersed. Geography has all but lost its meaning to participants of online communities.

4 **Disembodiment**—most Internet communication is textual and often anonymous.

Slater's framework stresses the fact that people do not have to reveal any of the offline cues used for SC such as age, sex, and race. The online identity can be very different from the offline identity.

Another analytical framework for the virtual social space claims that the interesting dimensions for internet research include: hypertextuality, synchronicity, topology, history, and interactivity (Newhagen & Rafaeli, 1996; Rafaeli, 2004). While these constructs sound rooted in an engineering culture, they are behavioral and perceptual in nature.

Both frameworks imply that the online CMC environment has qualities of its own. The character of the net is less in the constraints it places, and perhaps more in the opportunities it raises. Rather than gauging CMC against an external standard set by face-to-face communication, it might be more fruitful and interesting to understand the parameters of communication, perception, and thought that are specific to networked situations. Another central element in any research of online activity, is the distinction and fusing of sociability and usability as organizing concepts for the analysis and design of virtual communities (Preece, 2000).

Importance of social cognition in CMC

Besides being an interesting and novel area for research, why is it important to study and understand SC in networked contexts? We believe this is an important field of research because the online environment defines new loci, within which new rules for social behavior may be defined. The geographical and temporal limitations on social horizons may be lifted or reshaped. Upper limits for effective group size may be rewritten. Distance, location, and co-presence take on new meanings. Play, in general, has become more widely practiced. Frivolity and experimentation in playful forms are commonplace online, even in serious contexts (Rafaeli, 1986). People may experiment with their own SC and that of others when they assume different personalities online, when they introduce themselves by chosen nicknames, perhaps forfeiting age, gender, or other cues. Essentially, 'first impressions' are formed over and over again for the same person and shape that person's social behavior online. To paraphrase a famous quip, online you *do* get another chance to make a first impression.

Online SC is likely to be a very dynamic construct subject to different game rules. Is it more of the same? Is it a completely new ball game? Educational, managerial, regulatory and legal systems are being crafted to deal with new realities made possible by the new online social environments. Understanding SC feeds into the deep ethical issues raised by Weizenbaum. This understanding should inform moral, parental, legal, and managerial value judgments about employing online arrangements. Understanding SC on its own terms is crucial to the understanding of a rapidly growing segment of human and social life.

In the following sections we describe burgeoning research in broadening contexts: self, other, group, and then the computer and the network.

The self online

In the following section, we will look at the interaction between self concept and the online environment. As Shakespeare, and then Goffman (1959), suggested, the world is a stage, and we are engaged in presenting ourselves on it. On the

Internet too, people engage in multiple activities related to various aspects of their lives. They interact with others using several technologies, search for information (formal and informal), and perform work-related activities as well as commercial activities. They learn, affiliate, flirt, and amuse themselves. Does one's self concept have anything to do with all these online activities? How does self concept affect online presentation activities, and how do these activities affect self concept? We shall try to review some studies related to these questions bearing in mind that most of the research in this area has yet to be done.

Perception of self

Self perception or self concept may seem fixed or constant. In fact, self perception is very malleable. SC research has identified a variety of selves: self concept varies in private vs. public circumstances, it varies with the different roles we assume and contexts or situations we experience. Thus, self concept is dynamic, with attention focused on the context-specific self rather than on one 'global' self (Devine *et al.*, 1994). Sherry Turkle, in a seminal article, provided computers and networks' impact on perception of self with a slogan that captures the variability of self perception, perhaps amplified, by computers and networks (Turkle, 1980). In 'Computers as Rorscharch' she says that users project meaning to computerized activities, rather than being passive recipients. This sentiment was then echoed in much HCI (Human Computer Interaction) work on user-centered computing (Shneiderman, 1998), and naturally percolated into the very design of systems and networks. The projected meaning is influenced by a variety of environmental or social effects, in addition to personality of the actor.

One of the most overused clichés about the Internet and SC is the cartoon 'On the Internet no one knows that you are a dog'. It has become very popular to create take-offs on this sentiment. One suggested extension would be: 'On the internet no one knows that you are a dog. Do you know what you are?' Further research in Turkle's tradition evolved in the landmark book *The Second Self* and in *Life on the Screen* (Turkle, 1984, 1997). In more recent work Turkle describes computers as evocative objects (Turkle, 2004). In her work she documents how objects stir up the emotions of others, as well as increasingly react emotionally, thus playing active social roles. This socially evocative potential of computerized and networked objects may resonate with 'interactivity' as discussed in the following.

Ego and ego surfing

The Internet provides numerous opportunities to affect what Goffman would call 'the presentation of self' (Donath, 1998; Stone, 1991). The construction of a personal home page, the introduction one is required to make when entering an online forum, the short descriptions many provide as a rite of inclusion into various social software arenas, and the profiles one accumulates for oneself willingly or not on a variety of online systems, all have a narcissistic potential. Even earlier in this process, the act (performed more online than offline) of choosing a name involves self presentation (Bechar–Israeli, 1995).

Further, performing web searches on one's own name (often called 'ego surfing') turns this into a self-referential process. Are the acts of 'googling' others, and then oneself, the modern-day equivalents of facing the mirror? What is more natural, and even prudent, for any person than to run a search on her/his own name in a search engine? Granted, finding out what others say about us may satisfy some and not others. More interestingly, the Internet gives us a chance to see how we are portrayed online and what others are likely to find when they run a search on us. Since others (potential employers, colleagues, friends, competitors, etc.) are likely to run a search on our name, why shouldn't we do our homework by reading the same information and being prepared for discussion on any topic that came up in our 'online self'? Ego surfing may even be crucial, for example, if someone by the same name is found and who is known for activities that are contrary to one's own beliefs and norms. Why, then, does the term 'ego surfing' have such negative connotations? Using the web wisely means that we should portray ourselves online as we wish to be perceived. Ego surfing is an important step in assessing what's needed for better self portrayal online.

Role playing, false identities

There has been considerable work on role playing, false identities, and 'make believe' online. These forms of using the network are relatively widespread, and their effects are ambivalent. On the one hand, playing and entertainment can be viewed as harmless, innocuous, and well-intended. Perhaps role playing may even create social bonds. However, as Donath (1998) indicates, online identity deception is relatively easy to achieve because of the unreliable nature of identity cues online. Forms of deception can be harmful to self and surroundings. Role playing loci are experienced at an unprecedentedly deep psychological and social level. Participants are not looking at a painting—they are in it. And it is not a painting at all, but an immersive scenery that induces people to play parts in what becomes an evolving and unending collective drama (Castronova, 2001). The catch though, is that the painting we inhabit may be false, distorted, or completely absent from reality. And the only available reality checks are other deceivers or self deceivers. This makes for powerful psychological drama as well.

The Internet provides a backdrop for a duality of positive and negative. Enrichment and improvement of human functioning reside side by side with threatening environments that can expose individuals to great risks. 'Being' online facilitates sexual exploration, education, and pleasure; on the other hand, it furnishes an opportunity for criminal and other negative and harmful sexual conduct (Barak & King, 2000).

Information/social information overload

Perceiving others and one's relation to them requires some processing capacity. People have only finite resources for processing. In CMC, this capacity is often challenged, if not filled to the brim. Information overload has been noticed widely as a cognitive artifact of modern life and the tools it uses. Social information overload is a natural follow-up (Monge and Contractor, 1997; Markus, 1994) A sense of too much social information has measurable impacts on both individual behavior and social cohesion in the long term. Effects of exceeding 'cognitive processing load' limits are reported in large-scale empirical measures of online behavior (Jones & Rafaeli, 1999, 2000*a*, 2000*b*; Jones *et al.*, 2001*a*, 2001*b*; Sudweeks *et al.*, 1998).

At the extreme, online information overload as a social phenomenon may amount to a new form of crowding, with all the familiar social psychological attendants of such overpopulation. More commonly, a sense of exaggerated density of neighbors, social cues, and human demands must result in acts and attitudes of increased filtering and selective availability. Spamming may be one extreme expression of this. Of course, this all leads to an economic outlook on social life summarized by the term 'attention economy' (Davenport & Beck, 2001). An attention economy is a social arrangement where the value of attention is accentuated and a price sticker is affixed to it. It is also one where human caring and attentiveness are rationed more strictly and not provided as a matter of course.

Sociology has been paying attention to such shifts for over a century. Tonnies coined the notions of 'gemeinschaft' and 'gesselschaft' before the appearance of networks and computers. Beniger's 1986 importation of these notions to a networked environment only highlights the end of a cycle that starts with information inundation (Beniger, 1987).

The other online

The previous discussion connected the very intimate and internal perception of self to 'other' oriented cognitions. In fact, impersonating others, social information overload, and filtering others are all individual reactions to the other. In this section we will explore the way the others are perceived online, and the cognitive effects of meeting others online.

Online impression formation meets 'real world'

The perception of the 'other' online and how the impression of those we interact with online is formed has been a focus of research from the first days of online communications. The initial focus was on the gap between the impressions formed online and impressions in 'real life', with an emphasis on anecdotal cases of fraud and deception. This approach follows a historical pattern of focusing on the sensational, as well as on the faults and deficiencies of a new medium in relation to traditional communication media. Similar claims were made historically with the introduction of early electric media (Standage, 1998) and in social science research about the first days of telephone and telegraph (Pool, 1983). Much of the early work focused on the reduced social cues in comparison to face-to-face communication. The reduced social cues approach highlighted the surprise and disappointment that arose when those who formed the impressions were confronted with 'real life'. These works concluded that online impression formation is faulty and wrought with stereotypical and prejudiced assumptions used to 'fill in the blanks' (Albright, 2001) of the reduced social cues, and terms such as 'fluid identities' (Turkle, 1997) were used to warn about the unsound and shifting sands of CMC.

In retrospect it is clear that many of the early works on CMC may have failed to distinguish between the various contexts of online activities. Some popular activities such as MOOs and MUD were purposely structured for 'play', wherein impersonation and identity experimentation were the expressed aim. Such environments flourished among students, on university campuses, close to the eye and attention of researchers. This, too, may have given these contexts some increased salience. No wonder that a 'reality check' in such cases reveals that the (generally) young and often experimentally minded people behind the screen names are different than imagined.

As indicated above, impersonation (a form of self-presentation) ranges from simply using an alias in order to save typing or time or to avoid revealing one's real name through assuming an identity for playful purposes, through to creating a complete false identity in order to engage in criminal or terrorist activity. The latter form has been given the most media attention, but the other two forms of self-presentation are far more widely used. All these forms of self-presentations indicate a high degree of awareness of others, your own and others' perception, combined with a high degree of understanding of the computerized and networked environment.

Research shows that senders often try to optimize their self-presentation by mentioning information they perceive as impressive, while holding back information which is less so (Walther & Burgoon, 1992). The receiver in the online case often idealizes the sender, 'filling in the blanks' with information that tends to be too rosy. Such a combination can result in disillusion when a face-to-face meeting eventually occurs. This disenchantment has received much attention in literature dealing with online dating and online relationships (Turkle, 1997), but is apparent in other online contexts too (Rouse & Haas, 2003). As Rouse and Haas point out, inaccuracies in personality perception of online 'others' are mainly a result of three important differences between Internet-mediated factors and face-to-face communication:

1 That physical appearance has a less meaningful effect.

2 That people may behave different online than in a face-to-face situation.

3 That online there is a heightened level of ambiguity due to the lack of vocal inflection and facial expression.

In contrast, we wish to point out that before such assertions about the inferiority of online vs. offline impression formation are presented as conclusive, some more basic questions are called for. For example, is the ability to present an idealized self online similar to the ability to idealize one's physical appearance through the choice of clothing, haircut, makeup, accessories, and even plastic surgery? Are humans gradually becoming more skilled at detecting signs of such online attempts, integrating them into the emerging impression, just as an attempt to conceal physical imperfections is interpreted in traditional offline interaction? Is the ambiguity of an online 'smiley' analogous to some extent to the different interpretation a smile can have in an Eastern culture like Japan in comparison to its meaning in a Western country like England?

We contend that it may be too early in the evolution of human online communication to simply conclude that this ability is inferior to face to face. Research should focus on understanding the dynamics and evolution of the emergence of the human capability to communicate online, on the way skilled users are using it to fine tune their perceptions, or to influence the way they are perceived. For example, the ability to 'google' a person to find out valuable information not accessible otherwise, sheds new light on the 'inferiority' and 'poverty' of the web. Reeves and Nass (2000) point out in their discussion of the 'perceptual bandwidth' of computer-mediated communication: 'the assumption that more is always less is misguided. An increase in the breadth and depth of media representations certainly turns up the volume knob on perceptual responses, but greater presence does not translate into greater efficacy or desirability; intensity does not equal quality.' We believe that the importance of these issues to the design of online communication interfaces is fundamental.

Once the issue of the superiority of face to face over CMC is removed, the questions that arise are questions that focus on aspects of SC online, and mainly questions of what influences the way users translate the special social cues of CMC (especially text-based CMC) into impressions, and what influences these impressions.

How do impressions and heuristics form online?

Online impression formation occurs in stages. First impressions are formed based on very initial signs such as the e-mail addresses or the screen names as well as on the context of the online occurrence. As the interaction progresses, more information accumulates: the sentence structure, vocabulary, grammar, spelling, use of capitals letters, typographical marks such as emoticons, as well as self-testimonials about matters such as gender, age, location, occupation, and marital status. Additional elements that can influence this impression are less linked to pure linguistic aspects and can include the length of the message, the amount devoted to talking about oneself, number of opinions expressed, level of friendliness, the content of the message, strength of expressed opinions, etc. (Savicki et al., 1999). Some online cues are non-verbal. The response time to an online message, referred to as a chronemic, carries a message to the recipient (Tyler & Tang, 2003). Online silence, or lack of response, is a cue which is usually ambiguous to interpret, especially in an online context, raising the question of if the 'other' chose not to respond, or if the silence is a result of forgetfulness or a delay or possibly of a technical glitch. This chronemic non-verbal cue can result in strong negative feelings if interpreted as intentional (Williams et al., 2000).

As mentioned earlier, the network enables learning about online and offline others. This is commonly known as 'googling'—searching for web-based information about a person. Search results can include information made available by the person, as well as external information sources.

How do all of these cues translate into an impression of the 'other' online? As in offline situations, this process is in essence inductive, and may be based on social stereotypes, categorizing people according to the signals they give off. Success of this process depends on factors such as the context of the interaction, the interpreter's capabilities and information sources, the self- presentation of the 'other', and his or her willingness to present truthfully. Online, first impressions may be based on reduced information in comparison to traditional face-to-face interactions—the 'reduced cues' tradition of research. Kiesler (1986) described how the social effects of computers may be greater and more important than initially imagined. The main point was that computers have social effects, cut down hierarchies, and cut across norms and organization boundaries.

Cognitive psychology has developed a keen interest in the introspective notion of heuristics. How do people form impressions, perceptions, cognitions, and attitudes by relying on shortcuts. Prospect theory (Kahneman & Tversky, 1979) explains a wide variety of perceptual and attitudinal peculiarities of human choice, preference, and behavior. Much of prospect theory has been developed in traditional contexts. How does prospect theory translate to the online arena? It seems that, at least in the case of the 'endowment effect' (Thaler, 1980), the predictions that applied to the physical, tangential world work well for the abstract, virtual, and online milieu. In their experiments for instance, Raban and Rafaeli found that people apply similar decision-making biases and heuristics in online contexts (Raban & Rafaeli, 2004; Rafaeli & Raban, 2003). Consistency in behavior overpowers opportunity for change.

Groups online

All social cognitive aspects of interacting with others, as well as self-perception, are repeated and compounded in online groups. As in the previous sections, questions about the 'reality' of online groups are the focus of researchers who place face-to-face groups as the benchmark, and only after this question is addressed can we look at the actual way people interact online, perceive the group as an entity, socialize, work, entertain themselves, and learn.

What are online groups and how do they compare with face-to-face groups?

Many terms have been used to describe influential Internet based interactions between several participants, including 'virtual communities' (Rheingold, 1993), 'virtual teams' (Lipnack & Stamps, 2000), and 'virtual groups' (Wallace, 1999). In this chapter we will use the more generic term, virtual groups.

The tools used by people to congregate online are diverse, and include e-mail list forums, synchronous chat systems such as IRC, asynchronous discussion forums, MUDs, and MOOs, Usenet newsgroups, virtual classrooms, web logs, and groupware tools. Some of these are very rich media, allowing real-time transmission of audio, video, and text, as well as online application sharing, while others are very rudimentary, and based only on the asynchronous transmission of ASCII text. People participate in online groups for work, education, leisure, acquiring, disseminating, and sharing information and knowledge, collaborating, and socializing.

A central focus of research on online groups has been on understanding the differences between traditional groups and virtual groups. Why do people group online, how effective are online groups, and what influences this effectiveness? How does socialization happen online, and what expresses leadership in online groups?

Initially, there was a lot of excitement about the possibilities opened by online virtual groups, with the combination of a widely dispersed but closely-knit community. A good example is The Well, established in 1985 and described in the book *The Virtual Community* (Rheingold, 1993). At about the same time, virtual communities were contrasted with 'real' communities, mourning the damage inflicted by 'Technopoly' (Postman, 1992). Later, the term 'Internet paradox' was coined (Kraut *et al.*, 1998), showing that the Internet actually reduces the level of social involvement of its users. An additional element in this process of disillusion was the accumulation of online communities that disintegrated, or simply stopped functioning. Unlike 'real world' social connections which can disappear without leaving a trace, online communities often leave behind artifacts (Jones, 1997) which can confuse people who might attempt to join or interact with such communities, only to discover that they are totally silent (Wallace, 1999). The disillusion was supported by reports of discussions in online groups that resulted in flaming and polarization (Spears *et al.*, 1990).

When put into perspective such a dichotomous debate becomes meaningless (Etzioni & Etzioni, 1999; Wellman & Gulia, 1999). Online groups are as 'real' as any other groups, and are simply different in some aspects from traditional groups. Online groups are social units in which the participants are interdependent and behave according to explicit or implicit social norms. Online groups show, just like other groups, both examples of social compensation as well as social loafing, and even effects such as crowding and deindividuation (Spears *et al.*, 2002) have been documented. We will now look at a few of the main research questions about online groups.

How do people socialize in online groups?

Socialization occurs when people join a group. They learn the norms and normative behavior. Socialization is carried out by established members who provide information about the norms of the group to newcomers. Parts of this information are communicated directly and explicitly, while other parts are implicit. In online socialization, explicit information is often communicated through established sources such as a list of frequently asked questions (FAQs), an orientation provided to newcomers, or answers to questions posted by newcomers (Ahuja & Galvin, 2003; Burnett & Bonnici, 2003).

The notion of 'newbies' (recent new members) and group toleration of their needs is one of the first set of 'social' notions and norms to emerge in online community dynamics (Rheingold, 1993). The need to make such norms explicit is stronger in 'poor media' based communities such as text-based forums, as the absence of non-verbal cues hinders the ability to communicate them tacitly. The discussion of these 'published' norms is, necessarily, more common in online forums than in face-to-face communities, and these 'meta-discussions' offer a window into the emerging and evolving nature of such norms.

Despite the effort to document norms and make them explicit, online groups also have implicit norms, which can only be learned by newcomers through observation of the online behavior of others. Members of the group quite often debate such norms. Burnett and Bonnici (2003) extend Kemper's (1968) observation to online groups by saying that 'the process of newcomers reaching some kind of understanding of a group's implicit norms can be understood as a mechanism of socialization. As newcomers begin to enter into the discussion of a group's norms, they begin to become true participants.' The difficulty of deducing implicit information results in newcomers pro-actively requesting normative information from the group, and the provision of answers to such requests is often an important role for the established member who acts as a 'mentor' or 'liaison'.

Media richness and online groups

Online groups communicate using media that is defined by the media richness theory (MRT) as 'leaner' than face-to-face communication (Daft & Lengel, 1986). According to the MRT, such online groups are predicted to be less capable of resolving ambiguity, negotiating various interpretations, and facilitating understanding. Recently, critiques of MRT have appeared in a variety of contexts, providing empirical evidence in contrast to the predictions of MRT (El–Shinnawy & Markus, 1997; Kock, 1998; Workman *et al.*, 2003). These findings show that when faced with a choice between rich, offline communication alternatives, people sometimes still choose leaner online media. Moreover, such choices are not irrational, but actually ones that lead to group work which is more effective than face-to-face arrangements.

When revisiting MRT, it seems that the interpretation of the theory was too simplistic, and that effectiveness is linked not only to the richness of the medium chosen by groups but also to other needs of the group. For example, the theory of media synchronicity (Dennis & Valacich, 1999) looks at the extent to which the medium is synchronized with the recipient's communication needs, and proposes a set of five media capabilities that are important to group work. The match between these capabilities and the needs of the fundamental communication processes will affect communication effectiveness. Clearly, then, people choose to use leaner media to work with their colleagues not only because they are forced to do so and to compromise, but also because leaner media often better fits the cognitive and operational needs of the team members. Here, too, we see the fusion of the choices of technological determinism vs. social construction, and face-to-face vs. internally defined benchmarks.

Lurking

Lurking is a special form of SC. Participation in online groups, such as forum discussions, is not symmetric. A small number of participants contribute. A much larger number remain receivers. Often, reticent receivers are named 'lurkers'. Receivers who remain passive are either intimating a social cue, or at the very least are understood as imparting a message. Thus, lurking is not just a behavior. It is a perception and is perceived by others in social contexts. Lurking has been a social and cognitive concern since the early years of public CMC. Even in participatory virtual communities, many people limit their participation to reading and never post themselves. The reported proportion of lurkers varies from around 90% (Katz, 2003; Mason, 1999) to around 50% (Nonnecke & Preece, 2000; Soroka *et al.*, 2003).

Lurking usually means 'lying in wait', often with malicious intent. But interestingly, 'lurking' does not have to carry a negative connotation. The Merriam–Webster dictionary definition of the verb 'lurk' has one unexpected meaning—'to persist in staying'. Thus lurkers can be defined as a persistent but silent audience. Lurkers have been recognized by many researchers as an important and integral part of any community. Rafaeli and Sudweeks (1997) point out that though lurkers are an important part of any online group there is little information about their activity. Whittaker *et al.* (1998) also acknowledge lurking as a very popular activity among virtual community participants that leaves no traces.

The reasons for lurking range from concerns for privacy, through respect for others' time and attention limits, to those rooted in personality (Rafaeli *et al.*, 2004). In any case, both the reasons for lurking and its outcomes are central to the understanding of SC among the less salient and available (but probably more numerous) participants in online social behavior.

Prosocial behavior in online groups?

Anecdotal evidence and informal observation suggest that prosocial behavior occurs in online groups, perhaps at the same rate as it occurs offline. Social behavior online is, by definition, more clearly contingent on perceptions and cognition. The only avenue through which others are available is the cognitive, perhaps cerebral communication. Others are instantiated as bits, not atoms. We know that philanthropy, mobilization of social movements, altruism in the form of providing help, and individual and group emotional support are all hallmarks of novel online networks. How do such processes get launched? What are the ways in which people perceive other individuals and collectives via the prism of online interactions? How do these perceptions bias the orientations toward others? Online prosocial behavior remains mostly a challenge for future research. We are still unclear about the specific social and psychological underpinnings and peculiarities of prosocial organizing online. How, for instance, do you get a hundred strangers to agree (Sudweeks & Rafaeli, 1996)? The fact is, consensus and collective action do occur online, often to positive ends (Rheingold, 2002).

A central social cognitive question is why people contribute to online group efforts. How do people perceive fairness online, when evenhandedness is not as easily gauged, where justice is less tangible? Does equity theory apply here? Can social exchange theory help explain helpers' motives (Constant *et al.*, 1994)? There has been some very early work on reciprocity and perceptions of humans and computers, for instance in online prisoner pilemma studies (Rafaeli, 1988). However, of greater interest are field studies of the same issue (Adamic & Adar, 2003; Adamic *et al.*, 2003). To date, most of the work on online prosocial activity is not sufficiently distinguished from offline group behavior. Online, too, people will contribute time and effort for the good of the whole group for various reasons and benefits (Butler *et al.*, 2002). Effects such as the bystander effect, or diffusion of responsibility, appear online too (Barron & Yechiam, 2002).

Social cognitive aspects at work and in learning

The research, design, and management building and implementing of CMC-based collaboration tools should consider the psychological principles, as well as the social and cognitive processes of individual users (Olson & Olson, 2003). One such example, social facilitation, has been shown as important to e-commerce (Rafaeli & Noy, 2002). Commerce sites should apply this knowledge and develop tools for interaction with the vendor and among the customers. Elements that facilitate social interaction can increase the effectiveness of sites, for example by increasing the time users spend on the website. Adar and Huberman (2000) show that reciprocity in online peer-to-peer contexts is not as prevalent as expected. In other words, systems predicated on altruistic reciprocity may experience problems. The expectations and motivations brought to online arenas by the participants structure the outcome not just for the owners of such expectations and motivations; they enable or constrain the experiences and payoffs of all others as well. Here again, we see the powerful hand of social construction overruling the theoretical determinism of technological structure.

Social presence is the awareness of others' being there. As early as 1976, Short and Christie (1976) identified social presence as crucial to the understanding of mediated behavior. Presence was postulated to affect trust, compliance, attraction, motivation, and more. More recent work looks at virtual presence as both an independent and a dependent variable. As computerized systems and networks are designed by humans, the degree to which they elicit a sense of presence is an important variable. Thus, for instance, Biocca *et al.* (1995) experiment with the interaction effect between user factors and media factors on feelings of social presence. They provide strong evidence for human's automatic social responses to artificial representations possessing humanistic properties such as language and personality. Clearly, the more immersive CMC systems become, with a wider range of sensory and cognitive appeals and a longer average exposure to these systems, the degree to which such systems are actually social, in the full sense of the word, comes into focus. Lombard and Ditton (1997) remind us that virtual presence might be an illusion or a hoax, and that its effects are worthy of further examination.

Another example is online education. Kreijns *et al.* (2003) identified two 'pitfalls' that can hinder the success of online collaborative learning, and both of these are related to elements of social interaction between the members of the online class. The first pitfall they identify is technological determinism— the assumption that providing students with an environment that *can* support online collaboration is enough, and that collaboration will automatically follow. The second pitfall is focusing only on the cognitive aspects of learning, and ignoring the fact that social interaction is just as important for the development of an effective learning community. Online platforms that take social aspects of learning into account will fair better than those that ignore them. Data presented by Barak and Rafaeli (in press) indicate that efforts invested in sharing information with the group in online learning contexts correlate highly with actual performance.

People have been socializing in groups since the dawn of mankind, and social capabilities are believed to have strongly influenced human evolution (Dunbar, 2002). Amongst other things, Dunbar shows that the optimal size of classrooms, social networks, and other groups is a result of evolutionary selection, and predicts that technological developments will not effect these numbers significantly, since these numbers are 'etched' into the human genes by evolution. These questions regarding optimal group size for various online tasks still loom and call for further investigation.

Usability and sociability

As Preece describes, online groups are not homogenous (Preece, 2000). Some groups are successful, while others falter. Some communities enhance the lives of their members, while others are abandoned as a result of a low 'signal to noise ratio', shallow or no contributions, loss of interest, or even participant hostility. In addition, communities are not only an entity, but also a process, and any analysis of online groups needs to take into account their constantly evolving nature.

Preece distinguishes between the two aspects of online groups—usability and sociability. While the two are complementary, usability focuses on the aspects of the software that allow the participants to 'interact and perform their tasks intuitively and easily'. Software with good usability supports rapid learning, high skill retention, low error rates, and high productivity. It is consistent, controllable, and predictable, making it pleasant and effective to use. Sociability, on the other hand is focused on 'planning and developing social policies which are understandable and acceptable to members, to support the community's purpose'. Online groups should be understood in this context: just like offline groups of people, each one is different and evolving, and the fact that the interaction takes place online, thus linking participants separated by time and or space, should not result in a focus solely on the technical similarity between them, but rather should take into consideration socio-cognitive aspects that will affect the sociability of the group. In this sense, usability and sociability are synonyms for technological determinism and social construction.

Facing the computer

The computer as a socio-cognitive entity

We opened this chapter with the assertion that computers are cognitive. This is neither surprising, nor controversial. After all, computers are tools that were built to augment human calculating abilities. However, computers are turning out to be *social*, as well as cognitive entities. The sociability of computers stars prominently in science fiction writing. It has also been the subject of morality and philosophy, as in the case of Weizenbaum's Eliza (see p. 58) and the discussion of the limits of human and computer co-mingling.

In the last decade of the twentieth century CE, and the first years of the twenty-first century, computers stepped boldly into additional social roles.

Any discussion of SC in online communication must include communication directly to and with computers. Here, we mean social interaction with the machine itself, above and beyond (or beneath?) the interactions with others via the machine. This is not just the machine as conduit or container of others' personae. This is the machine itself, treated like a real person or group of people.

Reeves and Nass (1996) conclude that media in general, and computers in particular, 'can evoke emotional responses, demand attention, threaten us, influence memories, and change ideas of what is natural. Media are full participants in our social and natural world' (p. 251).

People's responses to computers (and not just content or others mediated through the computers) are fundamentally social. People respond to what is present. Thus, computers can be charismatic, likeable, and persuasive (Fogg, 1999, 2003). The emotion expressed by machines is taken seriously (Brave & Nass, 2002). Computers manifest mainstay social cognitive effects such as source credibility, politeness, attribution, reciprocity, mindlessness, fairness, and credibility (Fogg & Nass, 1997; Lee & Nass, 1999; Nass & Moon, 2000; Nass et al., 1999; Nass et al., 1994; Sundar & Nass, 2000).

The social role assumed by computers has been employed by game designers. The Tamaguchi of the early 1990s made way to Furbies in the early years of the twenty-first century. Children play with computers (see Turkle, forthcoming and 1997), and endow them with companionship, evocative relations, even love. Children of this generation, who play with computers as social actors, have come a long way from the cautious, critical approach of Eliza's first users. Will this generation grow into different modes of using computers? At the same time, computers are tools we are eager to 'think with'. In Turkle's terms, 'computers offer themselves as models of mind and as objects to think with'. To be sure, not all emotional reaction to computers is positive. Some of our reactions are negative. All too often we blame computers for misfortunes; we are very likely to accept fault or blame attributions to computers; and aggression toward computers has become a staple of work life.

Some research has been sparked by the warm, often embracing, but in any case emotional, not-just-cognitive reaction of humans to thinking machines. At the same time, design is further informed by the research into thinking about relations (SC). Thus, one of the leading thinkers about human–computer interaction now advocates an approach to design that adds visceral and reflective layers to the functional layer. In *Emotional Design: Why We Love (Or Hate) Everyday Things* Norman (2004) expands both his description of empirical findings, and his prescription of normative suggestions regarding the way humans do and ought to relate to machines, especially computers and robots. In fact, the field of human–computer interaction is increasingly enamored by social cognitive issues (cf. Donald Norman's work here *http://www.jnd.org* and Jakob Nielsen's site *http://www.useit.com*, as well as Murthi and Sarkar, 2003).

Across the designing universe, both practitioners and researchers are investing more attention in humanization and personalization. While empirical evidence is still scarce, the intuitive belief is that more personalized systems will be more attractive, captivating, and 'sticky'. Personalization and humanization are envisaged in varying manners. Some believe that pictures, avatars, and voices convey the psychological 'glue' between the person and other, endowing the computer and network with the 'self' and mind, otherwise absent. Thus, 'theory of mind' and 'intuitive psychology' are beginning to influence a theory of computers and an intuitive or even naïve psychology of the machine.

Personalization is an important concept harnessed of late by economists of information (Shapiro & Varian, 1999). Personalization as a strategy in managing the selling of information is amplified and used extensively on the Internet where every user leaves distinct digital footprints. The thought behind this economic principle is that approaching a prospective client in a more personal way may reduce hesitation or initial resistance to purchase. Our digital footprints are reflections of our online cognition, thus providing very useful information for personalization efforts. It would be interesting to trace the impact the economic notion of personalization may have in behavioral and cognitive domains.

Interactivity

One central driving force in the induction of computers into our social circles is the notion of interactivity. Interactivity refers to the extent to which communication reflects back on itself, feeds on and responds to the past. Interactivity is the degree of mutuality and reciprocation present in a communication setting. The term interactivity is widely used to refer to the way content expresses contact, and communication evolves into community. And, of course, interactivity is a major option in governing the relation between humans and computers (Rafaeli, 1984, 1988, 2004).

Communication to and with computers highlights the role of interactivity. Interactivity can be consciously 'programmed in' or kept out. While most human–computer exchanges are not interactive, the potential is there. It has been shown that interactivity accounts for attraction, motivation, openness, and commitment (between person and system). Good choices and crafty implementation of interactivity are often the difference between successful and failing websites. But do the genres residing on the web live up to the promise of interactivity? Are there costs to interactivity, or is it all rosy? When and where is interactivity achievable, and when should it be avoided?

The answer to these issues resides in applying SC theory (of the established, tried and true kind) to the design of human—computer interactions. The understanding of such interactions is best informed by traditional SC theory.

Facing the network

After discussing the SC of computers, we turn to SC of the network. Computer-mediated communication is, after all, about the work and play on networks (Sudweeks et al., 1998). The SC aspects of computer-mediated communication are to be understood fully only if we consider SC of the network as a whole. To do so, we propose a focus on the who-to-whom taxonomy, and on social network analysis tools.

CMC takes on a rich spectrum of forms. Imagine a two-dimensional matrix— the vertical axis describes the synchronicity of communication; the horizontal axis denotes the types of connections. At the far edge of this axis we encounter one-to-one settings, such as electronic mail or an instant message, located at the same point on this axis but separated by the vertical (synchronicity axis). Further along the horizontal axis we will place one-to-many settings, such as e-mail-based discussion groups, listerves, etc. Even further down this who-to-whom axis will be located the many-to-many arrangements, such as Usenet News.

On this matrix we can immediately identify a multitude of SC issues. What sort of interaction might one choose to use when generating an appeal for attention, help, love, information, intimacy, leadership, or plain human contact? Is there an obvious or better choice of avenue or locus for any of these needs? Is there a different answer for those searching to talk, listen, or connect?

In more general terms, does the availability of convenient, instant, and inexpensive contact change social relations? On the one hand, there seems to be an opportunity for cutting through barriers and obstacles that were imposed by earlier social structures. Take, for instance, the rise of the notion of disintermediation (i.e. the elimination of intermediaries). Disintermediation is about 'cutting out the middlemen' that used to govern social relations in whatever context (Rafaeli & Ravid, 2003). Disintermediation and other efficiency promises of networks may bring up hopes of a limitless, borderless, 'death of distance'(Cairncross, 2001). On the other hand, how are group measures of well-being, social capital and participation affected by these opportunities? (Rafaeli et al., 2004)

There have been several contributions to this discussion from the areas of sociology and social psychology on one hand, and from economics on the other hand. From the sociological vantage point, we observe that individuals' SC would be severely stressed in an environment where elemental notions of proximity, permanence, and local group affiliation are removed. There is a challenge on SC introduced by the attractions of online communication. This tension between the local and the global is addressed, recently increasingly, by the notion of 'glocalization' (Hampton, 2001; Wellman & Haythornthwaite, 2002).

The substitution of one means of social contact for another could lead to an erosion of social contact in general. However, it may also represent a more efficient or successful means of forming, controlling, or maintaining access to other people. The combination of global and local connectivity that may be facilitated by CMC is termed 'glocalization'. If these new technologies can increase communication with network members or increase the size or diversity of social networks, then computer-mediated communication portends major changes for SC.

Economists, too, have turned their attention to the meeting between cognition, social life, and mediating technology. For them, the interesting notion in much of the public communication activity on the Internet is how this activity is fueled by the notion of scarcity. Economists tend to seek scarcity, as value is determined by scarcity. And on the Internet, observe some economists, there seems to be more abundance than scarcity. However, human attention *is* scarce, and could therefore serve as a useful organizing notion (Goldhaber, 1997; Rafaeli, 1989). The economy of online interactions, claim some economists, is therefore an economy of attention. The crass marketing term for this is 'eyeball count'. From a SC point of view, the network then becomes a mechanism that turns a very personal quality and choice (attention) into a socially valued and traded asset.

Lastly, we turn to the budding field of social network analysis. Network analysis has been a practice in social research for several decades and is the study of social relations among a set of actors. Network researchers have developed a set of distinctive theoretical perspectives closely associated to SC issues. Among the insights contributed by social network analysis is the focus on relationships between actors rather than attributes of actors (i.e. SC), a sense of interdependence of actors in a network, the observation that structure affects substantive outcomes in behavior.

So networks are intellectual analysis and action tools at once. The suggestion to apply network analysis-based quantitative ideas of ties, similarity, density, and centrality to online behavior followed very shortly on the heels of the introduction of online communication networks. Thus, Rogers and Kincaid's *Communication Networks: Toward a New Paradigm for Research* and Rice's *The New Media: Communication, Research and Technology* were early harbingers of this trend (Rice, 1984; Rogers & Kincaid, 1981). In the first years of the twenty-first century, commercial implementations of social networking tools are becoming one of the most popular innovations on the network.

Methodologically, social network analysis extends SC research in directions quite unfamiliar to those accustomed to research based on self-report. Social network analyses use unobtrusively collected data about actual communication behavior. The networks carry both the acts of receiving and imparting content. Their analysis may utilize the patterns of such connections as both dependent and independent variables in explanatory models of who perceives whom in what way.

Online social cognition: new/emerging research issues

What are the emerging research issues relating to online social cognition? We propose the following questions and thoughts:

Are all traditional research areas applicable to online social cognition research? Do new areas emerge?

How does a medium, such as a networked computer, influence our self-perception, our perception of others, and the perception of a group? What changes are there in SC when communication is computer-mediated? If individuals are viewed as constantly processing information (Fiske & Taylor, 1991), it follows that when they engage in any kind of activity in front of an information delivery system, this effect should intensify. Do we respond to electronically-delivered social cues? Collective memory, for example, has been subject to social cognition research. Is there a reason to expect differential outcomes when interactions are online, are by and large textual, and can be recorded and retrieved?

Social cognition is a moving target

Technological advances in telecommunications and specifically in media have always generated some hype. Often, the hype was later reduced to its natural size and effect (Jankowski, 2002; Slater, 2002). The impact of radio and television on the family, the community, and society at large has been profound, but was still over-rated at first. While the Internet in its present form has been around for about ten years, it is still in the center of legal and moral controversies which might exaggerate its portrayal as either an evil or a blessing. The Internet may still be in an early 'hype' stage and has yet to mature in the minds of the various audiences that use it. Therefore, any discussion of SC online must be revisited and updated periodically. Our present understanding of this issue, in this evolutionary state of the Internet, is likely to evolve as more and more studies are published.

Technology is a moving target

Research itself, not just the technology, is therefore subject to short half-life limits. As technology evolves, the insights pertaining to it must evolve too. Thus, for instance, the lively debate over 'media richness' dates itself to the early 1990s, when bandwidth was at a premium. As circumstances evolve and bandwidth becomes more widely available, the very notion of poverty of a channel is changed and is now a function not of the richness of the medium itself, but rather of the richness of media alternatives that a person has to choose from for the task at hand.

Online usage and behavior are moving targets

The percentage of people involved in computerized networking is rapidly evolving. Many have noted the exponential rate of adoption of the technology. Others have viewed with concern slow-downs in acceptance, so called 'potholes on the information highway' (Pew Internet and the American Life, *http://www.pewinternet.org/*). Gartner's much cited 'hype curve' (*http://www4.gartner.com*) is another prognostication of the chronological contraction of the phenomenon and its subscribers. Two different theoretical frameworks may be applied to understanding this growth process—diffusion of innovations and network externalities.

General use of computers, and even more so, the use of networked computers for social activities, are still novel notions, though they are decades old by now. Like any innovation, these encounter initial resistance or suspicion. The adoption of innovations, even successful ones, is an involved mental and social process, as described by diffusion of innovation theory (Rogers, 1968–2003). Another force operates on networked environments and their growth—network externalities. While the diffusion of innovation tradition of research focuses on social and psychological determinants of early adoption, economists have raised the specter of network externalities, the idea that networks have built-in dynamics encouraging spurts in their own market expansion. The slope of the S-shaped diffusion adoption curve is especially steep with regards to networked computing.

Rapid adoption may imply less time for contemplation of its full potential. It could be that for many of the most recent recruits to computerized networks there was not enough time for full learning and maximum utilization of the new social environment. We believe that with the Internet we are now seeing the steepness of the S-curve, where some social technologies are adopted but they are not yet realized to their full potential for community building, political activity, and other social functions. The learning curve is still catching up with the adoption curve. SC is still seeking its full realization. It is a moving target which must be further monitored and studied.

Much attention has been given in the years following the first dot com bubble burst to so-called 'social networking'. Social networking applications such as Friendster, LinkedIn and Orkut.com are mushrooming. These are Internet-based attempts to map the web of affiliations or relations between people. Users are invited to identify their friends or acquaintances. Once recorded, these connections are harnessed to make introductions and further interests to create 'social capital'. The social and commercial implications are numerous. And, of course, social-networking based escalation is a prime example of adoption that may precede cognitive processing.

Adoption of any kind of online behavior cannot itself be taken for granted. The digital divide is still very much an issue along ethnic, geographic, age, and gender lines, even as it is shrinking as a socio-economic concern. Any discussion of SC must keep in mind the specific Internet demographics (Wellman & Haythornthwaite, 2002).

Degrees of social cognition online

The network is populated by evolving applications and content (from specific to prolific, from pornography to anything and everything). The online environment is versatile. It includes applications with various degrees of social presence. From synchronous to asynchronous, from video display to plain text correspondence, the network offers varying degrees of interactivity. It follows that various degrees of SC occur at each application and deserve special research attention. Is the channel the single appropriate perspective to use in evaluating the social impact or is it a multitude of considerations such as the skills and preferences of the communicator, the time of day, the amount of time available, the context, and the type of information sought (Ramirez et al., 2002)? Otherwise, how can we explain colleagues e-mailing immediately adjacent employees, or even the huge success of written text (SMS) embedded in voice-oriented appliances. We will return to this issue at the conclusion of the chapter.

At the start of this chapter, we presented Fiske and Taylor's (1984) definition of SC. This definition consists of constructs and processes present in traditional interaction environments. The online context places different emphases on SC. Online, we may have reduced social cues (Sproull & Kiesler, 1986), increased bandwidth, increased reach over time and distance, increased communication modalities, altered forms of personal and interpersonal memory, different potential for demands on attention allocation, different nature of linearity in messages and connections (Newhagen & Rafaeli, 1996; Rafaeli, 2004). Therefore, SC may have been accented otherwise in the first decades of research. Thus, future attention to SC online faces two challenges—to continue study of that which is special about online behavior, as well as close the gaps in studying traditional concepts of SC.

In summary, the study of SC in a computerized, networked environment raises many unique and novel questions and considerations for research. Our discussion of SC used a collapsing telescopic lens. We started with SC online and the conception of self, turned then to a discussion of the other online, and then to the group. We concluded with a treatment of social cognitive perception of the computer and the network.

Conclusions

One way to grasp the scope of SC online is to examine the timeline of theory development. While the structure of this chapter proposed zooming out from the self to other to the computer and the network, it might be appropriate to conclude by suggesting a chronological observation as an alternative perspective. Over the decades of research into SC and computer-mediated communication, the thinking, research, and policy/public interest formulations have developed from simplistic views toward sophistication. The evolution of theory has been from a pronouncedly defensive concern about alleged direct deficiencies to a more nuanced examination of the actual qualities of CMC, the process, and the network. Research has moved from a conservative position that (to an extent) glorified the available in critiquing the new, to a more forward-facing approach.

The initial critical reactions to CMC were expressed as reduced social cues theory, media richness theory, and the Internet paradox approach. All three approaches are rooted in using face-to-face interaction as the optimal mode and term of reference. Online interaction was found wanting. All three approaches took an unfavorable view of CMC, pointing out the weaknesses and insufficiencies in social behavior that relies on CMC as a vehicle. It is likely that some of the roots for these opinions were as reactions to the utopist, hyped introduction of these technologies in the first place. However, data did not seem to bear out the dire, dystopic predictions of these early critics. The pendulum of theory has now swung to a more central location.

The largest fact looming on the horizon of SC is the ongoing adoption of the technologies and the opportunities they suggest. Rather than heeding the call of reduced cues, the critique of 'poor' media, or the admonition of the 'Internet paradox', people seem to take to the technology. Many are conducting large and growing portions of their work, learning, social, and even intimate lives via CMC. The effects do not seem to be as dire as predicted. Nor do the gains seem to be as rosy as promised. Rather, the technologies that fit SC needs and serve them best, are those that survive the diffusion bustle. A recurring empirical finding of naturalistic studies, conducted in the field with real-life users of online technologies, is that online interactions are much more like those offline than is sometimes thought (Katz & Rice, 2002; Kendall, 2002; Wellman & Haythornthwaite, 2002). This finding of continuity and stability stands despite the extended and very much changed physical capabilities of reach, territory, speed, ease of copying, and boundary spanning that typify network technology.

The confluence of these findings is, again, a critique of technological determinism and further support for social construction of technology viewpoints (Nass & Mason, 1990). As Jackson *et al.* (2002) put it, the fundamental goal should be to the active effort to privilege neither social nor technical factors in constructing accounts of technology design, development, implementation, or use. It should be the aim of current and future research about SC online to aid in the selection, design, and evaluation of technology used in human activity.

References

Adamic, L.A. and Adar, E. (2003). Friends and neighbors on the web. *Social Networks*, 25(3), 211–30.

Adamic, L.A., Buyukkokten, O., and Adar, E. (2003). A social network caught in the web. *First Monday*, 8(6).

Adar, E. and Huberman, B.A. (2000). Free riding on Gnutella. *First Monday*, 5(10) *http://firstmonday.org/issues/issue5_10/adar/index.html*.

Ahuja, M.K. and Galvin, J.E. (2003). Socialization in virtual groups. *Journal of Management*, 29(2), 161–85.

Albright, J.M. (2001). *Impression formation and attraction in computer-mediated communication*. University of Southern California.

Barak, A. and King, S.A. (2000). The two faces of the Internet: introduction to the special issue on the Internet and sexuality. *CyberPsychology & Behavior*, 3, 517–20.

Barak, M. and Rafaeli, S. (in press) Online question-posing and peer-assessment as means for web-based knowledge sharing in learning. *International Journal of Human-Computer Studies*.

Barron, G. and Yechiam, E. (2002). Private e-mail requests and the diffusion of responsibility. *Computers in Human Behavior*, 18(5), 507–20.

Bechar–Israeli, H. (1995). FROM <Bonehead> TO <cLoNehEAd>:nicknames, play, and identity on internet relay chat. *Journal of Computer-Mediated Communication*, 1(2), *http://www.ascusc.org/jcmc/vol1/issue2/bechar.html*.

Beniger, J. (1987). Personalization of mass media and the growth of pseudo-community. *Communication Research*, **14**(3), 352–71.

Biocca, F., Kim, T., and Levy, M.R. (1995). The vision of virtual reality. In F. Biocca and M. R. Levy (eds), *Communication in the Age of Virtual Reality* (pp. 3–14). Hillsdale, NJ: Lawrence Erlbaum.

Brave, S. and Nass, C. (2002). Emotion in human-computer interaction. In J. Jacko and A. Sears (eds), *The Human-Computer Interaction Handbook: Fundamentals, Evolving Technologies and Emerging Applications*. Hillsdale, NJ: Lawrence Erlbaum.

Burnett, G. and Bonnici, L. (2003). Beyond the FAQ: explicit and implicit norms in Usenet newsgroups. *Library and Information Science Research*, **25**(3), 333–51.

Butler, B., Sproull, L., Kiesler, S., and Kraut, R. (2002). Community effort in online groups: who does the work and why? In S. Weisband and L. Atwater (eds), *Leadership at a Distance*.

Cairncross, F. (2001). *The Death of Distance: How the Communications Revolution Is Changing Our Lives* (2nd edn). Boston, MA: Harvard Business School Press.

Castronova, E. (2001). *Virtual Worlds: A First-Hand Account of Market and Society on the Cyberian Frontier*. *http://papers.ssrn.com/sol3/papers.cfm?abstract_id=294828*, from *http://papers.ssrn.com/sol3/papers.cfm?abstract_id=294828*.

Chapanis, A. (1975). Interactive Human Communication. *Scientific American*, **232**, 34–42.

Constant, D., Kiesler, S., and Sproull, L. (1994). What's mine is ours, or is it? A study of attitudes about information sharing. *Information Systems Research*, **5**(4), 400–21.

Daft, R.L. and Lengel, R.H. (1986). Organizational information requirements, media richness and structural design. *Management Science*, **32**(5), 554–71.

Davenport, T.H. and Beck, J.C. (2001). *The Attention Economy*. Boston, MA: Harvard Business School Press.

Dennis, A.R., Kinney, S.T., and Hung, Y.T.C. (1999). Gender differences in the effects of media richness. *Small Group Research*, **30**(4), 405–37.

Dennis, A.R. and Valacich, J.S. (1999). *Rethinking Media Richness: Towards a Theory of Media Synchronicity*. Paper presented at the 32nd annual Hawaii International Conference on System Sciences. Volume 1, Maui, Hawaii.

Devine, P.G., Hamilton, D.L., and Ostrom, T.M. (1994). *Social cognition: impact on social psychology*. San Diego, CA: Academic Press.

Donath, J.S. (1998). Identity and deception in the virtual community. In P. Kollock and M. Smith (eds), *Communities in Cyberspace*. London: Routledge.

Dunbar, R. (2002). *Grooming, Gossip, and the Evolution of Language*. Harvard University Press.

El–Shinnawy, M. and Markus, L.M. (1997). The poverty of media richness theory: explaining people's choice of electronic mail vs. voice mail. *International Journal of Human-Computer Studies*, **46**(4), 443–67.

Etzioni, A. and Etzioni, O. (1999). Face-to-face and computer-mediated communities, a comparative analysis. *Information Society*, **15**(4), 241–8.

Fiske, S.T. (1993). Social cognition and social-perception. *Annual Review of Psychology*, **44**, 155–94.

Fiske, S.T. and Taylor, S.E. (1991). *Social Cognition* (2nd edn). New York: McGraw—Hill.

Fogg, B.J. (1999). Persuasive technologies—now is your chance to decide what they will persuade us to do—and how they'll do it. *Communications of the Acm*, **42**(5), 26–9.

Fogg, B.J. (2003). *Persuasive Technology: Using Computers to Change What We Think and Do.* San Francisco, CA: Morgan Kaufmann.

Fogg, B.J. and Nass, C. (1997). *How Users Reciprocate to Computers: An Experiment that Demonstrates Behavior Change.* Paper presented at the CHI97, Atlanta, GA.

Fulk, J. (1993). Social construction of communication technology. *Academy of Management Journal,* 36(5), 921–50.

Fulk, J., Schmitz, J., and Ryu, D. (1995). Cognitive elements in the social construction of communication technology. *Management Communication Quarterly,* 8(3), 259–88.

Fulk, J., Schmitz, J., and Steinfield, C.W. (1990). A social influence model of technology use. In J. Fulk and C.W. Steinfield (eds), *Organizations and Communications Technology.* Newbury Park, CA: Sage.

Goffman, E. (1959). *The Presentation of Self in Everyday Life.* Garden City, New York: Doubleday.

Goldhaber, M.H. (1997). The attention economy and the net. *First Monday,* 2(4).

Hampton, K. (2001). *Living the Wired Life in the Wired Suburb: Netville, Glocalization and Civil Society.* University of Toronto, Toronto.

Jackson, M.H., Poole, M.S., and Kuhn, T. (2002). The social construction of technology. In L. A. Lievrouw and S. Livingstone (eds), *The Handbook of New Media* (pp. 236–53). London: Sage Publications.

Janis, I.L. and Mann, L. (1977). *Decision Making.* New York: Free Press.

Jankowski, N.W. (2002). Creating community with media: history, theories and scientific investigations. In L.A. Lievrouw and S. Livingstone (eds), *The Handbook of New Media* (pp. 34–49). London: Sage Publications.

Jones, Q. (1997). Virtual-Communities, Virtual Settlements & Cyber-Archaeology: A Theoretical Outline. *Journal of Computer-Mediated Communication,* 3(3).

Jones, Q. and Rafaeli, S. (1999). *User Population and User Contributions to Virtual Publics: A Systems Model.* Paper presented at the ACM International Conference on Supporting Group Work (Group 99), Phoenix, Az.

Jones, Q. and Rafaeli, S. (2000a). Time to Split, Virtually: 'Discourse Architecture' and 'Community Building' Create Vibrant Virtual Publics. In B.F. Schmid, U. Lechner, K. Stanoevska—Slabeva, Y.—H. Tan, and B. Buchet (eds), *Electronic Markets— Communities & Platforms* (Vol. 10).

Jones, Q. and Rafaeli, S. (2000b). *What do virtual 'tells' tell? Placing cybersociety research into a hierarchy of social explanation.* Paper presented at the 16th Annual Hawaii International Conference on System Science (HICSS), Hawaii.

Jones, Q., Ravid, G., and Rafaeli, S. (2001a). *Empirical Evidence for Information Overload In Mass Interaction.* Paper presented at the ACM Digital Library and CHI (Computers and Human Interaction) Conference.

Jones, Q., Ravid, G., and Rafaeli, S. (2001b). *Information Overload and Virtual Public Discourse Boundaries.* Paper presented at the INTERACT'01, Eighth IFIP TC.13 Conference on Human-Computer Interaction, Tokyo, Japan.

Kahneman, D. and Tversky, A. (1979). Prospect theory: an analysis of decision under risk. *Econometrica,* 47(2), 263–291.

Katz, J. (2003). *Luring the Lurkers.* Retrieved February 28th, 2004, from *http://slashdot.org/features/98/12/28/1745252.shtml.*

Katz, J. and Rice, R.E. (2002). *Social consequences of Internet use.* Boston, MA: MIT Press.

Kemper, T.D. (1968). Reference Groups, Socialization and Achievement. *American Sociological Review*, **33**(1), 31–45.

Kendall, L. (2002). *Hanging Out in the Virtual Pub: Relationships and Masculinities Online.* Berkeley, CA: University of California Press.

Kiesler, S. (1986). The Hidden Messages in Computer-Networks. *Harvard Business Review*, **64**(1), 46.

Kock, N. (1998). Can communication medium limitations foster better group outcomes? An action research study. *Information & Management*, **34**(5), 295–305.

Kraut, R., Patterson, M., Lundmark, V., Kiesler, S., Mukopadhyay, T., and Scherlis, W. (1998). Internet paradox—a social technology that reduces social involvement and psychological well-being? *American Psychologist*, **53**(9), 1017–31.

Kreijns, K., Kirschner, P.A., and Jochems, W. (2003). Identifying the pitfalls for social interaction in computer-supported collaborative learning environments: a review of the research. *Computers in Human Behavior*, **19**(3), 335–53.

Kunda, Z. (1999). *Social cognition: making sense of people.* Cambridge, MA: The MIT Press.

Lantz, A. (2001). Meetings in a Distributed Group of Experts: Comparing Face-to-Face, Chat and Collaborative Virtual Environments. *Behaviour & Information Technology*, **20**(2), 111–17.

Lee, E.J. and Nass, C. (1999). *Effects of the form of representation and number of computer agents on conformity.* Paper presented at the proceedings of the CHI99 Conference, Pittsburgh, PA.

Levine, J.M. and Resnick, L.B. (1993). Social Foundations of Cognition. *Annual Review of Psychology*, **44**, 585–612.

Lipnack, J. and Stamps, J. (2000). *Virtual Teams.* New York: John Wiley & Sons.

Lombard, M. and Ditton, T. (1997). At the Heart of It All: The Concept of Presence. *Journal of Computer-Mediated Communication*, **3**(2), http://www.ascusc.org/jcmc/vo13/issue2/lombard.html.

Mason, B. (1999). *Issues in Virtual Ethnography.* Paper presented at the Proceedings of Esprit i3 Workshop on Ethnographic Studies, Edinburgh.

Mazlish, B. (1993). *The Fourth Discontinuity: The Co-Evolution of Humans and Machines.* New Haven, CT: Yale University Press.

Metcalfe, B. (1995). From the Ether: Metcalfe's Law. *Infoworld*, **17**(40).

Morris, M. and Ogan, C. (1996). The internet as mass medium. *Journal of Computer-Mediated Communication*, **1**(4), http://www.ascusc.org/jcmc/vo11/issue4/morris.html.

Murthi, B.P.S. and Sarkar, S. (2003). The role of the management sciences in research on personalization. *Management Science*, **49**(10), 1344–62.

Nass, C. and Mason, B. (1990). On the Study of Technology and Task: A Variable-based Approach. In J. Fulk and C. W. Steinfield (eds), *Organizations and Communication Technologies* (pp. 29–45). Newbury Park, CA: Sage Publications.

Nass, C. and Moon, Y. (2000). Machines and mindlessness: social responses to computers. *Journal of Social Issues*, **56**(1), 81–103.

Nass, C., Moon, Y.M., and Carney, P. (1999). Are people polite to computers? Responses to computer-based interviewing systems. *Journal of Applied Social Psychology*, **29**(5), 1093–110.

Nass, C., Steuer, J., and Tauber, E. (1994). *Computers are Social Actors.* Paper presented at the Proceedings of SIGCHI, Boston, MA.

Newhagen, J.E. and Rafaeli, S. (1996). Why communication researchers should study the Internet: a dialogue. *Journal of Communication*, **46**(1), 4–13.

Nonnecke, B. and Preece, J. (2000). *Lurker Demographics*. Paper presented at the Proceedings of CHI2000, The Hague, Netherlands.

Norman, D. (2004). *Emotional Design: Why We Love (or Hate) Everyday Things*. New York: Basic Books.

Olson, G.M. and Olson, J.S. (2003). Human-computer interaction: psychological aspects of the human use of computing. *Annual Review of Psychology*, **54**, 491–516.

Pool, I.D.S. (1983). *Forecasting the Telephone: a Retrospective Technology Assessment Of The Telephone*. Norwood, NJ: Ablex Publishing.

Postman, N. (1992). *Technopoly: The Surrender of Culture to Technology*. New York: Knopf.

Preece, J. (2000). *Online Communities: Designing Usability and Supporting Sociability*. New York: John Wiley & Sons Inc.

Raban, D.R. and Rafaeli, S. (2004). The effect of source nature and status on the subjective value of information. (*Under review*).

Rafaeli, S. (1984). *If the Computer is the Medium, What is the Message?* Paper presented at the Annual Conference of the International Communication Association, Honolulu, Hawaii.

Rafaeli, S. (1986). The electronic bulletin board: a computer-driven mass medium. *Computers and the Social Sciences*, **2**(3), 123–36.

Rafaeli, S. (1988). Interactivity: from new media to communication. In *Sage Annual Review of Communication Research: Advancing Communication Science* (Vol. 16, pp. 110–34). Beverly Hills, CA: Sage.

Rafaeli, S. (1989). Soapware: the fit between software and advertising. *Information and Software Technology*, **31**(5), 268–75.

Rafaeli, S. (2004). In M. Consalvo, N. Baym, J. Hunsinger, *et al.* (eds), *Constructs in the Storm*. New York, NY: Peter Lang.

Rafaeli, S. and Noy, A. (2002). Online auctions, messaging, communication and social facilitation: a simulation and experimental evidence. *European Journal of Information Systems*, **11**(3), 196–207.

Rafaeli, S. and Raban, D.R. (2003). Experimental investigation of the subjective value of information in trading. *Journal of the Association for Information Systems*, **4**(5), 119–39.

Rafaeli, S. and Ravid, G. (2003). Information sharing as an enabler for the virtual team: an experimental approach to assessing the role of electronic mail in disintermediation. In *Information Sytems Journal*, **13**, 191–206.

Rafaeli, S., Ravid, G., and Soroka, V. (2004). *De-lurking in virtual communities: a social communication network approach to measuring the effects of social and cultural capital*. Paper presented at the 37th annual HICSS conference (Hawaii International Conference on System Sciences), Hawaii.

Rafaeli, S. and Sudweeks, F. (1997). Networked Interactivity. *Journal of Computer-Mediated Communication*, **2**(4), *http://www.ascusc.org/jcmc/vo12/issue4/rafaeli.sudweeks.html*.

Ramirez, A., Walther, J.B., Burgoon, J.K., and Sunnafrank, M. (2002). Information-seeking strategies, uncertainty, and computer-mediated communication—toward a conceptual model. *Human Communication Research*, **28**(2), 213–28.

Reed, D. (1998). Accounting in the age of Moore's Law. *Context Magazine*, **1**(3), *http://www.contextmag.com/archives/199806/technosynth.asp*.

Reeves, B. and Nass, C. (1996). *The media equation: how people treat computers, television and new media like real people and places.* Cambridge, MA: Cambridge University Press.

Reeves, B. and Nass, C. (2000). Perceptual bandwidth. *Communications of the Acm,* 43(3), 65–70.

Rheingold, H. (1993). *The virtual community: homesteading on the electronic frontier.* Reading, MA: Addison–Wesley.

Rheingold, H. (2002). *Smart Mobs: The Next Social Revolution.* Boulder, CO: Perseus Publishing.

Rice, R.E. (1984). *The new media: communication, research and technology.* Beverly Hills, CA: Sage.

Rogers, E.M. (1968–2003). *Diffusion of Innovations* (5th edn). New York: Free Press.

Rogers, E.M. and Chaffee, S.H. (1983). Communication as an academic discipline. *Journal of Communication,* 33(3), 18–30.

Rogers, E.M. and Kincaid, L.D. (1981). *Communication networks: toward a new paradigm for research.* New York: Free Press.

Rouse, S.V. and Haas, H.A. (2003). Exploring the accuracies and inaccuracies of personality perception following Internet-mediated communication. *Journal of Research in Personality,* 37(5), 446–67.

Savicki, V., Kelley, M., and Oesterreich, E. (1999). Judgments of gender in computer-mediated communication. *Computers in Human Behavior,* 15(2), 185–94.

Shapiro, C. and Varian, H.R. (1999). *Information Rules: A Strategic Guide to the Network Economy.* Boston: Harvard Business School Press.

Shneiderman, B. (1998). *Designing the user interface: strategies for effective human-computer interaction* (3rd edn). Boston, MA: Addison–Wesley.

Short, J., Williams, E., and Christie, B. (1976). *The Social Psychology of Telecommunications.* London: Wiley.

Slater, D. (2002). Social Relationships and Identity Online and Offline. In L.A. Lievrouw nd S. Livingstone (eds), *The Handbook of New Media* (pp. 533–46). London: Sage Publications.

Soroka, V., Jacovi, M., and Ur, S. (2003). We can see you: a study of communities' invisible people through reachout. *Communities and Technologies,* 65–79.

Spears, M., Russell, L., and Lee, S. (1990). De-individuation and group polarization in computer-mediated communication. *British Journal of Social Psychology,* (29), 121–34.

Spears, R., Postmes, T., Lea, M., and Wolbert, A. (2002). When are net effects gross products? The power of influence and the influence of power in computer-mediated communication. *Journal of Social Issues,* 58(1), 91–107.

Sproull, L. and Kiesler, S. (1986). Reducing Social-Context Cues—Electronic Mail in Organizational Communication. *Management Science,* 32(11), 1492–512.

Standage, T. (1998). *The Victorian Internet: The Remarkable Story of the Telegraph and the Nineteenth Century's On-Line Pioneers.* New York: Walker & Co.

Stone, A. (1991). Will the Real Body Please Stand Up? Boundary Stories about Virtual Cultures. In M. Benedikt (ed), *Cyberspace: First Steps.* Cambridge, MA: The MIT Press.

Sudweeks, F., McLaughlin, M., and Rafaeli, S. (1998). *Network and Netplay: Virtual Groups on the Internet.* Cambridge, MA: MIT Press.

Sudweeks, F. and Rafaeli, S. (1996). How do you get a hundred strangers to agree: computer mediated communication and collaboration. In T.M. Harrison and T.D. Stephen (eds), *Computer Networking and Scholarship in the 21st Century University* (pp. 115–36). Albany, NY: SUNY Press.

Sundar, S.S. and Nass, C. (2000). Source orientation in human-computer interaction—programmer, networker, or independent social actor? *Communication Research*, 27(6), 683–703.

Thaler, R.H. (1980). Toward a positive theory of consumer choice. *Journal of Economic Behavior and Organization*, 1(1), 39–60.

Turkle, S. (1980). Computers as Rorschach. *Society*, 17(2).

Turkle, S. (1984). *The Second Self: Computers and the Human Spirit*. New York: Simon & Schuster.

Turkle, S. (1997). *Life on the Screen: Identity in the Age of the Internet*. Carmichael, CA: Touchstone Books.

Turkle, S. (2004). Computer Games as Evocative Objects: From Projective Screens to Relational Artifacts. In J. Raessens & J. Goldstein (eds), *Handbook of Computer Game Studies*. Boston, MA: MIT Press.

Tyler, J.R. and Tang, J.C. (2003). *When Can I Expect an Email Response? A Study of Rhythms in Email Usage*. Paper presented at the ECSCW 2003.

Wallace, P. (1999). *The Psychology of the Internet*. Cambridge: Cambridge University Press.

Walther, J.B. and Burgoon, J.K. (1992). Relational Communication in Computer-Mediated Interaction. *Human Communication Research*, 19(1), 50–88.

Weizenbaum, J. (1966). Eliza—a Computer Program for Study of Natural Language Communication between Man and Machine. *Communications of the Acm*, 9(1), 35–6.

Wellman, B. and Gulia, M. (1999). Net Surfers Don't Ride Alone: Virtual Communities as Communities. In B. Wellman (ed), *Networks in the Global Village: Life in Contemporary Communities* (pp. 331–66). Boulder, CO: Westview.

Wellman, B. and Haythornthwaite, C. (2002). *The internet in everyday life*. Malden, MA: Blackwell Publishing.

Whittaker, S., Terveen, L., Hill, W., and Cherny, L. (1998). *The Dynamics of Mass Interaction*. Paper presented at the Proceedings of CSCW 98, Seattle, WA.

Williams, K.D., Cheung, C.K.T., and Choi, W. (2000). Cyberostracism: Effects of Being Ignored Over the Internet*1. *Journal of Personality and Social Psychology*, 79(5), 748–62.

Williams, R. and Edge, D. (1996). What is the social shaping of technology? *Research Policy*, 25, 856–99.

Workman, M., Kahnweiler, W., and Bommer, W. (2003). The effects of cognitive style and media richness on commitment to telework and virtual teams. *Journal of Vocational Behavior*, 63(2), 199–219.

Chapter 4

Online persuasion and compliance: social influence on the Internet and beyond

Rosanna Guadagno and Robert Cialdini

A colleague of ours once tried to count the number of influence appeals he received throughout a single day. Between the television commercials, t-shirt slogans, bumper stickers, telemarketing solicitations, radio ads, billboards, magazine and newspaper ads, and requests from colleagues, friends, and family, he very soon counted over 500 in less than an hour! The Internet, having been adopted for both personal and business use, has quickly become yet another channel for influence appeals. We now find advertisements in our e-mail inbox (also called 'junk mail' or 'SPAM'); and banner ads on web pages and 'pop-up' ads appear throughout our web surfing adventures. We also receive instant messages from strangers imploring us to visit their websites. Sometimes misleading advertisements appear telling us that there is something wrong with our computer when in fact it is really a ploy to get us to purchase the software being surreptitiously advertised. Corporations offer us free software as long as we agree to be direct marketed through ads embedded in the software. Additionally, colleagues, friends, and family use the Internet as a means to communicate influence appeals. Thus, this new communications channel has become yet another way for people to attempt to influence us.

Just as influence practitioners, novice and professional alike, have moved into this area, so have the researchers. Social scientists have been studying the impact of the Internet on social behavior across a variety of contexts ranging from the formation of romantic relationships and friendships with strangers without the barrier of geographic distance (see for example, McKenna *et al.*, 2002) to the consumption habits of online shoppers (see for example,

The authors would like to thank Tonio Loewald, Petia Petrova, and Brad Sagarin for their helpful comments on this chapter.

Iacobucci, 2003) to decision making in computer-mediated groups (see for example, Kiesler *et al.*, 1984). Additionally, the authors of this chapter have been involved in examining the impact of this relatively new, primarily text-based, communication modality on the interpersonal persuasion process (Guadagno, 2003; Guadagno & Cialdini, 2002).

Chapter overview

What has research on computer-mediated persuasion revealed? The purpose of this chapter is to review the research on social influence on the Internet, primarily via text-based communications. We will cover the research on social influence—examining both behavior change and attitude change—in computer-mediated contexts. Our focus will be on empirical work that has examined the following:

- text-based interactive influence appeals
- web-based non-interactive influence appeals
- non-text based forms of computer-mediated influence appeals.

First, we will define some core terms and then review the research on computer-mediated communication focusing on how it differs from other communication modalities (e.g. face-to-face interaction). Next, we will briefly review the relevant research on dual process models of persuasion. A review of the research conducted on persuasion in interactive and non-interactive computer-based modalities will follow. Then, we will provide an overview of the principles of influence and the research that has been conducted on compliance in online contexts. A discussion of the findings on non-text based forms of communication via the Internet (e.g. online virtual environments) will follow. We will conclude with limitations of this research and a discussion of the implications of the research reviewed on future work in this area.

Key definitions

Social influence, sometimes referred to simply as influence, refers to the change in one's attitudes, behavior, or beliefs due to external pressure that is real or imagined (Cialdini, 2001). We will be focusing on two specific types of influence: persuasion and compliance.

Compliance involves an area of social influence that focuses on change in behavior resulting from a direct request. For instance, if an individual is asked to sign an online petition advocating the continuation of the science fiction television series *Farscape* and agrees to this request, we would say that this individual is complying with this request. Persuasion describes an area of social influence that is focused on the change in a private attitude or belief as a result of receiving a message (Cialdini, 2001). So, for instance, if you read a 'blog' (personal web-based diary or 'weblog') entry that contains compelling reasons why the film *Battlefield Earth* is a better science fiction film than *Bladerunner*, and your opinion on this topic is changed as a result of reading the arguments, then you have been persuaded.

Additional terms that will appear throughout this chapter describe the individuals involved in an influence attempt. First, influence practitioner, communicator, or agent of influence are terms used to describe the individual who attempts to influence others. For instance, in the example above, the person who made the request to sign the petition to save the TV series is the influence practitioner. Next, the target or target of influence refers to the person who has the influence attempt directed at him/her.

Throughout this chapter, we will use the terms Internet, online, and cyber-space somewhat interchangeably. In all cases, we intend these terms to signify computer-mediated communication involving networked computers. However, it is also important to note that some research that has examined social influence online has been conducted using computers running Internet applications such as a web browser without actually being connected to the Internet, thus creating a realistic but controlled environment in which to study online behavior.

How does computer-mediated communication differ from other forms of communication?

Although people use the Internet for myriad things such as shopping, banking, obtaining information and news, downloading images and computer pro-grams, it is primarily a tool for communication (Kraut *et al.*, 1998). This fairly new communication technology is widely used and has a huge impact on the nature of our interactions with others. However, the nature of the interactions may be very different from that of the interactions we have with others via more traditional communications technologies.

McKenna and Bargh (2000) suggest that there are four novel and important aspects of online interactions. First, the Internet allows for greater anonymity. In cyberspace, we can meet new people but readily visible characteristics, such as our appearance, are not our most salient feature. Individuals may choose what others know about them: name, age, appearance, sex, and many other pieces of information can be concealed or revealed at will. For instance, if an individual chooses to call herself 'JellyBean' in her online interactions, and reveal nothing else, she can be just about completely anonymous. Conversely, our professional e-mail addresses convey our full names and our place of work, and, if one reads our e-mail signatures, one would know quite a bit about us, thus making us perhaps even less anonymous than over the telephone. The ability to be completely anonymous while in cyberspace has been related to a decrease in self-focus on internal standards for behavior (Matheson & Zanna, 1989). This may explain why individuals are far more likely to engage in non-normative behavior, such as 'flaming' or making rude or derogatory statements to others, when in a computer-mediated interaction than in a face-to-face interaction (Siegel *et al.*, 1986).

Social category salience, such as one's group membership (e.g. sex, ethnic group, university affiliation), has been demonstrated to impact the kind of behavior exhibited during anonymous computer-mediated communication. For instance, if an individual's social category is made salient by a username (e.g. '101Female') in an anonymous computer-mediated interaction, that individual is likely to exhibit behavior consistent with normative expectations for the behavior based on that social category (e.g. '101Female' may act more feminine in that specific context as opposed to other online contexts). For further information on this topic, we recommend an examination of the work of Postmes *et al.* (1998) on the SIDE (social identity model of deindividuation effects) model.

In addition to anonymity, McKenna and Bargh (2000) presented three other factors that make Internet-based communication different from other forms of communication. First, as we alluded to above, owing to the text-based nature of the typical online interaction, physical appearance is far less important than in face-to-face forms of communication. This aspect of online interaction is important for this is the dominant communication modality that allows us to meet people in the comfort of our own home with no concern about differential treatment owing to our physical appearance. Second, physical distance is no longer a barrier for interacting with others. Thus, our accessibility to new friends and colleagues is broader than before the advent of the Internet. Individuals can find others with similar interests with great ease. All one has to do is find the online community that best caters to one's interests and similar others will be found. And the variety is such that online communities range widely from Beanie Baby collectors to Star Trek fans to individuals seeking social support due to an abusive romantic relationship to individuals looking for advice, information, and support for their diabetic cat. Finally, individuals have greater control over the time and place of interactions. This experience is by and large empowering for the Internet user, but can sometimes be the exact opposite as the line between work and home life blur due to the ubiquity of the Internet.

Another aspect that makes online interactions different from interactions in visual and auditory modalities is the absence of available social cues, such as eye contact or voice tone. Although as we mention above, social category salience can impact behavior in certain online contexts, other research indicates that certain cues that may accompany a communication in other modalities are far less salient in computer-mediated communication. For instance, Dubrovsky *et al.* (1991) reported that status and expertise cues were less salient and had less of an impact on behavior in a computer-mediated interaction as compared to an analogous face-to-face interaction. Others have also found liking for a communicator to be linked to persuasion in face-to-face influence appeals but not in analogous online appeals (Guadagno & Cialdini, 2002; Matheson & Zanna, 1989). This decreased salience of social cues associated with an online communication suggests that communicator cues, such as liking and expertise, may be less important in a computer-mediated influence appeal as compared to a face-to-face appeal. We will have more to say about this later on in this chapter.

What factors impact on the persuasion process?

Persuasion researchers have proposed dual process models of persuasion—that there are two primary ways in which individuals process information (Chaiken *et al.*, 1996; Petty & Cacioppo, 1984). Individuals either process information centrally (also called systematic processing) or peripherally (also called heuristic processing). In the case of central route persuasion, individuals focus on the content of the message and make decisions as to their attitude on the topic based on factors such as the quality of the argument. Individuals are more likely to engage in central route persuasion if the topic is of importance to them, they have the cognitive resources available to process the message, they know something about the topic, and the arguments are written (Chaiken, *et al.*, 1996; Petty & Cacioppo, 1984).

Conversely, an individual who engages in peripheral route persuasion is likely to use decision cues or rules of thumb (also called heuristics) to make decisions about their attitude on the topic. For instance, a person engaging in peripheral route persuasion may be more swayed by the quantity of the persuasive arguments rather than the quality or may make a decision based on the perceived credibility of the influence agent rather than the veracity of his/her statements. People are most likely to engage in this type of message processing when the topic is of little relevance to them, they do not have the ability to process the message, the communication mode is one in which the influence agent is salient, and they know very little about the topic (Chaiken, *et al.*, 1996; Petty & Cacioppo, 1984).

Although individuals tend to process persuasive messages using either the central or peripheral route (depending on the features of the influence attempt), we do not mean to say that message processing will always be entirely central or entirely peripheral. Individuals will engage in both types of message processing under certain circumstances.

In an early attempt to examine persuasion in different communication modalities, Chaiken and Eagly (1983) examined the impact of the likeability of the communicator on persuasion in one of three communication modalities: written, videotape, or audiotape. To manipulate the appeal of the influence agent, participants also read a personal statement from the influence agent that portrayed him as a likeable or unlikeable individual. When the influence agent was likeable, influence targets in both video and audiotape conditions showed greater attitude change than those in the written communication condition. When the influence agent was not likeable, attitude change was greatest for targets who received the written communication. These results suggest that in the video and audiotape conditions, the personal cues of the communicator were salient and participants engaged in heuristic processing of the persuasive message. Conversely, in the written communication condition, where source cues were less salient, participants processed the message systematically. Thus, prior research in this field suggests that computer-mediated influence appeals may be akin to written appeals, in that the cues of the communicator are less salient and targets of influence may therefore be more focused on the characteristics of the message content than the message source when determining their attitude on a topic.

Persuasion online

In this next section, we will review the research that examines the impact of the Internet on the persuasion process. First, we will focus on non-interactive persuasive appeals, then on interpersonal influence attempts.

Non-interactive online persuasion

What may have been the first computer-mediated persuasion study compared written paragraphs to one another, with some participants reading the passage on a computer and some reading it in written form after a face-to-face interaction with other participants (Matheson & Zanna, 1989). The purpose of their study was to examine the impact of self-awareness on persuasion. They predicted that individuals in the computer-mediated communication condition would experience greater private self-awareness (e.g. heightened awareness of internalized personal values) than participants in the face-to-face condition, and that this increased private self-awareness would lead participants in the computer-mediated condition to process the persuasive message systematically. They also predicted that participants in the face-to-face condition would engage in heuristic processing of the persuasive message and therefore would experience more attitude change if the message was presented by a likeable source.

Participants completed several tasks. In the face-to-face condition, they each wrote a short paragraph on an assigned topic with paper and pencil. Next, they completed two decision-making problems with a partner. Finally, they read a persuasive communication printed on paper. Participants in the computer-mediated condition typed the paragraph on the computer, completed the decision-making problems via computer, and read the persuasive communication on the computer. After they read the persuasive communication, participants in both communication conditions filled out an attitude measure and a measure of private and public self-awareness. They defined private self-awareness as personal attitudes, beliefs, and feelings and public self-awareness as a focus on one's awareness of themselves from the view of others including self-presentational concerns.

Results indicated that, although there was no overall difference in attitude change between the online interaction and the face-to-face condition, there were differences in the way in which the persuasive message was processed. For instance, participants in the online interaction condition reported higher levels of private self-awareness than those in the face-to-face condition. Additionally, although the predicted communication modality difference did not occur, the authors did report that social cues had a direct influence on the message reception of the face-to-face condition participants, but not for the computer-mediated condition participants. The authors concluded that this difference in message processing may have been due to their finding that respondents in the computer-mediated condition reported greater private self-awareness than face-to-face respondents. Thus, the results of this study suggest that a message received through computer mediation is more likely to be centrally processed.

In another study on persuasion, this time in a web-based context, Duthler (2001) asked participants to read a series of persuasive statements that varied in argument strength, personal relevance, and the complexity of the peripheral cues associated with the message. Some participants read strong, well-reasoned arguments endorsing comprehensive exams as a new graduation requirement, while some participants read a set of weak, poorly reasoned arguments advocating the same. Personal relevance was manipulated by telling some participants that, if approved, the new graduation requirement would apply to them, thereby making the topic highly relevant to them. Participants in the low-relevance condition were told that, if approved, the exam would not be implemented for 10 years. Finally, complexity of peripheral cues was manipulated by amount of color and graphics in the website. In the low-complexity condition, the website was essentially in black and white, whereas in the high-complexity condition, the website was in color and had several colored graphics.

The results indicated that participants had a more positive attitude toward the comprehensive exam after reading the strong arguments as compared to the weak. However, there was no difference in positivity toward the exam based on whether they were personally relevant. In addition, the website that was high in complexity of peripheral cues (i.e. with full color and graphics) enhanced the attention paid by participants to the persuasive message when the personal relevance was low. The results of this study are comparable to written communication modes in traditional persuasion literature such as the Chaiken and Eagly (1983) study reviewed above, suggesting that when the persuasive attempt is non-interactive (e.g. web-based), participants respond to web-based influence attempts by engaging in a message-focused approach which makes systematic processing more likely.

In a series of studies designed to examine the persuasive impact of online ads, Sagarin *et al.* (2003) asked participants to solve anagrams on a computer while ads appeared at the edge of the screen throughout their exercise. Across three studies, the results indicated that these visually peripheral ads were both persuasive and a source of distraction even though participants reported that they were not attending to them.

Overall, the few studies that have been conducted using non-interactive methodologies akin to 'SPAM', banner ads, or 'pop-up' ads indicate that when there is no interaction between the influence agent and the target of influence, individuals respond in a manner similar to participants from prior studies who have read persuasive communications on paper. There is a tendency toward central processing of the message. Additionally, one implication of the studies reviewed here is that the online ads that frequently disrupt our web surfing actually do have a persuasive effect even when we do not actively attend to them.

Interpersonal persuasion online

What about when individuals use a computer as the mode through which to engage in a persuasive interaction? How is the persuasion process impacted by the features of online communication?

Two studies conducted by Guadagno and Cialdini (2002) examined these questions. In the first study, an influence agent attempted to persuade a same-sex participant in either a face-to-face discussion or via a non-anonymous e-mail discussion. The influence agent presented either strong or weak arguments adopted from Petty *et al.* (1980) to persuade research participants that a comprehensive exam as a new graduation requirement was a good idea. As would be expected, the results indicated that the strong arguments were more persuasive than the weak arguments. In addition, there was also an interesting gender effect. Regardless of the strength of the arguments, female participants who discussed the topic via e-mail reported less agreement with the message than did women in the face-to-face condition, whereas there was no communication mode difference for the male participants.

These results were interpreted in terms of gender-based expectations for behavior (Carli, 1989): female targets were oriented towards forming a bond with the influence agent, whereas male targets were oriented towards the task and maintaining their independence. Because the e-mail condition did not allow for bonding with ease, the female participants were less inclined to change their attitude in the direction expressed by the influence agent. However, this was not the case in the face-to-face discussion condition, which did lend itself to the formation of a bond between the female target and the female influence agent. Because the male targets were focused on maintaining their independence and on the task, the communication mode was not relevant to meeting these goals.

In support of this interpretation, Guadagno and Cialdini (2002) reported that participants' ratings of the likeability, knowledge, and trustworthiness of the influence agent were correlated with attitude toward the comprehensive exam only for women in the face-to-face condition. In contrast, men made their decisions based primarily on the arguments. Regardless of communication

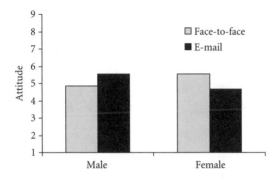

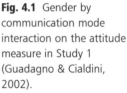

Fig. 4.1 Gender by communication mode interaction on the attitude measure in Study 1 (Guadagno & Cialdini, 2002).

modality, proximity and personality characteristics of the confederate did not have an impact on their opinions. There was also evidence (from the analysis of cognitive responses measured by examining the thoughts that participants recorded during the study) that participants in the e-mail condition engaged in central route processing of the message, whereas there was more communicator focus in the face-to-face condition indicating peripheral route processing.

To replicate and extend these findings, Guadagno and Cialdini (2002) conducted a follow-up study in which participants engaged in an interaction with the influence agent prior to the comprehensive exam discussion. This prior interaction was competitive, cooperative, or independent in nature and was always a face-to-face interaction. Next, half of the participants received a persuasive message from the influence agent in a face-to-face context, while the other half received the same message from the same influence agent via e-mail. The influence agent presented only strong, well-reasoned arguments.

Consistent with predictions, once the female influence target had an opportunity to interact with the female influence agent, the mode of communication did not impact the level of positivity toward the message. Only female participants who had no interaction with the influence agent (those who were in the independent prior interaction condition and who then communicated via e-mail) reported less positivity towards the message. For male participants, only those who competed with the influence agent during the prior interaction and then took part in a face-to-face discussion exhibited less opinion change than men in all other conditions. Thus, for women, it was the lack of social interaction with the communicator (in the independent prior interaction condition) coupled with the lack of social cues (in the e-mail communication condition) that led to the least willingness to adopt the communicator's sound arguments. For men, on the other hand, it was the presence of a competitive social interaction (in the competitive prior interaction condition) coupled with the presence of social cues (in the face-to-face communication condition) that most retarded acceptance of the communicator's position.

Additional research on gender differences in online interaction supports the interpretation of these results. Dennis *et al.* (1999) conducted research on gender and interaction in online versus offline contexts and reported that female dyads who completed a decision-making task in a face-to-face discussion made better decisions than did women in a comparable computer-mediated group. Communication mode had less of an impact on performance for mixed-sex and male dyads.

A third study was conducted to further examine these issues. In this study, Guadagno (2003) sought to replicate the basic finding that women report less positivity towards a topic after a persuasive attempt in an e-mail exchange as compared to face-to-face context, and to expand on this topic by investigating the extent to which perceived similarity impacts this. Men and women engaged in the same discussion of comprehensive exams with a same-sex influence agent. This time, however, prior to the interaction, participants received feedback as to their similarity with the other individual in terms of their personality and the way they perceived the world. This false feedback was intended to induce a perception of oneness. Oneness refers to a sense of merged or interconnected identity (Cialdini *et al.*, 1997).

Participants received one of three oneness manipulations: high, low, or none. In the high-oneness condition, participants were told that they were so similar to the influence agent that they could be siblings. Participants in the low-oneness condition were given the opposite feedback: they were told that they were so dissimilar from the influence agent that it was unlikely that two people would ever be so different. Finally, in a pair of conditions designed to replicate the findings of the Guadagno and Cialdini (2002) studies, some male and female participants were given no oneness information. As with the second study in Guadagno and Cialdini (2002), only strong arguments were used.

The results indicated that, regardless of communication mode, there was an overall effect for oneness—the higher the level of oneness, the greater the positivity towards the position on the comprehensive exams espoused by the influence agent. Across communication modality and gender, the amount of oneness reported predicted attitude toward the comprehensive exam proposal. Thus, the more the participants felt a sense of merged identity, the more likely they were to change their attitude to match the confederate.

As in the two Guadagno and Cialdini (2002) studies, in the absence of the oneness manipulation, women reported less positivity towards the message in the e-mail condition as compared to the face-to-face condition, while there was no communication mode difference for men. In terms of the oneness conditions, oneness eliminated communication mode difference for women: they either had very positive opinions or very negative opinions depending on the oneness condition, regardless of whether they received the persuasive communication in an e-mail or face-to-face context.

Specifically, across all the female conditions, women in the low-oneness condition, regardless of communication mode, reported the least positivity toward the exam. In the low-oneness condition, the female influence agent was a person from an outgroup, a person so dissimilar that participants did not attempt to cross group boundaries to bond with her. Given that research on adolescent friendships indicates that girls tend to strengthen their friendship groups in part through the exclusion of others (Henrich *et al.*, 2000), it may be that the women in this study chose to reject the influence agent and her message, regardless of communication mode, because there was no possibility of bringing her into their group.

For males, there was no communication mode difference for high oneness, but there was a difference for low oneness. Similar to Guadagno and Cialdini's (2002) second study, when faced with a face-to-face discussion with someone who they might categorize as a competitor or outgroup member, men reported the least positivity towards the message as compared to any other condition. However, in the low-oneness e-mail condition, the decreased salience of the influence agent appeared to neutralize this effect. Men in this condition reported levels of positivity toward the message that were equivalent to the other oneness conditions. The male participants may have felt competitive toward the dissimilar other. When he was salient in the face-to-face condition, they rejected his message. However, when he was not present in the same room and the competitive social cues were not salient, they were more open to his arguments delivered by e-mail. There is no doubt that men in this condition did project a competitive orientation onto the confederate: collapsed across communication modality, men in the low-oneness condition rated the confederate as more competitive than did participants in the no- and high-oneness conditions.

Taken together these studies indicated that, at least in same-sex interactions with strangers, women may have a hard time persuading other women via e-mail unless they are able to discover some sort of similarity or commonality. Whereas for men, the mode of communication is less important, except in the case of a competitor or outgroup member. In this case, men are likely to reject even the most sound arguments of such a person in a face-to-face interaction. Fortunately, the decreased salience of the interaction partner's social cues in e-mail appears to alleviate the competitive aspects of the interaction.

The final study on interpersonal, computer-mediated persuasion revealed by our literature review was conducted by Moon (1999). In two studies, Moon compared the impact of response latency (low: 0–1 sec. vs. medium: 5–10 sec. vs. high: 13–18 sec.) defined as the amount of time between sending a message and receiving a response, and perceived distance (several miles away vs. several hundred miles away) on computer-mediated persuasion. Participants completed a survival task that asked them to rank the importance of items needed to survive in the desert on their own. Then a computer agent tried to persuade them to change their responses. In the first study, participants were told that they were interacting with another human. In the second study, they were told that they were interacting with a computer program.

The results indicated that the medium-length response latency was the most persuasive as compared to the low- and high-latency conditions. Additionally,

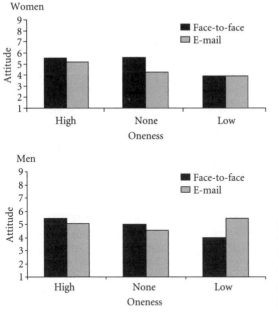

Fig. 4.2 Attitude toward the comprehensive exam broken down by oneness, communication mode, and gender (Guadagno, 2003).

the close perceived distance condition produced more persuasion than did the far perceived distance condition. Moreover, there was no difference in results based on being told that they were interacting with a real human versus a computer agent. The results of this study indicated that the length of time an individual takes to respond to a message may have a substantial impact on the way his/her message is received. Also, although the Internet provides us access to individuals all over the world, there is still an effect for proximity. Indeed, participants also rated the close proximity persuader as being higher in credibility and as providing higher quality information. Finally, these results suggest that the decreased salience of the interaction partner in online interactions is so strong that it does not matter whether the interaction partner is human or a computer program.

Influence principles online: do people comply?

We now turn our attention away from persuasion in cyberspace and on to compliance online. Cialdini (2001) suggested that many tendencies to comply with another's request can be explained in terms of six fundamental principles of influence: scarcity, reciprocity, consistency/commitment, authority, social validation, and friendship/liking. The principles serve as rules of thumb or decision heuristics (e.g. 'rare = valuable') that assist in decision making.

Influence agents often use decision heuristics to obtain compliance from their targets (e.g. an influence appeal involving a limited opportunity capitalizes on the 'rare = valuable' decision heuristic). Although these principles have been examined broadly across a variety of contexts and communication modes, we will only focus on those principles that have been examined in computer-mediated contexts.

One important aspect of examining compliance in online interactions is that, although non-verbal cues are not available in these situations, social category cues are still available and people may respond to influence appeals based on those cues. So, for instance, if the only thing you know about an online interaction partner is that she is a lawyer, you are likely to be more persuaded by her advice on legal matters.

Guégen and Jacob (2002) conducted a study that examined this salience issue and its impact on compliance. In this study, participants were e-mailed a request to fill out a survey on dietary habits. Half the participants received photographs of the influence agent along with the request. The results revealed that including photographs with the request increased compliance. There were also gender effects. Men were generally more compliant than women. Additionally, both men and women were more likely to comply with the request when the influence agent was female. Thus, in this case, the photographs increased the salience of the communicator and increased compliance, but across the board, men and women responded differently, in part based on the social category information of the sex of the influence agent.

Based on our review of the literature, only two of the six principles of influence have been examined empirically in online contexts: authority and commitment/consistency. The remainder of this section of the chapter will examine these principles and their ability to induce compliance online.

Authority online

We all want to make good choices and we frequently choose a course of action based on information such as the recommendation of an authority (Cialdini, 2001). Authority figures often influence others, in part because they are perceived as experts. This activates the 'believe an expert' decision heuristic. Although some of the literature on online behavior demonstrates a decrease in the transmission of social cues, are people still more likely to comply with the request of an authority figure? On the one hand, being an expert or an authority figure is a social category that can easily be made salient by an e-mail signature or e-mail address. In this case, we would expect that individuals who received an influence appeal from an authority figure to respond much in the same way as they would in a context where the authority figure was more salient. That is, we might expect individuals to be more compliant with an authority figure's request than compared to a low-status requestor. However, when the online context is interactive in nature, will authority cues be salient enough to alter the behavior of others in the group?

In a study designed to examine the impact of expertise and status in computer-mediated and face-to-face decision-making, Dubrovsky *et al.* (1991) asked groups comprising of one high-status group member (a graduate student) and three low-status group members (college freshmen) to discuss two topics in either a computer-mediated or a face-to-face interaction. The career choices available to college graduates was the topic in which the graduate student was an expert, while the other was a topic in which the low-status group members were experts.

The results indicated several significant differences between face-to-face and online interaction groups relevant to the transmission of authority cues online. In the face-to-face condition, the graduate student was more likely to be first advocate, to engage in greater participation in the discussion, and to have more influence over the ultimate group decision than a low-status first advocate. Thus, the high-status group member successfully maintained the position of authority in the group. However, this was only the case when the high-status group member was also an expert on the topic. In the computer-mediated discussion, status cue effects were reduced: both the high-status and low-status participants were equally likely to be the first person in the group to advocate a position on the topic because they were likely to start expressing themselves at the same time, regardless of the high-status member's expertise. Thus, these results support the notion that status and expertise are less salient in the computer-mediated decision groups (Dubrovsky *et al.*, 1991).

What about when it is not a discussion but rather a more traditional attempt to induce compliance? Guégen and Jacob (2002) tested this in a study designed to assess the effectiveness of status in online compliance. In this study, participants were asked to complete a short survey on dietary habits. The request was either from an influence agent who was either high in status (a professor) or low in status (a college student). This study was conducted with an ingroup sample (university students) and an outgroup sample (members of the surrounding community).

For students within the university, nearly all (97.5%) complied with the request from the professor, whereas 65% complied when the influence agent was low in status. Additionally, the latency in response rate (i.e. time taken to return the completed questionnaire) was lower with the high-status influence agent than with the low-status one. With the outgroup sample, compliance was lower in both conditions, but the same pattern of results was reported.

Thus, status does appear to serve as a meaningful social category in cyberspace and can translate into higher compliance, particularly when the influence agent is a high-status ingroup member.

It appears, therefore, that authority is successful in increasing compliance in online groups when it is used as a decision heuristic, but is far less influential when present in an interactive discussion. However, more studies on this topic need to be conducted before we draw a firm conclusion.

Commitment and consistency online

Another factor that may increase the likely success of an influence attempt is commitment and consistency: whether one has committed oneself to a similar position in the past. This consistency with prior commitments is a highly successful influence principle because it alters one's self-perception. We often look to our own behavior to understand who we are. However, the outcome of our actions based on self-perception information varies based on the level of internal consistency we desire and the way a request is presented (Guadagno *et al.*, 2001).

Although there are several commitment and consistency-based influence tactics, there is only one that has been examined in cyberspace: the 'foot-in-the-door' technique. This works as follows: first an influence agent asks for something small—usually a minor commitment, such as signing a petition to ban censorship on the Internet. The influence agent then builds upon that small commitment to gain compliance with a second (usually related) larger request, such as volunteering to spend five hours with an organization that supports free speech online. Freedman and Fraser (1966) initially investigated the foot-in-the-door technique. They gave this tactic its particular name because the small request is like the proverbial foot that allows a salesperson to get in the door of a potential customer.

Given the way the foot-in-the-door effect operates—that it is primarily a function of a desire for internal consistency—we would expect commitment and consistency-based influence attempts to be successful in online as well as in more traditional communication modes such as the telephone and face-to-face interactions.

The foot-in-the-door has been demonstrated to be effective across multiple computer-mediated contexts. For instance, Guégen (2002) examined the effectiveness of the foot-in-the-door through an e-mail solicitation for assistance. In this study, a (fictitious) university student asked half the participants for instructions on how to save a document in a rich text file format as the first request. For the second request, which all participants received, the same requester asked the participants to fill out a 40-item survey on their dietary

Table 4.1 Summary of the results of the online foot-in-the-door studies

Author(s)	First request	Second request	% compliance to the second request	
			FITD condition	Control condition
Guégen, 2002	Participants were asked to provide instructions on how to save a file as .RTF	Participants were asked to fill out a 40-item questionnaire on their dietary habits	76%	44%
Guégen & Jacob, 2001	Participants were asked to sign a petition on a web page	Participants' activity on the website (e.g. additional links clicked)	14%	3%
Markey et al., 2001 (Study 3)	Participants were asked to provide help to an Internet novice on using chat features	Participants were asked to send a test e-mail to the novice	16%	2%

habits. The results of this study indicated that there was a significant foot-in-the door effect: 76% of participants who had complied with the first request also filled out the dietary habits survey, as compared to 44% in the control group. Guégen and Jacob (2001) also demonstrated a significant foot-in-the-door effect using web pages. In this study, participants who were first asked to sign a website petition advocating a humanitarian cause were more likely to read further into the website and click links to other sites than were those who were not asked to sign the petition.

Markey *et al.* (2001, Study 3) also demonstrated the foot-in-the-door's effectiveness in a chat context. In this study, a 'novice' Internet user asked for assistance using the chat features as the first request; then asked the target of influence for a second request—an e-mail message to make sure his e-mail program was functioning properly. Although compliance rates were relatively low, there was still a significant foot-in-the-door effect: 16% of participants who complied with the first request, also sent the e-mail, as compared with only 2% of participants who only received the second request. See Table 4.1 for a summary of the methodology and results of all three studies reviewed above.

Finally, Petrova *et al.* (2003) examined the effectiveness of computer-mediated foot-in-the-door cross-culturally. In this study, American-born and Asian international students were first asked to fill out a short online survey, then one month later were asked to fill out a more lengthy similar survey. Interestingly, their results indicated that, although American participants were more likely to refuse the initial request, those who complied showed higher rates of compliance with the subsequent request than did the Asian participants. The authors interpreted these findings in terms of cultural differences: American students are more individualistic and, therefore, their internal commitments are centrally important, whereas Asian students are more collectivistic and their individual internal commitments are less directive because they define themselves in terms of their group membership rather than their past behavior.

Thus, overall, it appears that the foot-in-the door effect is effective in online contexts as well as in other communication modalities, presumably because it functions through an individual's internal consistency motives rather than the salience of the influence agent.

Beyond text-based computer-mediated social influence

What about when the online communication is *not* text-based? Individuals can also persuade others via the Internet in graphical formats. There are a wide variety of online role-playing games (e.g. Everquest) and communities (e.g. the Palace.com) that allow individuals to interact with others while appearing as a graphical avatar in a virtual world. This increased salience of the individual in the virtual world may drastically alter the nature of online interpersonal interactions as compared to traditional text-based computer-mediated communication.

Research on social behavior in virtual worlds is an emerging field. For instance, researchers have examined personal space in virtual worlds and found that the amount of realism in the behavior of a virtual human predicts the amount of personal space real humans give it (Bailenson *et al.*, 2003*b*). In terms of social influence, Blascovich (2002) has proposed a model of social influence in virtual environments which states that the more realistic the setting and the behavior of the virtual humans, the more influential a virtual other will be on the behavior of influence targets. Immersive virtual environments also have the advantage that they allow for both high experimental realism, due to the immersive aspect of the technology, and high experimental control, as all participants run through the same exact sequence of events generated by the computer program.

Additionally, research on persuasion in a virtual environment has reported results similar to Guadagno and Cialdini (2002)—in same-sex groups, the extent of social cues transmitted via non-verbal behavior did not impact men's attitude on a topic, but it did for women. Female participants exhibited the most positivity when the communicator was making full eye contact with them as compared to conditions with moderate to low levels of eye contact during the persuasive interaction (Bailenson *et al.*, 2003*a*; Beall *et al.*, 2003; Guadagno *et al.*, 2004). This suggests that women may respond differently than men across a variety of computer-mediated contexts.

Conclusions

Owing to the dearth of research on influence in cyberspace available to review, much remains to be learned about the nature of online influence. However, there are some conclusions that we can draw. We will also discuss limitations of this review and conclude with recommendations for future research in the area.

Overall, the studies we have reviewed indicate that sometimes online influence attempts function similarly to attempts of the same kind in other contexts, and sometimes they do not. Factors that determine this include the nature of the influence attempt (specifically whether it is interactive or static), the amount of prior exposure between the influence agent and target, and whether the influence agent is perceived as a member of the target's ingroup.

Influence attempts in cyberspace may operate differently owing to the increased internal focus prevalent in online interactions. So, as a general rule, influence appeals that are mediated by self-focus should operate similarly in online contexts as more traditional text-based modalities, but others that rely on an interpersonal interaction may function differently in an online interaction.

It also seems evident from some of the research reviewed in this chapter that gender is an important factor, at least in same-sex groups. Future research should examine this issue further to test if these effects are similar with mixed-sex groups. Additional work on this issue should also seek to deepen our understanding of women's seeming discomfort communicating with others via communication modes that limit the transmission of non-verbal cues.

Most of the research reported in this chapter examined strangers interacting once with each other, but this does not reflect what is really occurring in online contexts. Individuals use the Internet primarily to interact with people they know or to establish new relationships. Even comparatively anonymous activities often involve maintaining an ongoing virtual identity. The one-time interaction with a stranger is the exception, not the rule, and researchers should address this.

Additionally, we should mention the research conducted on computer-mediated group influence focusing primarily on decision making in the form of choice dilemmas that was outside the scope of this review. For more information on this topic, we recommend an examination of the following articles: Kiesler et al., 1984; Lee & Nass, 2002; McGuire et al., 1987; Sassenberg & Boos, in press; and Siegel et al., 1986.

We would also like to point out that there are other models of social influence that have yet to be tested in an online context. Although many of our computer-mediated interactions may take place with co-workers, this review failed to find any research examining online interpersonal influence from the theoretical perspective of organizational researchers (although Thompson and colleagues have conducted several studies on computer-mediated negotiation—e.g. Morris et al., 2002) . Raven's power/interaction model of social influence is one such perspective (Raven 1993; Raven et al., 1998). This model proposes that there are different bases of power from which people influence others, depending on the resources the influence agent has at his or her disposal. Thus, it would be interesting to investigate the conditions under which the decreased salience of the influence agent in a computer-mediated interaction could enhance or reduce the effectiveness of a power-based influence appeal.

As the Internet advances in both capacity and reach, the options for online communication will continue to diversify beyond primarily text-based interaction. Researchers should attempt to keep up with the advances in technology, not only to stay abreast of changes in society but for opportunities to study ways people interact in new modalities. For example, we recommend that researchers interested in influence and technology consider examining such behavior in immersive virtual environments, in addition to text-based, computer-mediated communication. With the different technologies emerging and the different theoretical perspectives from which to derive hypotheses, this area of research is wide open and sure to yield many interesting findings as our knowledge base is built.

References

Bailenson, J.N., Beall, A.C., Blascovich, J., Loomis, J.M., and Turk, M. (2003b). *Non-zero-sum gaze and persuasion.* Unpublished manuscript, University of California, Santa Barbara, CA.

Bailenson, J.N., Blascovich, J., Beall, A.C., and Loomis, J.M. (2003). Interpersonal distance in immersive virtual environments. *Personality and Social Psychology Bulletin,* **29**, 1–15.

Beall, A.C., Bailenson, J.N., Loomis, J., Blascovich, J., and Rex, C. (2003) Non-zero-sum mutual gaze in immersive virtual environments. *Proceedings of HCI 2003.*

Blascovich, J. (2002). Social influence within immersive virtual environments. In R. Schroeder (ed), *The social life of avatars* (pp. 127–45). New York: Springer–Verlag.

Carli, L.L. (1989). Gender differences in interaction style and influence. *Journal of Personality and Social Psychology,* **56**, 565–76.

Chaiken, S. and Eagly, A.H. (1983). Communication modality as a determinant of persuasion: the role of communicator salience. *Journal of Personality and Social Psychology,* **45**, 241–65.

Chaiken, S., Wood, W., and Eagly, A.H. (1996). Principles of persuasion. In E. T. Higgins and A. W. Kruglanski (eds), *Social psychology: handbook of basic principles* (pp. 702–44). New York: Guilford.

Cialdini, R.B. (2001). *Influence: Science and Practice* (4th edn). New York: Harper Collins.

Cialdini, R.B., Brown, S.L., Lewis, B.P., Luce, C., and Neuberg, S.L. (1997). Reinterpreting the empathy-altruism relationship: when one into one equals oneness. *Journal of Personality and Social Psychology,* **73**, 481–94.

Dennis, A.R., Kinney, S.T., and Hung, Y.C. (1999). Gender differences in the effects of media richness. *Small Group Research,* **30**, 405–37.

Dubrovsky, V.J., Kiesler, S., and Sethna, B.N. (1991). The equalization phenomenon: status effects in computer-mediated and face-to-face decision-making groups. *Human–Computer Interaction,* **6**, 119–46.

Duthler, K.W. (2001). *The influence of peripheral cues on the processing of persuasive messages on the World Wide Web.* Unpublished doctoral dissertation, University of Kentucky, Lexington, KY.

Freedman, J.L. and Fraser, S.C. (1966). Compliance without pressure: the foot-in-the-door technique. *Journal of Personality and Social Psychology,* **4**, 195–202.

Guadagno, R.E. (2003). *Online persuasion revisited: The impact of gender and oneness on computer-mediated interpersonal influence.* Unpublished doctoral dissertation, Arizona State University, Tempe, AZ.

Guadagno, R.E., Asher, T., Demaine, L., and Cialdini, R.B. (2001). When saying yes leads to saying no: preference for consistency and the reverse foot-in-the-door effect. *Personality and Social Psychology Bulletin*, **27**, 859–67.

Guadagno, R.E., Bailenson, J.N., Beall, A.C., Dimov, A., and Blascovich, J. (2004). Non-zero sum gaze and the cyranoid: the impact of non-verbal on persuasion in an immersive virtual environment. Unpublished manuscript, University of California, Santa Barbara, CA.

Guadagno, R.E. and Cialdini, R.B. (2002). Online persuasion: an examination of gender differences in computer-mediated interpersonal influence. *Group Dynamics: Theory Research and Practice. Special Issue on Internet Research*, **6**, 38–51.

Guégen, N. (2002). Foot-in-the-door technique and computer-mediated communication. *Computers in Human Behavior*, **18**, 11–15.

Guégen, N. and Jacob, C. (2001). Fund-raising on the web: the effect of an electronic foot-in-the-door on donation. *CyberPsychology & Behavior*, **4**, 705–9.

Guégen, N. and Jacob, C. (2002). Social presence reinforcement and computer-mediated communication: the effect of the solicitor's photography on compliance to a survey request made by e-mail. *CyberPsychology & Behavior*, **5**, 139–42.

Henrich, C.C., Kupermine, G.P., Sack, A., Blatt, S.J., and Leadbeater, B.J. (2000). Characteristics and homogeneity of early adolescent friendship groups: a comparison of male and female clique and nonclique members. *Applied Developmental Science*, **4(1)**, 15–26.

Iacobucci, D. (ed). (2003). Consumers in cyberspace. [Special Issue] *Journal of Consumer Psychology*, **13**(1/2).

Kiesler, S., Siegel, J., and McGuire, T.W. (1984). Social psychological aspects of computer-mediated communication. *American Psychologist*, **39**, 1123–34.

Kraut, R., Mukhopadhyay, T., Szczypula, J., Kiesler, S., and Scherlis, W. (1998). Communication and information: alternative uses of the Internet in households. In *Proceedings of the CHI 98* (pp. 368–83). New York: ACM.

Lee, E. and Nass, C. (2002). Experimental tests of normative group influence and representation effects in computer-mediated communication: when interacting via computers differs from interacting with computers. *Human Communication Research*, **28**, 349–81.

Markey, P.M., Wells, S.M., and Markey, C.N. (2001). Personality and social psychology in the culture of cyberspace. In S. P. Shohov (ed), *Advances in Psychology Research* (Vol. 9, pp. 103–24). Huntington, NY: Nova Science Publishers.

Matheson, K. and Zanna, M.P. (1989). Persuasion as a function of self-awareness in computer-mediated communication. *Social Behaviour*, **4**, 99–111.

McGuire, T.W., Kiesler, S., and Siegel, J. (1987). Group and computer-mediated discussion effects in risk decision making. *Journal of Personality and Social Psychology*, **52**, 917–30.

McKenna, K.Y.A. and Bargh, J.A. (2000). Plan 9 from cyberspace: the implications of the Internet for personality and social psychology. *Personality and Social Psychology Review*, **4**, 57–75.

McKenna, K.Y.A., Green, A.S., and Glason, M.E.J. (2002). Relationship formation and the Internet: what's the big attraction? *Journal of Social Issues*, **58**, 9–32.

Moon, Y. (1999). The effects of physical distance and response latency on persuasion in computer-mediated communication and human-computer communication. *Journal of Experimental Psychology: Applied*, **5**, 379–92.

Morris, M., Nadler, J., Kurtzberg, T., and Thompson, L. (2002). Schmooze or lose: social friction and lubrication in e-mail negotiations. *Group Dynamics: Theory Research and Practice. Special Issue on Internet Research*, **6**, 89–100.

Petrova, P.K., Cialdini, R.B., and Sills, S. (2003). *Personal consistency and compliance across cultures.* Unpublished manuscript, Arizona State University, Tempe, AZ.

Petty, R.E. and Cacioppo, J.T. (1984). The effects of involvement on responses to argument quantity and quality: central and peripheral approaches to persuasion. *Journal of Personality and Social Psychology*, **46**, 69–81.

Petty, R.E., Harkins, S.G., and Williams, K.D. (1980). The effects of group diffusion of cognitive effort on attitudes: an information-processing view. *Journal of Personality and Social Psychology*, **38**, 81–92.

Postmes, T., Spears, R., and Lea, M. (1998). Breaching or building social boundaries? SIDE-effects of computer-mediated communication. *Communication Research*, **25**, 689–715.

Raven, B.H. (1993). The bases of power: origins and recent developments. *Journal of Social Issues*, **49**, 227–51.

Raven, B.H., Schwarzwald, and Koslowsky, M. (1998). Conceptualizing and measuring a power/interaction model of interpersonal influence. *Journal of Applied Social Psychology*, **28**, 307–32.

Sagarin, B.J., Britt, M.A., Heider, J., Wood, S.E., and Lynch, J. (2003). Bartering our attention: the distraction and persuasion effects of online advertisements. *Cognitive Technology*, **8**, 4–17.

Sassenberg, K. and Boos, M. (in press). Attitude change in computer-mediated communication: effects of anonymity and category norms. *Group Processes and Intergroup Relations*.

Siegel, J., Dubrovsky, V., Kiesler, S., and McGuire, T.W. (1986). Group processes in computer-mediated communication. *Organizational Behavior and Human Decision Processes*, **37**, 157–87.

Chapter 5

'Detattachment': the unique nature of online romantic relationships

Aaron Ben–Ze'ev

Introduction

The appearance of computer-mediated communication has created a new type of distant romantic relationship. Although being conducted at a distance, it enjoys many of the benefits of close relationships. This chapter discusses some essential aspects of such relationships and compares them to those typical of offline relationships.

I begin by analyzing the role of distance in generating emotions. Although geographical and temporal distance usually reduce emotional intensity, sometimes the intensity is increased, and in other cases the direction of the correlation is unclear and non-linear. Then, the role of distance in romantic relationships is examined; again, that role is complex and sensitive to the given context. In the next section, I discuss the paradoxical nature of online romantic relationships; such relationships involve features of both close and remote relationships. I term these relationships 'detached attachment' or, in short, 'detattachment'. Then I turn to a discussion of what I consider to be two basic evaluative patterns of romantic love—praiseworthiness and attractiveness—and compare the role of these patterns in offline and online romantic affairs. I suggest that the relative weight of praiseworthiness is greater in online relationships; accordingly, conversations are more important than vision. Nevertheless, attractiveness is still an important factor in cyberlove.

Because of the unique nature of cyberspace, distance often exaggerates romantic and sexual intensity. Another important feature of online relationships (as well as of emotions in general) is their partiality: they focus upon partial aspects. Hence, they require fewer resources and people can be engaged in several romantic relationships at the same time. If such relationships are going to prevail, significant changes in our moral and emotional norms are expected.

The role of distance in emotions

Distance plays a crucial role in determining emotional significance. Since emotions are highly personal and practical attitudes, they are directed toward those who are close to us. Distance typically decreases emotional intensity (Ortony *et al.*, 1988).

In envy, for example, our attention is focused on those perceived close or similar to us. Those who are close to us, but still above us, emphasize our own inferiority more than do those who are distant from us (Ben–Ze'ev, 2000; Elster, 1999; Schoeck, 1969; Spinoza, 1985/1677). Love, which incorporates a profoundly positive evaluation of the other person, includes the wish to become as close as possible to that person. Increasing the subject–object distance can often decrease the intensity of hate. When the object of hate is no longer close or relevant, hatred is likely to diminish or fade completely (e.g. Temkin & Yanay, 1988). Temporal distance, like other types of distance, decreases emotional intensity. Thus, in hope and fear, a temporal distance between the agent and the emotional object will usually reduce emotional intensity (Breznitz, 1984; Ortony *et al.*, 1988). At a distance, events often seem less significant than they are when they are nearer. Accordingly, as the saying goes, sometimes time can heal a wounded heart.

Despite the above negative correlation between distance and emotional intensity, the situation is more complex for the following reasons:

- the correlation is not always negative
- the correlation is not linear
- the relevant distance is psychological and is measured by subjective means.

The correlation between distance and emotional intensity is not always negative and it is not linear. Although distance typically decreases emotional intensity, there are circumstances in which distance increases it. Thus, distance typically promotes admiration. Indeed, a typical difference between envy and admiration is that in envy, the subject–object distance is smaller. Admiration is different from love in that it implies distance and hence a lack of reciprocity. There are also circumstances in which temporal distance may amplify the event. In these cases, the time that separates us from the event is used for incessant rumination upon it; this makes the event more central for us and hence our emotions intensify (McIntosh & Martin, 1992).

There are also cases in which only a certain measure of closeness or distance increases emotional intensity; deviation from this precise measure may decrease or leave intact emotional intensity. Thus, envy may not be typical of some kinds of very close relationships. Similarly, pleasure in others' misfortune is not typical of very close and very distant relationships. In emotions such as envy, pity, and pleasure in others' misfortune, the relationship between emotional intensity and closeness (or rather, emotional distance) is somewhat similar to a bell-shaped curve. When very small or very great distance prevails, these emotions are not usually generated; they are typically aroused in cases of an intermediate distance (Cialdini *et al.*, 1976; Lyons, 1980; Ortony *et al.*, 1988; Smith, 1991; Tesser, 1988; for further discussions, see Ben–Ze'ev, 2000).

Another complication in determining the correlation between distance and emotional intensity is that distance is a psychological, rather than a geographical, feature (Ortony *et al.*, 1988). Geographical (or physical) proximity is usually emotionally significant because it is often relevant to our well-being. However, geographical proximity does not always lead to emotional intensity.

The above discussion indicates that distant relationships, such as online relationships, are not necessarily less intense. On the contrary, I shall indicate that some features of distant relationships in general, and online relationships in particular, make such relationships romantically more intense.

Distant romantic relationships

Contemporary personal relationships among primary groups, such as friends, family, and partners, are different from such relationships prevailing not long ago, in the sense that the physical distance among individuals has increased. Thus, individuals no longer live together from birth to death (Gerstel & Gross, 1984).

Physical proximity has long been considered a positive factor in both initiating and maintaining romantic bonds. Indeed, romantic relationships are partially differentiated from mere friendships by involving behaviors (such as fondling, caressing, kissing, and making love) that necessitate physical proximity (Rohlfing, 1995). The chances were good that the seeker's 'one and only' would be found not far from where the seeker lived (Kirkendall & Gravatt, 1984; Murstein, 1976). The resources and effort required in this case are considerably less than in the case of distant relationships. Accordingly, distance is often considered a negative factor in maintaining romantic bonds because, at great distances, it is much more difficult to carry on the activities typical of such bonds. In the absence of physical proximity and the activities that it allows, it is doubtful whether romantic relationships can flourish. Distant relationships often rely on either imagining physical proximity or expecting that such proximity to be achieved in the future.

Distance is important for gaining an adequate perspective. Thus, when we look at something from very close up, our vision is fragmented and often distorted. In the extreme case where there is no distance at all, that is, when we place the object right next to the eye itself, we do not see it for what it actually is. We need some distance in order to achieve a perspective that encompasses multiple aspects of the object and thereby makes the perspective less fragmented (Ben–Ze'ev, 1993).

In a similar manner, some kind of distance is important for personal relationships. Significant and temporally extended physical distance may harm them, but more limited distance may be beneficial. As the saying goes: 'Absence makes the heart grow fonder'. Several studies indicate that long-distance couples are more satisfied with their relationships and with their communication and more in love than are geographically close couples; accordingly, the former relationships enjoy a higher rate of survival (Joinson, 2003; Rohlfing, 1995; Stafford & Reske, 1990; Stephen, 1986). It seems that distance may focus the partners' attention on profound aspects of their relationships and help them to apportion appropriate weight to the more superficial aspects. These people are likely to value their relationships even more; in addition, the distance enhances the likelihood that they will idealize their partners.

In itself, distance is not necessarily harmful to romantic relationships. Finding the correct measures of temporal, physical, and psychological distance is crucial for a satisfactory romantic relationship, as indeed it is for all relationships. Distance may have its own costs, but an appropriate distance can minimize the impact of those costs.

Distant romantic relationships may use various communicative means, such as conventional letters, phone conversations, or SMS messages, in order to overcome the difficulties associated with the distance separating the two lovers. Without getting into a detailed discussion of these means, I may say that they are efficient tools for dealing with short-term hardships generated by the unique nature of distant relationships, but they do not present an alternative environment in which romantic relationships can flourish for a lengthy period of time (Ben–Ze'ev, 2004).

Falling in love through letter writing is not a new phenomenon (Gwinnell, 1998). Online relationships are based upon an improved version of an old-fashioned way of communicating: writing. In the new version, the time gap between writing, sending, receiving, and reading has been made almost instantaneous—the sender can receive a reply while still in the state of emotions in which he/she sent the original message. This difference, which may appear merely technical, is of great emotional significance, as emotions are typically brief and usually involve the urge to act immediately (Ekman,

1992; Frijda *et al.*, 1991). The great temporal gap between one letter and another does not suit the impetuous nature of romantic affairs. Accordingly, generating and maintaining loving relationships by merely using conventional letters is rare; it is used far less for this purpose than online communication.

Romantic relationships conducted exclusively via phone conversations are also rare. Such type of communication lacks some of the unique features of online communication. Thus, phone conversations involve a lesser degree of anonymity—typically, your gender, approximate age, and approximate physical location are detectable; hence, imagination has a lesser role in such communication. Moreover, unlike online communication, in which you choose when and how to respond without immediate time or psychological pressures, phone communication is more intrusive and insistent (Joinson, 2003).

Modern technology continues to improve the methods available for distant relationships. One such recent technological innovation is short message service (SMS), which is a kind of mobile texting. In comparison to online communication, mobile texting is more continuous, available, immediate, and spontaneous. Like online communication, mobile texting is not intrusive, but is less anonymous and less detached. Mobile texting is a very useful and convenient medium for flirting, as it suits the superficiality and brevity that characterizes flirting. It is less useful as the sole or major way of sustaining long-term distance relationships, as it does not lend itself to profound conversations. Mobile texting provides the modern and light version of written flirtatious communication. Indeed, a sizeable proportion of SMS users choose SMS for asking someone out on a date and for arranging casual sex (Joinson, 2003; Orr, 2004; Rheingold, 2002).

Relating by merely conventional letters, phone conversations, or SMS messages does not present a real alternative to conventional offline relationships. Accordingly, these means typically supplement such relationships—when those are not feasible or desirable—but do not replace them. Online relationships seem to be the first real alternative to face-to-face romantic relationships. As I shall indicate below, when an online romantic relationship is successful, its participants wish to transform it into a conventional offline relationship.

Detached attachment

Online communication involves a new type of interpersonal relationship in which features of close and remote relationships are combined. In online relationships, people are neither close, intimate friends nor complete strangers. Online relationships constitute a unique kind of relationship—termed 'detached attachment' or, in short, 'detattachment'—that includes opposing features whose presence in offline relationships would be paradoxical.

Detached attachment is difficult to conduct offline, as a romantic relationship is typically characterized by direct, continuous contact—settling for less is painful. However, what seems to be an obvious paradox in actual space (namely, intimate closeness at a distance) can prevail in cyberspace. Quite often an intense online romantic attachment is between people who are physically separated and who are committed in some way or another to a different romantic relationship. The other commitment and physical separation make the relationship detached, but the intense emotions sustain the great attachment.

Human beings have never before had access to such an ambivalent type of personal relationship. This possibility presents an entirely different ball game in the field of personal interactions. In this exciting, novel game, the rules and consequences are also different.

The following are major opposing aspects of online personal relationships:

- distance and immediacy
- lean and rich communication
- anonymity and self-disclosure
- deception and sincerity
- discontinuity and continuity
- marginal physical investment and considerable mental investment.

Distance and immediacy

In typical, offline relationships, two intimate friends are geographically close and, when they are not together, they are generally aware of each other's approximate location. Online relationships exist between people who are spatially separated. This separation can consist of great physical distance, and the two online friends may not even know each other's exact geographical location. Physical distance becomes irrelevant in cyberspace; some people even speak about the death of (physical) distance. Although each person uses the Internet from different locales, while they are in cyberspace they are actually in the same space (Cairncross, 1997; Kellerman, 2002).

Online personal relationships are immediate in a temporal sense—two lovers can communicate with no significant time delay—and in the sense that there is no human third party that mediates the conversation. In cyberspace, physical location is of less importance. We could say that this space enables a person to be in two places at the same time, or at least to be detached from her physical context. As one married woman testifies: 'We also have a very wonderful time when we chat, so wonderful that it actually feels like we are in the same room doing the things we are typing.'[1] In light of the temporal immediacy, emotional immediacy is present as well: people can express their spontaneous, authentic emotional reactions, as is done in offline relationships.

Lean and rich communication

Face-to-face communication relies on many sources of information in addition to the verbal one: facial expressions, voice, posture, hands, gaze, focus, and so on. Such sources provide crucial signals for communicating our emotions and understanding the other person's attitudes. Online communication relies on fewer sources and is often based merely on written messages. The lack of visual content seems to be a particularly significant deficiency. The lack of non-verbal information in text-based online communication has led some researchers to claim that such communication is leaner and hence online relationships are less involving, less rich, and less personal than offline relationships (for review and critique see Baym, 2002).

It is true that not all types of information available in face-to-face communication are also available in online communication; in this sense, the latter is leaner. However, this does not mean that online relationships are necessarily less involving, less rich, or less personal than offline relationships. Despite the fewer vehicles of communication, online communication provides rich information. In a certain type of communication, people may be ready to provide more profound information than they would in communication based on a greater number of communicative vehicles (and which is thus potentially richer). Text-based communication with a sincere person may provide richer information than a face-to-face meeting with another person. Indeed, as compared to face-to-face communication, online communication involves higher proportions of more intimate questions and lower proportions of peripheral questions (Tidwell & Walther, 2002). Although online impressions of the other, and hence personal relationships, may take longer to develop, over time they can become as profound and as intimate as in offline circumstances (Donn & Sherman, 2002; Lea & Spears, 1995; Sherman, 2001; Whitty, 2002; Whitty & Gavin, 2001). Thus, a married woman writes about her communication with a married man: 'We both knew what our hearts were feeling at the time without having to say a word. I feel like I've known Rob all of my life.'[2]

---

[1] Hawaii Chat Universe, *http://www.lovelife.com/CLS/story59.html*, Cyber Love Stories, 'Anonymous 2'.

[2] Hawaii Chat Universe, *http://www.lovelife.com/CLS/story151.html*, 'Married but not to each other'.

Anonymity and self-disclosure

Two seemingly contrasting features of online relationships are greater anonymity and greater self-disclosure. Anonymity is associated with concealment, which is contradictory to self-disclosure. However, greater anonymity typically facilitates greater self-disclosure, which is positively associated with intimacy (Hale *et al.*, 1989). As one man said: 'When you're on a one-on-one with somebody, people really reveal a lot of their soul to you. And you are entrusted to keep what you have there as sacred property, because they share a piece of theirselves with you.' (Miller & Slater, 2000, p. 68).

Several studies have found that often there is faster and more profound self-disclosure in online communication than in face-to-face meetings (Joinson, 2001; Parks & Floyd, 1996; Tidwell & Walther, 2002). This may be attributed to several major reasons:

- greater anonymity and reduced vulnerability (Baxter & Wilmot, 1985; McKenna *et al.*, 2001)
- lack of 'gating features' (that is, easily discernible features, such as unattractive physical appearance, which might be an obstacle to the establishment of a close relationship) (McKenna *et al.*, 2002)
- lack of other means to know each other
- greater ease in finding similar others (Baker, 2002).

Profound intimacy that might take months or years to appear in offline relationships may only take days or weeks online. In online relationships, people usually get to know each other more quickly and more intimately. In online relationships, the information may arrive at a slower pace (although sometimes it may even arrive faster), but it has a potential to reach a greater variety and deeper aspects of the partner's life and to do it at a faster pace (Cooper & Sportolari, 1997; Lea & Spears, 1995; McKenna *et al.*, 2002; Merkle & Richardson, 2000; Tidwell & Walther, 2002).

Sincerity and deception

The greater self-disclosure typical of online relationships is associated with greater sincerity. In offline relationships, people usually try not to hurt other people (even those they really want to) because they worry that in the future such behavior may, in turn, hurt them. Accordingly, in offline relationships people conceal some of their basic emotional attitudes and fantasies, becoming to some extent insincere.

The more voluntary nature of online self-presentation involves the risk of being more susceptible to manipulations; in such controlled exposure, there is much room for deception and misrepresentation, which may lead to disappointment when the relationship develops further. In both offline and online relationships, when the level of commitment is high, misrepresentation is low (Cooper *et al.*, 2000; Cornwell & Lundgren, 2001; Joinson, 2003; Schneider & Weiss, 2001; White, 2004). Online relationships, however, encourage many people to present a more accurate presentation of their true self, which is characterized as that version of self that a person believes he/she actually is, but is unable to present, or is prevented from presenting, to others in most situations (Bargh *et al.*, 2002; McKenna *et al.*, 2002).

Continuity and discontinuity

In one sense, offline romantic relationships can be regarded as continuous: the two intimate friends may not be together all the time, but they typically have an idea of each other's whereabouts. Such continuity is often absent in online romantic relationships where people can simply disappear, because they have suddenly decided not to communicate (temporarily or permanently) or because matters in their offline environment have become more important to them. Such a sudden termination is clearly expressed in the following description: 'I knew we were too different, but things didn't even GRADUALLY get worse. They just stopped.'[3] Sudden disappearance in cyberspace is easy; it merely requires not pressing a certain button. Indeed, the tactic of avoidance and escape is likely to prevail in online relationships more than in offline relationships (Merkle & Richardson, 2000).

In another sense, however, online romantic relationships can be regarded as more continuous than offline relationships. They are continuous in the sense that they can be conducted at any time; accordingly, online lovers are always on each other's mind. In this type of online continuity, there is no minimum associated with an online 'encounter': e-mail messages can be very brief, consisting of one sentence or even one word. This enables sending and receiving messages many times a day. In this regard, Karl writes: 'I usually picked up her messages in the morning, and when I didn't get mail from her, I really felt let down. I worried about her and wondered if she was safe. I'd log on every hour to see if she was just sending me mail late that day.'[4]

We can say that online romantic relationships may be discontinuous in a physical, temporal sense because online communication is not continuous; nevertheless, these relationships are continuous in an emotional sense, in that the online lovers are always on each other's mind.

---

[3] Cyber-Relations, *http://www.geocities.com/Paris/6278/*, 'Suddenly it stopped'.

[4] Joan Elizabeth Lloyd's website, *http://www.joanelloyd.com/fbcheat.htm*.

Physical and mental investment

Face-to-face romantic relationships are characterized by significant investment in the relationship by both partners. The investment can be physical (involving, for example, money, time, and obligations) or mental, which can include intense emotions and mental effort. Cyberspace seems to be in this sense a perfect world—by investing the minimum of physical resources, we can do almost anything we wish to do. Finding the right online partner and maintaining the ongoing relationship with this partner require fewer resources than finding a suitable, offline partner.

Needless to say that what people must pay for their seemingly online, unearned emotional salary is related to their actual partners, who suffer most from the occupation with online affairs. Another cost of online affairs is the mental price: the participants invest a lot of mental energy and time. It is as if such participants live in two parallel worlds—actual and virtual. In the virtual world, physical investment is considerably smaller, but investment in time and mental resources is of the same magnitude as in the physical world, and sometimes even greater.

In online relationships, people try to enjoy the benefits of both close and remote relationships, while avoiding their drawbacks. People enjoy the highly valued products of close relationships while paying the low cost of remote relationships. Thus, they are able to get away from people when they want to, and be instantly close to them, if they so desire. In this sense, online relationships help promote social relationships as they reduce the price of such relationships. The negative aspect of online relationships is related to their advantage: while the closeness is often illusory, there is a growing expectation of making it actual.

The varied value of online relationships is in line with the varied social value of the Internet in general. Indeed, there have been conflicting findings concerning the social value of the Internet. Some indicate that the Internet facilitates shallow and aggressive behavior as well as loneliness, depression, and lower social support and self-esteem. In contrast, other findings indicate the profound nature of online relating, as well as a decrease in loneliness and depression and an increase in social support and self-esteem (see for example Amichai–Hamburger & Ben–Artzi, 2003; Joinson, 2003; Wellman & Haythornthwaite, 2002).

These contradictory findings reflect the complex nature of the Internet and the difficulty in defining a typical Internet user. Thus, there may be general and individual differences in social value when reference is made to cyberlove, sex sites, or online support groups (such as groups for specific chronic illnesses, for weight loss, or for bereavement). The Internet suits most types of personalities, even though it is differently associated with each type. Despite the various prognoses, it may turn out to be the case that people with more extensive offline social contacts will use the new medium more frequently than shy people who have fewer contacts; however, the latter are more likely to achieve more intimate relationships (Birnie & Horvath, 2002; Peris *et al.*, 2002).

The last decades seem to have witnessed a striking diminution of regular contacts with our friends and neighbors. It appears that electronic communication to some extent overcomes this trend by enabling the formation of social ties without necessitating physical encounters. No wonder that such ties have also become increasingly popular in the romantic and sexual domains.

Basic evaluative patterns in love

After describing some features of distant romantic relationships in general, and of online romantic relationships in particular, I turn now to discuss the impact of distance upon the way we evaluate the beloved. In this regard, I shall claim that in online relationships the weight of appraising the beloved's personal characteristics is significantly increased and that of appraising external attraction decreases. This has profound implications upon the nature of the relationship.

The complex experience of romantic love involves two basic evaluative patterns referring to attractiveness (that is, an attraction to external appearance) and praiseworthiness (that is, positively appraising other characteristics). Romantic love requires the presence of both patterns (Ben–Ze'ev, 2000; Ortony *et al.*, 1988). In Yeats' poem, 'For Anne Gregory', a woman wants to be loved not for the yellow color of her hair, which stands for the element of attractiveness, but for herself alone, that is, her actions and traits. An old man tells her that 'only God, my dear, could love you for yourself alone and not your yellow hair'. People realize that genuine romantic love requires the presence of both evaluative patterns and they want to satisfy both, even if they are at an apparent disadvantage insofar as one pattern is concerned.

Some people would like to change the relative weight of one of these patterns—not regarding the beloved's attitude toward them, but regarding their own attitude. Thus, some people wish that they could attach less weight to attraction, which may carry less value in the long run. Other people may wish the opposite: that their love were more spontaneous and less calculated; they wish they could attach more weight to attraction. The familiar unsuccessful experience of trying to love the 'right' person indicates the importance of attraction in love.

The relative weight of the two evaluative patterns depends, to a certain extent, on personal and social factors. For example, with age, people may accord less weight to the issue of attraction. We can also expect to find that a given society influences the determination of the relative weight of the patterns (see for example Ben–Ze'ev, 2000; Buss, 1994; Etcoff, 1999; Illouz, 1997).

The two kinds of evaluative patterns involved in romantic love are not independent: a positive appraisal of your partner's characteristics is greatly influenced by his or her attractiveness. There is much evidence suggesting that attractiveness significantly influences ratings of intelligence, sociality, and morality (Buss, 1994; Etcoff, 1999; Lawson, 1971; Townsend & Levy, 1990; Zebrowitz et al., 1996). A common phenomenon in offline relationships is the 'attractiveness halo', in which a person who is perceived as beautiful is assumed to be good as well (Etcoff, 1999). People will usually not admit or even be aware of the great weight they assign to the pattern of attractiveness. They tend to claim that they assign greater weight to the pattern of praiseworthiness.

To further complicate the determination of the evaluative structure of romantic love, it seems that maintaining love requires something beyond the mere repetition of the variables that initiated it and something besides the mere absence of the variables associated with its failure. The variables underlying a short-term emotion may be different from those underlying its corresponding long-term sentiment.

As an acute emotion, love largely consists of gazing at each other and activating the pattern related to external attractiveness, but as a sentiment, love basically consists of the ability to communicate with each other and do things together. In this respect, praising personal characteristics which are not expressed in external appearance is important. It seems that online affairs produce the intensity of acute emotions, but this intensity is generated by written communication based primarily upon the pattern of praiseworthiness.

Basic evaluative patterns in online affairs

Online romantic relationships differ from offline relationships in that they are based upon written texts rather than visual content. Accordingly, online relationships attach less weight to external appearance, which is revealed by vision, and more weight to a positive appraisal of the other's characteristics, which are revealed by verbal communication. External appearance is typically not fully known in the early stages of online relationships, and therefore these relationships must rely on other characteristics for creating positive emotional attitudes toward each other. Online relationships prevent people from relying mainly on physical attributes when evaluating other people, and hence they avoid the unjustified advantages that are usually granted to attractive people. These relationships enable people to get to know each other without having to cope with the heavy burden of the stereotypes that are associated with physical appearance (Wallace, 1999). As Jennifer, 31, writes: 'The aspect I like most about online dating is that looks and physical attraction don't take part in the initial introduction of becoming acquainted with someone new. I learned about many aspects of the person's personality and characteristic traits without the obstacle of appearances'. (Hogan, 2001, p. 185)

In this chapter I have focused on profound online-only romantic relationships. Other types of online intimate activities are: online relationships intended to find an offline sexual or romantic partner; and cybersex. In the first type of relationships, the issue of external appearance is relatively significant right from the outset. In the second type, external appearance is also significant but the veracity of the description is less important.

In online romantic relationships, the 'attractiveness halo' may be replaced by the 'personality halo', in which a person who is perceived as having a specific, positive personality trait is assumed to have other good characteristics—even those connected to physical appearance. Online partners can be perceived, for example, as physically attractive, clever, witty, and possessing well-developed, uninhibited sexuality. One woman writes: 'This is the beauty of online romance. It gets past that whole physical attraction thing. Sure, it's still gotta be there, but it's not the major factor in the whole thing. He likes me for my personality. And he still thinks I am beautiful.' One man testifies: 'She is not even my type when it comes to physical attraction, but she is now the most beautiful girl I have ever and will ever meet; she is my better half, this I know.' Another man writes about a woman he had never seen: 'someone with such a heart can only be attractive.'[5]

In accordance with the 'personality halo', in cyberspace the perception of one positive personal characteristic is taken to indicate the presence of many other positive characteristics, including attractiveness. Since online correspondence provides scant information about attractiveness, people are not primarily distinguished in light of this feature, and the degree of attractiveness has less weight in choosing a partner. In the same way that the 'attractiveness halo' underlies love at first sight, the 'personality halo' underlies love at first chat. Indeed, people often say that, although they met online, 'they hit it off right away'. As one man writes: 'She was funny and sexy and cute, and I was immediately attracted to her personality.'[6] We may speak here about 'net

---

[5] *http://members.tripod.com/~VixenOne/index.html*, Story 30—'Two tales'; Lovingyou.com, 'If it's the Lords will'; Cyberlove101.com, Story 35—'Those who seek shall find'.

[6] Gloria G. Brame: 'How to have cybersex: Boot up and turn on', *http://gloria-brame.com/glory/journ7.htm*.

chemistry'. It should be noted that although beauty has a powerful impact at first sight, the weight of this impact decreases as time goes by and once we know other characteristics of the person. Likewise, wittiness has a powerful impact at first chat, but its impact may be reduced once we know other characteristics of the person. When wittiness is perceived to be superficial and more profound characteristics, such as kindness and wisdom, are found to be wanting, the weight of the positive initial impact of wittiness may vanish.

Online romantic relationships do not ignore then physical attractiveness, but merely attach relatively less weight to this aspect. Thus, in one study of the users of an online matchmaker, women who rated their own appearance as average were less likely to be contacted by men than those who rated their appearance as above average (Scharlott & Christ, 1995). Among women who rated their appearance as above average or very good, 57% received messages from more than 50 men; among women who rated their appearance as average, only 11% received messages from more than 50 men. There was no similar relationship concerning the appearance of the men; those who reported average appearance received as many messages as those who reported above-average appearance. (Interestingly, no one, either male or female, described himself or herself as below average.) However, there was no significant difference between appearance and the number of romantic partners they found online: 43% of those who rated themselves better looking started romantic relationships online, and 41% of those who reported average appearance did the same (Scharlott & Christ, 1995).

People often say that they value the inner side of their online partners and not what they look like on the outside. However, when asked if they would ever meet someone in person without knowing anything about the person's physical body, they reject such a possibility (Mileham, 2003). The relevance of attractiveness in cyberlove is clearly indicated in the following claim by a 39-year-old married man: 'I always ask whoever I'm chatting with to describe their body in detail. I don't want to chat with some 300lb woman. But maybe I have.' (Mileham, 2003, p. 70). Although interactions in online affairs are disembodied, the partner's body is quite important as well. The actual interaction may be mind to mind, but the emotional reactions are similar to those between people with physical bodies. Indeed, Mileham (2003) reports that in her study, virtually all participants reported developing physical attraction to their virtual partners although they never saw them in person; most of these participants are enchanted with the vision they form of their online partners.

In offline circumstances, no one is perfect and one's flaws are revealed during the interactions between the two people. In online relationships, all the information about the person's appearance and characteristics is gained by the person's own self-description. It is possible for people to describe their characteristics in an extremely positive manner. In such a case, there is a unique possibility of finding real angels on earth – or rather on the Internet. Consider the following statement by a 46-year-old married man:

> I've been chatting with a girl, the most unbelievable person I've ever met. I mean, this girl is tall and has short brown hair—which happens to be my favorite hairstyle. On top of that, she has the biggest blue eyes you can ever find. I haven't really seen a picture, but she described it in fine detail . . . Now, on top of all that, she's smart and she's getting a PhD. Not to mention the talks we have, very charismatic, sexy. Wow . . . my wife has become such a faint presence.   (Mileham, 2003, p. 71)

When attractiveness is taken into consideration in online relationships, it is typically viewed in a more positive light. In online affairs, people usually do not have a precise and detailed picture of the other's attractiveness, and imagination and wishful thinking fill the gaps in the data—the picture created is likely to be more attractive than in reality. Even if the two partners have met previously, prior to their online correspondence, or if they have exchanged (flattering) pictures of themselves, it is likely that they tend to imagine each other as more attractive than they actually are. As a result of an intimate online relationship, people may alter their notions of attractiveness and find themselves drawn to people to whom they were previously not attracted.

The more that factors from offline relationships are introduced to the online relationship (e.g. pictures, phone calls, and webcam shots) the more the online relationship will become similar to an offline one. In such circumstances, the online relationship may retain most of the advantages of an offline relationship, although it is likely to encounter its disadvantages as well. When the similarity is more superficial, the ability to retain the unique advantages of an online relationship (e.g. its focus upon personality traits rather than upon appearance) is considerably increased.

Online affairs involve positive appraisals of both attractiveness and praiseworthiness; however, praiseworthiness has relatively greater weight than in offline affairs. The increased importance of other personal characteristics is a positive feature in long-term considerations, as the latter are more fundamental for enduring relationships. Getting to know each other's qualities is important in building a strong relationship (Lafollette, 1996).

An interesting study concerning this issue indicates that when individuals interacted in a darkened room, where they could not see one another, they not only engaged in greater self-disclosure but also left the encounter liking one another more so than did those who interacted in a room that was brightly lit (Gergen *et al.*, 1973). McKenna argues that interacting on the Internet is similar in some respects to interacting in a darkened room, in that one cannot see one's partner, nor can one be seen. In both cases, first impressions are based upon considerable mutual self-disclosure. This is even more so in the case of online interactions (McKenna *et al.*, 2002).

In accordance with the above considerations, quite a few people, who are considered attractive in ordinary circumstances, are using the Internet to meet romantic partners because they want to be appreciated for characteristics other than their appearance (Levine, 2000). Likewise, a 35-year-old male says:

> I am considered very handsome by any standard you can think of. And I like that, of course. But in here I feel way more free than I feel in the real world. I can be myself and not have to worry about living up to my physical attractiveness. This sounds crazy to you? Believe me, handsomeness sucks sometimes. Women don't take the time to get to know you, and here they do, because I'm just a cyber guy like any other guy in here. My mind counts more. (Mileham, 2003, p. 75)

In face-to-face relationships, most people fall in love in response to what they see, and then that love is strengthened or weakened as further information is revealed. In online relationships, where self-disclosure is greater and hence intimacy is significant and occurs early in the relationship, most people first get to know each other and only then fall in love (Cooper & Sportolari, 1997; Merkle & Richardson, 2000; Rheingold, 2000; Wysocki, 1998).

In cyberspace, the beloved is mainly perceived by reference to personality traits; accordingly, the beloved is often characterized as the smartest, funniest, sweetest, kindest, most wonderful, sincere, honest, truthful, loving, and caring person—someone who is 'a little too perfect'. In cyberspace it is easier to possess virtuous traits, as it is just a matter of perfecting your writing skills. The reduced weight of external attraction forces correspondents to make the effort to be evaluated positively in other realms.

The development of an online relationship is similar to the development of a non-erotic friendship, where people first get to know the other person and only then become friends. As in friendship, in online relationships people spend a lot of time just talking and sharing. Indeed, many individuals report that their online romance was more meaningful because of this friendship. People often describe their online relationship as the most open, rewarding, and exciting friendship they have ever had (Adamse & Motta, 2000).

Dreams and idealization play a crucial role in our lives in general and in love in particular. Hence, it has been argued that the most tragic form of loss is the loss of the capacity to imagine that things can be different (Bloch, 1988). Since falling in love is the nearest most of us come to glimpsing utopia in our lifetime (Kipnis, 2003), a dull love life can have a depressing impact on a person's life. Online romantic relationships may provide many people with a much-needed sense of excitement and an opportunity to dream. This can be healthy, as long as we are careful that such dreams do not blur the boundaries between reality and fantasy.

The partial nature of online distant relationships

Distant romantic relationships are essentially partial, as they are limited to specific activities and to specific time; their participants cannot be involved in many activities typical of close, offline relationships. Having physical, sexual activities with each other is one example of such missing activities. In some distant relationships, such as commuter marriages, the partiality is merely temporary—when the two people actually meet each other, they can perform all types of activities. Online-only romantic relationships are partial in a fuller sense, as those missing activities cannot be performed at any time.

It should be noted that emotions are partial in two basic senses: they are focused on a narrow target, such as one person or very few people, and they express a personal and interested perspective. Focusing upon fewer objects increases the resources available for each and hence increases emotional intensity, just as a laser beam focuses upon a very narrow area and consequently achieves high intensity at that point. Accordingly, emotions have a magnifying nature: everything looms larger when we are emotional (Ben–Ze'ev, 2000; Derryberry & Tucker, 1994; Larsen *et al.*, 1987; Rubin, 1970).

In online romantic relationships, people's perspective is more partial than that typical of offline relationships: They do not have comprehensive knowledge about their cybermates. All they know is what their mate wants to tell them—and this typically focuses on positive information. The types of activities and resources required for maintaining online relationships are also more partial, as the relationships are limited to electronic correspondence.

The greater partiality of online relationships facilitates conducting a few romantic relationships at the same time. Generally, modern technology saves time and enables us to do various things at the same time. This is clearly the case of mobile phones that enable us to be in constant contact, even when we are doing something else, such as shopping (Katz & Aakhus, 2002). Online communication enables people to be engaged in a new romantic affair while maintaining the current one. The characteristic of multiconversing (i.e. conducting a conversation simultaneously, but nevertheless privately, with a few people at the same time, which prevails in chat rooms and instant messaging), further increases the ability to conduct several romantic relationships at the same time. Accordingly, online affairs with several people at the same time are common practice. When the affair merely consists of typing on a keyboard, having a few online romantic partners at the same time is both feasible and increasingly acceptable.

This possibility can liberate people and give them better control over their own romantic destiny. Indeed, according to one estimate, about 30% of those visiting American dating sites are married (Orr, 2004). However, cyberspace is remarkably seductive; people can become addicted to it and forget its illusory nature. Moreover, since multi-lovers do not live only in cyberspace, it is highly probable that their actual everyday relationships will suffer as a result of their multi-loving. As with other forms of extramarital liaisons, online affairs divert resources from the primary offline relationship to the online affair so that it becomes increasingly difficult to sustain the offline relationship, as someone else is competing for the time and attention of the partner. The more intense the online relationship is, the more resources are diverted to it. Thus, too much cybersex may make offline sexual activity a rarity: the person having the online affair may be less enthusiastic, less energetic, and less responsive to lovemaking with the offline partner, as it is difficult to compete with the novelty and excitement of a new, fantasy partner. In a survey of cybersex addicts, in only 30% of the offline relationships involving such an addict were the two partners still interested in offline sex with each other (Schneider & Weiss, 2001; Young *et al.*, 2000).

The great partiality of online romantic relationships renders these relationships the characteristic of 'unfinished business', since many conventional romantic activities are missing from them. In this sense, these relationships are incomplete. Such incompleteness generates instability and great intensity. It makes the relationship a neverending event that always requires our attention. A paradoxical aspect in this regard is that although online relationships are intense because of, among other factors, their incompleteness, such incompleteness involves the wish to transform the relationship into a more complete one—something that usually decreases the intensity and may lead to the termination of the relationship.

Numerous novels and movies deal with romantic affairs that are partial and hence incomplete; this partiality helps maintain the intense excitement of the affair. In one such circumstance, the two lovers meet every month (or year) for an intense sexual encounter while knowing virtually nothing about the life of their partners outside of their meetings. In other circumstances, the relationship is conducted solely via letters (written either before or after a passionate sexual encounter). Another type of incomplete romantic relationship involves close emotional ties, but no sexual intercourse. In all these examples, the intensity of the romantic relationship is due to its incomplete nature—to the implicit desire by the participants to reach a more fulfilled interaction.

Online relationships gain their emotional intensity by referring to a partial, imaginary environment that is better than the actual one. By ignoring various aspects of actual reality and limiting their attention to the exciting ones, they increase emotional intensity. However, because of the greatly enjoyable nature of such a relationship, people would like to upgrade it by transforming it to an actual, face-to-face relationship that is more complete, since it also involves the activities that are missing from the online affair. A 41-year-old male says: 'I was talking with someone about caresses and where we like to caress and be caressed. Suddenly I felt a huge urge to touch this woman and actually do what we were talking about.' (Mileham, 2003, p. 74). Making the affair more complete may, however, result in losing the emotional advantages of being incomplete. Indeed, a face-to-face meeting often terminates the online relationship—either because the meeting was so disappointing that the two cannot continue their communication or because the meeting was so enjoyable that the relationship is transferred offline. Ironically, the successful goal of an online romantic relationship is its termination. That is the sad aspect of online relationships. Since we cannot be content with our own limited online lot, we want to improve the relationship by extending it offline. The extension may prove to be suicidal. It should be mentioned that there is less, or even no, desire to transform the successful online relationship into an offline one when the former involves significant deception concerning, for example, gender and age.

Conclusions

Online romantic relationships are a unique type of distant relationship that seems to overcome some of the main problems of other types of distant relationships. The Internet allows a constant flow of communication that can lead to profound and intimate exchanges. The participants grow close to each other, love develops and becomes intense. Nevertheless, online relationships cannot remove the human desire for physical closeness.

Romantic love consists of two major evaluative patterns: the first is the attraction to external appearance, and the second is the positive appraisal of other characteristics. Attraction to external appearance is a pattern that is also found in online relationships, although its influence is more limited. The complete absence of such a pattern would make a relationship one of friendship, rather than romance (although it is arguable that friendship is also, to some small extent, influenced by physical factors, including attraction). Online lovers overcome the lack of full visual information concerning external appearance by using their imaginations; however, an essential element of romantic attraction is physical touching and sexual fusion. Mental fusion, which is successfully achieved in online romantic relationships, is seldom enough—most couples desire a physical fusion as well (Bargh *et al.*, 2002;

McKenna *et al.*, 2002). However, achieving the physical fusion may terminate the online relationship and may also sever the mental fusion.

The partial nature of distant relationships gives them certain advantages, in particular the ability to focus on the positive aspects of each other and on the satisfying aspects of the relationship in general. Online relationships can fulfill various needs that may not be fulfilled in proximate, offline relationships. However, their partial nature also indicates the incompleteness of these relationships; accordingly, they may not substitute for offline relationships that may theoretically achieve much greater sense of completion.

A significant measure of the value of online romantic relationships is, therefore, their ability to complement offline relationships. Such mutuality is difficult to achieve as conducting several intense romantic relationships at the same time involves difficulties with focus, commitment, and other factors. The Internet, which has already dramatically changed the romantic domain, has provided the technical means to sustain simultaneous online and offline relationships. We can thus expect further relaxation of norms concerning romantic exclusivity and an increase in romantic tolerance within committed relationships.

The impact of online communication upon emotions in general, and romantic attitudes in particular, is far from being clear. People know what to expect from a close relationship; they know what to expect from remote relationships. They do not know what to expect from relationships characterized as detached attachment. Our emotional system is not yet structured to deal with such opposing features. It seems that the new technology has not been accompanied by a corresponding mental change. In particular, we may not be ready to face living with seemingly highly available and desired romantic alternatives that cannot be actualized. The contradictions and uncertainty associated with online relationships make them less stable and more intense. Emotions play a much greater role in these relationships. Future research should indicate the types of emotional changes we are likely to witness in the long run.

References

Adamse, M. and Motta, S. (2000). *Affairs of the Net*. Deerfield Beach: Health Communications.

Amichai–Hamburger, Y. and Ben–Artzi, E. (2003). Loneliness and Internet use. *Computers in Human Behavior*, **19**, 71–80.

Baker, A. (2002). What makes an online relationship successful? Clues from couples who met in cyberspace. *CyberPsychology & Behavior*, **5**, 363–75.

Bargh, J.A., McKenna, K.Y.A., and Fitzsimons, G.M. (2002). Can you see the real me? Activation and expression of the 'true self' on the Internet. *Journal of Social Issues*, **58**, 33–48.

Baxter, L.A. and Wilmot, W.W. (1985). Taboo topics in close relationships. *Journal of Social and Personal Relationships*, **2**, 253–69.

Baym, N.K. (2002). Interpersonal life online. In L.A. Lievrouw and S. Livingstone (eds), *Handbook of new media: social shaping and consequences of ICTs*. London: Sage.

Ben–Ze'ev, A. (1993). *The perceptual system: a philosophical and psychological perspective*. New York: Peter Lang.

Ben–Ze'ev, A. (2000). *The subtlety of emotions*. Cambridge, MA: MIT Press.

Ben–Ze'ev, A. (2004). *Love online: emotions on the Internet*. Cambridge: Cambridge University Press.

Birnie, S.A. and Horvath, P. (2002). Psychological predictors of Internet social communication. *Journal of Computer Mediated Communication*, **7** (online).

Bloch, E. (1988). *The utopian function of art and literature*. Cambridge, MA: MIT Press.

Breznitz, S. (1984). *Cry wolf: the psychology of false alarms*. Hillsdale, NJ: Erlbaum.

Buss, D.M. (1994). *The evolution of desire: strategies of human mating*. New York: Basic Books.

Cairncross, F. (1997). *The death of distance: how the communications revolution will change our lives*. Boston: Harvard Business School Press.

Cialdini, R.B., Borden, R.J., Thorne, A., and Sloan, L.R. (1976). Basking in reflected glory: three (football) field studies. *Journal of Personality and Social Psychology*, **34**, 366–75.

Cooper, A., Delmonico, D., and Burg, R. (2000). Cybersex users, abusers, and compulsives: new findings and implications. *Sexual Addiction & Compulsivity*, **7**, 5–29.

Cooper, A. and Sportolari, L. (1997). Romance in cyberspace: understanding online attraction. *Journal of Sex Education and Therapy*, **22**, 7–14.

Cornwell, B. and Lundgren, D.C. (2001). Love on the Internet: involvement and misrepresentation in romantic relationships in cyberspace vs. actual-space. *Computers in Human Behavior*, **17**, 197–211.

Derryberry, D. and Tucker, D.M. (1994). Motivating the focus of attention. In P. M. Neidenthal and S. Kitayama (eds), *The heart's eye: emotional influences in perception and attention*. San Diego: Academic Press.

Donn, J.E. and Sherman, R.C. (2002). Attitudes and practices regarding the formation of romantic relationships on the Internet. *CyberPsychology & Behavior*, **5**, 107–23.

Ekman, P. (1992). An argument for basic emotions. *Cognition and Emotion*, **6**, 169–200.

Elster, J. (1999). Strong feelings: emotion, addiction, and human behavior. Cambridge, MA: MIT Press.

Etcoff, N. (1999). *Survival of the prettiest: the science of beauty*. New York: Doubleday.

Frijda, N.H., Mesquita, B., Sonnemans, J., and Van Goozen, S. (1991). The duration of affective phenomena or emotions, sentiments and passions. *International Review of Studies on Emotion*, **1**, 187–225.

Gergen, K.J., Gergen, M.M., and Barton, W.H. (1973). Deviance in the dark. *Psychology Today*, **7**, 129–30.

Gerstel, N. and Gross, H. (1984). *Commuter marriage: a study of work and family*. New York: Guilford Press.

Gwinnell, E. (1998). *Online seductions*. New York: Kodansha International.

Hale, J.L., Lundy, J.C., and Mongeau, P.A. (1989). Perceived relational intimacy and relational message content. *Communication Research Report*, **6**, 94–9.

Hogan, E.E. (2001). *Virtual foreplay*. Alameda, CA: Hunter House.

Illouz, E. (1997). *Consuming the romantic utopia: love and the cultural contradictions of capitalism.* Berkeley: University of California Press.

Joinson, A.N. (2001). Self-disclosure in compute-mediated communication: the role of self-awareness and visual anonymity. *European Journal of Social Psychology,* **31,** 177–92.

Joinson, A.N. (2003). *Understanding the psychology of Internet behavior: virtual worlds, real lives.* Hampshire: Palgrave Macmillan.

Katz, J.E. and Aakhus, M. (2002). *Perpetual contact: mobile communication, private talk, public performance.* Cambridge: Cambridge University Press.

Kellerman, A. (2002). *The Internet on earth: a geography of information.* Chichester: Wiley.

Kipnis, L. (2003). *Against love: a polemic.* New York: Pantheon Books.

Kirkendall, L.A. and Gravatt, A.E. (1984). Marriage and family: styles and forms. In L.A. Kirkendall and A.E. Gravatt (eds), *Marriage and the family in the year 2020.* Buffalo: Prometheus Books.

LaFollette, H. (1996). *Personal relationships: love, identity, and morality.* Oxford: Blackwell.

Larsen, R.J., Diener, E., and Cropanzano, R.S. (1987). Cognitive operations associated with individual differences in affect intensity. *Journal of Personality and Social Psychology,* **53,** 767–74.

Lawson, E.D. (1971). Hair colour, personality and the observer. *Psychological Report,* **28,** 311–22.

Lea, M. and Spears, R. (1995). Love at first byte. In J. Wood and S. Duck (eds), *Understudied relationships: off the beaten track* (pp. 197–233). Thousand Oaks: Sage.

Levine, D. (2000). Virtual attraction: what rocks your boat. *CyberPsychology & Behavior,* **3,** 565–73.

Lyons, W. (1980). *Emotion.* Cambridge: Cambridge University Press.

McIntosh, W.D. and Martin, L.L. (1992). The cybernetics of happiness: the relation of goal attainment, rumination, and affect. *Review of Personality and Social Psychology,* **14,** 222–46.

McKenna, K.Y.A., Green, A.S., and Gleason, M.E.J. (2002). Relationship formation on the Internet: what's the big attraction? *Journal of Social Issues,* **58,** 9–32.

McKenna, K.Y.A., Green, A.S., and Smith, P.K. (2001). Demarginalizing the sexual self. *Journal of Sex Research,* **38,** 302–11.

Merkle, E.R. and Richardson, R.A. (2000). Digital dating and virtual relating: conceptualizing computer-mediated romantic relationships. *Family Relations,* **49,** 187–92.

Mileham, B.L.A. (2003). *Online infidelity in Internet chat rooms.* Unpublished doctoral dissertation, University of Florida, Gainesville, FL.

Miller, D. and Slater, D. (2000). *The Internet: an ethnographic approach.* Oxford: Berg.

Murstein, B.L. (1976). *Who will marry whom? Theories and research in marital choice.* New York: Springer.

Orr, A. (2004). *Meeting, mating, and cheating: sex, love and the new world of online dating.* Upper Saddle River, NJ: Reuters.

Ortony, A., Clore, G.L., and Collins, A. (1988). *The cognitive structure of emotions.* Cambridge: Cambridge University Press.

Parks, M.R. and Floyd, K. (1996). Making friends in cyberspace. *Journal of Computer Mediated Communication,* **1(4)** (online).

Peris, R., Gimeno, M.A., Pinazo, D., *et al.* (2002). Online chat rooms: virtual spaces of interaction for socially oriented people. *CyberPsychology & Behavior*, 5, 43–51.

Rheingold, H. (2000). *The virtual community: homesteading on the electronic frontier.* Cambridge, MA: MIT Press.

Rheingold, H. (2002). *Smart mobs: the next social revolution.* Cambridge, MA: Perseus.

Rohlfing, M.E. (1995). 'Doesn't anybody stay in one place anymore?' An exploration of the under-studies phenomenon of long-distance relationships. In J. Wood and S. Duck (eds), *Understudied relationships.* Thousand Oaks: Sage.

Rubin, Z. (1970). Measurement of romantic love. *Journal of Personality and Social Psychology*, 16, 265–73.

Scharlott, B.W. and Christ, W.G. (1995). Overcoming relationship-initiation barriers: the impact of a computer-dating system on sex role, shyness, and appearance inhibitions. *Computers in Human Behavior*, 11, 191–204.

Schneider, J. and Weiss, R. (2001). *Cybersex exposed: simple fantasy or obsession?* Center City: Hazelden.

Schoeck, H. (1969). *Envy: a theory of social behaviour.* London: Secker & Warburg.

Sherman, R.C. (2001). The mind's eye in cyberspace: online perceptions of self and others. In G. Riva and C. Galimberti (eds), *Towards cyberpsychology: mind, cognition and society in the Internet age.* Amsterdam: IOS Press, 2001.

Smith, R.H. (1991). Envy and the sense of injustice. In P. Salovey (ed), *The psychology of jealousy and envy.* New York: Guilford Press.

Spinoza, B. (1985). *Ethics.* In E. Curley (ed), *The collected works of Spinoza.* Princeton: Princeton University Press. (Original work published 1677.)

Stafford, L. and Reske, J.R. (1990). Idealization and communication in long-distance premarital relationships. *Family Relations*, 39, 274–9.

Stephen, T. (1986). Communication and interdependence in geographically separated relationships. *Human Communication Research*, 13, 191–210.

Temkin, B. and Yanay, N. (1988). 'I shot them with words': an analysis of political hate-letters. *British Journal of Political Science*, 18, 467–83.

Tesser, A. (1988). Toward a self-evaluation maintenance model of social behavior. In L. Berkowitz (ed), *Advances in experimental social psychology.* New York: Academic Press.

Tidwell, L.C. and Walther, J.B. (2002). Computer-mediated communication effects on disclosure, impressions, and interpersonal evaluations: getting to know one another a bit at a time. *Human Communication Research*, 28, 317–48.

Townsend, J.M. and Levy, G.D. (1990). Effect of potential partners' physical attractiveness and socioeconomic status on sexuality and partner selection. *Archives of Sexual Behavior*, 19, 149–64.

Wallace, P. (1999). *The psychology of the Internet.* Cambridge: Cambridge University Press.

Wellman, B. and Haythornthwaite, C. (eds). (2002). *The Internet in everyday life.* Malden: Blackwell.

White, M. (2004). On the Internet, everybody worries that you're a dog. In P.M. Backlund and M.R. Williams (eds), *Reading in gender communication.* Belmunt, CA.: Wadsworth.

Whitty, M.T. (2002). Liar, liar! An examination of how open, supportive and honest people are in chat rooms. *Computers in Human Behavior*, 18, 343–52.

Whitty, M.T. and Gavin, J. (2001). Age/sex/location: uncovering the social cues in the development of online relationships. *CyberPsychology & Behavior*, **4**, 623–30.

Wysocki, D.K. (1998). Let your fingers do the talking: sex on an adult chat-line. *Sexualities*, **1**, 425–52.

Young, K.S., Griffin-Shelley, E., Cooper, A., O'Mara, J., and Buchanan, J. (2000). Online infidelity: a new dimension in couple relationships with implications for evaluation and treatment. *Sexual Addiction & Compulsivity*, **7**, 59–74.

Zebrowitz, L.A., Voinescu, L., and Collins, M.A. (1996). 'Wide eyed' and 'crooked faced': determinants of perceived and real honesty across the lifespan. *Personality and Social Psychology Bulletin*, **22**, 1258–69.

Chapter 6

Prosocial behavior on the net

Lee Sproull, Caryn Conley, and
Jae Yun Moon

Introduction

Subject: Thank you!
Date: Wed, 27 Nov 2002 17:55:49–0500
From: John <JohnDoe@here.net>
Reply To: XXXX@PEACH.EASE.LSOFT.COM
To: XXXX@PEACH.EASE.LSOFT.COM
I am fast approaching the fifth year of my subscription to this
listserv. I cannot begin to know how to count the number of hours and the
amount of frustration I would have suffered had it not been for the generosity
of members of this group.
I thank God that He allowed me to find and use the resources of this listserv.
To each of the members here, I want to say to you, 'Thank you for being here
and for contributing to me and to others in need'.
Thank you and God bless
John

This message was posted the day before U.S. Thanksgiving Day to an online
technical support group. It references one of the most striking social aspects
of the Internet, which is that every day, hundreds of thousands of people voluntarily help one another on the net with no expectation of direct reward.
Moreover, the helpers and those they help usually have never met face to
face. Yet the help is consequential and people are enormously grateful for it, as
the message above suggests. This chapter is about the kinds of behavior on the
net referenced in the above message—prosocial behavior, defined as 'voluntary intentional behavior that results in benefits for another' (Eisenberg &
Miller, 1987).

People voluntarily help one another in many ways on the net:

◆ They donate funds to worthy causes through charitable organizations online.

◆ They donate idle computing power from their PCs to help scientists
  analyze large data files.

- They contribute software and documentation that they have written to open-source (free) software communities.
- They donate time and attention to electronic groups organized for socially worthwhile causes, such as electronically mentoring disadvantaged students or making public domain literature freely available on the web.
- They contribute time and attention to organize and maintain voluntary online discussion groups.
- Within voluntary discussion groups, they contribute information and emotional support to one another.

The first two examples above (donating money or unused computing power) illustrate the Internet equivalent of 'checkbook voluntarism', which entails electronically contributing resources with economic value to a worthy cause. Many people use the efficiencies of online financial transaction processing to support charitable giving over the net. In the first month after the World Trade Center attack, for example, more than three million Americans made online financial donations to relief efforts (Rainie & Kalsnes, 2001). Many not-for-profit organizations in the offline world are beginning to explore online fundraising (e.g. *http://www.nonprofits.org/*).[1] People can donate not only money but also other resources with economic value. For example, some people donate unused computing power from their PCs to advance scientific research. They voluntarily download software and scientific data from the net to their PC for processing while their PC would otherwise be idle; results are uploaded to a central server where software performs quality checks and aggregates results. In this way more than four million people have donated processor cycles from their PCs to a deep-space astronomy

----

[1] As we were writing this chapter, we saw our first instance of someone collecting donations for charity by acquiring sponsors to support the organizer's 'blogging' non-stop for 24 hours (*http://www.blogathon.org*). A blog is short for a 'weblog', the equivalent of a personal diary on the Internet, where people can report on anything ranging from personal news for friends to commentary on various social and political issues. In the summer of 2000, one such blogger decided to see if she could blog for 24 hours, at the rate of one entry every 15 minutes. The marathon was a success, and the blogger decided that if she did it again it would be for a socially worthwhile purpose. Thus, the concept of the 'blogathon'—a blog marathon running non-stop for 24 hours at the rate of one blog every 30 minutes—was born. Sponsors support the blogger and charity of their choice by pledging a fixed amount or hourly rate. In the first charity blogathon, held in 2001, approximately 100 bloggers raised more than $20 000 for 77 different charities; in 2002, roughly 200 bloggers raised more than $50 000; in the third annual blogathon in 2003, 401 participants raised $102 000 from 1312 sponsors. (See *http://www.esztersblog.com/blogathon03* for an example of one volunteer's 24-hour log of blog entries.)

project (*http://setiathome.ssl.berkeley.edu*); additional millions of people have donated processor cycles from their PCs to other scientific projects (see *http://www.aspenleaf.com/distributed/* for examples). Online charitable donation of money or other resources with economic value produces benefits for society, but because it represents arms-length prosocial behavior, we do not consider it further in this chapter. This chapter focuses on people who voluntarily help others through interacting with them directly on the net.

Direct prosocial behavior on the net can be found among friends and family in private e-mail and buddy lists (e.g. see Wellman & Gulia, 1999), among organizational employees behind corporate firewalls in corporate intranets (e.g. Constant *et al.*, 1996), and among people who may be strangers to one another in publicly accessible electronic groups and websites (e.g. Galegher *et al.*, 1998). This chapter focuses on prosocial behavior among people who may be strangers to one another in publicly accessible contexts, for both pragmatic and theoretical reasons. Pragmatically, these contexts are often more accessible to researchers than are private or corporate contexts. Theoretically, they represent an opportunity to understand behavior about which the offline world offers few opportunities for study, namely, social contexts that are organized in such a way that large numbers of strangers voluntarily help one another.

One of the ways to understand prosocial behavior on the net is to compare and contrast it with prosocial behavior in the offline world. Prosocial behavior in the offline world is found in a variety of social contexts. These can be characterized by the strength of the social relationship among participants and the degree of organizational structure of the contexts. Social psychological research on prosocial behavior in the offline world has focused on social contexts with minimal formal organizational structure, either single acts of bystanders helping strangers or ongoing support among people with strong interpersonal bonds such as close friends or relatives (e.g. Bolger *et al.*, 2000; Kiesler *et al.*, 2000; Latané & Darley, 1970; Wellman & Wortley, 1990). Sociological research on prosocial behavior in the offline world has focused on more highly organized social contexts, such as the self-help group and the volunteer organization (e.g. Akera, 2001; Knoke, 1981; Popielarz & McPherson, 1995; Wilson, 2000 for a review). See Table 6.1 for a matrix of voluntary helping contexts studied by researchers in the offline world.

In some ways, prosocial behavior on the net resembles bystanders helping in the offline world. Typically, helpers, and those they help, have no pre-existing face-to-face relationship. Usually there is no expectation of direct reciprocity or even of any ongoing relationship. Requests for help come at random times. At the same time, however, in some ways prosocial behavior on the net

Table 6.1 Matrix of voluntary helping contexts

Degree of organization	Strength of social relationship		
	Strangers	Acquaintances	Close friends and relatives
Unstructured	Bystander helping (e.g. Latané & Darley, 1970)		Ongoing support (e.g. Bolger et al., 2000; Kiesler et al., 2000; Latané & Darley, 1970; Wellman & Wortley, 1990) Long-term care (e.g. Brennan et al., 1995)
Informal or self-organized groups		Self-help and support groups (e.g. Akera, 2001) Neighborhood groups (e.g. Portney & Barry, 1997)	
Formal groups and organizations	Checkbook voluntarism (e.g. Callero et al., 1987)	Volunteer organizations (e.g. Grube & Piliavin, 2000; Knoke, 1981; Popielarz & McPherson, 1995; Simon et al., 1998) Organizational citizenship (e.g. Constant et al., 1996; Perlow & Weeks, 2002; Smith et al., 1983)	

resembles behavior in voluntary organizations in the offline world. It occurs in organized social contexts in which helping is supported and rewarded. Therefore, this chapter draws upon research from both social psychology and sociology to characterize prosocial behavior on the net.

In the following, there are five sections. Section one characterizes the electronic helping context; section two examines why people engage in prosocial behavior on the net in the light of relevant theoretical perspectives; section three presents evidence of the effects of electronic prosocial behavior; section four offers implications and suggestions for future research; and section five concludes with final comments.

The electronic helping context

Public discussion groups and public collaborative work groups are the settings in which this chapter considers prosocial behavior on the net. Public discussion groups exist for hundreds of thousands of topics: hobbies, entertainment, social issues, politics, technical support, and health and lifestyle support, among others. These groups are supported by a variety of different technologies: mailing lists or listservs, Usenet groups, bulletin boards, chat rooms, web forums, etc. Each group focuses on a particular discussion topic; anyone who wants to participate in discussing that topic may do so. Public collaborative work groups always have a goal beyond discussion, although discussion is usually an important group component. Some online groups work on scientific projects; some engage in software development; others engage in social projects such as electronic mentoring or electronic proofreading. Anyone who wishes to participate in any of these projects may do so. Opportunities to seek and offer help in all of these contexts are visible, easy, and organized.

Visible opportunities

People can use software tools such as search engines and directory listings to find social contexts where help can be sought or given. These tools make visible many opportunities to seek or give help. Within these social contexts, requests for help are visible to all. Everyone who goes to a public discussion group will see messages that ask for help and discussions that could use help. Everyone who goes to a volunteer work group will see explanations for how and why to help displayed prominently. Helping behaviors in response to requests for help are equally visible. Additionally, many groups retain searchable archives, which means that the history of prior helping behavior in the group can also be visible.

While requests for help are visible, people making the requests are not visible. In the offline world, bystander helping is influenced by the physical appearance of the person needing help. Physically attractive people are more likely to be helped in the offline world than are unattractive people (Athanasiou & Green, 1973; Byrne et al., 1971; Chaiken, 1979; Dommeyer & Ruggiero, 1996; Harrell, 1978; Mims et al., 1975; Piliavin & Piliavin, 1975; West & Brown, 1975; Wilson, 1978). Social similarity also affects helping in the offline world (Eagly & Crowley, 1986; Emswiller et al., 1971; Simon et al., 1998, 2000; Wellman & Wortley, 1990). In the online world, however, people reading a request for help have no information about the requestor's physical appearance or social similarity that is conveyed by visible attributes such as age, gender, or race. In the offline world, one of the impediments to asking for help is the perceived threat to one's public self-image (Karabenick & Knapp, 1988). Physical invisibility may reduce that perceived threat in the online world; so, too, may the use of pseudonyms, screen names, or anonymous postings.

Not only are the people asking for help physically invisible, but so also are the people receiving the request who might potentially offer help. In the offline world, bystander helping is influenced by the number of other people available to provide help (Latané & Darley, 1970). In the online world, potential helpers are invisible unless they actually offer help. The combination of visible helping contexts and physically invisible potential helpers may make the felt (perceived) need to offer help more prominent. Potential help providers are unaware of how many others online have the ability to provide the help requested. Until one person actually offers help, every potential helper may assume that he or she is the only one who could help. Physical invisibility also reduces the barriers for help providers whose age, gender, race, or other visible attributes lead people to discount their contributions in the offline world, regardless of their actual usefulness. Help provided is not spurned on the basis of physical attributes that are invisible, but can be judged based solely on the content of the help.

Easy opportunities

It is relatively easy to make a contribution to a public discussion group or volunteer work group, including a contribution that asks for help or that offers help to someone in need. People can participate in these contexts at any hour of the day or night from any place with technology and net access. People can read or send messages at their convenience and can fit their contributions into their own time schedule. If they have discretionary net access at work, they can participate during the day in the interstices between work activities, or they can do so from home. The message is the basic unit of contribution behavior: it consumes a rather small unit of time and attention and represents a voluntary micro-contribution to the community. Some people may devote many hours a week to online prosocial activity, but they can do so in small units of time at their own convenience. In one survey of online volunteers, convenience and schedule flexibility were the two most common reasons people cited for choosing to volunteer online (*http://www.serviceleader.org/old/vv/admin/99vols/stats.html*).

Not only is it easy to make a helpful contribution, it is also easy to control the extent of further involvement. In the offline world, a person may hesitate to offer help for fear that a helpful response will lead to further demands on one's time or emotional energy. In the online world, a person offering help may feel in complete control of how much further involvement will ensue; he or she can simply ignore further requests.

Organized opportunities

A combination of software and social norms organizes human behavior in online discussion groups. Someone posts a message containing a question or request for help and others reply with messages containing answers, comments, or suggestions. Software allows people to indicate that their message is a response to a previous post and lets them display messages as 'threads' (a seed message and all responses to it). Threads organize messages by topic so that everyone can view related messages, making it easy for potential contributors and beneficiaries to see what has already been contributed and where there are opportunities for further contribution. Discussion groups may have tens or hundreds of threads active at any given time, which creates the need for a level of aggregation beyond the self-organizing thread in order to help readers find their way. In these cases, a human designer may suggest or impose a topic map in order to organize contributions into more general topic categories.

A topic common across most electronic groups is the FAQ (frequently asked questions), a compilation of messages about the goals of the group and how to behave in the particular group. The FAQ typically states the group's 'rules of the road' explicitly, including expectations about asking for and providing help and discussions appropriate for each topic category. In addition to the FAQ, the substantive focus of a group usually implies the structure of its topic map. For example, health support groups usually have topics for symptoms, medications and side-effects, negotiating the healthcare system, and managing relationships with family and friends. Within any discussion group, organizing devices like threads, topic maps, and FAQs demonstrate where and how to ask for and provide help.

Volunteer work groups use software that is specialized to the particular group to organize people's contributions. The software typically includes a code that records each person's contribution and that aggregates across contributions. Collaborative software development groups use specialized software to keep track of changes to it. They use bug-tracking systems to keep track of bug reports and bug status. Many types of groups use collaborative authoring software that allows anyone to change a document, and stores a history of those changes. Groups also use software to display contribution totals to the group as a whole and to give contributors feedback on their contributions. Volunteer work groups also typically support organized discussion among their members, using the organizing methods described in the previous paragraph for discussion groups.

We have suggested that the electronic context is one in which helping opportunities are visible, organized, and easy; but convenience is not the only determinant of prosocial behavior. We must ask: Why do people help when they cannot see the potential recipient and so may find it difficult to judge if he or she is worthy? Why do people help when they cannot see other potential helpers and so may find it difficult to judge if their help would be useful?

Why do people help when they have no tangible reminders of the social benefit of their help? The theoretical perspectives of social learning and social identification are useful in answering these questions.

Theoretical perspectives applied to helping in the electronic context

Social learning theory

Social learning theory suggests that prosocial behavior is learned (Bandura, 1977; Bandura & McDonald, 1963; Batson, 1998, for a recent review). Observing role models who are loved or respected, such as parents or authorities, engaged in prosocial behavior, demonstrates how people can and should behave prosocially. Rewards reinforce helping behavior; punishments reduce unhelpful or hurtful behavior. Within a group context, social recognition, not just private reward, increases prosocial behavior (Fisher & Ackerman, 1998). Observational modeling processes with reinforcement will result in learning over time (Compeau & Higgins, 1995; Lim et al., 1997). Although social learning theory was developed within the context of physically co-located actors and observers, it can be applied within the electronic context to the extent that prosocial behavior is observable and socially reinforced in that context.

Public discussion groups and collaborative work groups often explicitly encourage newcomers to read the group for a while before posting their first message. The visibility of behavior on the net insures that everyone who does read a discussion group will see examples of prosocial behavior (i.e. helpful messages). Moreover, they will also see that some of these messages are explicitly recognized as helpful, either by the recipient or by another reader. That is, sometimes a helpful reply to a question receives a thankful reply from the person who asked for help or a message of commendation from another reader. These recognition messages are also visible to everyone and thus constitute social recognition, not just private reward. Social recognition for helpful behavior can go beyond ad hoc public acknowledgment messages. Some groups use software that allows participants to reward helpful messages with recognition points. Points are tallied automatically and the most helpful participants (people whose messages receive the greatest number of recognition points) for a given period of time are publicly acknowledged.

In some volunteer work groups, the quality of the contribution is assessed directly by software; in still other groups, the software lets the recipient of the help, or any other participant, rate the quality of the contribution. In addition to helpful messages, readers will occasionally see unhelpful or erroneous ones. These, too, may engender a visible response in the form of complaints or negative feedback messages. Visible peer recognition—whether textual or numeric, ad hoc or systematic, positive or negative—is a powerful learning reinforcement mechanism for both direct and vicarious learning. The combination of visible messages with peer feedback suggests that the minimum criteria for learning how to behave prosocially in the electronic context are met.

Social learning theory also suggests that low-cost trials are more effective than high-cost ones in the initial stages of learning. We have noted that the cost of a single micro-contribution is relatively low in the electronic context. Studies of various Internet discussion groups and volunteer work groups have reported a mean message length ranging from 8 to 30 lines of new text (Galegher *et al.*, 1998; Sproull & Faraj, 1995; Wasko & Faraj, 2000; Winzelberg, 1997). They have also reported a mean participation time of 10–20 minutes per session (Boberg *et al.*, 1995; Brennan *et al.*, 1995; Lakhani & von Hippel, 2003). The newcomer to a group can learn vicariously about how to behave prosocially by viewing small demonstrations of it, and can learn directly by making small prosocial contributions and receiving (small, easy-to-make, visible to all) positive reinforcements for doing so.

Motivation to help

Theorists differentiate altruistic prosocial behavior from egoistic prosocial behavior depending upon the motivation of the helper (Batson, 1991; Nelson, 1999; Piliavin & Charng, 1990). Altruistic prosocial behavior is motivated purely by the desire to increase another person's welfare; egoistic prosocial behavior is motivated by the desire to increase one's own welfare or that of one's group or cause through helping others (Batson, 1998; MacIntyre, 1967). Both motivations are likely to be present in ongoing volunteer contexts. Help providers in electronic groups describe having been motivated by empathy, community interest, generalized reciprocity, and the personal return of learning and reputation enhancement (e.g. Butler *et al.*, forthcoming; Lakhani & von Hippel, 2003; Pope, 2001; Wasko & Faraj, 2000). In discussion groups, participants who report being motivated by community or group interest often provide the most valuable contributions (Butler *et al.*, forthcoming; Constant *et al.*, 1996).

In electronic contexts, as in offline ones, a majority of the help is often provided by a minority of the members who incur substantial costs in terms of their own time. Table 6.2 displays participation rates across several different types of online discussion groups and volunteer work groups and demonstrates the unequal nature of participation. Most studies report aggregate participation rates (i.e. they do not differentiate messages that ask for help from

Table 6.2 Inequality in participation with electronic voluntary groups

Participation rate	Total no. of active participants*	Duration of observation	Type of group	Authors
10% of participants contributed 63% of msgs	70	3 month	Eating disorder	Winzelberg (1997)
50% of participants contributed 94% of msgs	33	18 months	Caregivers of people with mental illness	Perron (2002)
9% of participants contributed 27% of msgs	119	3 weeks	Arthritis	Galegher et al. (1998)
14% of participants contributed 38% of msgs	274	3 weeks	Attention deficit disorder	Galegher et al. (1998)
3% of participants contributed 23% of msgs	733	3 weeks	Depression	Galegher et al.(1998)
2% of participants contributed 50% of answers	11 510	4 years	Support for free software	Lakhani & von Hippel (2003)
2% of participants contributed 55% of msgs	13 000	5 years	Creating free software	Moon & Sproull (2002)
63% of people identified craters more than once; 1.9 million crater identifications	>85,000	10 months	Volunteer science: identifying Martian craters	*http://clickworkers.arc.nasa.gov/documents/crater-marking.pdf*

* People who posted at least one message during the period of observation.

those that offer it). However, because each question or request for help usually receives multiple replies, aggregate rates are more a function of responding (which includes providing help) than initiating (which includes asking for help). Occasional ad hoc positive feedback for a helpful message is probably sufficient to offset the cost to the infrequent helper. However, when people repeatedly respond to individual requests for help or contribute to the group in other ways, even if they do so in small increments, then more systematic recognition, as well as other forms of benefit, will reinforce sustained helping behavior. That is, the greater the cost of the helping behavior, the greater the need for personal rewards if the helping is to be sustained (Field & Johnson, 1993; Omoto & Snyder, 1995).[2]

Social identity theory

Social identity theory and self-categorization theory (Tajfel & Turner, 1986; Turner *et al.*, 1987) are helpful in understanding why some people exhibit substantial prosocial behavior over time. Social identity theory is based on the premise that people identify with particular groups in order to enhance their self-esteem. Identification leads to selective social comparisons that emphasize intergroup differences along dimensions that favor the ingroup and confer positive distinctiveness on the ingroup when compared to the salient outgroup (Hogg & Abrams, 1988). Categorizing the self and others in terms of groups accentuates the similarities between group members with respect to their fit with the relevant group prototype or 'cognitive representation of features that describe and prescribe attributes of the group' (Hogg & Terry, 2000). The prototype guides the participants' understanding of the group and its expected behaviors and attitudes. People identified with a group will thus be more likely to exhibit behaviors (and more behaviors) that are consistent with shared group norms and will cooperate with the group and its members.

In a discourse analysis of electronic health support groups, Galegher *et al.* (1998) found that people legitimated their requests for help in their messages by describing their membership in the group and by appealing to the group's shared history. Even frequent posters framed their requests for help in terms that referenced the group. Requests that did not reference the group were much less likely to receive a reply. In a linguistic analysis of discussion groups, Sassenberg (2002) demonstrated that people in cohesive groups exhibited greater linguistic norm conformity than people in ad hoc groups. Thus, in electronic groups, message interactions among participants can both define and express the group norms. Group prototypes are negotiated and redefined through member message interactions (McKenna & Green, 2002; Postmes *et al.*, 2000). In other words, participants collectively define who is an admired member and what is a high-quality contribution through comments and feedback provided in response to member contributions.

In both offline and online contexts, frequent participants are likely to form relational bonds with one another (Lawler *et al.*, 2000), especially if they expect the group to persist over the long term (Chidambaram, 1996; Walther, 2002).

---

[2] In some groups, however, the rewards and benefits provided in order to sustain helping behaviors, such as recognition points, can actually reduce contributions to the group by inducing competition rather than cooperation with other participants (Gu & Jarvenpaa, 2003).

In voluntary electronic groups, as people participate over time they become aware of other members who repeatedly provide valuable help. Moon (in progress) suggests that eventually active members will form a sense of community with other core members and become committed to this core subgroup of the larger group. These highly identified volunteers will help other members, not only as a service to those needing help and as a matter of self-interest, but also in order to demonstrate their identification with and commitment to the core group of volunteers who sustain the group as a whole. In a study of volunteer Linux developers, Hertel *et al.* (2003) found that identification with the developers in the Linux subsystem in which the respondent was participating, but not identification with the Linux user community as a whole, was positively related to the number of hours spent on the Linux project.

Group identification is an important antecedent to cooperative behaviors related to group maintenance and survival (Ashforth & Mael, 1989; Kramer, 1993; Mael & Ashforth, 1995; Tyler, 1999). Volunteerism studies in the offline world have generally found that participation in voluntary association management can foster commitment (Simon *et al.*, 1998; Wilson, 2000). In this literature, participation refers to having an active role in the decisions made by the association, and not mere participation by showing up.

A study of 212 voluntary e-mail lists found that the volunteer who maintains a list (often called a list 'owner') spends substantially more time than other members in infrastructure maintenance, social control, and external promotion (Butler *et al.*, forthcoming). Typically, owners take responsibility for such time-consuming work as regular maintenance and upgrades of the technical infrastructure and dealing with problems such as viruses and junk e-mail. Infrastructure administration also involves developing and maintaining components that are unique to the needs of the particular group, such as an up-to-date content archive, ancillary files such as group descriptions and FAQs, and the list of people who have access to the group. Owners also take some responsibility for the social management of listservs. They remind members about the rules and the norms of the group, manage disputes, prevent exploitation of individual members, chastise those who engage in inappropriate behavior, and deny serious offenders access to the group (usually as a last resort). Owners frequently encourage members and membership as well. They promote desirable behavior by recognizing people who contribute especially informative or supporting messages, and those who create interesting or useful group activities.

Social learning processes and social identification processes help explain how prosocial behaviors can be learned and sustained on the net. Social identification processes are instrumental in the group's collective definition of what constitutes helpful, as opposed to harmful, behavior in the context of the group. Long-term participants identified with the core subgroup, including group owners or founders, are committed to enforcing these group norms. Just as people learn from respected authorities in the offline context, software that makes valued long-term contributors of the group visible and salient facilitates people's learning from members most representative of the respected group prototypical member.

The value of electronic prosocial behavior

Value to beneficiaries

Discussion group members benefit from prosocial behavior and are grateful for it, as the message quoted at the beginning of the chapter illustrates. Even 'lurkers' (people who read group messages but never post them) receive informational benefits from passive participation in electronic discussion groups (e.g. Butler *et al.*, forthcoming; Nonnecke & Preece, 2000*a*, 2000*b*; Wasko & Faraj, 2000). Nonnecke and Preece (2000*a*) estimate that up to 90% of group members never post or do so less than once a month, with software discussion groups exhibiting up to 30% higher lurking than health support groups on average. Because lurkers may constitute a substantial fraction of electronic group membership, benefits to lurkers should not be ignored even if such lurkers are invisible to the group and to researchers. Nevertheless, consonant with research on offline groups and communities, passive participants derive fewer benefits than do active ones (e.g. Callero *et al.*, 1987; Omoto & Snyder, 1995). Passive participants report mostly information benefits; their total level of benefits is lower than that for more active participants; and they are more likely to drop out (Butler *et al.*, forthcoming; Cummings *et al.*, 2002).

There is little systematic research that explicitly examines the impact of electronic prosocial behavior on its recipients. Research generally investigates the impact of actively participating in online discussion groups, especially in support groups. 'Active participation' is measured by the number of posts a person makes, which does not differentiate between posts that ask for help, posts that offer help, and posts unrelated to help. A particularly important point in the process of becoming an active electronic group member is the first time a person posts to a group. Prosocial responses to an initial post may offer information, encouragement, and/or emotional support. If these positive responses occur, they increase the likelihood that the new poster will become more engaged with the group. A study of electronic groups dealing with stigmatized and marginalized identities found that people in these marginalized identity groups whose initial post received more positive than negative responses were more likely to continue to participate in these groups (McKenna & Bargh, 1998).

Many studies have documented that active participants incur benefits from their voluntary interaction with others. Most studies of members of online discussion groups and volunteer collaborative work groups report that information benefits are important to them (Baym, 1999; Lakhani & von Hippel, 2003; Wasko & Faraj, 2000). Some members also derive the social benefits that can come from interacting with other people: getting to know them, building relationships, making friends, having fun (Baym, 1999; Butler *et al.*, forthcoming; Cummings *et al.*, 2002; Kendall, 2002; Quan y Hasse *et al.*, 2002). Protégés in online mentoring report positive attitudinal and behavioral outcomes (Barsion, 2002; Bennett *et al.*, 1998). Members of medical and psychological support groups may derive health benefits from their participation in addition to information and social benefits. The evidentiary base for health benefits is small, but it comes from studies that use either random assignment or statistical procedures to control for other factors that could influence health status. Health-status benefits for active participants include shorter hospital stays (Gray *et al.*, 2000), decrease in pain and disability (Lorig *et al.*, 2002), decrease in social isolation (Galegher *et al.*, 1998), and increase in self-efficacy and psychological well-being (Cummings *et al.*, 2002; McKenna & Bargh, 1998).

Value to helpers

A few studies have focused specifically on benefits to those who help others. As predicted by social learning theory, people who devote substantial time and attention to helping others report receiving both egoistic and altruistic benefits, but relatively greater altruistic benefits than those who are less involved.

In their study of 212 listservs, Butler *et al.* (forthcoming) found that listserv owners (who spent more time helping the group than did other members) reported receiving different levels and types of benefits compared to other members. They reported lower levels of information benefits and higher levels of prosocial benefits, such as the satisfaction of helping other people and supporting the real world community associated with the listserv's topic. This finding is consistent with the role identity theory, and research by Piliavin and her colleagues who suggest that in-role volunteer activity (i.e. behavior specified by a person's role as a volunteer) encourages an altruistic self-image and commitment to the community (see for example, Callero *et al.*, 1987; Piliavin & Callero, 1991).

A study of people who help others by answering questions in an open-source software support group found that participants derived learning benefits, reputational benefits, and benefits related to advancing the group (Lakhani &

von Hippel, 2003). A study of volunteer programmers found that people who donated the code were more likely to report identification with the software development group, whereas people who merely used the code were more likely to report only egoistic benefits from participation (Hertel *et al.*, 2003). A study of electronic mentoring of college undergraduates found that mentors reported they derived satisfaction from 'helping the next generation move ahead' and insight into their own career experiences (Barsion, 2002). This finding is consistent with research on mentoring in the offline world which finds that those who mentor derive both altruistic and egoistic benefits from so doing (Higgins & Kram, 2001).

Value to society

There is no rigorous empirical evidence for how prosocial behavior on the net might benefit the larger society. Extrapolating from studies that document benefits to individual people, we can speculate on broader social benefits. If members of health and lifestyle groups achieve improved health status, the cost of their medical or psychological care could decrease. (Alternatively, better-informed members may seek additional tests or treatments, thereby increasing the cost of their care.) If members of special populations like schoolteachers, female science students, or senior citizens derive cognitive, social, and emotional benefits from participating in electronic discussion groups, then the larger society may benefit as well. Online volunteer discussion groups, in which people ask and answer questions about open-source software, have received industry awards for providing high-quality help (Foster, 1998, 1999, 2000). All open-source users benefit indirectly from the resulting high-quality software.

Public volunteer work groups suggest most clearly the potential societal benefits that may arise from prosocial behavior on the net. For example, NASA invited net-based volunteers to identify and mark craters on images of Mars in an experiment to see if 'public volunteers (clickworkers), many working for a few minutes here and there and others choosing to work longer, can do some routine science analysis that would normally be done by a scientist or graduate student working for months on end' (*http://clickworkers.arc.nasa.gov/top*). More than 85 000 volunteers marked and classified craters.[3] The quality of their work was 'virtually indistinguishable from [that] of a geologist with years of experience in identifying Mars craters' (*http://clickworkers.arc.nasa.gov/documents/crater-marking.pdf*). In another example, Project Gutenberg, whose

---

[3] Every crater was marked an average of 50 times and classified an average of seven times. Thirty-seven percent of the contributions were made by one-time visitors.

goal is to make the world's public domain literature freely available online, relies upon volunteers to scan images of book pages, to proofread electronic pages, and to manage the consolidation and digital archiving of resulting texts. Volunteers proofread more than half a million pages in 2002, resulting in more than 800 books being archived for public access (*http://www.pgdp.net*) in that one year alone. In total, Project Gutenberg volunteers have made more than 6000 books freely available online.

Implications and future research

Prosocial behavior is widespread on the net. Evidence of the consequences of prosocial behavior is beginning to accumulate in studies of the effects of participating in online public discussion groups and volunteer work groups. Yet, as noted above, these studies rarely focus explicitly on prosocial behavior and rarely differentiate receiving help from offering help. Moreover, with few exceptions, studies that have focused on understanding the motivations for helping have not assessed the quality of the help provided. However, the quality of help provided is what determines its value to individual recipients. (See Hoch *et al.*, 1999, for one exception that found that informational help provided in online public medical discussion groups is of comparable quality to expert medical advice.) We should also note that some types of 'helping' behavior on the net, while rare, may be defined by many observers as anti-social rather than prosocial. A stark example of this can be found in volunteer 'pro-ana' (pro-anorexia) online groups, whose members support one another in their 'personal choice' to become dangerously thin. In sum, there is much research to be done at the individual level focusing on the costs and benefits of online prosocial behavior. Similarly, there are opportunities for systematic studies of broader social benefits accruing from prosocial behavior on the net.

Studies of offline helping have found that people help less when they observe more people in the helping context (Latané & Darley, 1970). However, in the electronic context there are no salient cues regarding group size. Both the help-seekers and potential help-providers are invisible. Research on the role of perceived group size could provide a fuller account of some of the situational determinants of helping behavior in the electronic context.

Individual differences affect help-seeking and offering behaviors offline (Nadler & Fisher, 1986). For example, individual differences in self-esteem affect tendencies for asking and providing help. People with low self-esteem are less likely to ask for help because they feel threatened. The invisibility of the electronic context makes it psychologically less taxing for everyone, but this effect may be stronger for people of low self-esteem. Studies that do not control for individual differences when measuring the perceived benefits of the help provided and received online may lead to incomplete or even wrong conclusions. McKenna and Bargh (1998) found, for example, that although active participation in support groups was beneficial, the benefits accrued only to those for whom identity as a member of the group was important. Future research on the causes and effects of prosocial behavior at the individual level should incorporate important individual person variables.

Studies using one-time (cross-sectional) questionnaires that ask people to self-report their motivations for helping others are problematic. Cross-sectional studies cannot distinguish the role of motivation from pre-existing group differences, such as the (often) higher educational attainment of volunteers than non-volunteers. Researchers have made some progress in untangling people's *ex ante* motivations for helping from their *post hoc* justifications of helping by conducting laboratory experiments and longitudinal surveys in which causal links among motivations, attributions, and contributions can be assessed more accurately than in cross-sectional surveys (e.g. Penner & Finkelstein, 1998). The archives of public discussion groups offer the opportunity to design and conduct unobtrusive longitudinal studies of prosocial behavior.

McKenna and Bargh (1998) demonstrate how positive responses to a first post increase the likelihood of the newcomer's subsequent active involvement in a group (with attendant changes in self-efficacy in the case of people with socially marginalized identities). No one has yet investigated how repeated positive responses to a person's posts over time increase the likelihood that the person who receives positive responses will increasingly exhibit prosocial behavior toward other online group members. Such a study could offer a direct investigation of the reinforcement aspects of social learning theory. A comparative content analysis of posts from frequent posters with those from infrequent posters could illuminate developmental processes associated with identification with a prosocial subgroup.

Galegher *et al.* (1998) demonstrate how referencing group membership in a request for help increases the likelihood that help will be provided. See Sassenberg (2002) for an example of a cross-sectional linguistic analysis of conformity to group communication norms; see Moon (in progress) for one of a longitudinal study of subgroup identification in public volunteer work groups.

Researchers are becoming more sensitive to ethical issues involved in conducting Internet research on any topic (e.g. Bruckman, 2002; Frankel & Siang, 1999; Nosek *et al.*, 2002; Thomas, 1996). Archival or contemporary studies of prosocial behavior must attend to these ethical issues. In addition, because public discussion groups and volunteer work groups *are* public, it is easy to post an online questionnaire to the group as a whole or to the e-mail addresses of people who have posted to the group. As more and more social scientists and their students try to study groups by using online questionnaires, the potential subjects of study may react with increasing hostility to what are viewed as 'off-topic' posts. It is important to remember that one person's research instrument is another person's SPAM.

Conclusions

In 2002, a father whose infant son died of sudden infant death syndrome (SIDS) posted a message on the net asking people to help him develop sensor technology to possibly reduce the future incidence of SIDS. Two weeks after his initial post, he had heard from more than one thousand volunteers. As he said:

> And the quality of those volunteering has been remarkable. Engineers with deep experience in medical devices and sensors stand out, of course, but the very breadth of talents offered is staggering. Programmers and poets, big idea guys and assembly coders, they just keep coming in . . .

> This is the Internet equivalent, I suppose, of a barn raising. People come together and volunteer their talents toward a common and laudable cause. And this type of volunteerism . . . is the real essence of the Internet. It is something that literally couldn't happen any other way or through any other medium . . . Such collaboration simply wouldn't work without the Internet. When some engineer offers . . . two hours of labor per week, which is about the norm, the only way to get anything done is to eliminate meetings, eliminate travel, eliminate the effects of time zones, eliminate as much over-head and friction from the process as possible. And what's left over is the work, itself. (Cringley, 2002)

In sum, the net offers the opportunity to engage in meaningful prosocial behavior, the opportunity to theorize about who engages in these behaviors and why they do, and the opportunity to study these behaviors in a wide variety of electronic contexts.

References

Akera, A. (2001). Voluntarism and the fruits of collaboration: the IBM user group, SHARE. *Technology and Culture*, **42**(4), 710–36.

Ashforth, B.E. and Mael, F. (1989). Social identity theory and the organization. *Academy of Management Review*, **14**(1), 20–39.

Athanasiou, R. and Green, P. (1973). Physical attractiveness and helping behavior. *Proceedings of the 81st Annual Convention of the American Psychological Association*, **8**, 289–90.

Bandura, A. (1977). *Social learning theory*. Englewood Cliffs, NJ: Prentice-Hall.

Bandura, A. and McDonald, F.J. (1963). Influence of social-reinforcement and behavior of models in shaping children's moral judgments. *Journal of Abnormal and Social Psychology*, **67**(3), 274–81.

Barsion, S.J. (2002). *MentorNet: the E-mentoring network for women in engineering and science.* Retrieved, from the world wide web: *http://www.mentornet.net/Documents/About/Results/Evaluation/*

Batson, C.D. (1991). *The altruism question: toward a social psychological answer.* Hillsdale, NJ: Erlbaum.

Batson, D. (1998). Altruism and prosocial behavior. In D.T. Gilbert, S.T. Fiske, and G. Lindzey (eds), *Handbook of social psychology* (4th edn) (Vol. II, pp. 282–316). New York: McGraw-Hill.

Baym, N.K. (1999). *Tune in, log on: Soaps, fandom, and online community.* Thousand Oaks, CA: Sage.

Bennett, D., Tsikalas, K., Hupert, N., Meade, T., and Honey, M. (1998, September). The benefits of online mentoring for high school girls: telementoring young women in science, engineering, and computing project. Retrieved from the world wide web: *http://www2.edc.org/CCT/admin/publications/report/telement_bomhsg98.pdf*

Boberg, E.W., Gustafson, D.H., Hawkins, R.P., *et al.*(1995). Development, acceptance, and use patterns of a computer-based education and social support system for people with AIDS/HIV infection. *Computers in Human Behavior,* **11**(2), 289–311.

Bolger, N., Zuckerman, A., and Kessler, R. (2000). Invisible support and adjustment to stress. *Journal of Personality and Social Psychology,* **79**(6), 953–61.

Brennan, P.F., Moore, S.M., and Smyth, K.A. (1995). The effects of a special computer network on caregivers of persons with Alzheimer's disease. *Nursing Research,* **44**(3), 166–72.

Bruckman, A. (2002). Studying the amateur artist: a perspective on disguising data collected in human subjects research on the Internet. *Ethics and Information Technology,* **4**(3), 217–31.

Butler, B.S., Sproull, L., Kiesler, S., and Kraut, R.E. (forthcoming). Community effort in online groups: who does the work and why? In L. Atwater (ed), *Leadership at a distance.* Mahwah, NJ: Erlbaum.

Byrne, D., Baskett, G., and Hodges, L. (1971). Behavioral indicators of interpersonal attraction. *Journal of Applied Social Psychology,* **1**(2), 137–49.

Callero, P.L., Howard, J.A., and Piliavin, J.A. (1987). Helping behavior as role behavior: disclosing social structure and history in the analysis of prosocial action. *Social Psychology Quarterly,* **50**(3), 247–56.

Chaiken, S. (1979). Communicator physical attractiveness and persuasion. *Journal of Personality and Social Psychology,* **37**(8), 1387–97.

Chidambaram, L. (1996). Relational development in computer-supported groups. *MIS Quarterly,* **20**(2), 143–65.

Compeau, D.R. and Higgins, C.A. (1995). Application of social cognitive theory to training for computer skills. *Information Systems Research,* **6**(2), 118–43.

Constant, D., Sproull, L., and Kiesler, S. (1996). The kindness of strangers: the usefulness of electronic weak ties for technical advice. *Organization Science,* **7**(2), 119–35.

Cringley, R.X. (2002, May 2). *Chase 2.0 Is that a supercomputer in your jammies?* Retrieved from the world wide web: *http://www.pbs.org/cringely/pulpit/pulpit20020502.html*

Cummings, J.N., Sproull, L., and Kiesler, S. (2002). Beyond hearing: where real world and online support meet. *Group Dynamics: Theory, Research and Practice,* **6**(1), 78–88.

Dommeyer, C.J. and Ruggiero, L.A. (1996). The effects of a photograph on a mail survey response. *Marketing Bulletin,* **7**, 51–7.

Eagly, A.H. and Crowley, M. (1986). Gender differences in helping behavior: a meta-analytic review of the social psychological literature. *Psychological Bulletin*, **100**, 283–308.

Eisenberg, N. and Miller, P.A. (1987). Empathy and prosocial behavior. *Psychological Bulletin*, **101**, 91–119.

Emswiller, T., Deaux, K., and Willits, J. (1971). Similarity, sex, and requests for small favors. *Journal of Applied Social Psychology*, **1**, 284–91.

Field, D. and Johnson, I. (1993). Satisfaction and change: a survey of volunteers in a hospice organisation. *Social Science & Medicine*, **36(12)**, 1625–33.

Fisher, R.J. and Ackerman, D. (1998). The effects of recognition and group need on volunteerism: a social norm perspective. *Journal of Consumer Research*, **25(3)**, 262–75.

Foster, E. (1998, February 2). *Best technical support award: Linux user community*. Retrieved from the world wide web: *http://www.infoworld.com/cgi-bin/displayTC.pl?/97poy.supp.htm*

Foster, E. (1999, November 29). *Best technical support: it may not be the guy on the telephones anymore*. Retrieved from the world wide web: *http://www.infoworld.com/articles/op/xml/99/11/29/991129opfoster.xml*

Foster, E. (2000, January 14). *Best customer support? The award goes to Sybase Internet newsgroups*. Retrieved from the world wide web: *http://www.infoworld.com/articles/op/xml/00/01/17/000117opfoster.xml*

Frankel, M.S. and Siang, S. (1999, November). *Ethical and legal aspects of human subjects research on the Internet: A report of a workshop*. Retrieved from the world wide web: *http://www.aaas.org/spp/dspp/sfrl/projects/intres/main.htm*

Galegher, J., Sproull, L., and Kiesler, S. (1998). Legitimacy, authority, and community in electronic support groups. *Written Communication*, **15(4)**, 493–530.

Gray, J.E., Safran, C., Davis, R.B., *et al.* (2000). Baby CareLink: using the Internet and telemedicine to improve care for high-risk infants. *Pediatrics*, **106(6)**, 1318–24.

Grube, J.A. and Piliavin, J.A. (2000). Role identity, organizational experiences, and volunteer performance. *Personality and Social Psychology Bulletin*, **26(9)**, 1108–19.

Gu, B. and Jarvenpaa, S. (2003, December). *Online discussion boards for technical support: the effect of token recognition on customer contributions*. Paper presented at the Proceedings of the 24th International Conference on Information Systems, Seattle, WA.

Harrell, W.A. (1978). Physical attractiveness, self-disclosure, and helping behaviour. *The Journal of Social Psychology*, **104**, 15–17.

Hertel, G., Niedner, S., and Herrmann, S. (2003). Motivation of software developers in open source projects: an Internet-based survey of contributors to the Linux kernel. *Research Policy*, **32(7)**, 1159–77.

Higgins, M.C. and Kram, K.E. (2001). Reconceptualizing mentoring at work: a developmental network perspective. *Academy of Management Review*, **26**, 264–88.

Hoch, D.B., Norris, D., Lester, J.E., and Marcus, A.D. (1999). Information exchange in an epilepsy forum on the world wide web. *Seizure*, **8(1)**, 30–4.

Hogg, M.A. and Abrams, D. (1988). *Social identifications: a social psychology of intergroup relations and group processes*. London: Routledge.

Hogg, M.A. and Terry, D.J. (2000). Social identity and self-categorization processes in organizational contexts. *Academy of Management Review*, **25(1)**, 121–40.

Karabenick, S.A. and Knapp, J.R. (1988). Effects of computer privacy on help-seeking. *Journal of Applied Social Psychology*, **18(6)**, 461–72.

Kendall, L. (2002). *Hanging out in the virtual pub: masculinities and relationships online*. Berkeley: University of California Press.

Kiesler, S., Zdaniuk, B., Lundmark, V., and Kraut, R. (2000). Troubles with the Internet: the dynamics of help at home. *Human-Computer Interaction*, **15(4)**, 323–51.

Knoke, D. (1981). Commitment and detachment in voluntary associations. *American Sociological Review*, **46(2)**, 141–58.

Kramer, R.M. (1993). Cooperation and organizational identification. In J.K. Murnighan (ed), *Social psychology in organizations: advances in theory and research* (pp. 244–268). Englewood Cliffs, NJ: Prentice-Hall.

Lakhani, K.R. and von Hippel, E. (2003). How open source software works: 'free' user-to-user assistance. *Research Policy*, **32(6)**, 923–43.

Latané, B. and Darley, J.M. (1970). *The unresponsive bystander: why doesn't he help?* New York, NY: Appleton–Century–Crofts.

Lawler, E.J., Thye, S.R., and Yoon, J. (2000). Emotion and group cohesion in productive exchange. *American Journal of Sociology*, **106(3)**, 616–57.

Lim, K.H., Ward, L.M., and Benbasat, I. (1997). An empirical study of computer system learning: comparison of co-discovery and self-discovery methods. *Information Systems Research*, **8(3)**, 254–72.

Lorig, K.R., Laurent, D.D., Deyo, R.A., Marnell, M.E., Minor, M.A., and Ritter, P.L. (2002). Can a back pain e-mail discussion group improve health status and lower health care costs? *Archives of Internal Medicine*, **162**, 792–6.

MacIntyre, A. (1967). Egoism and altruism. In P. Edwards (ed), *The encyclopedia of philosophy* (Vol. 2, pp. 462–6). New York: Macmillan.

Mael, F.A. and Ashforth, B.E. (1995). Loyal from day one: biodata, organizational identification, and turnover among newcomers. *Personnel Psychology*, **48(2)**, 309–33.

McKenna, K.Y.A. and Bargh, J.A. (1998). Coming out in the age of the Internet: identity 'demarginalization' through virtual group participation. *Journal of Personality and Social Psychology*, **75(3)**, 681–94.

McKenna, K.Y.A. and Green, A.S. (2002). Virtual group dynamics. *Group Dynamics: theory, Research and Practice*, **6(1)**, 116–27.

Mims, P.R., Hartnett, J.J., and Nay, W.R. (1975). Interpersonal attraction and help volunteering as a function of physical attractiveness. *The Journal of Psychology*, **89**, 125–31.

Moon, J.Y. (in progress). *Identification processes in distributed electronic groups: a study of voluntary technical support groups on the net*. Unpublished doctoral dissertation, New York University, New York, NY.

Moon, J.Y. and Sproull, L. (2002). Essence of distributed work: the case of the Linux kernel. In P. Hinds and S. Kiesler (eds), *Distributed work* (pp. 381–404). Cambridge, MA: MIT Press.

Nadler, A. and Fisher, J.D. (1986). The role of threat to self-esteem and perceived control in recipient reaction to help: theory development and empirical validation. *Advances in Experimental Social Psychology*, **19**, 81–122.

Nelson, T.D. (1999). Motivational bases of prosocial and altruistic behavior: a critical reappraisal. *Journal of Research*, **4(1)**, 23–31.

Nonnecke, B. and Preece, J. (2000*a*). *Lurker demographics: counting the silent*. Proceedings of the CHI 2000 Conference on Human Factors in Computing Systems, 73–80.

Nonnecke, B. and Preece, J. (2000*b*). *Persistence and lurkers in discussion lists: a pilot study.* Proceedings of the 33rd Hawaii International Conference on System Sciences.

Nosek, B.A., Banaji, M.R., and Greenwald, A.G. (2002). E-research: ethics, security, design, and control in psychological research on the Internet. *Journal of Social Issues,* **58**(1), 161–76.

Omoto, A.M. and Snyder, M. (1995). Sustained helping without obligation: motivation, longevity of service, and perceived attitude change among AIDS volunteers. *Journal of Personality and Social Psychology,* **68**(4), 671–86.

Penner, L.A. and Finkelstein, M.A. (1998). Dispositional and structural determinants of volunteerism. *Journal of Personality and Social Psychology,* **74**(2), 525–37.

Perlow, L. and Weeks, J. (2002). Who's helping whom? Layers of culture and workplace behavior. *Journal of Organizational Behavior,* **23**(4), 345–61.

Perron, B. (2002). Online support for caregivers of people with a mental illness. *Psychiatric Rehabilitation Journal,* **26**(1).

Piliavin, I.M. and Piliavin, J.A. (1975). Costs, diffusion, and the stigmatized victim. *Journal of Personality and Social Psychology,* **32**(3), 429–38.

Piliavin, J.A. and Callero, P.L. (1991). *Giving blood: the development of an altruistic identity.* Baltimore: Johns Hopkins University Press.

Piliavin, J.A. and Charng, H.-W. (1990). Altruism: a review of recent theory and research. *Annual Review of Sociology,* **16**, 27–65.

Pope, W.G. (2001). *The use of computer conferencing as an organizational knowledge transfer tool.* Unpublished doctoral dissertation, Pace University, New York, NY.

Popielarz, P.A. and McPherson, J.M. (1995). On the edge or in between: niche position, niche overlap, and the duration of voluntary association memberships. *American Journal of Sociology,* **101**(3), 698–720.

Portney, K.E. and Barry, J.M. (1997). Mobilizing minority communities: Social capital and participation in urban neighborhoods. *American Behavioral Scientist,* **40**(5), 632–44.

Postmes, T., Spears, R., and Lea, M. (2000). The formation of group norms in computer-mediated communication. *Human Communication Research,* **26**(3), 341–71.

Quan y Hasse, A., Wellman, B., Witte, J., and Hampton, K. (2002). Capitalizing on the Internet: social contact, civic engagement and sense of community. In B. Wellman and C. Haythornthwaite (eds), *The Internet in everyday life* (pp. 291–324). Oxford: Blackwell.

Rainie, L. and Kalsnes, B. (2001, October 10). *The commons of the tragedy: how the Internet was used by millions after the terror attacks to grieve, console, share news, and debate the country's response.* Washington, DC: Pew Internet and American Life Project. Retrieved from the world wide web: *http://www.pewinternet.org/reports/pdfs/PIP_Tragedy_Report.pdf*

Sassenberg, K. (2002). Common bond and common identity groups on the Internet: attachment and normative behavior in on-topic and off-topic chats. *Group Dynamics: Theory, Research and Practice,* **6**(1), 27–37.

Simon, B., Loewy, M., Stürmer, S., *et al.* (1998). Collective identification and social movement participation. *Journal of Personality and Social Psychology,* **74**(3), 646–58.

Simon, B., Stürmer, S., and Steffens, K. (2000). Helping individuals or group members? The role of individual and collective identification in AIDS volunteerism. *Personality and Social Psychology Bulletin,* **26**(4), 497–506.

Smith, C.A., Organ, D.W. and Near, J.P. (1983). Organizational citizenship behavior: Its nature and antecedents. *Journal of Applied Psychology,* **68**(4), 653.

Sproull, L. and Faraj, S. (1995). Atheism, sex, and databases: the net as a social technology. In B. Kahin and J. Keller (eds), *Public access to the Internet* (pp. 62–81). Cambridge, MA: The MIT Press.

Tajfel, H. and Turner, J.C. (1986). The social identity theory of intergroup behaviour. In S. Worchel and W.G. Austin (eds), *Psychology of intergroup relations* (pp. 7–24). Chicago: Nelson–Hall.

Thomas, J. (1996). Introduction: a debate about the ethics of fair practices for collecting social science data in cyberspace. *Information Society*, 12(2), 107–17.

Turner, J.C., Hogg, M.A., Oakes, P.J., Reicher, S.D., and Wetherell, M.S. (1987). *Rediscovering the social group: a self-categorization theory*. Oxford, UK: Basil Blackwell.

Tyler, T.R. (1999). Why people cooperate with organizations: an identity-based perspective. *Research in Organizational Behavior*, 21, 201–46.

Walther, J.B. (2002). Time effects in computer-mediated groups: past, present and future. In P. Hinds and S. Kiesler (eds), *Distributed work* (pp. 235–257). Cambridge, MA: MIT Press.

Wasko, M. and Faraj, S. (2000). 'It is what one does': why people participate and help others in electronic communities of practice. *Journal of Strategic Information Systems*, 9(2–3), 155–73.

Wellman, B. and Gulia, M. (1999). Net surfers don't ride alone: virtual community as community. In B. Wellman (ed), *Networks in the Global Village* (pp. 331–367). Boulder, CO: Westview Press.

Wellman, B. and Wortley, S. (1990). Different strokes from different folks: community ties and social support. *American Journal of Sociology*, 96(3), 558–88.

West, S.G. and Brown, T.J. (1975). Physical attractiveness, the severity of the emergency and helping: a field experiment and interpersonal simulation. *Journal of Experimental Social Psychology*, 11, 531–8.

Wilson, D.W. (1978). Helping behaviour and physical attractiveness. *The Journal of Social Psychology*, 194, 313–14.

Wilson, J. (2000). Volunteering. *Annual Review of Sociology*, 26(1), 215–40.

Winzelberg, A. (1997). The analysis of an electronic support group for individuals with eating disorders. *Computers in Human Behavior*, 13(3), 393–407.

Chapter 7

The Internet and aggression: motivation, disinhibitory, and opportunity aspects

Neil Malamuth, Daniel Linz, and
Mike Yao

Introduction

Claims about the Internet and aggression

As part of research for this chapter, we decided to type on an Internet search engine the phrase 'Internet and aggression'. Among the top 'hits' that emerged was an ABC News Online story dated November 26, 2003, with the provocative headline 'Internet linked to kids' sexual aggression'. It suggested that the Internet may be at least partly responsible for a growing number of young, sexually aggressive children because it enables them to freely access really violent and sexually explicit material that teaches them such aggression. Immediately following this ABC story, the next 'hit' was a site titled 'Tech dirt' that commented on the above story, with one of the contributors, named Mike, raising thoughtful questions about what evidence, if any, actually exists to substantiate such 'blame'. A third 'hit' included two entries from a site titled 'Kate's eye view' posted on June 28, 2003. One bemoaned the high levels of aggressive communications in chatrooms and similar Internet sites. Then, she discussed several potential explanations for such aggression and asked others to suggest additional explanations for such attacks. A response by Steph was as follows: 'Fuck you and your blog. And fuck your aggression too. I fucking hate aggression . . .'

In this chapter we offer our thoughts and describe related research on the intersection of two domains—the social psychology of the Internet and its implications for aggression. As the above 'hits' illustrate, there are interesting paradoxes that researchers face in addressing this topic. Claims abound of powerful negative effects, as illustrated in the ABC headline story. Yet, as Mike correctly argues, such claims are often made without sufficient evidence, since there is relatively sparse research currently available that directly assesses such claims. Interestingly, certain features of the Internet provided Mike with an opportunity to 'correctively respond' in a manner that gave his commentary much more equal prominence with the ABC story than would have been typical of individuals' responses to news stories in other media outlets, such as television or newspapers. Yet, as the next 'hit' by Kate notes, there are some features of the Internet that may indeed allow greater expression of aggression, although as the response to her posting illustrates, some of it may (or may not) be 'tongue in cheek' rather than truly hostile.

Discussing the full range of these intricate and fascinating issues is beyond the scope of this chapter, although we elected to address some of them in detail. We begin by outlining here the general theoretical framework that guides our conceptualization.

Our theoretical framework

Our approach recognizes the important interrelationship between the medium and the messages. Every communication medium has certain unique features that shape the characteristics of the messages conveyed on it: In other words, enhance the effectiveness of certain types of messages and correspondingly limit the effectiveness of other types of messages. In that sense, the introduction of the Internet—much like television some fifty years earlier, and radio before that, and the telephone even before—affected the types of communications transmitted.

Consider, for example, the link between terrorism and the Internet (a topic we discuss in greater length later in this chapter). The following quote is from the Internet site of the Hizbollah organization (quoted in *Yediot Aharonot*, Dec. 16, 1998, p. 7) (Tsfati & Weimann, 2002): '*By means of the Internet Hizbollah has succeeded in entering the homes of Israelis, creating an important psychological breakthrough*—Ibrahim Nasser al–Din, Hizbollah military leader.'

Although we recognize that exactly the same type of 'breakthrough' by terrorist organizations would not have been achieved with another medium, it is important to briefly consider what type of psychological breakthrough the Internet permitted and what other types of psychological effects have resulted from the use of other media. In media such as television, terrorists may actually achieve a much more powerful 'shock' impact on a larger number of people by widespread broadcast of their threatening acts—a primary goal of the terrorists. With the Internet, on the other hand, the terrorists may be better able to target specific segments of the population with a more subtle and complicated 'informational' strategy.

Tsfati and Weimann (2002) conducted content analyses of various terrorists' Internet sites, focusing on the way terrorists communicate through this medium as compared to more traditional means of communication. While some similarities with conventional types of communication were found, the researchers described three key differences. First, on the Internet the terrorist groups played down their violence and were much more 'pacificistic' in their rhetoric than in other media outlets. The researchers suggested that their intent here was to attract web surfers sympathetic to issues of human rights and free speech. A second difference is that the web pages contained a great deal of detailed information, not possible on mass media channels that operate with more limited space constraints and where some journalists may be loathe to allow certain information favorable to terrorists to be widely disseminated. A third difference is that the sites offered visitors ample and varied possibilities to take action such as soliciting donations, protesting, disseminating messages, but advocating violence was rarely one of the approaches (at least directly; violence was indirectly advocated through calls for Jihad on Islamic sites).

In other words, both media may have served the interests of such terrorist groups, and each in its own way. Messages designed to elicit terror among the widest audience might be most effectively communicated via broadcast television, with its dramatic visual potential and wide audience, whereas messages designed to elicit sympathy among certain segments of the population might be much more effectively communicated via the Internet. However, a recent exception to such a generalization occurred with the beheading of the American, Nicholas E. Berg, on May 8, 2004 in Iraq. The terrorist group that murdered him released a videotape of the gruesome beheading with the stated goal of demonstrating their revenge against Americans and creating fear. While traditional media outlets generally refused to show the videotape, it was posted on the Internet and was very widely viewed throughout the world, including being shown in some high school classes (*CNN News* report on May 13–15, 2004). This event may represent a relatively new tactic by which such groups may be able to reach very wide audiences without being subjected to restrictions that might be placed on them by more traditional media outlets. In fact, this beheading was soon followed by several others also broadcasted on the Internet. In addition, the Internet has become what has been described as a " . . . virtual classroom for terrorists . . ." (p.1, Franz, Meyer & Schmitt, 2004).

We accept that it is difficult to disentangle the effects of the Internet *per se* since its use is typically embedded within the context of various other media uses and other experiences. Even in the example of the beheading of Nicholas Berg, knowledge about the Internet videotape reached most people by reports about it in more traditional media, such as television, with some of the audience then searching for the Internet videotape. And, we certainly do not assume that the Internet always makes the potential for aggression worse. We do, though, focus here on the possibility that aggression can become more widespread and easier to accomplish, but we also recognize that it holds the promise of making some situations involving aggression arguably better.

As with each of the previous communication innovations mentioned above, there are a number of distinctive features of this new technology that invoke social psychological processes. While earlier communication technologies may have revolutionized the way and, at times, even the content of what was communicated, they did not offer the same capacity for invoking as many fundamental social psychological processes that may be related to aggression as does the Internet. In this chapter we emphasize some risk factors for aggressive action based on the social psychological features that are in many ways unique to the Internet. Although the research data directly addressing the Internet and the risk factors we present below are quite limited, we not only consider these, but also emphasize various other relevant data sources that provide a basis for extrapolating to theorizing about the Internet environment.

The general theoretical perspective on media effects that we subscribe to recognizes the need to study media effects within the context of other factors and the importance of considering bi-directional interactive influences (Malamuth *et al.*, 2000; Slater *et al.*, 2003). It is hypothesized that individuals with certain predispositions (e.g. relatively more aggressive tendencies) are likely to seek out media that are consistent with those pre-existing predispositions, which are then likely to strengthen those predispositions. In other words, our underlying model postulates that different types of people seek out and respond to media content differently in accordance with their individual predispositions and their ongoing social relationships, and media exposure in turn may reinforce certain tendencies.[1] Research seeking to identify the effects of Internet experiences *per se* may attempt to systematically focus on these while controlling for other factors, but it may often prove more realistic to analyze such exposure as part of a larger set of media and other experiences within which Internet experiences are often largely embedded.

Defining aggression for studying the Internet

Although the concept may not be easy to define precisely, most social psychologists have agreed to define aggression as a behavior directed toward the goal

---

[1] Certain features of the Internet, though, may result in people being more likely than with other media to be exposed to material that they did not necessarily seek out. We have, for example, heard of the child of a colleague who was attempting to gather information on the Internet for a book report and typed the phrase 'Little Women'. She was connected to various pornography sites.

of harming or injuring another living being, who is motivated to avoid that harm (e.g. Baron & Richardson,1994). This definition includes several key elements, wherein:

- aggression is a behavior, not an attitude, motive, or emotion
- an intention exists to cause harm to the victim
- some type of aversive consequences occur
- the victim is a living being
- the victim is motivated to avoid the harm (Berkowitz, 1993).

Social psychologists are fascinated by the fact that a vast range of people, depending on the situation, can participate in various forms of aggression (see Malamuth & Addison, 2001, for further elaboration), on a continuum of behavior ranging from verbal assaults to extreme forms of physical violence.

A widely used distinction in the social psychological literature is between *hostile* and *instrumental* aggression (Geen, 2001). Definitions of *instrumental* aggression emphasize that any harm is primarily a tactical means of attaining other goals, such as social status or money (e.g. Berkowitz, 1993). Typically, the definition of *hostile* aggression emphasizes that harm or injury to the target is the primary goal of the behavior. Berkowitz (1993) links hostile aggression with anger in response to frustration. His model is based on the network theory of emotion which argues that emotions, cognitions, and even action tendencies are connected in memory through association. The activation of one element (e.g. anger) can spread to other 'nodes' in the associative network, such as aggression.

Rather than considering hostile and instrumental aggression as distinct entities, some researchers have argued that both types of aggression actually share some common underlying mechanisms. For instance, Huesmann (1998) suggests that a key distinguishing element is the degree to which emotional anger underlies the aggressive response. He proposes that a continuum is the most suitable conceptualization, with instrumental and hostile aggression being at opposite ends of this emotional anger continuum.

These definitions and distinctions are especially important when thinking about aggression and the Internet. As expanded upon in this chapter, certain characteristics of the Internet result in some forms of aggression being rare and other forms much more common. A discussion of aggression and the Internet cannot be limited to a consideration of only extreme forms of violence such as homicide with guns, or terrorism with explosives, committed directly against a victim. Aggression as a social psychological phenomenon accomplished through the communication medium of the Internet is often both more subtle and more encompassing. What we recognize as aggression on the

Internet often has little to do with directly hitting, stabbing, or shooting. For example, aggression from senders whose identities are shielded may take the form of written or audio-verbal messages designed to hurt or humiliate. Indirect aggression (Lagerspetz *et al.*, 1988), which may take such forms as telling lies or stealing in the form of destructive messages, codes, 'viruses' or 'worms' designed to hinder or destroy others' work or computer software, also occurs. Hate words designed to incite other people, unseen by and usually unknown to the message composer, are used to urge others to engage in violent behavior. Attempts are now routinely made to steal the 'identities' and credit information from victims who are never seen. In all of these cases, the broad definition of aggression would still apply because of the intention to harm the victim.

Internet characteristics and aggression risk

The features of the Internet that may facilitate aggression may be organized within a general framework suggested by social learning theorists focusing on the causes of aggressive behaviors (e.g. Bandura, 1973, 1977). They emphasize that it is essential to consider the role of interactive multiple factors, such as those creating the motivation to commit aggression, those reducing internal and external inhibitions that might prevent acting out of the desire to aggress, and those factors providing the opportunity for the act to occur. These headings serve as broad categories that are useful for discussing various relevant features of the Internet and, therefore, our detailed discussion below will be organized by such a framework consisting of motivational, disinhibitory, and opportunity aspects.

Motivational aspects

The Internet is ubiquitous

A critical social feature of the Internet as a social communication device is that it is always 'on', thereby increasing the possibility of extensive exposure to cognitive scripts and emotions potentially priming and thereby motivating aggression. Moreover, the images and ideas are often accessed with little if any discernible cost. The Internet's ubiquitous availability also creates the potential for high levels of exposure to violence that may be highly graphic.

The Internet is a network of connected information, and because the ideas and information are connected through hypertext links, people can follow one node to another. A user can rapidly build exposure to information. The same images can be viewed repeatedly, and similar content can be pursued with greater and greater depth and specialization. Research has shown that people may habituate or become desensitized to repeated exposures to scenes of violence (Linz *et al.*, 1989).

The social cognitive approach to aggression is the most applicable to this set of features. The cognitive or information-processing approach to aggression is the most fully explicated social psychological approach and is based on the assumption that memory can be represented as a complex associative network of nodes representing cognitive concepts and emotions. Research has shown that the processes by which hostile schemas or aggressive 'scripts'—indeed, all types of knowledge structures—are activated involves awareness but with practice may become 'automatic' and operate without awareness (Schneider & Shiffrin, 1977; Todorov & Bargh, 2002).

Many can access

The Internet is available to virtually anyone. Unlike older technologies, there is no 'family viewing' time, or 'daytime programming' wherein there is a guarantee that certain ideas and images that are potentially harmful or offensive to certain audiences are restricted. The Internet provides widespread access to images and ideas not normally present in many people's social environment—especially children's. They may use the Internet to download games, watch video clips, and generally have access to information around the clock which would often be restricted to them were it not for this medium. Valkenburg and Soeters (2001) conducted a survey among 194 Dutch children (aged 8–13 years) who had home access to the Internet. Children's spontaneous descriptions of their positive experiences with the Internet most frequently included playing or downloading computer games (17%), watching video clips and songs (13%), visiting kids' entertainment sites (12%), and seeking information about animals (7%). As a negative experience, children most frequently reported a virus or computer crash (10%), violence (4%), and pornography (4%).

The Internet is interactive and more engaging

Unlike older forms of mass media, the Internet is interactive and may therefore be an especially potent source of social psychological factors that may increase the risk for aggression. This may be illustrated by focusing on video games, since the Internet has become an important arena for such interactions. For example, the website of the Entertainment Software Association reports that 43% of game players play games online one or more hours per week, which reflects an increasing trend, up from 37% in 2003 and 31% in 2002 (see *http://www.theesa.com/pressroom.html*). This increase is likely to be continued since, in 2002, various video games (e.g. PlayStation 2, Xbox, and GameCube) all introduced online services. According to ABC Online, even the U.S. Army has 'jumped into the game scene to capitalize on people's increased interest in the Internet and America's military prowess'. They have created freely available army experience video games on the Army's Website that have already been downloaded millions of times.

Although not the majority of the content, considerable video game content portrays violence.[2] Slater *et al.* (2003) found support for the assertion that more alienated individuals seek out violent website content. Moreover, they found evidence that visiting violence-oriented Internet sites contributes to youths' aggressiveness above and beyond the effects due to other factors, including other media experiences.

Researchers have described how violent video games, including those experienced on the Internet, differ from violent TV programs and films. There are at least four such important differences, all of which have been found to increase the risk for increasing aggressive tendencies (for reviews see Anderson *et al.*, 2003; Anderson & Bushman, 2001; Anderson & Dill, 2000; Bushman & Anderson, 2002). The first difference relates to the *involvement level of individuals and identification with violent characters*. Whereas TV viewing is a relatively passive activity, video game playing is highly active. Viewers of violent TV programs and films watch other characters behave aggressively; players of violent video games 'become' the aggressive characters—they are the ones who pull the trigger and throw the punches. Viewers of violent films might identify with the characters they see. Such role-taking is covert. However, players of some violent video games are required to take on the identity of a violent game character. This form of role-taking is overt. In first-person games, the player controls the actions of the violent game character and sees the game environment from the character's visual perspective. In third-person games, the player can 'become' one of an array of characters that differ in gender, appearance, and special fighting skills. In some games, the player can apply scanned images to characters in the game (called 'skins').

The second difference is to do with *reinforcement of violent acts*. In the mass media, aggression often pays (e.g. the fighter is rewarded by getting what he or she wants). When people watch a TV program or film, this reinforcing effect is indirect and vicarious. In contrast, the violent video game player is directly reinforced for aggressing by seeing visual effects, hearing sound effects (e.g. groans of pain from the enemy), hearing verbal praise (e.g. when an enemy is killed the computer says 'nice shot' or 'impressive'), receiving points, and advancing to the next highest level of the game.

---

[2] Some video game violence has particularly alarmed parents and legislators. For example, 'Grand Theft Auto: Vice City' purportedly prominently features the rape and mutilation of young women and the assault of police officers (see the *Seattle Post-Intelligencer*, Friday, March 21, 2003).

The *frequency of violent scenes* is another important difference. Compared to violent TV programs and films, the violence shown in violent video games is almost continuous. The player must constantly be on the alert for hostile enemies, must constantly choose and enact aggressive behaviors, and is reinforced for doing so. In addition, the violent video game player is exposed to constant gory scenes filled with blood, screams of pain, and suffering. All of this takes place in a context in which emotions, incompatible with normal empathic feelings, are at the fore. Instead, the scenes of gory death evoke emotions such as excitement and exhilaration. Thus, desensitization is likely to proceed at a faster and more effective pace for the violent video game player than for the violent TV/film viewer.

The final important difference lies in the *perceived realism*. Video games are becoming increasingly more realistic. In fact, CBS's '60 Minutes' program (broadcast August 6, 2003) reported that the richest man in the world, Bill Gates (Chairman of Microsoft), has decided to seriously invest in video games and to help create technology which makes the games so realistic that 'people forget they are playing a game'.

As noted above, all of these four elements may be expected to make violent video games more harmful than violent TV programs and films. Violent video games can contribute to the learning and enactment of aggression via classical conditioning processes, instrumental conditioning processes, and higher order observational learning processes. This combination of learning strategies has been shown to be more powerful than any of these methods used alone (Chambers & Ascione, 1987).

Disinhibitory aspects

Content is unregulated

The Internet was designed as a highly decentralized system. This decentralization defies regulation. Unlike television and radio in the past, it is a decentralized, distributed network. This decentralization poses a challenge to would-be inhibitors or censors who wish to impose normative limitations. The decentralization and associated lack of normative limitations is important for aggression. Violent material previously inaccessible is now available; there are no external inhibitors. Broadcast television was the primary source of media depictions of violence and censorship was imposed upon this medium, although it has come to be far less restricted recently. The Federal Communications Commission has not yet attempted to regulate the Internet, as it has the older communication technologies of radio and television.

Because of this lack of regulation the content found on the Internet may be much more extreme than that found on other media. Barron and Kimmel

(2000) conducted a content analysis of the degree of sexual violence in various types of popular media. They found that sexual violent content was the highest on the Internet. They concluded that the relatively 'democratic' unregulated characteristics of the Internet enabled content that would otherwise be strongly discouraged (e.g. by pressures from women's groups) to be more widely distributed.

Participation is often private and anonymous

Rubin (1994) describes certain characteristics of electronic technologies that increase the propensity for acts that transgress moral boundaries. One element of the cyber world is that it is possible for users to simultaneously maintain both privacy and public contact. Using the Internet is often a solitary activity and inhibitors normally present in face-to-face interaction with others are absent.

Although many researchers suggest that it is overly deterministic to view the computer-mediated environment as an inherently impersonal medium that always fosters anti-social behavior (e.g. Lea *et al.*, 1992; Spears & Lea, 1994; Walther, 1992, 1994, 1996; Walther *et al.*, 1994), they generally believe that a computer-mediated environment decreases or eliminates cues and sources of information that have been identified as important in the development of polite, friendly, courteous interpersonal interactions (Daft & Lengel, 1984; Kiesler *et al.*, 1984; Rice, 1993). Communication via a network of computers 'seems to comprise some of the same conditions that are important for deindividuation—anonymity, reduced self-regulation, and reduced self-awareness' (Kiesler, *et al.*, 1984, p. 1126). More specifically, the reduction of social cues in a computer-mediated environment is believed to decrease users' overall self-awareness, leading to a state of deindividuation. Such deindividuation effects were emphasized by Demetriou and Silke (2003) to account for the findings of their innovative study, which was designed to determine whether people who visited for the purposes of gaining access to legal pornographic material would also attempt to access illegal and/or deviant pornographic material. Over about a three-month period they found that 803 visitors entered the site and that the majority of visitors also accessed the illegal and/or deviant content.

Fisher and Barak (2000) expanded on some of the features of the Internet that may lead some individuals who are otherwise not likely to seek out various types of sexual content to encounter it in this media environment. As part of this discussion, they note that erotophobic individuals (those who typically have negative reactions to sexuality) might, in this Internet environment, 'import such information and expectancies into fantasies consistent with his or her affective predisposition (e.g. imagery of depraved sexual behavior with unwilling victims that resulted from a pervert's contact with the Internet).' (Fisher & Barak, p. 583). The wide availability on the Internet of relatively 'deviant' material may create the impression that there is considerable interest by others in what you are interested in. Thus, it may facilitate great social support for the images, ideas, and messages that the user is interested in (Fisher & Barak).

One such content area that has aroused concern relates to the various sites devoted entirely to rape depictions as entertainment. For example, in a content analysis of Internet rape sites, Gossett and Byrne (2002) note that discussions about violent pornography are incomplete without an understanding of the Internet as a unique and rapidly expanding medium for disseminating images of sexual violence against women. They address that gap by examining violent pornography in a sample of 31 free Internet sites. Each site was analyzed for its portrayal of women victims, male perpetrators, and its story of rape. The authors found that the iconography of Internet pornography strongly emphasizes the depiction of the victims. Victims of rape are either shown in a picture or alluded to in the text, while information about the perpetrator is left to one's own imagination. The presence of a perpetrator is rare. The pictures do not present rape as a romantic seduction. In contrast, the pain caused to the victim, the level of realism is a primary selling point for the sites.

In some cases, governments have focused on prosecuting Internet sites with such extreme content. For example, in a recent Canadian case (see *Fort Frances Times Online*, December 4, 2002) Don Smith was found guilty of creating and distributing material that featured 'undue exploitation of sex and violence' over the Internet. The site was closed down and the defendant was ordered to pay a $100 000 fine. In the U.S., a federal jury in Dallas convicted a Fort Worth couple of violating federal obscenity laws by selling videos featuring graphic rape and sexual torture via a website. Legal experts, prosecutors, and defense attorneys say it is the first federal obscenity case involving adult pornography in North Texas in at least 10 years (Heinzl, 2003).

Participation is unmonitored by others

Unlike other media experiences, viewing and interacting on the Internet can be free of the social costs associated with viewing socially unapproved deviant material. There are no embarrassing or social mores to inhibit the user. This may be particularly important for children and their access to the Internet, which is sometimes unmonitored by parents. There has been considerable discussion concerning parental controls, an issue that will not be discussed here.

Kahn–Egan (1998) conducted a study of the ease of accessibility of various types of sexually explicit media, including the Internet, and also surveyed several hundred 3rd-8th graders about their actual exposure to such media.

She found evidence for easy accessibility to such media, including many sites on the Internet that are supposed to be restricted to adults only. In addition, a high percentage of youths (48%) reported having visited Internet sites with various types of 'adult' content. Sexual content was the most popular type of adult sites visited. Moreover, the Internet has resulted in many more adults accessing sexually explicit images that otherwise they may have been more reluctant to access. According to Nielsen NetRatings, 17.5 million web surfers visited porn sites from their homes in January 2000—a 40% increase from four months earlier. That escalated to 20.7 million in October (or roughly 23% of the web-surfing population in the U.S.). With bigger sites taking in more than $100 million a year through X-rated portals, e-porn is the most successful of all Internet ventures, according to Nielsen NetRatings.

The fact that participation on the Internet is not monitored or controlled may make it a powerful tool for terrorists. Terrorism is 'the purposeful act or the threat of the act of violence to create fear and/or compliant behavior in a victim and/or audience of the act or threat' (Stohl, 1988, p. 1). The act of terrorism on the Internet is a special form of aggression in that it combines a specific target with its important impact on a wider audience. In other words, terrorism is unique in that the actual target that is attacked serves as a gateway to influencing a larger audience. 'Cyber terrorism' is unlawful attacks against computers, networks, and the information stored therein when done to intimidate or coerce a government or its people in furtherance of political or social objectives (Denning, 2000). Cyber terrorism is unique from other terrorist tactics in that it does not exist beyond its intimate relationship with computers. It can be international, domestic, state, or political, but the core act involving a combination of the terrorist act and computers always remains the same.

Flemming and Stohl (2001) note that there is increasing concern that the threat of terrorism in a global environment is reliant on the Internet. Similarly, Tsfati and Weimann (2002), in referring to the origins of the Internet, note that:

> Paradoxically, the very decentralized structure that the American security services created out of fear of a Soviet nuclear attack now serves the interests of the greatest foe of the West's security services since the end of the Cold War, namely international terror. The nature of the network, its international character and chaotic structure, the simple access, the anonymity—all furnish terrorist organizations with an ideal arena for action. (p. 317).

Terrorist groups engaging in cyber terrorism are noted for threats to commerce, public safety, and national security.

These threats can take any number of forms, but are generally parlayed into computer *versus* computer confrontations. Flemming and Stohl (2001) note that conventional terrorist tactics and those involving computers differ in three key ways: ease of operations; developing potential; and increased anonymity. None of these activities is easily detected or readily countered and thus, they enable terrorist groups to take advantage of computer technology and use it to create support structures to further their goals. These goals are accomplished on the Internet through political propaganda (including disinformation programs), recruitment, financing, intra/inter-group communication, and coordination in information/intelligence gathering. Stealth and anonymity are used in both routine activity and tactical operations. Of benefit to terrorists is the ease of Internet operations, both in terms of resources expended and ability to strike worldwide.

Specific examples of the facilitation of terrorism through use of computer technology illustrate the appeal this technology can have to terrorist groups. The use of the Internet for propaganda is an especially popular one. Many exiled political opposition groups emanating from such countries as Iran, Iraq, Mexico, Northern Ireland, and Saudi Arabia have used the world wide web for just such purposes (Rathmell, 1997). While the Internet may not be the primary instrument of terrorists, they do use it for ancillary purposes. The Internet is fast and cheap. Terrorists can and do communicate with each other with great efficiency. Their communications may be very difficult to detect and trace. In addition to communication among themselves, terrorists can use the Internet and web-based technologies to disseminate messages about their aggressive objectives. This expression can be symbolic (as in the case of website defacement), or it can be used in furtherance of propaganda, recruitment, or fund raising.

As well as aiding terrorist propaganda, computer networks also enhance terrorist recruitment and financing. Damphousse and Smith (1998) report that international terrorist groups such as Peru's Shining Path (Sendero Luminoso) have websites seeking to export the 'revolutionary message' and attempt to raise funds by selling revolutionary products such as T-shirts, posters, and videos. All in all, cyber technology, especially in the form of the Internet, is an attractive tool for terrorist groups desiring to strengthen their basic infrastructures.

The nature of the Internet allows groups eager to expand their activities to reach and influence others in ways that were previously available only to well-organized, state-funded terrorist organizations. Physical distance and national borders that once separated terrorists from their co-conspirators, their audience, and their targets do not similarly exist in the world of modern telecommunications and the Internet. Organizations such as the Islamic fundamentalist groups that follow Osama Bin Laden (Arquilla & Karasik, 1999) and Hamas (see Anti-Defamation League web site at *www.adl.org/terrorism/*)

rely on computers to coordinate their activity. The Revolutionary Armed Forces of Colombia (FARC), for example, is known to respond to press inquiries via e-mail (Anti-Defamation League, 1998).

The terrorists' ability to engage in 'growth activity' via the Internet for recruitment, communication, and especially financing, without the knowledge of state authorities, is likely to lead to stronger and, hence, more resilient terrorist groups. In turn, the potential for terrorist groups to engage in activity that focuses less on threats and more on tangible actions is significantly heightened. Terrorist groups utilizing computers for communication are likely to move beyond hierarchical organizational structures and employ networked ones.

Contact with similar others provides social support

Even without actually interacting with anyone else, the Internet can give the impression to the user that many others share his/her interests. One can access links to droves of images and ideas similar to the content at hand almost no matter how obscure, specialized, or even deviant the images may be. Thus, the impression is fostered of great social support and potentially disinhibiting effects on exposure to the images, ideas, and/or messages in which the user is interested.

Because it is possible to seek out others and make contact with those who share your interests in message-sharing centers, through personal addresses, or on websites devoted to shared content, social support for even the most aggressive images can be generated. Personal identity can be enhanced by identifying with others and through social support given by others with whom you share interests on the Internet (Bennett, 2003).

As a distributed network, the Internet is not only very difficult to monitor or censor, but it allows for expression of an identity through participation in a group that shares your interests. Identities can be made whole by participating with others in this interactive communication medium. Likewise the fact that identities can be changed and shielded is an import aspect of the following forms of aggression. Other Internet participants with whom a user can interact can come from nearly anywhere on earth. In addition, the aspect of the Internet that we identified as one person 'fishing' for many people is critical here. Many of the forms of aggression we describe in this chapter involve one person contacting many others in order to eventually locate a particular target, such as a child, with the intention of aggression. Finally, the technical feature of the Internet that allows one computer to find many others is important. This feature allows the Internet to be used for accomplishing indirect violence on a large scale.

Certain extremist groups, such as those that advocate outgroup ethnic hate and aggression, may find the relatively uninhibited context of the Internet as a fertile ground for growth and expression. In an investigation of hate crime with the Internet, Glaser *et al.* (2002) asked what makes racists advocate racial violence. They conducted semi-structured interviews with 38 participants in White racist Internet chatrooms. They examined the extent to which people would, in this unique environment, advocate interracial violence in response to purported economic and cultural threats. The authors experimentally manipulated the nature and proximity of the threats. Qualitative and quantitative analyses indicate that the respondents were most threatened by interracial marriage and, to a lesser extent, Blacks moving into White neighborhoods. In contrast, job competition posed by Blacks evoked very little advocacy of violence. Various supremacist groups in the U.S. have also used the Internet for financial gain (Damphousse & Smith, 1998).

The technical feature of the Internet that allows one computer to find many others may also facilitate violence against oneself, via social support and conveying of information reducing potential inhibitory mechanisms. Information that may be nearly impossible to obtain by other means about methods of suicide may be obtained from the Internet. It is now extremely easy to access information about suicide from the Internet using search engines. Websites offering advice on suicide may be found by teenagers trawling the internet for information on the best way to kill oneself (Beaston *et al.*, 2000). Several websites actually rate suicide in terms of ease and success rate (Alao *et al.*, 1999). One such site, calling itself 'Church of Euthanasia', advises people to 'do a good job' when they commit suicide. It reads: 'Suicide is hard work. It's easy to do it badly, or make rookie mistakes. As with many things, the best results are achieved by thorough research and careful preparation.' The site goes on to discuss the pros and cons of death by shooting, hanging, crashing a car, jumping, slitting your wrists, drowning, freezing, overdosing, or gassing yourself with nitrous oxide, exhaust fumes, and oven gas. One site described using guns, overdosing, slashing one's wrists, and hanging as the 'best methods to commit suicide'. Other site titles suggested various suicide methods. One site illustrated various methods including lethal doses of poison, their availability, estimated time of death, and degrees of certainty.

In fact, 90% of hospital contacts resulting from self-harm involves self-poisoning. Thompson (2000) has found that information on how to commit suicide and the number of pro-suicide groups on the Internet are burgeoning (especially concerning self-poisoning) and the number of high-traffic newsgroups encouraging suicide present on the Internet is increasing, compared to an earlier baseline. Thompson reports that details of how lethal chemicals can be purchased over the Internet, and lethal doses, are very explicit.

Not everyone is equally affected by exposure to these sites, of course, and there is no suggestion among mental health experts that merely viewing suicide websites will instigate an attempt from an otherwise healthy individual

(Adekola *et al.*, 2001). The problem, according to these authors, is that especially vulnerable individuals have been sharing information about suicide with one another. There are examples of interactive notes on the Internet followed by a suicide fatality (Baume *et al.*, 1997). Adekola *et al.* (2001) caution that, although surfing the Internet for information from the Internet may be useful for patients with other disorders, the potential hazard makes it inappropriate for use among those prone to extreme depression and suicide. These authors recommend that mental health care providers should counsel patients about alternatives to surfing the Web at times of crisis. Staying off the Web may be the best idea for these individuals. Instead they should seek help by calling crisis lines and talking to clinicians, friends, or family members.

Opportunity aspects

Targets of aggression are readily available

One of the various 'opportunity' aspects provided by the Internet environment pertains to the ability of one person to 'fish' or 'troll' for many others. Many people can be contacted and stalked, and children can be contacted for aggressive purposes. Stalking is legally defined by most statutes as the willful, malicious, and repeated following and harassing of another person (Sfiligoj, 2003). Typical stalking behavior involves physically following the victims, telephone harassment, and vandalism. Stalkers also often use binoculars, cameras, hidden microphones, and public records to keep track of the whereabouts of their victims. The development of the Internet and the rapid growth of digital communication have dramatically increased the efficiency and convenience of information gathering, exchange, and processing. However, many attributes of the Internet—low cost, ease of use, anonymity, ease of data gathering and cross-referencing—make it an attractive medium for stalkers. Given the enormous amount of personal information available through the Internet, a stalker can easily locate private information about a potential victim with a few mouse clicks or keystrokes.

In the past few years, stalking has increasingly received attention from popular press, legal opinion, law enforcement, and social scientists (Best, 1999; Spitzberg & Cupach, 2003). Although obsessive relational behaviors such as stalking have always existed in the human society (Meloy, 1999), it was not explicitly criminalized in the U.S. until the late 1980s. In 1989, an obsessed stalker named Robert John Bardo murdered actress Rebecca Schaeffer after obtaining her address and personal information from a private detective agency. In response to this high-profile murder, California enacted an anti-stalking law in 1990. This law gained immediate momentum. By the end of 1993, all 50 states and the District of Columbia had passed similar anti-stalking legislations

(Spitzberg & Cupach, 2003). In 1996, Congress passed the Federal Anti-Stalking Act to criminalize future violent crimes committed by stalkers.

The use of the Internet, e-mail, or other electronic communications devices to stalk another person is known as 'cyber stalking'. Although cyber stalking involves an array of activities, it shares important characteristics with offline stalking, including the desire to exert control over the victims. The Internet, though, provides new avenues for pursuit of a victim. A cyber stalker may send repeated, threatening, or harassing messages by the simple push of a button or use programs to send these messages without being physically in front of a computer terminal. A cyber stalker can also easily dupe other Internet users into harassing or threatening a victim by posting the name, phone number, or e-mail address of the victim in public chatrooms or Internet bulletin boards. In addition to its ease of use, the anonymity of the Internet also makes cyberspace a place where stalkers can conceal their true identity from law enforcement agencies.

Sfiligoj (2003) has found that whilst the majority of stalkers have been in relationships with their victims, some have never met their victim or they are merely acquaintances (e.g. neighbor, friend, or co-worker). Scientific information on stalking has been limited, despite unprecedented media, legal, and legislative attention over the past 10 years. In 1997, the National Institute of Justice (NIJ) collected data from 8000 men and 8000 women on the prevalence of stalking, characteristics of offenders, stalking behaviors, and co-occurrence of stalking and domestic violence. The survey showed that stalking was strongly linked to controlling behavior, and emotional, physical, and sexual abuse.

Sometimes when individuals are seeking useful information on the Internet, they might increase the likelihood of their being victimized by stalkers and/or other aggressors. For example, Finn and Banach (2000) have identified problems and dangers that may be encountered when females seek health and human services on the Internet, and the implications of these problems and dangers for human service organizations. Participation in online self-help groups may be harmful to some members for the following reasons:

◆ Members may encounter cyber stalkers.

◆ Communication may become disinhibited online, exposing participants to threats, profanity, seduction, and personal attacks.

◆ The qualifications of moderators are not regulated.

◆ The identity of members is unknown, which can cause problems in self-help groups concerned with issues of violence and abuse.

◆ Groups can be disrupted by 'cyber terrorists'.

- Members may receive misinformation from other group members.
- Messages may be forwarded or archived and searched by search engines, resulting in a loss of privacy.

Identity can be easily disguised

The fact that interaction with others on the Internet enables the disguising of one's identity can contribute greatly to the potential of aggression, such as the sexual abuse of children, whereby pedophilic predators may have the opportunity to reach children who otherwise would be better protected (Quayle & Taylor, 2002a, b, 2003). Barnitz (2001) discusses the need for a coordinated local and global response to the commercial sexual exploitation of children (CSEC) as one of the most destructive forms of child abuse. He stresses that although some efforts have been made to stop the trafficking in children and youth, they are far from sufficient. The scope of the child sex trade in physical and sexual violence for profit is outlined by Barnitz, and he notes that the Internet has made high-tech trade profitable.

The ability to hide identity has also enabled law enforcement agencies to conduct Internet stings directed at pedophiles (Fulda, 2002). After the Supreme Court upheld laws prohibiting child pornography in 1982, law enforcement agencies embarked on a large-scale effort to track and arrest purveyors of child pornography. With the rise of the Internet, child pornography proliferated. In the latter half of the 1990s, U.S. law enforcement agencies began directing their efforts online. This era also witnessed the rise of greater cooperation between federal, state, and local law enforcement agencies and between nations. One such sting operation, 'Operation Candyman' conducted in 2002, centered on a Yahoo! e-group that invited people to trade pictures of child pornography. The FBI estimates that there were more than 7000 subscribers to the group, with around 2400 living abroad.

Targets are unseen

A social psychological feature of the Internet includes the remoteness of victim to perpetrator. Albert Bandura has written extensively about the ways in which we excuse or allow ourselves to engage in moral transgressions that would otherwise be repugnant to us. He notes that on the Internet, transgressive acts can be performed in anonymity toward depersonalized or faceless victims located thousands of miles away (Bandura, 1990a, b, 2004). There are no consequences in terms of the victim's reactions. There is no ability for the victim to retaliate. The victim can be easily dehumanized. Bandura's writings on this topic emanate from his more general focus on moral disengagement.

Bandura (1990*a, b*) has outlined a set of conditions that disinhibit people and make it possible for them to engage in immoral behavior such as aggression. He identifies three sub-mechanisms: self-monitoring, judgmental, and self-reactive (Bandura, 1990*a, b*, 2004). The first step to exercising control over one's conduct is self-monitoring. Actions give rise to self-reactions through a judgmental function in which the individual's conduct is evaluated against their internal standards and situational circumstances. If an internal standard is violated, a self-sanction may occur.

People usually do not engage in reprehensible conduct unless they have justified to themselves the rightness of their actions or disassociated themselves from the consequences of their actions. Social cognitive theory of moral agency identifies mechanisms by which moral self-sanctions are selectively disengaged from detrimental conduct (e.g. Bandura, 1996). Moral disengagement may center on the cognitive restructuring of transgressive conduct into a benign or worthy one by using the mechanism of moral justification. Other psychological restructuring mechanisms which may be employed to justify a moral construct are:

- sanitizing euphemistic language
- advantageous comparison
- disavowal of a sense of personal agency by diffusion or displacement of responsibility
- disregarding or minimizing the injurious effects of one's actions
- attribution of blame to, and dehumanization of, those who are victimized.

Most important for our discussion of the social psychological features of the Internet that facilitate aggression are the last three of these mechanisms. (We will return to the other mechanisms in the discussion below on 'hacking'.) Cyber crimes such as virus attacks, hacking, or identity theft are particular difficult to combat due to the unique environment of cyberspace. The accessibility of an immense audience, coupled with the anonymity of the subject, make the Internet a perfect vehicle for locating victims, and it provides an environment where the victims don't see or speak to the attackers.

In such an environment, 'flaming' may be relatively common. Flaming refers to antagonistic or aggressive messages on computer networks (Joinson, 2003). Particular research attention within this area has focused on a sequence of written exchanges on a discussion topic that begins with a disagreement and gets more heated. The exchange often involves character attacks and foul language (Douglas & McGarty, 2001). Wallace and others have speculated that flaming is attributable to the psychological state of deindividuation (i.e. people lose their identity or sense of uniqueness as individuals). According to the theory of deindividuation (Zimbardo, 1969), under some social and psychological conditions (e.g. being in a large crowd or being anonymous), individuals are not able to view themselves as distinct individuals (i.e. they are deindividuated). Deindividuation will lead to a reduction of self-evaluation because of a lack of self-awareness (Duval & Wicklund, 1972). Consequently, a decreased self-evaluation would be conducive to anti-normative and uninhibited behavior (Zimbardo, 1969). In addition, Aiken and Waller (2000) reported that the same individuals engaged in flaming across two different discussions, suggesting that the characteristics of the flamer, as well as the technologies they use to flame, need to be considered (Joinson, 2003).

In considering the technological aspects, it is important to recall that the Internet was designed as a highly decentralized system that defies regulation. Because anybody can have access, and there is no central authority, Internet participants can use it for destructive purposes. The damage done may be enormously magnified because virtually all of the systems on which people depend in their everyday life are interdependently run by computer network systems. Therefore, hacking, virus attacks, and identity theft are becoming increasingly destructive and are forms of aggression made possible by features of the Internet, particularly those that increase depersonalization, lack consequences in terms of victim's reactions, and typically do not enable victims to retaliate.

At the same time, computer systems are vulnerable to a variety of forms of aggressive retaliation by disgruntled employees, former employees, or contractors. The CSI/FBI Computer Crime and Security Survey between 1996 and 2000 found that insiders topped the list of likely sources of cyber attacks, with more than 80% of respondents citing them as a likely source. In the 2000 survey, 71% of the respondents reported insider unauthorized access incidents (Power, 2000). In 2001, a disgruntled employee was convicted of hacking into the computerized waste management system of Maroochy Shire, Queensland, causing millions of gallons of raw sewage to spill out into local rivers and parks (Tagg, 2001). The individual in question appears to have been acting alone. However, to the extent that other 'insiders' are able and willing to act in concert with 'outsiders' (potential terrorists or otherwise), vulnerabilities to aggressive hackers or saboteurs may be exponentially greater because of the deindividuation features of the Internet.

A person may steal someone else's identity or break into a computer in order to steal information for financial gain, but the same acts can also be committed purely for the purpose of sabotage. Unlike crimes in the physical world, such as a bank robbery, it is often difficult to identify and assess the nature of cyber crimes due to the technological features of the Internet.

A computer virus is a program or piece of code that is loaded on to a computer without its user's knowledge and runs against the user's wishes. Viruses can also replicate themselves: a simple virus can make a copy of itself over and over again, and is relatively easy to produce. All computer viruses are man-made. Even a simple virus can be dangerous, because it can quickly use all available memory and bring the system to a halt. An even more dangerous type of virus is one capable of transmitting itself across networks and bypassing security systems.

One of the most dangerous aspects of a virus attack is that one person can cause catastrophic damages and affect the lives of millions of people in a very short period of time. In 1999, the infamous 'Melissa' virus infected thousands of computers in a few hours, causing an estimated $80 million in damage. On December 4, 2000, a 23-year-old Filipino hacker 'accidentally' sent out a very simple computer virus that was attached to an e-mail message proclaiming 'I LOVE YOU'. It raced over the world via e-mail, crashed e-mail systems, and destroyed data on millions of computers in a few hours. This 'love bug' caused an estimated $10 billion in damage worldwide, and affected the White House, Congress, the Pentagon, and the British House of Commons, along with numerous corporations. Also in 2000, dozens of high-profile websites such as Yahoo, e-Bay, Amazon, and Datek were knocked offline for several hours following a series of so-called distributed denial-of-service attacks.

Investigators later discovered that these attacks, in which a flood of traffic from hundreds of computers disables a target system simultaneously, were orchestrated when the hackers remotely 'borrowed' innocent computers at the University of California, Santa Barbara. The 'code red' worm infected tens of thousands of systems running Microsoft Windows NT and Windows 2000 server software, causing an estimated $2 billion in damages in 2001. Most recently in 2003, a virus, allegedly created by an 18-year-old high school student in Minnesota, infected more than 500, 000 computers worldwide.

Web page defacement is also a frequent form of cyber attack that is often perpetrated by hackers to express personal or political opinions. To deface a web page, a hacker first gains access to the system server on which the website is stored, and then changes the content of the website. In March, 2001, on the second anniversary of the NATO bombing of the Chinese embassy in Belgrade, a hacking group defaced numerous U.S. commercial and government websites with pro-Chinese and anti-American slogans.

Interviews with students who have engaged in web page defacement and other forms of hacking reveal that they engage in several forms of moral disengagement, including the cognitive restructuring of transgressive conduct into a benign or worthy act, by moral justification, sanitizing euphemistic language, and advantageous comparison. In Marc Roger's article, 'Modern-day Robin Hood or moral disengagement: understanding the justification for criminal computer activity', he used moral disengagement as a foundation to hypothesize that hackers and computer criminals are employing moral disengagement mechanisms in an attempt to reduce self-censure (Chantler, 1996; Denning, 1998; Rogers, 1999).

Several studies and articles quote hackers as stating that their activities are purely an intellectual activity and that information should be freely available to everyone (e.g. Chantler, 1996). Individuals engaged in criminal computer activity routinely minimize or misconstrue the consequences (Chantler, 1996; Denning, 1998; Shaw *et al.*, 1998). These individuals have stated that they never intentionally damage any files. They lay responsibility on the victims, claiming that besides, companies have or should have backups of their data and systems (Chantler, 1996). Other individuals dehumanize the victims and refer to them in terms such as multi-national corporations, or just networks and systems. They usually do not comment on the impact to the end users and system administrators, the cost to potential consumers, or the long-term effects (Spafford, 1997). The attribution of blame to the victim is possibly the most common mechanism employed by computer criminals and hackers (Rogers, 1999). The majority of researchers, who have used interviews and self-report surveys, quote the hacker subjects as blaming the system administrators or programmers for lax security, and stating that the victims deserved to be attacked (Chantler, 1996). Stealing music is also justified with these moral disengagement tactics.

Conclusions

The introduction of television and radio greatly changed the way we communicated with each other. Like these earlier innovations, the Internet is a human communication environment with certain unique characteristics that can activate and shape various psychological mechanisms, some of them pertaining to the potential for aggression. We have emphasized in this chapter that to analyze the conditions that contribute to aggression, it is essential to consider the role of interactive multiple factors, such as those creating the motivation to commit aggression, those reducing internal and external inhibitions that might prevent acting out of the desire to aggress, and those factors providing the opportunity for the act to occur. Within each of these categories, we have suggested that there are certain features of the Internet that are particularly relevant to increased risk for aggressive conduct. For example, we have suggested that the Internet is ubiquitous and interactive and thus likely to often be particularly engaging. We have also emphasized that Internet content is unregulated and consumption of information is often private and unmonitored, so that contact with similar others provides social support, and the user is often anonymous. Concealment and depersonalization can bring out the worst in people by removing personal and social sanctions for pernicious conduct, particularly since targets are often readily available, unseen, and may be reached in ways not available via other communication media. Such characteristics can disinhibit aggressive tendencies.

Depending on the motives of the users, many of the features that have been shown by social psychological research to increase aggression might also be used to decrease violence; for instance, the fact that the Internet is ubiquitous, available to virtually anyone, and often a medium for contact with similar others who may provide social support that can serve to reduce aggressive tendencies.

More specifically, one major function of the Internet for reducing aggression may lie in its capacity to help organize individuals to be vigilant with regard to possible acts of aggression and thereby to help prevent them. For example, listing of sex offenders in the neighborhoods is one strategy that has been employed (albeit a controversial example of the use of the Internet to help prevent future violence). Less problematic, from an individual civil rights' perspective, is the Internet's capacity for tracking violence more generally. Miller and DiGiuseppe (1998) discuss the development and implementation of the Violence Information Network (VIN)—a community database devoted to the surveillance of violence and its related factors. The purpose of the VIN is to provide communities within a metropolitan area with a comprehensive understanding of a complex social problem by integrating multiple violence-related data sources into a centralized location. The VIN is accessible via the Internet and is specific to the geographic areas of local communities, and tracks violence-related trends over time. The organizing function of the Internet may also allow for a counterweight to the vast amount of violence as entertainment by allowing parents' groups the opportunity to easily access relevant information, such as the violence ratings of video games and entertainment programs.

Organizing victims groups, such as women who have been victims of domestic and sexual violence, is also much easier over the Internet. The Internet offers the possibility of creating support groups of victims who would have much greater obstacles to meet through traditional means such as family, church, school, or job. Victims may find that they belong to a group that may be global and that shares the same modes of thinking and acting. A kind of group-based identity formation that can be useful in curbing the psychological effects of interpersonal violence is therefore possible, that would not be possible with more conventional communication.

In this chapter we have focused on the potential intersections of Internet and aggression by considering how the particular characteristics of this medium may interface with knowledge derived from social psychological research regarding the risk factors for aggression. These Internet characteristics allow the potential victim to be easily dehumanized. Yet, there is also remarkable potential for 'humanization' of social relationships on the Internet, resulting in activating psychological mechanisms that decrease the likelihood of aggression. We also found various sites emphasizing that the Internet can help foster understanding, respect, love, and peace because it 'connects people to each other'.

References

Adekola, O.A. Yolles, J.C., and Armenta, J. (2001). The Internet and suicide. *Psychiatric Bulletin* **25**, 400.

Aiken, M. and Waller, B. (2000). Flaming among first-time group support system users. *Information and Management*, **37**, 95–100.

Alao, A.O., Yolles, J.C., and Armenta, W.R. (1999). Cybersuicide: the Internet and suicide. *American Journal of Psychiatry*, **156**, 1836–7.

Anderson, C.A., Berkowitz, L., Donnerstein, E., *et al.* (2003). The influence of media violence on youth. *Psychological Science in the Public Interest*, **4**, 81–110.

Anderson, C.A. and Bushman, B.J. (2001). Effects of violent video games on aggressive behavior, aggressive cognition, aggressive affect, physiological arousal, and prosocial behavior: a meta-analytic review of the scientific literature. *Psychological Science*, **12**, 353–9.

Anderson, C.A. and Dill, K. (2000). Video games and aggressive thoughts, feelings, and behavior in the laboratory and in life. *Journal of Personality and Social Psychology*, **78**, 772.

Arquilla, J. and Karasik, T. (1999). Chechnya: a glimpse of future conflict? *Studies in Conflict & Terrorism*, **22**, 207–29.

Bandura, A. (1973). *Aggression: a social learning analysis*. Oxford, England: Prentice–Hall.

Bandura, A. (1977). *Social learning theory*. Oxford, England: Prentice–Hall.

Bandura, A. (1990*a*). Mechanisms of moral disengagement. In W. Reich (ed), *Origins of terrorism: psychologies, ideologies, theologies, states of mind* (pp. 161–91). New York: Cambridge University Press.

Bandura, A. (1990*b*). Selective activation and disengagement of moral control. *Journal of Social Issues*, **46**, 27–46.

Bandura, A. (1996). Moral disengagement in the perpetration of inhumanities. *Journal of Personality and Social Psychology*, **71**, 364–74.

Bandura, A. (2004). The role of selective moral disengagement in terrorism and counterterrorism. In F.M. Moghaddam and A.J. Marsella (eds), *Understanding terrorism: psychosocial roots, consequences, and interventions* (pp. 121–50). Washington, DC: American Psychological Association.

Barnitz, L. (2001). Effectively responding to the commercial sexual exploitation of children: a comprehensive approach to prevention, protection, and reintegration services. *Child Welfare. Special Issue: International Issues in Child Welfare*, **80**, 597–610.

Baron, R.A. and Richardson, D.R. (1994). Human aggression. *Perspectives in social psychology* (2nd edn). New York: Plenum Press.

Barron, M. and Kimmel, M. (2000). Sexual violence in three pornographic media: toward a sociological explanation. *Journal of Sex Research*, **37**, 161–8.

Baume.P., Cantor, C.H., and Rolfe, A. (1997). Cybersuicide: the role of interactive suicide notes on the Internet. *Crisis*, **18**, 73–9.

Beaston, S., Hosty, G.S., and Smith, S. (2000). Suicide and the Internet. *Psychiatric Bulletin*, **24**, 434.

Bennett, L. (2003). Lifestyle politics and citizen-consumers: identity, communication, and political action in late modern society. In J. Corner and D. Pels (eds), *Media and political style: essays on representation and civic culture*. Thousand Oaks, CA: Sage.

Berkowitz, L. (1993). Aggression: its causes, consequences and control. New York: McGraw–Hill.

Best, J. (1999). *Random violence: how we talk about new crimes and new victims*. Berkeley, CA: University of California Press.

Bushman, B.J. and Anderson, C.A. (2002).Violent video games and hostile expectations: a test of the general aggression model. *Personality & Social Psychology Bulletin*, **28**, 1679–86.

Chambers, J.A. and Ascione, F.R. (1987). The effects of prosocial and aggressive videogames on children's donating and helping. *Journal of Genetic Psychology*, **148**, 499–505.

Chantler, N. (1996). *Profile of a computer hacker*. Seminole, Florida: Interpact Press.

Daft, R.L. and Lengel, R.H. (1984). Information richness: a new approach to managerial behavior and organizational design. *Research in Organizational Behavior*, **6**, 191–233.

Damphousse, K.R. and Smith, B.L. (1998). The Internet: a terrorist medium for the 21st century. In H.W. Kushner (ed), *The future of terrorism: violence in the new millennium* (pp. 208–24). Thousand Oaks, CA: Sage.

Demetriou, C. and Silke, A. (2003). A criminological Internet 'Sting': experimental evidence of illegal and deviant visits to a website trap. *British Journal of Criminology*, **43**, 213–22.

Denning, D. (1998). *Information warfare and security*. Reading: Addison–Wesley.

Denning, D. (2000). *Cyberterrorism*. Testimony before the Special Oversight Panel on Terrorism Committee on Armed Services U.S. House of Representatives, May 23, 2000.

Douglas, K.M. and McGarty, C. (2001). Identifiability and self-presentation: computer-mediated communication and intergroup interaction. *British Journal of Social Psychology*, **40**, 399–416.

Duval, S. and Wicklund, R.A. (1972). *A theory of objective self-awareness*. New York: Academic Press.

Finn, J. and Banach, M. (2000). Victimization online: the downside of seeking human services for Women in the Internet. *CyberPsychology & Behavior*, **3**, 785–96.

Fisher, W.A. and Barak, A. (2000). Online sex shops: phenomenological, psychological, and ideological perspectives on Internet sexuality. *CyberPsychology & Behavior*, **3**, 575–89

Flemming, P. and Stohl, M. (2001). Myth and realities of cyberterrorism. In A. Schmid (ed), *Countering Terrorism Trough Enhanced International Cooperation. ISPAC (International Scientific and Professional Advisory Council of the United Nations Crime Prevention and Criminal Justice Program)* (pp. 70–105).

Frantz, D., Meyer, J., and Schmitt, R.B. (2004). *Los Angeles Times*, August 15th, Section A, p.1.

Fulda, J.S. (2002). Do Internet stings directed at pedophiles capture offenders or create offenders? And allied questions. *Sexuality & Culture: An Interdisciplinary Quarterly*, **6**, 73–100.

Geen, R.G. (2001). Human aggression (2nd edn). Taylor & Francis.

Glaser, J., Dixit, J., and Green, D.P. (2002). Internet for self and society: is social life being transformed? *Journal of Social Issues. Special Issue*, **58**, 177–93.

Gossett, J.L. and Byrne, S. (2002). A content analysis of Internet rape sites. *Gender and Society*, **16**, 689–709.

Heinzl, T. (October 23, 2003). *Couple guilty in obscenity trial. Dallas Star-Telegram.*

Huesmann, L.R. (1998). The role of social information processing and cognitive schema in the acquisition and maintenance of habitual aggressive behavior. In R.G. Geen and E. Donnerstein (eds), *Human aggression: Theories, research, and implications for social policy* (pp. 73–109). San Diego: Academic Press.

Joinson, A.N. (2003). *Understanding the psychology of Internet behaviour: virtual worlds, real lives.* Palgrave Macmillan: New York.

Kahn–Egan, C.N. (1998). *Pandora's boxes: children's reactions to and understanding of television and internet rules, ratings, and regulations.* Unpublished doctoral dissertation, Florida State University.

Kiesler, S., Siegel, J., and McGuire, T.W. (1984). Social psychological aspects of computer-mediated communication. *American Psychologist*, **39**, 1123–34.

Lagerspetz, K.M., Bjoerkqvist, K., and Peltonen, T. (1988). Is indirect aggression typical of females? Gender differences in aggressiveness in 11–12-year-old children. *Aggressive Behavior*, **14**, 403–14.

Lea, M., O'Shea, T., Fung, P., and Spears, R. (1992). 'Flaming' in computer-mediated communication: observations, explanations, implications. In M. Lea (ed), *Contexts of computer-mediated communication* (pp. 89–112). Hertfordshire: Harvester Wheatsheaf.

Linz, D., Donnerstein, E., and Adams, S. (1989). Physiological desensitization and judgments about female victims of violence. *Human Communication Research*, **15**, 509–22.

Malamuth, N. and Addison, T. (2001). Integrating social psychological research on aggression within an evolutionary-based framework. In G.J.O. Fletcher and M.S. Clark (eds), *Blackwell Handbook of Social Psychology: Interpersonal Process.* (pp. 129–161). Malden, MA: Blackwell.

Malamuth, N., Addison, T., and Koss, M. (2000). Pornography and sexual aggression: are there reliable effects and can we understand them? *Annual Review of Sex Research*, **11**, 26–91.

Meloy, J.R. (1999). Stalking: an old behavior, a new crime. *Forensic Psychiatry*, **22**, 85–99.

Miller, D.B. and DiGiuseppe, D. (1998). Fighting social problems with information: the development of a community database—the Violence Information Network. *Computers in Human Service*, **15**, 21–34.

Power, R. (2000). *Tangled WEB: tales of digital crime from the shadows of cyberspace.* Indianapolis: Que/Macmillan.

Quayle, E. and Taylor, M. (2002a). Child pornography and the Internet: perpetuating a cycle of abuse. *Deviant Behavior*, **23**, 331–62.

Quayle, E. and Taylor, M. (2002*b*). Paedophiles, pornography and the Internet: assessment issues. *British Journal of Social Work*, **32**, 863–75.

Quayle, E. and Taylor, M. (2003). Model of problematic Internet use in people with a sexual interest in children. *CyberPsychology & Behavior*, **6**, 93–106.

Rathmell, A. (October 1997). Cyber-terrorism: the shape of future conflict. *Royal United Service Institute Journal*.

Rice, R.E. (1993). Media appropriateness: using social presence theory to compare traditional and new organizational media. *Human Communication Research*, **19**, 451–84.

Rogers, M. (1999). *Psychology of hackers: steps toward a new taxonomy*. Available: *http://www.infowar.com*

Rubin, A.M. (1994). Media uses and effects: a uses-and-gratifications perspective. In J. Bryant and D. Zillmann (eds), *Media effects: advances in theory and research. LEA's communication series* (pp. 417–36). Hillsdale: Erlbaum.

Schneider, W. and Shiffrin, R.M. (1977). Controlled and automatic human information processing: I. Detection, search, and attention. *Psychological Review*, **84**, 1–66.

Sfiligoj, T.M. (2003). A comparison of stalkers and domestic violence batterers. *Journal of Psychological Practice*, **8**, 20–45.

Shaw, E., Post, J., and Roby, K. (1998). *Information terrorism and the dangerous insider*. Paper presented at the meeting of InfowarCon'98, Washington, DC.

Slater, M.D., Henry, K., Swaim, R.C., and Anderson, L.L. (2003). Violent media content and aggressiveness in adolescents: a downward spiral model. *Communication Research*, **30**, 713–36.

Spafford, E. (1997). Are hacker break-ins ethical? In Ermann, Williams, and Shauf (eds), *Computers, Ethics, and Society* (pp. 77–88). New York: Oxford.

Spears, R. and Lea, M. (1994). Panacea or panopticon? The hidden power in computer-mediated communication. *Communication Research*, **21**, 427–59.

Spitzberg, B.H. and Cupach, W.R. (2003). What mad pursuit? Obsessive relational intrusion and stalking related phenomena. *Aggression & Violent Behavior*, **8**, 345–75.

Stohl, M. (ed). (1988). *The politics of terrorism* (3rd edn). New York: Marcel Decker.

Tagg, L. (2001). *Aussie hacker jailed for sewage attacks*. Iafrica.com, 1 November. Available: *http://cooltech.iafrica.com/technews/archive/november/837110.htm*

Thompson, S. (2000) Suicide and the internet. *Psychiatric Bulletin*, **24**, 434.

Todorov, A. and Bargh, J.A. (2002). Automatic sources of aggression. *Aggression & Violent Behavior*, **7**, 53–68.

Tsfati, Y. and Weimann, G. (2002). www.terrorism.com: terror on the Internet. *Studies in Conflict & Terrorism*, **25**, 317–32.

Valkenburg, P.M. and Soeters, K.E. (2001). Children's positive and negative experiences with the Internet: an exploratory survey. *Communication Research*, **28**, 652–75.

Walther, J.B. (1992). Interpersonal effects in computer-mediated interaction: a relational perspective. *Communication Research*, **19**, 52–90.

Walther, J.B. (1994). Anticipated ongoing interaction versus channel effects on relational communication in computer-mediated interaction. *Human Communication Research*, **20**, 473–501.

Walther, J.B. (1996). Computer-mediated communication: impersonal, interpersonal, and hyperpersonal interaction. *Communication Research,* **23,** 3–43.

Walther, J.B., Anderson, J.F., and Park, D.W. (1994). Interpersonal effects in computer-mediated interaction: a meta-analysis of social and antisocial communication. *Communication Research,* **21,** 460–87.

Zimbardo, P.G. (1969). The hyman choice: individuation, reason, and order vs. individuation, impulse and chaos. In W.J. Arnold & D. Levine (eds), *Nebraska symposium on motivation* (pp. 237–307). Lincoln: University of Nebraska Press.

Chapter 8

You, me, and we: interpersonal processes in electronic groups

Katelyn McKenna and Gwendolyn
Seidman

Large vs. small, task-related vs. social, online vs. face-to-face—the way in which groups function and the effects of membership on the people within them have long been of interest to the academic researcher and layman alike. People are social animals. We largely define ourselves in terms of the social connections we form with others, and by the contrasts we make with those with whom we do not. We will develop feelings of affiliation based only on the most tenuous of connections—as Tajfel (1970) discovered to his initial dis-concertion when attempting to create a situation in which people do not develop a sense of group identity. It is not surprising, then, that a keyword search through the last 20 years of research in social psychology alone turns up some 26 300 articles focusing on groups and group behavior. The advent of a new form of communication—one mediated by computers—has thus understandably generated a flurry of speculation, theory, and research on its effects on groups and their members.

We know from research on traditional groups that there are some basic tenets and processes that apply to virtually all groups. We also know that groups can differ in a wide variety of ways, not only in terms of their size and purpose, but also in their character and functioning. Such is also the case for electronic groups. Although that may seem self-evident today, when electronic groups first arrived on the scene no such assumptions were made. If anything, the opposite was true.

Because computer-mediated communication was initially limited mainly to those within corporate settings,[1] early research focused on the effects of this

---

[1] E-mail and electronic bulletin boards (the predecessors of today's Usenet newsgroups and listservs) also existed but were available only to those few who had the computer skills and know-how to access them.

new medium within organizations and the workplace. In the 1980s (before the Internet *per se* existed) Sara Kiesler and her colleagues (e.g. Sproull & Kiesler, 1985) pioneered research in this area and generated influential theories about the nature and effects of interpersonal interaction conducted electronically, such as their 'limited bandwidth' model. According to this model, computer-mediated communication limits the 'bandwidth' of social communication because there is an absence of non-verbal features of communication (e.g. tone of voice, facial expressions) that have been found to be so influential and important in face-to-face communication. An environment that so reduces social cues, the model suggests, will produce an impoverished communication experience.

Then the 1990s arrived—with the 'age of the Internet'. No longer limited to the corporate world and those who were computer savvy, communication with others via computer was increasingly adopted by the population at large. Groups of all kinds sprung up online. Based on the theoretical models generated from observing electronic groups within the workplace, the initial assumption was that these models would apply to all electronic groups. That, however, turned out not to be the case.

Much of the research conducted in the 1990s was concerned with to what extent, if any, the theoretical assumptions made in the 1980s applied to the various kinds of groups now being observed. A second 'hot' issue concerned how online groups compared with face-to-face groups. The ways in which the qualities of Internet communication (e.g. anonymity, lack of physical cues) uniquely affect interpersonal and group processes were much researched. There was a strong emphasis on 'main effects' accounts in much of the research in the 1980s and 90s. A good example of this was the question 'does using the Internet make people lonely and depressed?'

Today, researchers have advanced beyond the stage of overly simplistic 'main effects' accounts. There is recognition of the fact that not all electronic groups function alike. There is a growing appreciation of the fact that the effects produced by the qualities of online communication depend on the interaction context, the way in which these qualities combine with one another (as well as with other factors), and the nature of the group itself. In other words, researchers have moved on to more sophisticated and complex analyses.

Our purpose here is to provide a discussion of the effects of participating in, and belonging to, electronic groups on the individual members and the group as a whole. In doing so, we hope to make clear that there are as few 'main effects' of communicating electronically as there are of communicating face to face. Online interactions can be as rich and as varied as traditional interactions; the processes that produce given outcomes can be as complex and multiply determined as those that occur in traditional interaction venues. Research is only beginning to demonstrate just how complex the 'online world' can be.

This chapter is organized into six sections. We begin with briefly defining what we mean by 'group' and then discuss some of the factors that influence, and processes that occur within, electronic and conventional groups alike. Next we discuss the qualities of communication that are unique to the Internet. We then turn to an examination of the different types of groups that exist online and the ways in which interpersonal effects of electronic interaction vary as a function of the social context. In the section that follows, we narrow our focus to discuss influential factors that may be operating at the individual level of membership. Finally, we examine the effects that electronic communication can have on dyadic relationships and broader social and community ties.

What is a group?

Before we can discuss how groups function, we must first answer the question, 'What is a group?' Within social psychology, the term 'group' has been viewed and defined in many different ways. For instance, some definitions suggest that a group is limited to a numerically small number of participants who all interact face to face with one another (e.g. Hogg, 1992). Others focus on the necessity of interdependence among the members (e.g. Cartwright & Zander, 1968). Still others assert that, for a collection of individuals to be considered a group, there must be strictly defined status and role relationships among those members, and norms and values that are distinct to that group as a whole and which serve to regulate the behavior of the individual members (e.g. Sherif & Sherif, 1953). For the purposes of this chapter, we are taking a page from Turner's (1982) conception of the social group and arguing that the perception of membership in some common social identity is sufficient for a group to exist. According to Turner's social identity model, it is the psychological state of 'the subjective sense of togetherness, we-ness, or belongingness' (1982, p. 16) that constitutes group formation, rather than the physical make-up of the group or other factors.

It is certainly the case that the other definitions above aptly encompass critical criteria for some groups (e.g. traditional face-to-face work groups in the case of Hogg) or for all groups (e.g. Sherif and Sherif's criteria of the development of shared norms and values). It is Turner's (1982) more inclusive model of social identity, however, that best seems to capture the essence of what 'groupness' means, as it applies equally to groups large and small, socially oriented and task-oriented, with members co-present and geographically separated, and that meet face to face and virtually (see McKenna & Green, 2002). Indeed, we would (and do) argue that romantic relationships also fall under the rubric of 'groups', not only because they meet Turner's definition of a group, but also because romantic dyads typically meet many of the important criteria for 'groupness' as defined by others (e.g. Cartwright & Zander, 1968; Sherif & Sherif, 1953). We, therefore, devote a section in this chapter to romantic relationships that form and develop over the Internet.

In summary, we define a group as consisting of two or more members who feel that they belong to a common social unit that has its own identity. The size and purpose of the social unit and the nature of the shared identity may vary dramatically between different groups. As is discussed later, the way groups function and the kinds of effects on members that are produced in groups depend to a large extent on the characteristics and type of the group in question, as well as other situational factors.

Group functioning online and off

Social interaction and group functioning on the Internet follow many of the same rules that govern socializing and group dynamics in traditional, face-to-face venues. As Spears and colleagues (Spears *et al.*, 2002) have argued, whether interactions take place in person or electronically, group processes and effects will evolve in much the same way. Theoretical models that were developed based on research on face-to-face groups (e.g. social identity theory, self-categorization theory, self-completion theory) have been tested and shown to also apply to online group behavior. Self-categorization theory (e.g. Turner, 1985; Turner *et al.*, 1987) for instance, posits that at different times and in different contexts we see ourselves as unique individuals and at other times as members of our groups. Gollwitzer and colleagues' self-completion theory (e.g. Gollwitzer, 1986; Wicklund & Gollwitzer, 1982) argues that people strive to make important aspects of their identity into a 'social reality'—that is, to have others notice and validate the identity-important aspect. Below, we touch on but a few of the processes and influential factors that apply to both electronic and non-electronic groups.

The emergence of (and conformity to) group norms

Early research and theory suggested that the reduction of social cues inherent in electronic communication, particularly when coupled with anonymity of the users, would result in the deindividuation of the participants. Kiesler and her colleagues (e.g. Kiesler *et al.*, 1984; Sproull & Kiesler, 1991) argued that the deindividuating nature of computer-mediated communication (CMC) produces an increase in hostility and aggression in exchanges between communication partners and a reduction in the usual inhibitions that one has when interacting with one's superiors. In other words, this sense of deindividuation would lead to anti-normative rather than normative behavior, to non-conformity rather than to conformity.

However, it is clear that norms do form within electronic groups, just as they do within face-to-face groups. Anarchy does not rule on the Internet. As with traditional groups, sometimes the rules or norms of an online group are explicitly stated, and sometimes they are implicit. Members of online groups rather quickly develop their own special paralangue (e.g. Spears & Lea, 1992) that is used in communication with the other group members and is differentiated from communication with outgroup members.

Many groups draw up stated rules of behavior and they develop means of censuring those who violate the stated norms of the group. For instance, there are moderated chatrooms, newsgroups, interactive websites, and listservs, many of which provide charters and guidelines of expected behavior (e.g. 'abusive language toward another member will not be tolerated', 'off-topic (OT) messages are not welcome and repeat violators will be banned from the group'). Should an individual member violate such explicit rules, he or she may receive a warning or, as in the example above, be banned from participation in the group. Implicit rules are those that are not stated in any kind of official document that has been drawn up by the group and to which a member can refer, but rather are unstated rules that must be gleaned through participation and the observation of other members' behavior in the group. In some cases the implicit rules of a group may, in essence, be much the same as those that are explicitly stated in other groups, as in the examples above; in others, they may be along the lines of good citizenship ('don't make a general nuisance of yourself') or they may be more subtle or capricious ('don't disagree with particular respected members of the group if you know what is good for you').

Violations of implicit rules within electronic groups are dealt with in much the same way as are such violations in traditional groups: the offending member may receive negative feedback from other members of the group, he or she may be publicly ostracized, or simply ignored (e.g. McKenna & Bargh, 1998; Williams *et al.*, 2002). Norms develop and evolve within particular groups, and what is considered normative behavior in one group may be quite different from that in another. Some groups may develop quite rigid expectations of behavior for members, while other groups embrace a 'free for all' mentality.

The social identity model of deindividuation (e.g. Spears & Lea, 1994) provides an alternative explanation for the 'anti-normative' behavior observed within some groups than that proposed by Kiesler and colleagues. From the perspective of social identity theory, proponents of this model (e.g. Reicher *et al.*, 1995; Spears *et al.*, 2002) have argued that electronic communication is not so much deindividuating as much as it is *depersonalizing*. They suggest that the decreased salience of personal accountability and identity makes group-level social identities all the more important. The real effect of CMC then is to *increase* conformity to those local group norms. Thus, whether the depersonalizing effect of CMC leads to more negative or more positive behavior relative to face-to-face interactions is said to depend on the content of those group norms (Postmes & Spears, 1998). An important component of this process is the extent to which the group identity is salient or important to the group members, as is discussed in more detail below.

The importance of group identity

In face-to-face groups and groups that form and function over the Internet, the degree to which the group identity is salient and the extent to which a member has incorporated the group identity into his or her self-concept are important mediators of the effects of group membership for the individual. Individuals typically feel themselves to be members of many different groups, and particular situations can make one's membership in one group versus the others more salient. Further, individuals incorporate some of their group identities into their self-concept to a greater extent than they do others. In other words, we consider our membership in some groups to be more self-defining and important to us than we do our membership in other groups. Thus, the extent to which a particular group identity is currently salient and the extent to which that identity is important to one's sense of 'this is who I am' are important mediators of the effects of group membership. Some examples of research that demonstrate the mediational role of salience and identity importance are discussed next.

Spears *et al.* (1990) found that when members of online groups interacted under anonymous conditions and group salience was high, normative behavior increased in those groups. In electronic groups in which members were anonymous but the salience of the group was low, there was significantly less conformity to the group norms. Again, however, there was no main effect of identity salience (or anonymity): whether group salience was high or low, participants who interacted under individuating conditions displayed an intermediate level of conformity to group norms. Thus, it is the way in which identity salience and anonymity (or lack thereof) interact that produces these outcomes.

Further attesting to the pivotal role that identity importance can play, Deaux (1996) has shown that an individual's behavior will be shaped by the opinions, values, goals, and so forth of the other group members only to the extent that group membership is important to the person's identity. When the group identity is highly important to an individual's sense of self, participation in the group can lead to powerful changes in the self, whether one is participating in a traditional group (Deaux, 1996) or in an Internet group (McKenna & Bargh, 1998).

The emergence of group leaders

In online groups and in face-to-face groups, as group membership becomes increasingly salient, members tend to become highly sensitive to prototypical characteristics of the group—that is, to the characteristics that distinguish that group from other groups. They also become sensitive to how they themselves, and other members, compare to that prototype. As the social identity theory of leadership (e.g. Hogg & Reid, 2001) suggests, when there is a high degree of overlap between an individual's characteristics (e.g. goals, values, attitude) and the group prototype, that individual is likely to emerge as a group leader. Research by Hogg (1992) and others has shown that people have a heightened awareness for even subtle differences in prototypicality among their fellow group members. They are able to clearly delineate which members most closely conform to the prototype (the leaders) and which fit the mold to a lesser degree (the followers). In other words, group leaders are those individuals who seem to best embody the behaviors and norms to which the other group members are attempting to adhere.

We tend to think of leaders as not only embodying the group prototype, but also as individuals who actively influence the behaviors of the other group members. In the case of established groups that is certainly the case. Perhaps surprisingly, however, such is not the case when it comes to newly formed groups. In new groups, individuals who best fit the prototype do emerge as leaders, but not because they are actually exerting any influence over the group. Rather, they are perceived (by the other group members) to be exerting an influence over the less prototypical members. In reality, however, it is the prototype (that the leader happens to most closely fit) that is exercising the influence (e.g. Hogg & Reid, 2001).

We would expect that the social identity theory of leadership would apply even more strongly in electronic groups than in face-to-face groups. Why? Factors that have been shown to be quite influential in determining who will be seen as best fitting the group prototype, such as physical appearance and interpersonal dominance, are not generally in operation in online interactions. In face-to-face groups, the individual who most closely fits the goals, values, and ideals of the group might still be dismissed as a potential leader by other members because biasing factors such as the prospective leader's age, physical attractiveness, and race may be playing a role in their assessment. Age and race are often counter-prototypical features and people are often not aware (and would be shocked to discover) that such factors are negatively affecting their judgments about someone (see Bargh, 1989; Brewer, 1988). Because such factors are not generally in evidence in online groups, they would not play an influential role and thus would not hinder the most proto-typical individual's rise to leadership.

Et tu Brute?

Online groups are just as vulnerable to friction from within as are groups existing in traditional venues. Indeed, early research on computer-mediated interaction (e.g. Kiesler *et al.*, 1984) indicated that the qualities of the communication media, such as anonymity and the lack of physical presence, produce far greater friction and hostility within online groups than is found in face-to-face groups. However, more recent meta-analytic reviews of the litera-ture have concluded that CMC does not, in fact, generally produce these heightened effects (e.g. Postmes & Spears, 1998; Walther *et al.*, 1994). Along these lines, Straus (1997) conducted a study comparing 36 CMC and 36 face-to-face work groups, composed of three members each, and found that 'the incidence of personal attacks in groups in either communication mode was exceedingly small and was not associated with cohesiveness or satisfaction, suggesting further that the impact of this behavior was trivial' (p. 255).

As a general rule, and one that applies to both face-to-face and electronic groups, smaller groups tend to be more cohesive than do larger groups. As groups grow in size, cliques are likely to develop and to then conflict and com-pete with the larger group and other cliques within the group (e.g. Bass, 1980). Take, as an example, the two major political parties in the U.S. Members of the Democratic and Republican parties are generally united in terms of the overarch-ing goals, beliefs, and values of their respective parties. There are factions within each party, however, that strongly disagree about how those goals should best be achieved, on subsidiary issues, and so forth. Should the conflicts become too entrenched and acrimonious over time, these smaller cliques are likely to splinter away from the larger group to form a group of their own (e.g. the Green Party largely comprises those dissatisfied with the Democratic Party; and the Reform Party, unhappy Republicans). A look at the history of some of the more popular Internet usenet newsgroups shows that they have followed this pattern as well, with flame-wars developing between cliques and the larger group and dis-satisfied subsets eventually splintering off to form separate but related groups.

External influences

As are traditional groups, electronic groups can also be affected by external pressures and factors. For instance, if the local bowling alley closes, then the members of the bowling league who play there will have to seek out another venue to meet and play, perhaps with a loss of old and a gain of new members (which may cause other changes in the dynamics of the group) or, should no other venue be available, simply dissolve. In the same way, electronic groups can lose their established meeting places due to server difficulties, website closures, and so forth. Unmoderated usenet newsgroups have been overrun with SPAM (off-topic advertisements), disrupting the sense of community in many of the groups and causing some previously vibrant forums to be abandoned entirely by the legitimate members.

Online versus traditional interaction

Although many of the social processes do unfold over the Internet in the same way as they do in face-to-face situations, there are also aspects of electronic communication that can and do produce new and different psychological and social effects. The comparison between qualities of face-to-face and electronic interaction and the resulting effects these differences may bring about have been discussed extensively elsewhere (e.g. McKenna & Bargh, 2000; McKenna *et al.*, 2002; Spears *et al.*, 2002). Therefore, we provide only a brief discussion of these differences below. In the following sections, we will revisit the unique qualities of electronic interaction to examine the ways in which they often interact with one another and with other situational, interpersonal, and individual differences to produce quite distinct results within the online environment itself.

Anonymity versus nonymity

One of the major differences between online and face-to-face interaction is the ability to engage in anonymous interaction with others should one so choose. Through popular service providers such as America On-Line and Hotmail, people can elect to communicate with others anonymously (i.e. with their true identity hidden). It is certainly rare for us to develop feelings of closeness and intimacy with those we meet in face-to-face environments while retaining our anonymity. On the Internet, however, close relationships can and do emerge between participants who, at least at the time such feelings begin to develop, are wholly anonymous to one another (e.g. McKenna *et al.*, 2002; Parks & Floyd, 1995; Walther, 1996).

Intimately linked with anonymity is the issue of identifiability. In our face-to-face lives we frequently, and often repeatedly, interact with others (e.g. the waiter in a favorite café, the woman who daily walks her dog in a similarly frequented area) to whom we do not reveal our names, occupations, place of residence, and so forth. Yet, these anonymous face-to-face contacts may well be able to easily recognize us in a different setting or pick us out in a police line-up. We do sometimes engage in what Zick Rubin (1975) termed the 'strangers on a train' phenomenon (sharing quite intimate details with an anonymous seat-mate about ourselves and our lives of which not even our closest friends and relations are aware). However, for the very reason that we are identifiable, such in-person disclosures are generally made only to those we expect to never see again.

In contrast, even when people interact nonymously on the Internet (i.e. using their true names; providing information about their profession, their home town, and so forth), they often still feel relatively anonymous or non-identifiable (McKenna & Bargh, 2000; McKenna *et al.*, 2002). Under such conditions, they often engage in the 'strangers on the Internet' phenomenon, in which they disclose quite intimate information to others whom they have a reasonable expectation of encountering online again. Such disclosures can thus lay the foundation for a continuing and close relationship.

As mentioned previously, when participants interact under anonymous and non-identifiable conditions online, even greater conformity to group norms can emerge than occurs in interactions that take place face to face (e.g. Spears *et al.*, 2002). Further, the ability to interact anonymously allows people to join groups and explore aspects of self on the Internet that, because of embarrassment or fears of rejection, they might otherwise not have dared to explore within their physical communities (e.g. Davison *et al.*, 2000; McKenna & Bargh, 1998; McKenna *et al.*, 2002).

Presence or absence of gating features

Physical appearance and mannerisms play an incredibly important role not only in impression formation, but also in determining whom we will approach and, of those whom we do approach, with whom we will develop friendships and romantic relationships (e.g. Hatfield & Sprecher, 1986). We tend to immediately and nonconsciously categorize others based on physically available features (e.g. their ethnicity, attractiveness, age) (Bargh, 1989; Brewer, 1988). For instance, research on zero-acquaintanceships (i.e. when the only information we have about another person is their physical appearance) has shown that there is extremely high consensus in impression formation, across a wide variety of measurements, based solely on physical appearance (e.g. Allbright *et al.*, 1988). In these studies, participants were shown photographs (generally taken from high school yearbooks) of people they had never met and, based only on the picture, asked about the qualities and characteristics they believed that person to possess.

Furthermore, research has shown that initial impressions are difficult to overcome (e.g. Fiske & Taylor, 1991). In subsequent interactions, people tend to selectively focus on information that confirms rather than disconfirms one's initial judgment (e.g. Higgins & Bargh, 1987). Thus, readily discernable features such as physical appearance (attractiveness), an apparent stigma (e.g. stuttering), or apparent shyness or social anxiety often serve as gates in our face-to-face interactions—opening to allow the more physically attractive and outgoing into our social or romantic circles and closing when we encounter the less socially skilled or physically attractive.

When interactions with new online acquaintances take place online in newsgroups, listservs, chatrooms, and so forth, such features are not usually in evidence initially, and thus do not serve as a barrier to potential relationships. Instead, impressions are formed on the basis of the opinions expressed and the information about the self that is revealed, rather than on more superficial physical features. However, to the extent that such features are in evidence initially (for example, online dating services such as Match.com provide member profiles with an accompanying picture), then the same biases that operate in our face-to-face lives will come into play and we are likely to similarly bypass or reject out of hand from the outset potentially satisfactory and mutually profitable relationships.

The degree of control over the interaction

Online interactions, as compared to those that take place face-to-face and on the telephone, provide participants with more control over how and when they will respond, how they present themselves, and the degree to which they can 'have their say'. When talking in person or on the telephone, communication norms dictate that one responds immediately and 'off the cuff'. Norms also dictate that we communicate in short reciprocal bursts rather than engaging in long soliloquies, and we often interrupt or talk over one another.

In contrast, we generally (although not always, as is discussed in the next section) expect there to be delays in receiving responses back from our online interaction partners. When we send an e-mail we generally do not know when the other party will check his or her mail, and we understand that he or she may not have time to respond immediately upon receiving it. When he or she does respond, there is the option of saying as much or as little on the subject at hand without fear of interruption. Chatting online more closely approximates the conventions of spoken interaction, but nonetheless there is an awareness that it takes time to type in a response (and some of us type more slowly than others). Interaction partners, therefore, have more time to prepare and plan what they wish to say, they can edit responses before sending them, and so forth. In other words, they have greater control over how they wish to present themselves and their ideas and opinions to others than generally occurs in face-to-face or telephone exchanges.

Is there a kindred spirit in the house?

Identifying others who share a particular interest of ours can also be easier on the Internet than in our physical communities. Neighbors do not generally put signs in their front gardens proclaiming their interests, but they may well put up a personal web page on the Internet doing just that. We may be aware of groups that meet and share our interests within our community but may not have the time or means to attend those get-togethers. Online, participation in interest groups can often take place at any time that it is convenient for the individual members, thus allowing those connections to be made. The Internet can be particularly useful for locating others who share very specialized interests (such as butterfly collecting) or who share aspects of identity that are socially sanctioned and thus are often not readily identifiable in one's physical community.

The nature of the electronic group

The different qualities of computer-mediated communication can produce different outcomes than those that result from face-to-face communication. However, it is not the case that the unique features of the Internet produce one globally applicable outcome and face-to-face communication another. Rather, the kinds of effects on members that are produced in groups, electronic or face to face, depend to a large extent on the characteristics and type of the group in question. In other words, the various features of communication will interact with the character and purpose of the group; the interpersonal effects of electronic interaction will vary as a function of the social context.

Getting down to business

Organizational groups, whether conducted online or face to face, differ in many ways from groups that have a more social purpose. Within social settings online, features of electronic communications (such as anonymity, the lack of physical presence, and the ability to exercise greater control over one's side of the exchange) can lead to greater self-disclosure and feelings of closeness. Within the business setting, these same features can lead to the opposite result: research has shown them to produce greater distrust between parties when it comes to negotiations.

Thompson and colleagues (see Thompson & Nadler, 2002 for a review) have conducted an extensive program of research on electronic negotiations. They argue that the main problem with 'e-gotiation' is that the participants make implicit assumptions about the time delays that occur in hearing back from their opponents. The motivations that negotiation partners attribute to such delays are quite different from the motivations that are assumed to be behind such delays in social settings. For instance, in a negotiation situation, people tend to assume that the other party will receive and read an e-mail just as soon as it has been sent. They therefore expect an immediate response and tend to attribute any delays in receiving a response to stalling, power-plays, or disrespect by the other party. As a result, their exchanges can become acrimonious and they are less likely to reach a satisfactory agreement.

In other work-related settings, however, electronic communication can function in much the same way, and as effectively, as does face-to-face communication. For instance, a U.S. national survey of college students (Cummings *et al.*, 2002*a*) found that e-mail was considered as useful as face-to-face interactions for getting work done and building school-related relationships.

The quilting bee

Surprisingly, the least researched kind of group, both online and off, is perhaps the most common. The majority of group-related research has focused on business or organizational groups (as discussed above), political, civic, or community-at-large groups, highly specialized or stigmatized groups, or support groups (discussed below). The run of the mill knitting circle, 'Mommy and me', chess club, 'a bunch of good friends just hanging out', and the like have but rarely been the sole focus of research. Such mainstream and innocuous groups have mainly been studied as the foil to more specialized and less mundane types of groups.

One line of research specifically focusing on such mainstream groups concerns the distinction between common bond and common identity groups. In common bond groups (such as among a group of friends), attachment to the group is based on the bonds that exist between the group members; in common identity groups (such as a sports team) attachment to the group is based on identification with the group as a whole (i.e. its purpose and goals) rather than on bonds between individual members (see Prentice *et al.*, 1994). Prentice and her colleagues examined traditional groups that fell into these two categories, and Sassenberg (2002) has examined equivalent groups on the Internet. Results from the studies in these two different communication venues dovetail: in common identity groups, as compared to common bond groups, there is greater adherence to group norms, indicating that the former have a greater impact on individual members' behavior. Thus, the kind of group to which one belongs (online or offline) matters. As is discussed next, when the common identity is a stigmatized one, even further distinctions can be made.

Stigmatized groups

For those with socially stigmatized aspects of identity, participation in an electronic group devoted to that identity aspect can prove to be particularly beneficial for the individual. Because of the embarrassing or socially sanctioned nature of the identity, finding others who share that interest in one's everyday life can be quite difficult. Through the Internet, however, one can locate others who share that interest. The protective cloak of anonymity allows people to share these aspects of self online with far fewer costs and risks to their everyday social life. As there is no equivalent 'offline' group, membership and participation in a relevant virtual group can become an important part of one's social life and can have powerful effects on one's sense of self and identity.

In line with, and extending, the findings of Prentice *et al.* (1994) and Sassenberg (2002) discussed above, are the results of a study comparing mainstream and socially stigmatized common identity groups on the Internet. McKenna and Bargh (1998, Study 1) reasoned that people with stigmatized and concealable social identities (see Frable, 1993; Jones *et al.*, 1984), such as homosexuality or fringe ideological beliefs, would be more responsive to the feedback they received from other group members than would individuals taking part in non-marginalized groups. In other words, the norms of such groups should exert a stronger than usual influence over members' behavior. These members should be motivated to behave in such a way as to gain acceptance and positive evaluation from their fellow group members. This prediction was confirmed by an archival and observational study of the frequency with which members posted messages to (i.e. participated in) the group: compared to the mainstream Internet groups, within the stigmatized identity groups, participation significantly increased when there was positive feedback from the other group members, and decreased following negative feedback.

Further, according to Deaux's (1996) model of social identity, active participation in a stigmatized-identity group should, because of the importance of that identity, lead to the incorporation of the virtual group membership into the self. Individuals then tend to be motivated to make this important and new aspect of self into a social reality (e.g. Gollwitzer, 1986) by sharing it with important others. In line with this are the results of structural equation modeling analyses of survey responses across two replications of quite different types of socially stigmatized identities (McKenna & Bargh, 1998, Studies 2 & 3). The average respondent was in his or her mid-30s, and many of them, as a direct result of their Internet group participation, had come out to their family and friends about this stigmatized aspect of themselves for the first time in their lives. They benefited from increased self-acceptance and felt less socially isolated and different. Such results support the view that membership and participation in Internet groups can have powerful effects on one's self and identity.

Support groups

Similarly, a study of online support provision for those with grave illnesses (Davison *et al.*, 2000) found that people used Internet support groups particularly for embarrassing, stigmatized illnesses such as AIDS, alcoholism, and prostate cancer, because of the relative anonymity of the online community. The authors point out that these patients feel anxiety and uncertainty and are thus highly motivated by social comparison needs to seek out others with the same illness. When the illness is an embarrassing, disfiguring, or otherwise stigmatized one, they are more likely to seek support online because of the anonymity afforded by Internet groups.

However, online support groups that focus on non-stigmatized illness can also be quite beneficial to their members. McKay *et al.* (2002) studied those who participated in diabetes self-management and peer support over the Internet. These participants experienced the same improvements in physiologic, behavioral and mental health, and in dietary control as did those participating in conventional diabetes management programs. Another study of diabetics (Barrera *et al.*, 2002) found that those assigned to participate in online diabetes support groups felt that they had received more support, in general, than did those asked to use the Internet only to gather information about their illness (and to thus rely only on their offline social network for support). Greater participation in community support websites for the elderly, such as SeniorNet, is associated with lower perceived life stress (Wright, 2000). Similarly, participation in an online support group for the hearing impaired was particularly beneficial for participants with little 'real world' support (Cummings *et al.*, 2002b).

One of the interesting findings of the Cummings *et al.* (2002b) study, was the fact that many of the hearing-impaired participants had family members and friends from their offline network also taking part in the online support group. In other words, there was a blending of online and offline support. How such a combination of support affects members is a new and exciting area for future research.

Old friends well met

Much of the research conducted on the effects of online interaction within social settings has focused on people's interactions with those whom they get to know over the Internet (e.g. in chatrooms, newsgroups, online games).

However, many Internet users interact online mainly, or even solely, with those whom they initially became acquainted with in person. For instance, a study of California adolescents (Gross *et al.*, 2002) found that they spend the majority of their online time chatting with friends from school. Similarly, a study conducted by the Pew Internet and American Life Project (2002) found that university students interact online mainly with family members, friends from high school, and friends they've met in college.

Qualities of online communication that can affect the formation and development of new relationships, such as anonymity and the lack of traditional gating features, are not in operation when old friends interact online. Impressions have already been formed and the participants may well share a long and rich history. We can thus expect that there will be some different outcomes from these kinds of interactions than from interactions and relationships that form with new people met within online environments. Research into the ways in which existing relationships function and evolve over the Internet and the effects of such online communication on these relationships is just beginning. The dearth of research thus far in this area is not because researchers find these relationships less interesting or important than those that develop initially over the Internet, but rather is a function of a more practical reason. Until a few short years ago, it was rare that many of an Internet user's existing family and friends would also be online, and thus the people most often encountered on the Internet tended to be new acquaintances. As more and more of the population has 'gotten connected', the effects of communicating online with existing relationships have become an increasingly important area of research.

The me within the we

Individuals influence the groups in which they participate and are in turn influenced by the group. In addition to (and interacting with) the social context, particular aspects of the Internet environment interact with the goals, motivations, and personal characteristics of the individuals involved, producing effects on psychological and interpersonal outcomes.

Individual motivations of members

According to classical motivation theorists such as Lewin (1951) and Atkinson (e.g. Atkinson & Birch, 1970), all behavior is motivated in some way and one engages in particular behaviors in order to further a desired end. Motivations are enduring and pan-situational and they find expression through situationally appropriate goals. Different motives and goals may underlie the same surface behavior. For instance, someone may join and participate in an illness support group online with the goal of gathering more information about the illness. Another individual might participate in the same group in order to gain social support. The social and psychological consequences of participation in this group may thus be quite different for these two individuals, despite the fact that they are engaging in the same kinds of activities online (see McKenna & Bargh, 1999; McKenna et al., 2001).

A person's motivations and goals for using the Internet will determine how he or she generally uses the available resources online. The goals of individual group members can interact not only with the Internet communication situation to produce social and psychological effects for that individual, but can also affect the processes and functioning of the group as a whole.

Further, similar outcomes may result from different underlying motivational processes. For instance, as mentioned previously, when anonymity is coupled with high group salience, the outcome is increased adherence to the group norms. Greater conformity to group norms can also occur, however, when participants are identifiable if certain self-presentational motivations (e.g. to make a positive impression) are in operation (e.g. Barreto & Ellemers, 2000; Douglas & McGarty, 2001).

What self am I presenting?

People express different versions of self, both on the Internet and in traditional interaction settings, depending on the context. Different social settings (e.g. a business meeting, a family cook-out) will bring to the fore certain aspects of self while inhibiting others. We also tend to incorporate important group identities (e.g. Deaux, 1996; Tajfel & Turner, 1986) and important close relationships (e.g. Baldwin, 1997; Chen & Andersen, 1999) into our sense of self. The particular aspects of self, as well as the goals, behaviors, and so forth that we associate with those important identities and relationships can then become situationally activated and expressed. Indeed, as Andersen and colleagues have shown (see Andersen & Chen, 2002 for a review), these relational aspects of self do not just become activated when we are with these important others, but also when these important mental representations or associations are brought to mind. For instance, if we encounter someone who reminds us of our sister, the goals we have in terms of our relationship with our sister, the self-attributes we generally feel and express around her, and even the ways in which we behave around her, may not just become activated in memory but may also be acted out, without our even being aware of it, in this new situation and with this other person.

Moreover, one's sense of self is not just made up of the various attributes and goals that one currently possesses and expresses to others. As Markus and

Nurius (1986) argue, the potential or possible selves that we feel we could become are also included in our sense of who we are. Higgins (1987) has shown that the 'ought' self (made up of the attributes a person feels obligated to possess) and the 'ideal' self (containing those characteristics an individual strives to possess) can also serve as important self-guides to one's behavior in the present. In other words, an individual has alternative senses of him or herself that are distinct from the public or 'actual' self generally presented to others.

How do the way in which we present ourselves in different contexts, the particular aspects of self and relational goals that become activated and expressed, and the attributes and goals we have that serve to guide our behavior relate to group processes and group dynamics? In particular, what does this have to do with our discussion of online groups? Quite a lot, it turns out. First, it is important to remember that groups are composed of individuals, and processes that are operating on the individual level will in turn affect the group. Secondly, as is discussed in more detail below, research has shown that the unique qualities of computer-mediated communication bring forth different, generally unexpressed, and important (to the individual) aspects of self than occurs in traditional interaction settings. These different aspects of self that become accessible and expressed online affect the formation and development of the dyadic relationships one forms in that venue and one's sense of group identity in significant ways.

As Turkle (1995) pointed out, the Internet is a prime venue for the exploration and experimentation with different versions of self. The particular version of self that the typical person will be most motivated to express and explore over the Internet with new interaction partners is that of his or her 'true' self. Rogers (1951) defined the true self as those inner qualities and aspects of identity and personality a person possesses but which he or she is not able to easily express in everyday (face-to-face) interactions. Importantly, these are aspects of self which the individual would very much like to be able to express to others.

In support of this contention, Bargh *et al.* (2002, Experiment 1) found that the average person's true self-concept becomes more activated and accessible than his or her actual self-concept (the aspects of self one typically expresses in daily life) during an online interaction with a new acquaintance, whereas the reverse is true during face-to-face interactions. In this study, when participants first arrived at the lab, each listed five traits or other characteristics that they believed they actually possessed and readily expressed to others in social settings (the *actual self* measure) and, separately, five traits that they believed they possessed and would like to be able to express but were not usually able to in most social settings (the *true self* measure). They were then randomly assigned to interact with another participant either face-to-face or in an Internet chatroom. Participants who had just interacted with a new acquaintance online responded significantly faster to true self-descriptors in a reaction-time task than did those who had interacted with a new acquaintance face to face. A second experiment (Bargh, McKenna, & Fitzsimons, 2002) ruled out the possibility that the observed effect was the result of *strategic* self-presentation in the one venue versus the other. When participants were led to believe that they were about to engage in an interaction with another participant online or face to face, true self qualities were equally inhibited for those expecting to interact online as for those expecting to interact face to face.

As it turns out, not only do electronic interactions with new others more readily bring forth aspects of a person's true self, but these aspects are also perceived more by one's new interaction partners over the Internet than face to face (Bargh *et al.*, 2002, Experiment 3). As is discussed next, the expression and validation of one's true self over the Internet has important implications for an individual's sense of self and for relationships. Again, however, the expression of different kinds of selves (e.g. possible selves, the ideal self, the true self) will interact with the individual's motivations or goals, with individual differences in personality, and with the social context, to produce different outcomes. For instance, those who are socially anxious and those who are lonely are more likely than those who are gregarious to feel that they are better able to express important aspects of the true self over the Internet than they can in face-to-face situations. When interacting online with friends whom we initially met offline, our actual self qualities still prevail (McKenna *et al.*, 2004).

Yours, mine, and ours

Relationship formation

Relationships can and do form over the Internet, and these relationships can become quite close (e.g. McKenna *et al.*, 2002; Parks & Floyd, 1995). Critically important to whether or not close relationships will form online, however, is the extent to which an individual feels better able to express his or her true or inner self online than in traditional interaction settings. McKenna *et al.* (2002) tested this prediction through structural equation modeling analyses of survey responses provided by hundreds of randomly selected Internet newsgroup members. The critical mediator of whether an individual would form close Internet relationships was his or her responses to a 'real me' scale (see Bargh *et al.*, 2002). This scale measured whether or not the participant felt better able to express aspects of self and personality in Internet interactions than in his or her offline social life. Compared to those who reported feeling more their true, inner self in traditional social settings, those who felt they expressed more of the 'real me' on the Internet were significantly more likely to have formed close, intimate relationships there and to have taken steps to integrate those online friends and romantic partners into their face-to-face interaction world. And, as a two-year follow-up study showed, these close Internet relationships turned out to be remarkably stable and durable over time.

Another important ingredient for the formation of close relationships over the Internet is the tendency to engage in greater self-disclosure there. Anonymity, connecting with similar others, and interacting in the physical absence of one's communication partner can produce this heightened disclosure tendency. The fact that people tend to more readily engage in acts of self-disclosure on the Internet has been well-documented (e.g. Joinson, 2001; Levine, 2000; Walther, 1996). According to a number of theorists (e.g. Derlega et al., 1993; Laurenceau et al., 1998), self-disclosure is important to the development of closeness and intimacy, as it entails being able to express and have accepted one's inner or true feelings and personality. Situation-appropriate self-disclosure breeds feelings of liking between communicants: we tend to like those to whom we self-disclose, to like those who disclose to us, and to disclose more to those we like (e.g. Collins & Miller, 1994). Early self-disclosure should lead to faster relationship development.

McKenna et al. (2002, Study 3) tested this premise in a laboratory experiment. Undergraduates were randomly assigned (in cross-sex pairs) to meet one another for the first time in an Internet chatroom or face to face. In line with predictions, those who met online both liked each other more and felt that they had gotten to know one another better than did those who interacted face to face. This effect held when participants met one another twice, once in person and once over the Internet, unaware that it was the same interaction partner in both situations. There was a significant correlation between the degree of liking for the partner and how well the participant felt he or she had gotten to know the other person for those who met over the Internet. However, there was no such correlation in the face-to-face condition. Along similar lines, Walther (1996, 1997) found that new acquaintances can achieve greater intimacy through online communication than they do in parallel face-to-face interactions.

To summarize, the average person's true self tends to become more accessible when interacting with new acquaintances on the Internet, his or her inner qualities are more readily perceived by online partners, and the Internet facilitates this greater liking for others. Yet, not everyone who uses the Internet forms close and intimate relationships with online acquaintances. Other factors, such as the way in which an individual uses the Internet, play an important role in determining whether one will form an online relationship. For instance, we would not expect new and important online relationships to develop for people who mainly use the Internet to interact with existing family and friends and only rarely, or sporadically, with people they meet online. It may depend on whether an individual becomes cognizant that he or she is expressing the true self more with others on the Internet than in his or her face-to-face interactions. The degree of felt discrepancy between one's inner and actual self (e.g. Horney, 1946; Rogers, 1951) and the extent to which the true self serves as an important self-guide to one's behavior (e.g. Higgins, 1987) may also be important moderators.

Family and community ties

Although early research seemed to indicate that Internet use may be detrimental to the everyday social fabric of family and community life (Kraut *et al.*, 1998; Nie & Erbring, 2000), subsequent research has reached the opposite conclusion. A number of national surveys have found that Internet users are just as likely as non-users to visit or call friends on the phone, or that Internet users actually have the larger social networks (see DiMaggio *et al.*, 2001). For instance, Howard *et al.* (2001) found. from a large random-sample survey. that the Internet enables people to keep in touch with family and friends and to even extend their social networks. The researchers note, 'A sizeable majority of those who email relatives say it increases the level of communication between family members . . . these survey results suggest that online tools are more likely to extend social contact than detract from it' (p. 399). Wellman *et al.* (2001) concluded that heavy users of the Internet do not use e-mail as a substitute for face-to-face and telephone contact, but instead use it to maintain longer distance relationships. Kraut and colleagues (Kraut *et al.*, 2002) found that those who use the Internet more also engage in more face-to-face and telephone contact with their family and friends than do lighter users. Thus, the effect of Internet use on one's immediate and extended social network seems to be to strengthen those ties and to increase contact, not only electronically but also face to face and by telephone.

Those who use the Internet more also tend to be more involved in their physical communities. A longitudinal study by Kraut *et al.* (2002) found that greater Internet use was associated with increased civic involvement, compared to baseline. Along similar lines, a random national survey by Katz *et al.* (2001) found that Internet users who spend more time online were also more likely to belong to offline religious, leisure, and community organizations, compared to non-users. There were no differences between Internet users and non-users in this study as far as awareness of and knowledge about one's neighbors. Similarly, a study of Californian teenagers (Gross *et al.*, 2002) found that even teenagers who used the Internet regularly continued to spend most of their after-school time on traditional activities, many of which involved peer interaction (e.g. participating in clubs or sports, hanging out with friends).

A 1998 survey of nearly 40 000 visitors to the National Geographic website found that heavy Internet use was associated with greater levels of participation in voluntary organizations and politics (Wellman *et al.*, 2001). Finally, based on evidence from the Blacksburg (VA) Electronic Village study, Kavanaugh and Patterson (2001) concluded that 'the longer people are on the Internet, the more likely they are to use the Internet to engage in social-capital-building activities' (p. 507). Thus, it does not appear that people are turning to participation in electronic communities at the expense of their involvement in their physical communities. If anything, Internet use appears to be bolstering real world community involvement.

Conclusions

Over time, the assessment of the effects of engaging in computer-mediated communication has changed and evolved. Theoretical premises have been revised and refined, new theories and models have been developed and tested, and analyses have become more sophisticated and complex. Advances within the structure and capabilities of the medium itself (e.g. the introduction of user-friendly browsers, instant messaging, and digital cameras) have changed the way people use the Internet and necessitated re-evaluations of some prior assumptions. Changes in the online population have also forced us to re-examine previous findings and spurred new research. As electronic communication has become a feature of everyday life, people have adapted to it—and adapted it to fit their needs. Researchers have adapted right along with them.

People are complex, social creatures. There are few universal truths when it comes to our interactions and relationships with others, whether those interactions take place in person or electronically. The Internet has unique, even transformational qualities as a means of communication, but there is often greater ambiguity surrounding the interactions that take place online. The desires and goals that an individual brings to the interaction and the goals he or she holds regarding the communication partner(s) make a dramatic difference in the assumptions and attributions made in the face of that ambiguity.

Not all interaction situations are alike. The online and the offline social spheres in which individuals move are various and many, as are the outcomes that can be produced by them. The individual differences of the users often interact with the social situation, as well as with the unique features of electronic (or face-to-face) communication, to produce different outcomes. The online and the offline world are becoming increasingly blended, with our face-to-face friends and family members also interacting with us online and our virtually initiated friendships being brought into our face-to-face lives. Researchers can expect that more theoretical shifts and insights will undoubtedly be on the way, as these communication spheres continue to meld and ever newer communication advances get thrown into the mix.

References

Allbright, L., Kenny, D.A., and Malloy, T.E. (1988). Consensus in personality judgments at zero acquaintance. *Journal of Personality & Social Psychology*, **55**, 387–95.

Andersen, S.M. and Chen, S. (2002). The relational self: an interpersonal social-cognitive theory. *Psychological Review*, **109**, 619–45.

Atkinson, J.W. and Birch, D. (1970). *The dynamics of action.* New York: Wiley.

Baldwin, M.W. (1997). Relational schemas as a source of if-then self-inference procedures. *Review of General Psychology*, **1**, 326–35.

Bargh, J.A. (1989). Conditional automaticity: varieties of automatic influence in social perception and cognition. In J.S. Uleman and J.A. Bargh (eds), *Unintended thought* (pp. 3–51). New York: Guilford Press.

Bargh, J.A., Fitzsimons, G.M., and McKenna, K.Y.A. (2002). The self, online. In S. Spencer and S. Fein (eds), *Motivated social perception: the 9th Ontario Symposium on Social Cognition* (pp. 195–214). Mahwah, NJ: Erlbaum.

Bargh, J.A., McKenna, K.Y.A., and Fitzsimons, G.M. (2002). Can you see the real me? Activation and expression of the 'true self' on the Internet. *Journal of Social Issues*, **58**, 33–48.

Barrera, M., Jr., Glasgow, R.E., McKay, H.G., Boles, S.M., and Feil, E.G. (2002). Do Internet-based support interventions change perceptions of social support? An experimental trial of approaches for supporting diabetes self-management. *American Journal of Community Psychology*, **30**, 637–54.

Barreto, M. and Ellemers, N. (2000). You can't always do what you want: social identity and self-presentational determinants of the choice to work for a low-status group. *Personality and Social Psychology Bulletin*, **26**, 891–906.

Bass, B.M. (1980). *Stogdill's handbook of leadership.* New York: Free Press.

Brewer, M.B. (1988). A dual process model of impression formation. In T.K. Srull and R.S., Wyer, Jr. (eds), *A dual process model of impression formation: advances in social cognition, Vol. 1*, (pp. 1–36). Hillsdale, NJ: Erlbaum.

Cartwright, D. and Zander, A. (1968). *Group dynamics: research and theory.* New York: Harper & Row.

Chen, S. and Andersen, S.M. (1999). Relationships from the past in the present: significant-other representations and transference in interpersonal life. *Advances in Experimental Social Psychology*, **31**, 123–90.

Collins, N.L. and Miller, L.C. (1994). Self-disclosure and liking: a meta-analytic review. *Psychological Bulletin*, **116**, 457–75.

Cummings, J.N., Butler, B., and Kraut, R. (2002). The quality of online socialrelationships. *Communications of the ACM*, **45**, 103–8.

Cummings, J., Sproull, L., and Kiesler, S. (2002). Beyond hearing: where real world and online support meet. *Group Dynamics: Theory, Research, and Practice*, **6**, 78–88.

Davison, K.P., Pennebaker, J.W., and Dickerson, S.S. (2000). Who talks? The social psychology of illness support groups. *American Psychologist*, **55**, 205–17.

Deaux, K. (1996). Social identification. In E.T. Higgins and A.W. Kruglanski (eds), *Social psychology: handbook of basic principles* (pp. 777–98). New York: Guilford Press.

Derlega, V.L., Metts, S., Petronio, S., and Margulis, S.T. (1993). *Self-disclosure.* London: Sage.

DiMaggio, P., Hargittai, E., Neuman, W.R., and Robinson, J.P. (2001). Social implications of the internet. *Annual Review of Sociology*, **27**, 307–36.

Douglas, K.M. and McGarty, C. (2001). Identifiability and self-presentation: computer-mediated communication and intergroup interaction. *British Journal of Social Psychology*, **40**, 399–416.

Fiske, S.T. and Taylor, S.E. (1991). *Social cognition* (2nd edn). New York: Scott, Foresman.

Frable, D.E.S. (1993). Being and feeling unique: statistical deviance and psychological marginality. *Journal of Personality*, **61**, 85–110.

Gollwitzer, P.M. (1986). Striving for specific identities: the social reality of self-symbolizing. In R. Baumeister (ed), *Public self and private self* (pp. 143–59). New York: Springer.

Gross, E.F., Juvonen, J., and Gable, S.L. (2002). Internet use and well-being in adolescence. *Journal of Social Issues*, **58**, 75–90.

Hatfield, E. and Sprecher, S. (1986). *Mirror, mirror: the importance of looks in everyday life.* Albany: State University of New York Press.

Higgins, E.T. (1987). Self-discrepancy theory. *Psychological Review*, **94**, 1120–34.

Higgins, E.T. and Bargh, J.A. (1987). Social cognition and social perception. *Annual Review of Psychology*, **38**, 369–425.

Hogg, M.A. (1992). *The social psychology of group cohesiveness.* London: Harvester-Wheatsheaf.

Hogg, M.A. and Reid, R.A. (2001). Social identity, leadership, and power. In A.Y. Lee-Chai and J.A. Bargh (eds) *The use and abuse of power: multiple perspectives on the causes of corruption* (pp. 159–80). Philadelphia: Psychology Press.

Horney, K. (1946). *Our inner conflicts: a constructive theory of neurosis.* London: Routledge & Kegan Paul.

Howard, P.E.N., Rainie, L., and Jones, S. (2001). Days and nights on the Internet. *American Behavorial Scientist*, **45**, 383–404.

Joinson, A.N. (2001). Knowing me, knowing you: reciprocal self-disclosure in internet-based surveys. *Cyberpsychology and Behaviour*, **4**, 587–91.

Jones, E.E., Farina, A., Hastorf, A.H., Markus, H., Miller, D.T., and Scott, R.A. (1984). *Social stigma: the psychology of marked relationships.* San Francisco: W.H. Freeman.

Katz, J.E., Rice, R.E., and Aspden, P. (2001). The Internet, 1995–2000. *American Behavioral Scientist*, **45**, 405–19.

Kavanaugh, A. and Patterson, S. (2001). The impact of community computer networks on social capital and community involvement. *American Behavorial Scientist*, **45**, 496–509.

Kiesler, S., Siegel, J., and McGuire, T. (1984). Social psychological aspects of computer-mediated communication. *American Psychologist*, **39**, 1129–34.

Kraut, R., Kiesler, S., Boneva, B., Cummings, J., Helgeson, V., and Crawford, A. (2002). Internet paradox revisited. *Journal of Social Issues*, **58**, 49–74.

Kraut, R.E., Patterson, M., Lundmark, V., Kiesler, S., Mukhopadhyay, T., and Scherlis, W. (1998). Internet paradox: a social technology that reduces social involvement and psychological well-being? *American Psychologist*, **53**, 1017–32.

Laurenceau, J., Barrett, L., and Pietromonaco, P.R. (1998). Intimacy as a process: the importance of self-disclosure and responsiveness in interpersonal exchanges. *Journal of Personality and Social Psychology*, **74**, 1238–51.

Levine, D. (2000). Virtual attraction: what rocks your boat? *Cyberpsychology & Behaviour*, **3**, 565–73.

Lewin, K. (1951). *Field theory in social science*. New York: Harper.

Markus, H. and Nurius, P. (1986). Possible selves. *American Psychologist*, **41**, 954–69.

McKay, H.G., Glasgow, R.E., Feil, E.G., Boles, S.M., and Barrera, M. (2002). Internet-based diabetes self-management and support initial outcomes from the diabetes network project. *Rehabilitation Psychology*, **47**, 31–48.

McKenna, K.Y.A. and Bargh, J.A. (1998). Coming out in the age of the Internet: identity demarginalization through virtual group participation. *Journal of Personality and Social Psychology*, **75**, 681–94.

McKenna, K.Y.A. and Bargh, J.A. (1999). Causes and consequences of social interaction on the Internet: a conceptual framework. *Media Psychology*, **1**, 249–69.

McKenna, K.Y.A. and Bargh, J.A. (2000). Plan 9 from Cyberspace: the implications of the Internet for personality and social psychology. *Personality and Social Psychology Review*, **4**, 57–75.

McKenna, K.Y.A., Buffardi, L., Seidman, G., and Green, A.S. (2004). *Strange but true: differential activation of the 'true-self' to friends and strangers online and in person.* Manuscript under review.

McKenna, K.Y.A. and Green, A.S. (2002). Virtual group dynamics. *Group Dynamics: Theory, Research and Practice*, **6**, 116–27.

McKenna, K.Y.A., Green, A.S., and Gleason, M.E.J. (2002). Relationship formation on the Internet: what's the big attraction? *Journal of Social Issues*, **58**, 9–31.

McKenna, K.Y.A., Green, A.S., and Smith, P.K. (2001). Demarginalizing the sexual self. *Journal of Sex Research*, **38**, 302–11.

Nie, N.H. and Erbring, L. (2000). *Internet and society: a preliminary report*. Stanford, CA: Stanford Institute for the Quantitative Study of Society. (Available online at *http://www.stanford.edu/group/siqss*)

Parks, M.R. and Floyd, K. (1995). Making friends in cyberspace. *Journal of Communication*, **46**, 80–97.

Pew Internet and American Life Project. (2002, September 15). *The Internet goes to college: How students are living in the future with today's technology*. (Available online at *http://www.pewinternet.org/reports/toc.asp? Report=71*)

Postmes, T. and Spears, R. (1998). Deindividuation and anti-normative behaviour: a meta-analysis. *Psychological Bulletin*, **123**, 238–59.

Prentice, D.A., Miller, D.T., and Lightdale, J.R. (1994). Asymmetrics in attachments to groups and their members: distinguishing between common-identity and common-bond groups. *Personality and Social Psychology Bulletin*, **20**, 484–93.

Reicher, S.D., Spears, R., and Postmes, T. (1995). A social identity model of deindividuation phenomena. *European Review of Social Psychology*, **6**, 161–98.

Rogers, C. (1951). *Client-centered therapy*. Boston: Houghton–Mifflin.

Rubin, Z. (1975). Disclosing oneself to a stranger: reciprocity and its limits. *Journal of Experimental Social Psychology*, **11**, 233–60.

Sassenberg, K. (2002). Common bond and common identity groups on the Internet: Attachment and normative behavior in on-topic and off-topic chats. *Group Dynamics: Theory, Research, and Practice*, **6**, 27–37.

Sherif, M. and Sherif, C.W. (1953). *Groups in harmony and tension*. New York: Harper & Row.

Spears, R. and Lea, M. (1992). Social influence and the influence of the 'social' in computer-mediated communication. In M. Lea (ed), *Contexts of computer-mediated communication* (pp. 30–65). Hemel Hempstead: Harvester–Wheatsheaf.

Spears, R. and Lea, M. (1994). Panacea or panopticon? The hidden power in computer-mediated communication. *Communication Research*, **21**, 427–59.

Spears, R., Lea, M., and Lee, S. (1990). De-individuation and group polarisation in computer-mediated communication. *British Journal of Social Psychology*, **29**, 121–34.

Spears, R., Postmes, T., Lea, M., and Wolbert, A. (2002). When are net effects gross products? The power of influence and the influence of power in computer-mediated communication. *Journal of Social Issues*, **58**, 91–107.

Sproull, L. and Kiesler, S. (1985). Reducing social context cues: electronic mail in organizational communication. *Management Science*, **11**, 1492–512.

Sproull, L. and Kiesler, S. (1991). *Connections: new ways of working in the networked organization*. Cambridge: MIT Press.

Straus, S.G. (1997). Technology, group process, and group outcomes: testing the connections in computer-mediated and face-to-face groups. *Human-Computer Interaction*, **12**, 227–66.

Tajfel, H. (1970). Experiments in intergroup discrimination. *Scientific American*, **223**, 96–102.

Tajfel, H. and Turner, J. C. (1986). The social identity theory of intergroup behavior. In S. Worchel and W.G. Austin (eds), *Psychology of intergroup relations* (pp. 7–24). Chicago: Nelson–Hall.

Thompson, L. and Nadler, J. (2002). Negotiating via information technology: theory and application. *Journal of Social Issues*, **58**, 109–24.

Turkle, S. (1995). *Life on the screen: identity in the age of the Internet*. New York: Simon & Schuster.

Turner, J.C. (1982). Towards a cognitive redefinition of the social group. In H. Tajfel (ed), *Social identity and intergroup relations* (pp. 15–40). Cambridge: Cambridge University Press.

Turner, J.C. (1985). Social categorization and the self-concept: a social cognitive theory of group behavior. In E.J. Lawler (ed), *Advances in group processes: theory and Research*, **2** (pp. 77–122). Greenwich: JAI Press.

Turner, J.C., Hogg, M.A., Oakes, P.J., Reicher, S.D., and Wetherell, M.S. (1987). *Rediscovering the social group: a self-categorization theory*. Oxford: Blackwell.

Walther, J.B. (1996). Computer-mediated communication: impersonal, interpersonal, and hyperpersonal interaction. *Communication Research*, **23**, 3–43.

Walther, J.B. (1997). Group and interpersonal effects in international computer-mediated collaboration. *Human Communication Research, 23*, 342–69.

Walther, J.B., Anderson, J.F., and Park, D.W. (1994). Interpersonal effects in computer-mediated interaction: a meta-analysis of social and antisocial communication. *Communication Research, 21*, 460–87.

Wellman, B., Haase, A.Q., Witte, J., and Hampton, K. (2001). Does the Internet increase, decrease, or supplement social capital? *American Behavioral Scientist, 45*, 436–55.

Wicklund, R.A., and Gollwitzer, P.M. (1982). *Symbolic self-completion.* Hillsdale, NJ: Erlbaum.

Williams, K.D., Govan, C.L., Croker, V., Tynan, D., Cruickshank, M., and Lam, A. (2002). Investigations into differences between social and cyber ostracism. *Group Dynamics: Theory, Research, & Practice, 6*, 65–77.

Wright, K. (2000). Computer-mediated social support, older adults, and coping. *Journal of Communication, 50*, 100–18.

Chapter 9

Leadership and decision making

Michael Coovert and Jennifer Burke

The Internet has changed the world in which we live. It has changed not only our social lives through enabling new channels of communication and the way individuals connect, but it has changed the business world as well. E-commerce drives a respectable portion of the world's economy and the way businesses and individuals exchange information, goods, and products. Organizations must strive to sustain a competitive advantage in the world market place. Businesses following a business-to-business (B-to-B) model can directly exchange supplies and products with one another. Similarly, individuals can purchase items directly from a company via online shopping or from one another through direct sales or even auctions. These changes in both connectedness and the ability to directly exchange goods and services with businesses and individuals are two of the forces impacting the way we must consider constructs fundamental to organizations and individuals. This connected world of ours has demonstrated that never before has an understanding of leadership and decision making, two constructs central to both individual and organizational effectiveness, been more important.

Our chapter examines these two constructs from the perspective of the social net. Having stated that, it is important to recognize that research on leadership and decision making fills volumes. Our goal here is to introduce the reader to what we believe are the classic or seminal perspectives within each area. Furthermore, within each we describe research that has been conducted critically, examining issues in the area that are targeted at the social net. We also highlight what we believe are deficiencies within the research that has been conducted to date in each area.

The first portion of the chapter focuses on leadership. Three theories of leadership are described: leader–member exchange, Fiedler's (1967) contingency theory, and transformational vs. transactional leadership. E-leadership is then defined along with our raising the issue of technology replacing (or substituting) leadership. Traditional leadership issues are discussed as presenting new challenges to the e-leader. These issues include: vision and goal setting, management and performance appraisal, communication, trust, and the dynamics of virtual teams. After a summary, the chapter moves to consider decision making. We present three classic paradigms that have driven research in the area: Bayes' theorem, multi-attribute utility, and subjective-expected utilities. Following is a description of decision biases—those 'human characteristics' that may lead to making a decision which is non-optimal. Finally, the computer-mediated influences of anonymity and critical thinking on decision making are considered.

One conclusion we reach is that, while many traditional leadership constructs and models apply to e-leadership, the research that considers decision making via the computer as opposed to traditional models of decision making seems to suggest something quite different. So, with that as a background, let us now move on to consider leadership.

Leadership: an introduction

As the transformation from an industrial, mechanized economy to a knowledge-information based, networked economy takes place, the Internet has changed the way organizations function. This has implications for leadership in organizations. The permeable boundaries both within and between organizations open the door for leadership to be based on factors other than titles or functional roles. Indeed, there is some question as to whether the traditional view of leadership is applicable in the Internet economy (Pulley *et al.*, 2000), though few would argue the continuing need for authentic leadership qualities in the people who step into these roles.

One of the challenges of defining leadership today is the lack of a 'face' to put on it: if no one knows who the leader is, is there a leader at all? Leadership in a virtual world may take different forms that are not immediately recognizable and the search may require looking in unfamiliar places. To find it, however, we need some sort of definition to go by, something to hold up and say, 'Does it look like this?' If so, 'Then it could be leadership'. For our exploration of leadership and decision making in the Internet world, we offer this definition from Bass and Stogdill:

> Effective leadership can be characterized . . . as the interaction among members of a group that initiates and maintains improved expectations and the competence of the group to solve problems or to attain goals. (Bass & Stodgill, 1990, p. 20)

In this section of the chapter, we present some of the current theories and models of leadership and discuss their relevance to leadership in an Internet world. We introduce the emergent term 'e-leadership' to highlight the differences in leader attributes, tasks, and challenges faced in this unique domain. Finally, we make some concluding comments on the topic.

Theories and models of leadership

Theories of leadership began with the 'great man' perspective and others that looked for the human traits that exemplified an effective leader. Current theories of leadership take a hybrid approach, focusing on environmental or situational influences as well as the cognitive, social learning, and relational aspects of the leader–follower system. Some of the more influential models relevant to Internet leadership are now discussed.

Leader–member exchange

In leader–member exchange theory (LMX), leadership is seen as the dyadic interaction of the leader and each individual subordinate, with the assumption that the leader's relationship with individual subordinates will vary. The quality of the exchange is based on three elements: the perceived contribution to the exchange by both the leader and the subordinate; each individual's loyalty to the other; and affect—that is, a mutual regard for each other based on factors other than work-related values. These exchanges tend to foster the development of an ingroup and an outgroup. The ingroup is composed of those subordinates with closer relationships to the leader, who are generally more likely to receive preferential treatment and higher status. The outgroup subordinates tend to interact with the leader at a more formal, role-defined level. The competence level of the subordinate is a determinant of becoming a member of the inner circle. Both laboratory and field studies have provided at least some support for LMX theory (Dansereau *et al.*, 1975; Wayne & Ferris, 1990).

LMX theory poses interesting questions for the Internet world: suppose a leader has both local subordinates he/she deals with face to face as well as through the Internet, and distributed subordinates whose sole communication channel is through the Internet. It is possible that subordinates who have the opportunity to communicate with their leader in person may form an ingroup based on proximity, making those whose contact with the leader is solely through the Internet an automatic outgroup. On the other hand, distributed members of the organization may develop a richer, more intimate personal relationship with the leader based upon the easy access to personal contact via e-mail, instant messages, or other Internet-channeled technologies. Future research on LMX theory should focus on the Internet's effects on development of ingroups and outgroups.

The contingency model: task-oriented vs. relations-oriented

Leaders are often described in terms of their primary focus of attention. Some are more concerned with getting the work done (task-oriented), while others place more emphasis on the interpersonal side of the work process (relations-oriented).

Fiedler's (1967) contingency theory posited that the effectiveness of either type depends on the situation in terms of task structure, position power, and leader–group relations. The least preferred co-worker (LPC) scale was developed to assess leader traits, with high LPC leaders classified as relations-oriented and low LPC leaders classified as task-oriented. Fiedler saw high LPC leaders as most effective in moderately favorable circumstances, that is, when situational factors are neither very good nor very bad. Task-oriented, low LPC leaders, in contrast, are most effective in extreme situations—when conditions are either very favorable or very unfavorable to the leader. Fiedler's perspective is that the leader's style is not changeable, and that the leader should be chosen according to the situation (or the situation should be changed). This is markedly different from other leadership models, and though the contingency model has been widely researched and validated, it is still perceived as controversial.

Leadership via the Internet offers new research questions for contingency model theorists, one of which is whether there are situational factors directly related to the Internet which would be classified as very favorable or unfavorable, thus creating an environment in which low LPC, task-oriented leaders would be most effective. A broader question is whether the Internet itself might be perceived as a situational factor that determines whether a task-oriented, low LPC leader or a relations-oriented, high LPC leader would be most effective.

Transformational vs. transactional leadership

Burns (1978) first used the labels transactional and transformational to describe leadership styles that differed in how subordinates were motivated to perform their work. Transactional leaders use exchange-based negotiations with subordinates, creating an interdependent relationship in which each party provides something of value to the other in return for desired rewards or outcomes. Transformational leaders move beyond the exchange-based nature of leader–follower relationships by promoting end values like integrity and truth, thus inspiring subordinates to work for reasons beyond self-interest.

Most leadership research in the past ten years has focused on transformational leadership (Judge & Bono, 2000); however, both transactional and transformational leader behaviors have been linked with positive performance outcomes at the subordinate and organizational levels (Bass & Avolio, 1990; Dubinsky et al., 1995; Howell & Avolio, 1993; Howell & Frost, 1989). Transformational leadership via the Internet is discussed further in later sections of this chapter.

As the Internet and organizational globalization transform the way business operates throughout the world, it begs the question as to the relevance of these traditional theories of leadership. As such, this leads us to a central purpose of this chapter: how will leadership be expressed in a virtual environment? Will the same behaviors and approaches apply or will new paradigms of leadership evolve? We examine the current zeitgeist, and propose a set of expected challenges that e-leaders will face in the networked economy.

E-leadership defined: leadership as a social system

In the business world, buzzwords and trendy terms are quickly coined and discarded just as quickly; it remains to be seen whether the e-leadership term survives, but it serves our purpose well in this chapter. We present it as our word for leadership via the Internet, expanding on Bass and Stogdill's (1990) earlier definition to include the unique situational focus:

> Effective *e-leadership* can be characterized . . . as the interaction among members of a group *mediated by information technology* that initiates and maintains improved expectations and the competence of the group to solve problems or to attain goals. (1990, p. 20)

The term *e-leadership* underscores a point made by Avolio *et al.* (2000) that the Internet is not just the context in which leadership takes place, but is part of the construct itself. It also supports the notion of leadership behaviors being shared across members of a group and, perhaps by the information technology as well.

Though research on e-leadership is in its infancy, there are some emergent theories and models that present a logical framework from which to examine technology-channeled leader behaviors. One theory that addresses the influence of information technology is adaptive structuration theory (AST). AST views the interaction of advanced information technology with organizational structures (including leadership) and how it transforms those organizational structures (Avolio *et al.*, 2000). Before describing the theory we must introduce a central term in the theory—*advanced information technology*.

Advanced information technology (AIT) is defined as the tools, techniques, and knowledge that enable multi-party participation in organizational and inter-organizational activities through sophisticated collection, processing, management, retrieval, transmission, and display of data and knowledge (DeSanctis & Poole, 1994). An AIT-enabled economy has real-time information availability, greater knowledge-sharing with stakeholders, and customized relationships based on this knowledge and information.

Leadership in an AIT economy occurs on many levels, as described in Yammarino *et al.* (2001), and can be temporally synchronous or asynchronous.

E-leadership is seen as a social influence process mediated by AIT, which occurs at any level in an organization (Avolio *et al.*, 2000). Leadership behaviors can come from one person or are shared by several.

Now with the concept of AIT in mind, we can return to the theory. AST proposes that human actions are guided by structures designed to facilitate planning and accomplishing tasks. These structures come from two sources: the work group and AIT. Some examples of structures in the work group are the tasks, environment, interaction styles, members' expertise, and shared mental models. AIT comes with pre-determined structures that can be characterized in terms of design features and the spirit of those features. For example, a group support system could have a feature that enables anonymous communication. The spirit of that feature is to promote participation for those reasons discussed later in the decision-making portion of the chapter under the heading of *anonymity*.

Leadership in a work group can influence not only whether an AIT is accepted and used by the group, but also how it changes or affects the existing internal structures of the group. What leadership style is most effective in this process? Some research has been done examining the effects of participative, directive, transformational, and transactional leader behaviors when using group support systems. Results appear mixed (Kahai *et al.*, 2003; Sosik *et al.*, 1997). The opening of new paths of information and knowledge sharing and collaboration seem to follow the spirit of a participative-style leader who seeks to involve organization members in decision making by encouraging and promoting use of new technology. The nature of the task, however, may influence the effectiveness of a participative leader style—more structured problems may call for directive leader behaviors. In studies comparing transactional and transformational leader styles, anonymity emerged as a determinant of the impact of leadership style. Groups working with a transactional leader had higher group levels of efficacy and satisfaction when individual inputs were identified, but transformational leaders were more effective when inputs were anonymous.

Anonymity is something of a double-edged sword in AIT. It enhances the sharing of sensitive information and minimizes biases, but can also lead to questioning the credibility of information. Additionally, the lack of recognition may foster a 'why bother' attitude among workers. Transformational leadership, with its emphasis on the collective nature of work, may be the key to the successful incorporation of AIT into an organization, as anonymity is a common element in many technologies. Avolio *et al.* (2000) proposed a model illustrating the effects of transformational leadership and media richness on trust in virtual teams. Media richness refers to a technology's capacity for providing immediate feedback, the number of cues and channels utilized, personalization of messages, and language variety (Daft & Lengel, 1986).

Generally stated, the model postulates that higher levels of media richness combined with transformational leader behaviors such as individualized consideration, inspirational motivation, and intellectual stimulation, will promote higher levels of trust in virtual teams. Media richness is expected to influence the emergence of trust by influencing the perception of team members' ability, benevolence, and integrity. (Lower media richness would inhibit forming judgments, potentially reducing the amount of interaction as well as blocking the formation of trust.) Leadership is likely to influence the appropriation of trust among members of a virtual team by affecting perceptions of other members' ability, benevolence, and integrity and team members' emotions and moods. Avolio *et al.* (2000) hypothesize an interactive effect between media richness and transformational leadership behaviors, such that when media richness is low, transformational leadership behaviors can produce higher levels of trust.

Another approach to understanding e-leadership is the multiple-level multidimensional model (see Figure 9.1)—a leadership mosaic comprising five critical areas: fundamental human processes, leadership core processes, leadership outcomes, other multi-level outcomes, and substitutes for leadership (Yammarino *et al.*, 2001). In the model, fundamental human processes are those that focus on explaining the underlying reasons why people develop relationships that they think of as leadership. These processes include affect and cognition, interpersonal attraction, organizational climate and group norms, cultural values, and styles of communication. Leadership core processes refer to the characteristics of the leader at several levels: individual traits as a person, dyadic relationships between leaders and followers (empowerment), group dynamics (i.e. the degree to which leaders provide task and relationship functions to their teams), and collective supervision or management (defined as the ability to function in a (formal) role system). Leadership approaches— team building, delegation and participation in decision making, leader– member exchange, and vertical dyad leadership—focus on leadership outcomes such as performance, satisfaction, absenteeism, and turnover. Substitutes for leadership, such as the knowledge and skills of individuals (person level), informal relationships (dyad level), group cohesiveness (team level), and various collective-level variables such as organizational formalization, task design, and communication systems (e.g. the Internet), may serve as enhancers to, neutralizers of, or replacements for the leadership core processes.

This model allows not only examination of the influence of e-leadership at several levels (person, dyad, group, and collective), but also provides

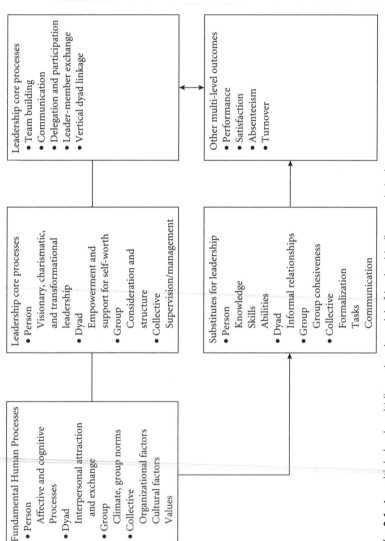

Fig. 9.1 A multiple-level multidimensional model of leadership (by permission).

consideration of the information technology itself as a substitute for certain behaviors. Four levels of analysis are presented in this model, each of which highlights a particular facet of leadership:

- *Person*: the importance of individual differences.
- *Dyad*: the importance of one-to-one relationships between a leader and each follower.
- *Group*: face-to-face relationships among a set of subordinates that a leader interacts with as a unit; can be characterized as leadership style (e.g. relations-oriented or task-oriented).
- *Collective*: systems in which large numbers of people (groups of groups) are connected by shared expectations (mission statements, core values, etc.).

The four levels of analysis may be used to look at aspects of leadership: fundamental human processes, leadership core processes, leadership outcomes, other multi-level outcomes, and substitutes for leadership. Though this model is not specifically focused on the influence of the Internet on leadership, its structure provides a broad range of work perspectives, from global impact to the individual worker, for examining the effects of Internet technology. At the person level, for example, a leader's comfort level with technology is likely to affect how it is incorporated into an organization. A leader who acts as a champion of Internet technology can tie its use to a greater variety of positive organizational outcomes (Howell & Boies, 2004). At the dyadic level, frequency and the content of one-to-one e-mail communications with subordinates may influence the judgments made by each subordinate as to whether the superior is viewed as a leader or not. Group and collective level interactions can facilitate communication of the leader's vision, core values, and goals throughout the organization. The core processes of leadership (leader style, empowerment, task and relationship functions, organizational management) can manifest within an organization and beyond through AIT.

Technology as a substitute for leadership

The multiple-level multidimensional model of leadership presents leadership outcomes (e.g. team building, communication, delegation, and participation) along with other multi-level outcomes such as performance, satisfaction, absenteeism, and turnover (Yammarino *et al.*, 2001). Internet technology may serve not only as a conduit for the leadership core processes that can influence these outcomes, but also as a substitute. That is, technology may actually fulfill some of the roles typically ascribed to leaders.

In research that examined team members' role perceptions after working in teams using group support software (GSS), Zigurs and Kozar (1994) found that members attributed several leader roles to the software itself (proceduralist, motivator, opinion seeker). Other studies have suggested that the structural features of GSS (e.g. process facilitation, anonymity) may supplant the team leader's direction in guiding team decision making (Ho & Raman, 1991). Dennis *et al.* (1998) found GSS to be a useful tool in overcoming the biased decision making that often occurs when there is a majority within a group. The GSS enabled the group minority to deflect the group's inertia toward the majority viewpoint, something the minority was unable to do without the GSS. Decision making will be further discussed shortly.

Leader attributes

What does it take to lead organizations in a web-centric world? A trait theory approach would argue that the situation might have changed, but the knowledge, skills, and abilities required have remained the same. In contrast, the contingency theory approach described earlier would cite the contextual variables of task environment, workforce characteristics, and organization life-cycle stages as key differences that require different leadership traits and behaviors. As is often the case, the truth probably lies somewhere in the middle. In surveys and interviews of traditional 'bricks-and-mortar' leaders and e-leaders, both cite the value of universal leadership traits, such as being intelligent, adaptable, energetic, decisive, inspiring, motivational, able to convey a shared vision, having the capacity to anticipate new opportunities, and possessing strong communication and strategic analysis skills (Horner–Long & Schoenberg, 2002; Pulley *et al.*, 2001).

However, the respondents in these studies also recognize that not only will certain leadership traits be more critical than others in effective e-leadership, but certain new attributes will also play a role. E-leaders emphasize the importance of being entrepreneurial, risk-taking, and less conservative. Predictably, information technology and project management skills are seen as more critical, along with the ability to network extensively and prioritize activities.

Interestingly, the skills and abilities rated as important leadership characteristics needed for the future are those that distinguish e-leaders from traditional leaders (Horner–Long & Schoenberg, 2002). Cross-field experience (the ability to transfer ideas from one field to another) and 'a cool head under fire' have also been identified as valuable attributes (Kissler, 2001). Cultural awareness is acknowledged as an increasingly salient leadership characteristic, and the globalization of many organizations has intensified the necessity for leaders to be cognizant of the many cultural influences that may affect employees, customers, and suppliers on organizational, national and societal levels (Avolio & Kahai, 2003; Avolio *et al.*, 2000; Kayworth & Leidner, 2000).

Old tasks present new challenges for the e-leader

What new tasks face the e-leader? Very few, really—but the traditional tasks that fall to a leader present new challenges to the e-leader. Various conjectures fall into organizational and interpersonal categories. Organizational tasks include creating organizational mind-share—introducing new information into the organization quickly will require rapid access. Strategic planning elements must take into account the emergence of new business designs; changes in infrastructure and workflow processes, with the incumbent changes in workforce skill requirements, call for more fluidity in strategic planning, and both long- and short-scope plans. In implementing new technology, leaders may need to provide 'air cover' for those on the front line—that is, support spontaneous decisions that, in hindsight, may not have been optimal (Kissler, 2001). As we shall see shortly, what is optimal in a decision model can be defined differentially (e.g. Bayes, MAU), thus further complicating what is considered 'optimal'.

Vision and goal setting, project management, and performance appraisal each present new organizational challenges for leaders in virtual environments. The interpersonal tasks of leadership cannot be separated from organizational tasks, for they are the oil that keeps the organization running. Communication, trust, and team dynamics are areas that present new challenges to e-leaders.

Vision and goal setting

Leaders can set superordinate goals in an organization that capture the heart and imagination of followers, galvanizing them to action by sharing a vision of the organization's future and values, and setting out the steps to make that vision a reality (Latham, 2003). The accessibility and interconnectedness of information technology offer the e-leader a powerful tool for sharing the core values and shared vision of an organization, and gaining goal commitment from employees. E-leaders can communicate directly with all members of an organization (including customers), rather than indirectly through a hierarchy of managers and supervisors, thus keeping a finger on the pulse of the organizational 'body'.

E-leaders can also use the tools of technology to set goals that are SMART: specific, measurable, attainable, relevant, and time-framed (Locke & Latham, 1990). Setting SMART goals gives employees a means to manage their own performance as well as monitor their progress. In the dynamic, fast-paced Internet environment, the rapid dissemination of information facilitates error management, allowing goals to be adjusted or refined as needed. The technology-increased accessibility of the e-leader provides a way to recognize and acknowledge employee efforts toward goal attainment both individually and collectively, increasing a sense of organizational unity and goal commitment.

The Internet can also provide subordinates with a conduit for direct (or anonymous) expression of dissent with organizational goals to leaders—healthy behavior in terms of avoiding the occurrence of group-think. Group-think occurs when individuals go along with a group decision or action they disagree with in order to be perceived as a team player (Spector, 2000). The sense of urgency that purveys web-centric business (Kissler, 2001) can exacerbate this phenomenon; increased customer expectations regarding service forces organizations to keep pace or they will be left behind. Encouraging constructive debate using groupware or other technology can be an integral factor in an e-leader's organizational alignment of goals and decisions.

Management and performance appraisal

An increasing number of employees work at home or off site on a part- or full-time basis. In addition, many projects are pieced out among organizational departments or teams across several geographic locations. This makes it difficult for supervisors to control and manage progress on projects and to keep track of employee performance. Effective project management in a virtual environment requires leaders to be clear at the outset in establishing responsibilities, schedules, and work process norms. Regular one-to-one performance checkpoints with subordinates and continuous feedback throughout the work process can prevent problems from going undetected. Leaders accustomed to relying on traditional temporal metrics, both formal (absenteeism) and informal (whose car is still in the parking lot after 5.00 pm) must adapt to managing and judging employee performance by tasks and objectives, not hours.

Flexibility in dealing with situations that arise is necessary, especially when dealing with employees whose work hours do not coincide with those of the central organization. E-leaders must recognize the potential for the formation of ingroups and outgroups based on proximity to the leader, and do more than stay accessible (some workers will never take advantage of the 'open door' policy, so leaders must initiate contact). Another factor to consider is that many workers are part of a traditional workplace in their physical location along with being a remote participant in the virtual work environment, and have to maintain two types of interpersonal relationships at work. It is important to recognize efforts and achievements of the virtual employee, which often go unnoticed when the worker is not present.

Communication

In a study of new product development team leaders, Barczak and Wilemon (1991) found that successful leaders communicated more with different groups both within the organization and across organizational boundaries about different subjects according to team type. Effective leaders in this kind of networked economy will use multiple channels of information and communication technologies—and will be experts in choosing the right one depending on whom they're talking to and what they're talking about (Pulley *et al.*, 2000). We shall see in a moment, in the decision-making section, how similar this is to a finding that the effective decision maker matched strategies to the task.

Communication skills are the number one priority identified by leaders in response to a survey which asked what skills, experiences, and traits are important for being an effective leader in the digital economy (Pulley *et al.*, 2001). Follow-up interviews indicated two needs for effective communication: speed and boundary spanning. Not only do e-leaders need to be able to reach people quickly, but they must also be able to influence those beyond the scope of formal authority, since many projects involve stakeholders outside organizational boundaries (e.g. customers or suppliers).

Differences in technological experience and expertise are also a factor. Younger people in the workforce grew up with the Internet and are used to its interactive, collaborative, non-hierarchical system of communication. This can present challenges for the leader and co-workers with less experience and expertise. Changing team membership is also a consideration. Many times the team that exists at the completion of a project is vastly different from the team that began the project, due to turnover, contractual sourcing of portions of the project, and changes in the project itself.

Specific communication skills and styles have been studied in recent research (Cascio & Shurygailo, 2003; Hart & McLeod, 2003; Weisband, 2002). In a field study of seven geographically dispersed work teams, Hart and McLeod (2003) reported that strong personal work relationships were characterized by frequent, short communications that were work-related rather than personal in content. Moreover, these relationships were developed and strengthened through proactive efforts to solve problems. The shared knowledge and understanding that characterize strong personal work relationships are important in time-critical work; therefore, leaders may promote relationship development through facilitation of communications exchanges between co-workers (making time available, technology accessible) and by sharing tasks across virtual teams to promote task-related interaction. In a study of 15 distributed teams, Weisband (2002) found that certain types of leader communications (initiating pressure and maintaining awareness of others), particularly in the early stages of a project, were associated with team performance. When leaders initiated structure of work processes and information exchange, team members communicated more frequently and performed more effectively.

The challenges of organizing and conducting virtual meetings were among the communication issues examined by Cascio and Shurygailo (2003). Providing adequate advance notice of such meetings (or having a standing meeting scheduled) is important, as is following procedural structure (e.g. beginning the meeting with a roll call and having an identification protocol so that members are aware of who is speaking at any given time). Indirect communication methods, such as e-mail, are best for group communications and the development of formal or complex ideas. The most effective use of this asynchronous technology will move the work process forward with each communication. More direct methods, such as instant messaging, offer more expedient communication, but should be brief and limited to important information to minimize work interruptions. Keeping up with current information and project status is critical to effective virtual team performance; having a project librarian post all written documentation on an established website is preferable to sifting through multiple e-mail exchanges.

These suggestions for facilitating communication are predicated on the leader establishing both the infrastructures and the processes, and on the team members' participation. Distributed and virtual teams offer new challenges to team cohesiveness, and suggestions vary as to how to build the important relational cornerstones. Should face-to-face contact come first or intensive task communication from a distance? Arguments have been presented on both sides (Cascio & Shurygailo, 2003; Hart & McLeod, 2003). If the task involves decision making, some guidance can be gleaned from the research described in the decision-making portion of this chapter. The reality is often that face-to-face interaction may not be an option. In those circumstances, how does one build trust in a virtual environment?

Trust

The rapid speed at which business is conducted in the networked economy has made the traditional establishment of trust through long-term relationships an impractical approach. Transformational leaders can build trust in others through individual consideration and inspirational interactions (Sosik *et al.*, 1997).

The challenge is that trust must be established at the outset. Lack of trust in teams is associated with low productivity and stress (see Coovert *et al.*, in press, for a full discussion), and in virtual teams, the building of rapid trust is critical to effective team performance. Positive, action-oriented messages and close monitoring for negative feedback are good initial leader behaviors, as first impressions are important in eliciting rapid trust. Trust is established through repeatedly setting expectations and then meeting or exceeding those expectations. The leader can promote the formation of this trust through structuring simple, clearly defined and understood interactions between team members to initiate the expectation–delivery cycle (Cascio & Shurygailo, 2003). This could include introductory e-mails (where each team member completes and shares a basic 'about me' form, including a picture); establishment of roles and communication channels by assigning certain team members as points of contact for various aspects of the team project; and modeling communication norms by example (i.e. making regular, consistent contact that requires a (brief) response).

In an empirical analysis of trust development within 29 global virtual teams, Cascio and Shurygailo reported initial social contact (good first impressions), clear roles, and positive attitude as characteristics of teams with high levels of trust. Trust is also created through the sharing of information and knowledge. New methods of information exchange, however, pose some threats to trust. These include undesired disclosure, loss of competitive advantage, and misuse of sensitive organizational data. Forwarding of e-mail to team members other than those originally addressed, (hitting 'reply to all' instead of 'reply'), and omitting (intentionally or unintentionally) certain team members from the list to receive an important communication, are examples of small actions that can erode trust in teams and organizations.

'Virtual team' dynamics

One of the more intriguing aspects of leadership in the Internet world is the management of teams composed of individuals separated by the dimensions of time and space. The terms used to describe these teams are varied and include: distributed, dispersed, co-located, and virtual. In this chapter, we use the term 'virtual team', as it conveys the unified presence of the team in a technological dimension that spans the constraints of physical location. Anyone who has led or participated in a group project is familiar with the complexities of scheduling meetings to match several individual calendars, co-ordinating tasks among team members, and keeping everyone informed and focused (and that's when you have them all in the same room!) A team dispersed in different geographic locations and time zones poses the same challenges, but given the available technology, the nuts and bolts of team work described above may not be more difficult. The creation of a sense of team cohesion among members who might never meet face to face by a leader they might never meet face to face is the real issue. Cultural differences, organizational norms, and varying levels of technical access and expertise among team members are all potential stumbling blocks.

Leaders that exhibit cultural awareness, set clear goals, provide feedback on a continuous basis, and are flexible and empathic toward team members can contribute to the success of virtual teams (Kayworth & Leidner, 2000). Weisband (2002) found teams with leaders who initiated task structure and sought awareness of team members' progress and general team status early in the project were more successful. Indeed, team members who take on the roles of initiator, scheduler, and integrator may find themselves regarded as the team leader. In a recent study of emergent leaders in virtual teams, researchers found that emergent leaders sent more and longer e-mail messages than did their team members. The number of task-oriented messages, particularly those that were related to logistics co-ordination, sent by emergent leaders, was higher than that of non-leaders (Yoo & Alavi, 2004). This suggests a large part of e-leadership may be 'leading by example' through utilizing the Internet communication channels to facilitate virtual team activities.

Recent studies in remote leadership (defined as technology-based interaction between geographically and physically isolated leaders and followers) suggest that team members can distinguish between leadership styles in e-mail messages. Kelloway *et al.* (2003) reported that team members (students) who read e-mail messages from a transformational leader had significantly higher scores on motivation, supervision satisfaction, and individual performance than those who read messages from a *laissez-faire*, management by exception, or contingent reward leader; moreover, group performance was better when group members read transformational leader e-mail messages. This suggests that the charismatic influence, individual consideration, and intellectual stimulation provided by transformational leaders in traditional face-to-face settings can be successfully transmitted through the Internet. Research expanding these findings to include field studies in organizations is the next logical step in exploring transformational leadership via electronic channels.

Leadership: summary

Leadership is a complex construct. This is true in a bricks-and-mortar economy, and even more so when considering e-leadership. The traditional theories examined here appear to be holding up well, although much research needs to be done to fully understand the nature of effective leadership in an social net environment. We move now to consider decision making—certainly a characteristic of an effective leader, but also a topic worthy of consideration in its own right for our understanding of the social net.

Decision making

Having considered leadership, we move to decision making. We provide a description of three dominant paradigms in the area and a brief discussion of decision biases. A review of findings in the computer-mediated environment is presented, although a brief one due to space constraints. Topics covered include face-to-face vs. computer-mediated, anonymity, and critical thinking. Our use of references in this section is judicious, using them to point the interested reader to a full discussion of the topic at hand.

Decision making has a rich history of research in many areas, including the social and behavioral sciences, management science, and the medical arena. A decision is defined simply as the process of choosing one course of action that has value-relevant consequences from among several alternatives. A very general, six-step process describes decision making:

1 Define the problem.

2 Gather information.

3 Identify alternative actions.

4 Evaluate the alternatives.

5 Select an alternative (the best).

6 Implement the selected alternative.

Three perspectives dominate the decision-making literature (Edwards & Fasolo, 2001). These are: Bayes' theorem;, multi-attribute utility; and subjective expected utility. Most decision making or decision-aiding technologies implement a version of one of these three models. Recently, Edwards and Fasolo (2001) proposed a 19-step model to integrate the three perspectives into one decision-making process. We refer interested readers to their work.

Bayes' theorem

A normative model of decision making that has lots of application is Bayes' theorem. It is quite straightforward in the sense that if one has a belief about an event, and the event has a probability distribution (Prior; $P(E)$), and additional information with known reliability (Likelihoods; $P(I|E)$) is available (or attainable), then the initial belief can be revised (Posterior; $P(E|I)$) according to the new information. Following this notion of conditional probability, Bayes' theorem is stated as:

$$P(A \mid B) = P(A \text{ Ç } B) / P(B).$$

Computerized help systems often rely on Bayes' theorem to try and predict a user's intention and/or behavior. As an example, consider a person working with a browser on the Internet and event E is the probability the person will click the 'help' button at the ACME company website. The indicator event, I, is a pop-up window (additional information) explaining how to navigate the site. The pop-up window may or may not be helpful, given nothing is known about the users who enter the ACME site, and if the provided information fits their mental model for site navigation.

The prior probability of E is $P(E)$, and it turns out that $0 < P(E) < 1$. We are trying to determine the probability of someone clicking the help button given that a pop-up window explaining site navigation has already been provided to the user. Mathematically this is stated as:

$$P(E \mid I) = P(E \cap I) / P(I)$$

Through rearranging terms we have:

$$P(E \cap I) = P(E \mid I) \times P(I)$$

Bayes deduced that through symmetry the following also had to be true:

$$P(E \cap I) = P(I \mid E) \times P(E)$$

Through further manipulations, Bayes' theorem is given as:

$$P(E \mid I) = \frac{P(I \mid E) \times P(E)}{P(I \mid E) \times P(E) + P(I \mid E') \times P(E')}$$

where E' is the complement of E.

Bayes' approach can be very useful. It is also intuitive in that it states that we can make a prediction about the probability of one event occurring given another event. Furthermore, the probabilities can be updated given new information.

Multi-attribute utility

Multi-attribute utility (MAU) tools are mathematical approaches for comparing alternatives and ultimately helping a decision maker to make the right decision. To apply the MAU strategy, first all the alternatives are identified, as well as the attributes that will be used to compare them. As an example, consider a decision maker deciding which of three computer systems to buy: A, B, or C. Each computer (alternative) has certain attributes (e.g. memory, hard disk size, CPU speed, screen display). Weights are assigned to each attribute according to its importance to the decision (e.g. 1, 2, 3, 4; or spreading 100 points over the alternatives). Each alternative is scored on each attribute using a scale (e.g. 1–10). Multiplying the importance weight by the attribute weight

Table 9.1 Example of MAU for a computer purchase decision

Alternative	Attributes				Utility (sum)
	Memory (20)	Hard disk size (25)	CPU speed (15)	Screen display (40)	
Brand A	1×20	2×25	3×15	1×40	155
Brand B	2×20	3×25	1×15	3×40	250
Brand C	3×20	1×25	2×15	2×40	195

and summing those determine the utility of each alternative. Table 9.1 presents a simple example.

MAU makes it easy to determine which alternative should be chosen, given the attributes, their values, and the ranking of each alternative on those attributes. Having an explicit model like this can be very useful in group decision making since everyone can see how an alternative was chosen. In our example, computer Brand B has the greatest total points, so it is the chosen alternative. With MAU it is also easy to change the attribute value weights to determine the impact on the decision outcome.

Maximized subjective expected utilities

This decision model is quite simple as well. It recognizes that for individuals, values and utilities can be quite different. The probabilities that enter into expected utilities are judgments; there is a psychological 'tainting' of the probabilities. This perspective of decision makers states that individuals will behave in such a manner as to choose the alternative that has the maximum expected utility. According to Edwards and Fasolo (2001), this often includes ascertaining if additional information is available and its cost, obtaining the information if it is inexpensive, and aggregating the cost of new information and the gain from having it.

The models described above are by no means exhaustive, but arguably, are the dominant approaches to understanding decision making. We now take a brief look at decision biases and then move to computer-mediated decision making.

Decision biases

It is interesting that many models of the individual as a decision maker assumes that one is always attempting to maximize the decision and/or arrive at the 'correct' decision. More and more research is demonstrating that individuals often violate predictions of this rational choice model. Effects that can bias decisions include framing effects, response modes, stimulus contexts, and the environment (Payne *et al.*, 1992).

Moving away from this perspective is a theory that views the decision maker as a 'rule follower' (March, 1994). Following rules or heuristics minimizes effort and allows individuals to avoid difficult trade-offs (Mellers *et al.*, 1998). Fiske (1992) argues that social decisions can be covered by the application of only four rules: communal sharing, authority ranking, equality matching, and market pricing. See March (1994) for a complete treatment of rule following as a model for decision making.

Summary

Having provided a brief highlight of the traditional decision-making literature, we now move to issues of decision making when technology is involved. The literature in the area is becoming quite large; therefore, our review is selective. Interested readers can obtain more complete reviews from many different sources (cf. Coovert & Thompson, 2003).

Computer-mediated influences

There are many themes of research examining the impact of taking a task, such as decision making, and moving it to a computerized environment to examine the impact on the task or the task outcome. A couple of main streams of research have focused on comparing face-to-face (FTF) versus computer-mediated (CM) decision making. It is interesting to note that, for the most part, these studies have not followed the classic models of decision making (e.g. Bayes', MAU), but rather have merely compared the results of a decision-making task when conducted FTF versus CM. For example, Jonassen and Kwon (2001) examined communication patterns in FTF versus CM groups and found that CM groups more closely followed the classic, general problem-solving process (problem definition, orientation, and solution development), while the FTF groups tended to follow a linear sequence of interactions. Interestingly, the participants in the CM groups also reported higher satisfaction with the process and also believed their proposed solutions were of higher quality.

Maznevski and Chudoba (2000) studied virtual teams in globally dispersed organizations and found that the most effective teams fit their communication patterns to the task and use a combination of FTF communications supplemented by CM communication. It also appears that the order of the FTF and CM discussions may be important. Dietz-Uhler & Bishop-Clark (2001) compared FTF groups with synchronous and asynchronous CM groups that needed to discuss topics. They reported that FTF discussions that are preceded by CM discussions (either synchronous or asynchronous) are perceived to be more enjoyable by the participants and include a greater diversity of ideas than are FTF discussions not preceded by CM communication.

Thompson and Coovert (2002) explored FTF versus CM decision making for groups using the stepladder decision-making technique. The stepladder technique (Rogelberg *et al.*, 1992) is thought to improve decision making by staggering members' entry into a discussion. Thompson and Coovert (2002) compared both traditional decision-making groups and stepladder groups in both FTF and CM conditions. They found that FTF participants felt more influential and satisfied than did the CM groups, regardless of which decision-making technique (traditional or stepladder) was used.

Exploring the notion that the type of task might moderate some findings in the FTF and CM literature, Murthy and Kerr (2003) focused on a communication process task that required either the conveyance of information (idea generation) or convergence to a best solution (problem solving). They found an interaction between communication mode and communication process goals. When the individual's goal was merely to convey information, the FTF and CM teams performed equally well. When the goal was to converge on a best solution, however, the FTF communication resulted in better performance.

Anonymity

Traditional decision-making research has held that if the identity of individuals in a group is not known, the group can make better decisions. There are many reasons for this, such as low-status individuals not wanting to express their views in front of high-status individuals; individuals making incorrect attributions about another's expertise and incorrectly deferring to them; high-power individuals commanding too much discussion time; and conformity to the group. (These are some of the reasons the stepladder technique mentioned above was developed.)

In CM communications, anonymity can be easily manipulated, and a few studies have examined its impact on decision-making performance of the group. One study (Sia *et al.*, 2002) focused on the effects of anonymity on group polarization. Polarized groups do not always make the best decisions, as the 'group think' literature has effectively demonstrated. Sia and colleagues conducted two experiments and found in both that anonymity increased group polarization by causing individuals to generate more novel arguments and also to engage in more one-upmanship behaviors. They also reported that identified CM conditions result in less polarization, while anonymous CM groups led to stronger polarization.

Postmes and Lea (2000) conducted a series of meta-analyses to carefully evaluate the studies published on anonymity and group-decision support systems. They focused on a variety of performance indicators to see if anonymity always led to better group decisions. Their conclusion was that the only reliable effect of anonymity was to lead to more contributions to the group, especially critical contributions. The authors further developed a model in which social norms and the social context of the decision must be considered for anonymity to lead to better group decisions.

Finally, a study conducted by Hayne *et al.* (2003) examined the issue of whether anonymous comments entered by group participants are truly anonymous. They looked at the influence of comment length, evaluative tone, prior group membership, and prior communication among group members on attributions made about the identity of the comment's author. The question they were asking is really as simple as 'Can group members who have a history with other group members look at an anonymous comment and determine from whom it came?' Examining data from 32 groups on a brainstorming task, it turned out that the study's participants made attributions that were significantly more accurate than chance guessing. Factors that positively influenced the accuracy of the attributions were the evaluative tone (especially the use of humor) and the amount of prior communication among the group members. Even though the attributions were significantly better than chance, most of the attributions were, however, incorrect.

Critical thinking

A special type of decision making occurs when individuals need to think critically about a problem or issue. This is especially important when individuals work in a group or team and need to tackle the problem collaboratively. Work in this area is extremely important for both organizations and institutions dealing with defense issues (Alberts *et al.*, 2001). Research has begun to address the nature of decision making in these situations (Freeman *et al.*, 2003). In addition to the work by Freeman and colleagues, others are conducting work that has implications for collaborative critical thinking and decision making. We now review a couple of seminal studies.

Focusing on comparing FTF and CM groups for a judgmental decision-making task, Cornelius and Boos (2003) sought to augment CM chats with training to see if performance could equal that obtained by FTF groups. Their premise was that individuals who engage in CM chats rarely understand the mechanisms whereby effective communication occurs, as it does in FTF encounters, and that technology often gets in the way as well. Their view is that effective performance is competency based, both in terms of communication and use of the technology. These authors developed a competency-based training program for media-adopted conversation management strategies that focused on both communication and media competency, aimed at increasing coherence to compensate for low mutual understanding. Experimental tests of the training showed it increased mutual understanding and satisfaction within the CM groups, and their performance approximated that achieved in FTF conditions.

Whitworth *et al.* (2001) examined agreement in groups when the groups must work in a CM environment. Agreement is an important social outcome of group processes. The authors were examining a proposed cognitive model in which agreement does not depend on the exchange of rich information, but can be obtained through the exchange of 'lean' text information. In an experimental context, groups of five individuals exchanged a few characters of text information while solving three rounds of choice problems. Results indicated that agreement can be achieved in asynchronous anonymous CM groups while exchanging only a few characters of information about their respective positions. Conclusions indicate that the key software design criteria for obtaining agreement is not richness, but dynamic many-to-many linkages between the group members.

Decision making: summary

Traditional approaches for studying decision making have been around for quite some time and have developed robust models of the decision maker, such as Bayes' theorem, multi-attribute utility theory, and maximized subjective expected utilities. We are also gaining a well-grounded base of decision biases and how they affect the decision outcome. Comparatively less is known about decision making on the Internet or through other computer-mediated modalities. However, we are gathering a solid foundation of research in the area.

It is interesting to note, however, that the focus of decision making on the Internet, or computer-mediated decision making for that matter, is not following the paradigms (e.g. Bayes') of classic decision making. Rather, the focus tends to be on how the medium might be impacting a decision outcome—that is, do individuals (groups) who use a computer to arrive at a decision achieve the same outcome as individuals (groups) who do not use the computer. The focus is on how the technology is changing the decision-making process, as opposed to understanding the core cognitive strategies involved with human decision making. This implies either that we know all we need to know about fundamental human decision making and need to move on, or that the medium (computer, Internet) has changed decision making so drastically that we first need to identify if it is different or not before we move to modeling it as part of the system of human—computer (Internet) decision making. It will be interesting to see how researchers define the criterion space for future research in the area.

Conclusions

Our chapter has been an overview of leadership and decision making on the Internet. Within each of those two main sections we described major classic topics and then went on to present selected research in the area. We structured the chapter according to the main sections, discussing leadership first, and then decision making.

For leadership, we presented theories and models of leadership both old (LMX theory, contingency model, transformational leadership) and new (adaptive structuration theory, the multiple-level multidimensional model of leadership) and discussed their relevance to leadership in an Internet world. We introduced the emergent term 'e-leadership' to highlight the differences in leader attributes, tasks, and challenges faced in this unique domain.

We discussed the attributes that are shared by traditional 'bricks-and-mortar' leaders and e-leaders (intelligence, adaptability, decisiveness, being a visionary and a motivator), as well as those attributes that distinguish e-leaders from their traditional counterparts (being entrepreneurial, a risk-taker, having cross-field experience and a cool head under fire). Cultural awareness—an important attribute for all leaders—is particularly salient for e-leaders in light of the globalization of many organizations and the resulting distribution of virtual teams across geographic and cultural borders. We then looked at some of the tasks and challenges facing the e-leader: vision and goal setting, project management and performance appraisal, communication, trust, and virtual team dynamics.

We conclude that e-leaders must develop the technical expertise necessary to effectively exploit the vast communication capabilities of the Internet and be flexible in dealing with the novel work complexities it creates. These complexities open doorways to new paths of research, ranging from the examination of the applicability of established leadership theories to leadership in an Internet world, to the development of new measures and constructs that emerge as we identify those leadership attributes, styles, and behaviors unique to e-leaders. As Yammarino *et al.* (2003) so aptly remind us, people are the basis of all leadership; let us remember that as we move forward into the Internet world.

Our presentation of decision making began with classic paradigms in the area: Bayes' theorem, multi-attribute utility theory, and maximized subjective expected utilities. Rule following as an alternative, and also decision biases, are mentioned. The background in each area provides a context in which to understand current research relative to how computer mediation and the Internet are transforming findings in each area. For decision making, we see that there are clear differences in decision outcomes that are reached via face-to-face as opposed to a computer-mediated process. Concomitantly, autonomy and critical thinking are impacted by the medium as well.

We conclude our chapter by saying that the Internet is bringing both great promise and challenges to the areas of leadership and decision making. The future will be an exciting one for individuals and teams that occupy leadership and decision-making roles in organizations.

References

Alberts, D.S., Gartska, J.J., Hayes, R.E., and Signori, D.A. (2001). *Understanding information age warfare*. Washington, D.C.: CCRP Press.

Avolio, B. and Kahai, S. (2003). Adding the 'E' to e-leadership: how it may impact your leadership. *Organizational Dynamics*, **31**, 325–38.

Avolio, B., Kahai, S., and Dodge, G. (2000). E-leadership: implications for theory, research and practice. *The Leadership Quarterly*, **11**, 615–68.

Barczak, G. and Wilemon, D. (1991). Communication patterns of new product development leaders. *IEEE Transactions on Engineering Management*, **38**, 101–9.

Bass, B. (1990). *Bass and Stogdill's handbook of leadership: theory, research, and managerial applications* (3rd edn). New York: Macmillan.

Bass, B.M. and Avolio, B.J. (1990). *Manual for the multifactor leadership questionnaire*. Palo Alto: Consulting Psychologists Press.

Burns, J.M. (1978). *Leadership*. New York: Harper & Row.

Cascio, W. and Shurygailo, S. (2003). E-leadership and virtual teams. *Organizational Dynamics*, **31**, 362–76.

Coovert, M.D. and Thompson, L.F. (2003). Technology and workplace health. In J.C. Quick and L.E. Tetrick (eds), *Handbook of occupational health psychology* (pp. 221–41). Washington, DC: American Psychological Association.

Coovert, M.D., Thompson, L.F., and Craiger, J.P. (in press). *Technology as a stressor*. In J. Barling, K. Kelloway, and M. Frone (eds), *Handbook of work stress*. Thousand Oaks: Sage.

Cornelius, C. and Boos, M. (2003). Enhancing mutual understanding in synchronous computer-mediated communication by training trade-offs in judgmental tasks. *Communication Research*, **30**, 147–77.

Daft, R. and Lengel, R. (1986). Organizational information requirements, media richnessand structural design. *Management Science*, **32**, 554–72.

Dansereau, F., Graen, G., and Haga, W.J. (1975). A vertical dyad linkage approach to leadership in formal organizations. *Organizational Behavior and Human Performance*, **13**, 46–78.

Dennis, A.R., Hilmer, K.M., and Taylor, N.J. (1998). Information exchange and use in GSS and verbal group decision making: effects of minority influence. *Journal of Management Information Systems*, **14**, 61–88.

DeSanctis, G. and Poole, M.S. (1994). Capturing the complexity in advanced technology use: adaptive structuration theory. *Organization Science*, **5**, 121–47.

Dietz-Uhler, B. and Bishop-Clark, C. (2001). The use of computer mediated communication to enhance subsequent face-to-face discussions. *Computers in Human Behavior,* **17,** 269–83.

Dubinsky, A.J., Yammarino, F.J., Jolson, M.A., and Spangler, W.D. (1995). Transformational leadership: an initial investigation in sales management. *Journal of Personal Selling and Sales Management,* **15,** 17–29.

Edwards, W. and Fasolo, B. (2001). Decision technology. *Annual Review of Psychology,* **52,** 581–606.

Fiedler, F.E. (1967). *A theory of leadership effectiveness.* New York: McGraw–Hill.

Fiske, A.P. (1992). The four elementary forms of sociality: framework for a unified theory of social relations. *Psychological Review,* **18,** 255–97.

Freeman, J., Hess, K.P., Spitz, G., *et al.* (2003). Collaborative critical thinking. In *Proceedings of the 8th International Command and Control Research and Technology Symposium.* Washington, DC.

Hart, R. and McLeod, P. (2003). Rethinking team building in geographically dispersed teams: one message at a time. *Organizational Dynamics,* **31,** 352–61.

Hayne, S.C., Pollard, C.E., and Rice, R.E. (2003). Identification of comment authorship in anonymous group support systems. *Journal of Management Information Systems,* **20,** 301–29.

Ho, T.H. and Raman, K.S. (1991). The effect of GSS and elected leadership on small group meetings. *Journal of Management Information Systems,* **8,** 109–33.

Horner-Long, P. and Schoenberg, R. (2002). Does e-business require different leadership characteristics? An empirical investigation. *European Management Journal,* **20,** 611–19.

Howell, J.M. and Avolio, B.J. (1993). Transformational leadership, transactional leadership, locus of control, and support for innovation: key predictors of consolidated-business-unit performance. *Journal of Applied Psychology,* **78,** 891–902.

Howell, J.M. and Boies, K. (2004). Champions of technological innovation: the influence of contextual knowledge, role orientation, idea generation, and idea promotion on champion emergence. *The Leadership Quarterly,* **15,** 123–43.

Howell, J.M. and Frost, P.J. (1989). A laboratory study of charismatic leadership. *Organizational Behavior and Human Decision Processes,* **43,** 243–69.

Jonassen, D.H. and Kwon, H.I. (2001). Communication patterns in computer mediated versus face-to-face group problem solving. *Educational Technology Research and Development,* **49,** 35–51.

Judge, T.A. and Bono, J.E. (2000). Five factor model of personality and transformational leadership. *Journal of Applied Psychology,* **85,** 751–65.

Kahai, S.S., Sosik, J.J., and Avolio, B.J. (2003). Effects of leadership style, anonymity, and rewards on creativity-relevant processes and outcomes in an electronic meeting system context. *The Leadership Quarterly,* **14,** 499–524.

Kayworth, T. and Leidner, D. (2000). The global virtual manager: a prescription for success. *European Management Journal,* **18,** 183–94.

Kelloway, E., Barling, J., Kelley, E., Comtois, and Gatien, B. (2003). Remote transformational leadership. *Leadership & Organization Development Journal,* **24,** 162–71.

Kissler, G. (2001). E-leadership. *Organizational Dynamics*, **30**, 121–33.

Latham, G. (2003). Goal setting: a five-step approach to behavior change. *Organizational Dynamics*, **32**, 309–18.

Locke, E.A. and Latham, G.P. (1990). *A theory of goal setting and task performance.* Upper Saddle River, NJ: Prentice-Hall.

March, J.G. (1994). *A primer of decision making.* New York: Free Press.

Maznevski, M.L. and Chudoba, K.M. (2000). Bridging space over time: global virtual team dynamics and effectiveness. *Organizational Science*, **11**, 473–92.

Mellers, B.A., Schwartz, A., and Cooke, A.D.J. (1998). Judgment and decision making. *Annual Review of Psychology*, **49**, 447–77.

Murthy, U.S. and Kerr, D.S. (2003). Decision making performance of interacting groups: an experimental investigation of the effects of task type and communication mode. *Information & Management*, **40**, 351–60.

Payne, J.W., Bettman, J.R., and Johnson, E.J. (1992). Behavioral decision research: a constructive processing perspective. *Annual Review of Psychology*, **43**, 87–131.

Postmes, T. and Lea, M. (2000). Social processes and group decision making: anonymity in group decision support systems. *Ergonomics*, **43**, 1252–4.

Pulley, M., McCarthy, J., and Taylor, S. (2000). E-leadership in the networked economy. *Leadership in Action*, **20**, 1–7.

Pulley, M., Sessa, V., Fleenor, J., and Pohlmann, T. (2001). E-leadership: separating the reality from the hype. *Leadership in Action*, **21**, 3–6.

Rogelberg, S.G., Barnes–Farrell, J.L., and Lowe, C.A. (1992). The stepladder technique: an alternative group structure facilitating effective group decision making. *Journal of Applied Psychology*, **77**, 730–7.

Sia, C.L., Tan, B.C.Y., and Wei, K.K. (2002). Group polarization and computer-mediated communication: effects of communication cues, social presence, and anonymity. *Information Systems Research*, **13**, 70–90.

Sosik, J.J., Avolio, B.J., and Kahai, S.S. (1997). Effects of leadership style and anonymity and group potency and effectiveness in a group decision support system. *Journal of Applied Psychology*, **82**, 89–103.

Spector, P.E. (2000). *Industrial and organizational psychology: research and practice.* New York: John Wiley & Sons.

Thompson, L.F. and Coovert, M.D. (2002). Stepping up to the challenge: a critical examination of face-to-face and computer-mediated team decision making. *Group Dynamics: Theory, Research, and Practice*, **6**, 52–64.

Wayne, S.J. and Ferris, G.F. (1990). Influence tactics, affect, and exchange quality in supervisor-subordinate dyads: a laboratory experiment and field study. *Journal of Applied Psychology*, **75**, 487–99.

Weisband, S. (2002). Maintaining awareness in distributed team collaboration: implications for leadership and performance. In P. Hinds and S. Kiesler (eds), *Distributed work* (pp. 311–33). Cambridge, MA: MIT Press.

Whitworth, B., Gallupe, B., and McQueen, R. (2001). Generating agreement in computer-mediated groups. *Small Group Research*, **32**, 625–65.

Yammarino, F., Dansereau, F., and Kennedy, C. (2001). A multiple-level multidimensional approach to leadership: viewing leadership through the elephant's eye. *Organizational Dynamics*, **29**, 149–63.

Yoo, Y. and Alavi, M. (2004). Emergent leadership in virtual teams: what do emergent leaders do? *Information and Organization*, **14**, 27–58.

Zigurs, I. and Kozar, K. (1994). An exploratory study of roles in computer-supported groups. *MIS Quarterly*, **4**, 277–97.

Chapter 10

Prejudice, discrimination, and the Internet

Jack Glaser and Kimberly Kahn

That which makes the study of prejudice and discrimination on the Internet exciting also makes it particularly challenging. Specifically, there are many topics and questions that have not yet been empirically explored, so while we currently have only a partial, nascent literature to draw upon, the opportunities are great. Nevertheless, while a small number of hypotheses have been directly tested, there is a growing literature that helps to establish a useful framework for the study of intergroup bias on the Internet. First, we would be well advised to look for relevant precedents regarding major communications innovations, really paradigm shifts, such as the advent of the telegraph, telephone, radio, and television. The Internet represents a shift in human communication and entertainment of comparable proportions. Thus, we may at the very least identify and describe a useful context for understanding the impact of communications technology on social psychology in general, if not intergroup bias more specifically.

Not surprisingly, others before us have made this connection. For example, Kraut *et al.* (1998), in discussing social involvement, noted that the advent of television has likely had a negative effect. This has relevance for intergroup bias because social involvement, or at least intergroup contact, is a demonstrated mechanism for reducing bias (e.g. Pettigrew & Tropp, 2000). To the extent that the Internet reduces direct personal contact it may undermine progress in this regard, as we will discuss further below. McKenna and Bargh (2000) have noted that the telephone and television, as with many technological innovations, were first met with considerable skepticism and apprehension, and that a similar reaction has occurred to some extent with the Internet, due in no small part to perceptions of the prevalence of pornography on the web.

What is not in doubt is that the Internet facilitates communication in many respects. Information, including music, graphics, and videos, is easily posted and retrieved from the world wide web. Audio-visual two-way communication on the Internet is possible, although not yet widely utilized. Electronic mail and chatrooms allow for free and, in some cases, real-time communication without borders. To the extent that communication builds bridges and breaks down barriers, one would expect the Internet to be a bias-reducing force. That, of course, depends on the type of information being shared and the nature of the interactions.

The nature of Internet-based interactions is crucial to the understanding of prejudice and discrimination on the Internet. Because these interactions have been, to date, mostly text-based, they lack much of the information conveyed in traditional, face-to-face, or even audio-only communication, such as tone, volume, gesture, facial expression (Bargh, 2002), as well as communicator characteristics such as age, size, gender, race/ethnicity, or physical stigma. This state of affairs leads us to make some interesting projections about prejudice and discrimination in cyberspace. Some of these projections are informed by classical research on prejudice and discrimination, but diverge meaningfully because of historical changes and the unique qualities of the Internet and the nature of computer-mediated social interaction.

In 1934, LaPiere published his now classic study investigating the relation between attitudes and behaviors, specifically with regard to racial prejudice and discrimination. LaPiere found that formal, written requests for hotel and restaurant accommodations for minorities were almost always rejected, but most of these people were accommodated when the services were requested in person. Wax (cited in Allport, 1954) and Linn (1965) observed similar discrepancies. Thus, one might predict that people's felt and expressed prejudice exceeds their discriminatory capacities. However, in a post civil rights era, where modern (McConahay, 1986), aversive (Gaertner & Dovidio, 1986), ambivalent (Glick & Fiske, 2001), and implicit (Banaji & Greenwald, 1995) forms of bias prevail and explicit expressions of prejudice are taboo, subtle, perhaps unintended forms of discrimination appear to persist (e.g. Correll *et al.*, 2002; Greenwald *et al.*, 2003) in the absence of overt bias. Consequently, we are inclined to predict the opposite of what LaPierre (1934) and his contemporaries observed. Specifically, decision makers today would not be likely to make an explicit decision to deny some resource or service on the basis of group membership, but, in the moment, might find an excuse to behave discriminatorily, as is borne out in research employing unobtrusive measures (Crosby *et al.*, 1980).

These conditions lead us to make some interesting, and seemingly paradoxical predictions about prejudice and discrimination on the Internet. Specifically, due to the anonymous, spontaneous, impersonal, and disinhibited nature of much Internet-based communication, prejudice may, in many ways, be more likely to be expressed overtly. On the other hand, due to automation and the ability of potential targets to also remain anonymous, perhaps concealing group-identifying cues, many forms of discrimination may be less common in cyberspace. Consequently, even though the Internet is in many ways the epitome of societal progress, prejudice and discrimination online may at least superficially resemble the pre-civil rights state of being reflected in LaPiere's (1934) research better than it does contemporary face-to-face interaction.

In this chapter, we will explore the important relation between the unusual mode of social interaction the Internet engenders and intergroup prejudice and discrimination. In doing this, we will attempt to apply theoretical coherence while covering the numerous interesting social and psychological aspects of the Internet as it relates to prejudice and discrimination. Making a distinction between the internal mental processes of stereotyping and prejudice as opposed to the behavior of discrimination, this chapter will discuss these separately. First, we will consider the role of the anonymity emblematic of Internet-based communication in promoting stereotyping and prejudice, as well as the proliferation of hate-group activity online. We will then discuss the potential of the Internet to promote the reduction of bias, including the facilitation of research on that topic. With regard to discrimination, we will review the various means by which it can be reduced and enhanced online, including, again, the role of anonymity, but also such phenomena as cyberostracism, harassment, and institutional discrimination. Given the breadth of this topic and the relative dearth of extant research, this discussion will not be definitive, but we hope it will serve, at the least, as a useful foundation for further analysis.

Stereotyping and prejudice on the Internet

The 'triarchic' theory of attitudes in social psychology divides this important construct into affective, cognitive, and behavioral components (e.g. Hilgard, 1980; McGuire, 1985, 1989). Similarly, intergroup bias (a specific type of attitude) can be broken down into its corresponding components—prejudice, stereotypes, and discrimination. Traditionally, the term 'prejudice' has often been used as the overarching rubric, under which there are attitudes, stereotypes, and discrimination (e.g. Allport, 1954). However, this strikes us as awkward and tautological, so we prefer to use the global term 'intergroup bias' (Blair, 2001) and to reserve 'prejudice' for the more affective (emotional or evaluative) component.

Having said that, we are going to group stereotyping and prejudice together for the sake of this discussion. This is not because we conflate these two distinct constructs (quite the contrary, e.g. Glaser, 1999). Rather, given our thesis about the paradoxical effects of the Internet, it makes sense to group together the internal, mental processes (stereotyping and prejudice) and contrast them with the outward, behavioral process (discrimination).

There are many theories, such as realistic group conflict theory (Sherif et al., 1961) and social identity theory (Tajfel & Turner, 1979) that seek, with considerable success, to explain the origins of intergroup bias and conflict. We do not have space here to review them, or the vast literature on stereotype content, structure, formation, and change that indirectly informs the present discussion. In the interest of clarity and parsimony, we will take a simpler approach, assuming that there are multiple, non-mutually exclusive determinants of intergroup bias, and we will discuss them where they are specifically relevant to some feature of Internet-based social processes.

Our primary, and admittedly simple thesis with regard to stereotypes and prejudice is that they are more likely to be expressed and transmitted on the Internet than in most modes of communication. This would be the case because of the unusual level of anonymity that prevails online, thus leading people to express themselves in less self-conscious and socially desirable ways. On a less banal level, this same anonymity, coupled with the efficiency and unbounded nature of Internet-based communication, has led to the proliferation of racist hate-group activity, thus promoting intergroup bias. Lest one be thoroughly discouraged by these implications of the Internet for intergroup relations, it is heartening to consider that the web offers promising opportunities for reducing bias as well. Each of these premises will be considered below, before turning to the effect of the Internet on discrimination.

The effect of anonymity on prejudice

Anonymity is one of the most distinctive and influential features of Internet-based communication (Back, 2002; Friedman & Resnick, 2001; McKenna & Bargh, 2000; Spears et al., 2002; Winter & Huff, 1996) and is perhaps the most important aspect with regard to stereotyping and prejudice. McKenna and Bargh (2000) have rightly noted that the remarkable anonymity afforded on e-mail and in chatrooms can disinhibit and even 'deindividuate' (Zimbardo, 1969) people, leading to relatively high degrees of expression of prejudice. Compounding this, they say, is the possibility that people expressing such attitudes will be reinforced by those who write in support, perhaps creating an 'illusion of large numbers' (McKenna & Bargh, 2000, p. 64). Winter and Huff (1996), in their analysis of women's efforts to find safe environments online, also indicate that this anonymity can lead to high levels of gender harassment on the Internet. Spears et al. (2002) caution that anonymous interaction should

not be confused with non-social interaction and, in fact, argue that group identification can even be strengthened in anonymous, computer-mediated communication. Such enhanced ingroup identification could, in turn, contribute to
stronger prejudice above and beyond the disinhibiting effects of anonymity.

Reference to the general literature on intergroup bias indicates that people are
less likely to express biases when their identity is knowable (e.g. Fazio *et al.*,
1995; Plant & Devine, 1998). Furthermore, the relation between anonymity and
setting (i.e. private vs. public) has been more generally explored in the domain
of computer use. Richman *et al.* (1999) performed a meta-analysis of computer-
administered questionnaires, pencil-and-paper questionnaires, and face-to-face
interviews to examine their effects on the social desirability of responses, finding
that less social desirability distortion was exhibited when people's computer use
occurred in private. Computer use most often occurs in private; therefore, the
private environment effects may be a better simulation of real computer use.
The private setting may instill a greater assurance of anonymity and the ability
to respond more freely with relative impunity. With regard to Internet-based
expressions of prejudice, this possibility was tested directly by Evans *et al.* (2003)
who found that on Internet-based questionnaire measures of racial bias,
respondents exhibited greater degrees of bias when giving their responses in a
private setting, specifically, in the absence of an experimenter.

Spears *et al.* (2002) offer another manner in which the protection of anonymity
may promote the expression of bias. They argue that online social behavior
combined with anonymity augment group identities, making individuals more
'socially responsive'. Results of experiments on identity salience conclude that
social influence reaches its highest and most pronounced effects when individuals are isolated (in private) and when their identity is effectively hidden from the
salient group. Therefore, group-based social effects including stereotyping,
discriminatory actions, and group conformity are more likely to occur.

Postmes *et al.* (2001) conducted an experiment testing the effect of
anonymity on social behavior occurring on the Internet. Group members
were either anonymous or identifiable, and then primed with a social norm of
efficiency or prosocial behavior. Anonymous group members exhibited the
social norm primed to them consistently more often than identifiable members. In a second study, non-primed group members followed the behavior of
primed group members only in the anonymity condition. It appears that
anonymity can bolster group normative behavior, enhancing the potential for
the expression of prejudice or discrimination if it is a group norm. Postmes
et al. (1998) reached similar conclusions.

When online users form common identity groups, and a feature of those
groups is anonymity, adherence to group influence is enhanced. Instead of

breaking down social boundaries, quite the opposite effect occurs: the social boundaries are strengthened. Hence, the substance of group norms signifi- cantly affects behavioral responses online (Postmes *et al.*, 1999). Furthermore, in a study on self-stereotyping in online discussions, anonymity was shown to actually breed gender-stereotypic behavior (Postmes & Spears, 2002). Hence, intergroup biases are not necessarily reduced, but may still persist, and even be enhanced, in spite of anonymity's barriers.

In summary, for a variety of reasons, it seems reasonable to infer that people will be more likely to express bias in the anonymous and impersonal condi- tions that much of cyberspace affords. Nevertheless, this would be a worth- while and fruitful direction of further study. Specifically, it would be useful to determine if, given increased expression of bias in anonymous computer- mediated communication, transmission of such biases occurred. One must consider that persuasiveness of messages is dependent to some degree on the reputation of the source (McGuire, 1985) and it is possible that anonymity undermines source credibility (Friedman & Resnick, 2001).

Hate groups online

Less subtle than the effects of anonymity on normal discourse on the Internet is the proliferation of extremist activity. Estimates of the number of 'hate sites' on the web range in the hundreds (e.g. Anti-Defamation League, 2000; Back, 2002; Franklin, 2003; Gerstenfeld *et al.*, 2003) and, by some accounts, the thousands (Simon Wiesenthal Center, 2002), extending at least across the U.S., Canada, South America, and Europe (Beckles, 1997). The Anti-Defamation League (ADL, 2000), having compiled an extensive inventory and analysis of Internet-based extremism, warns that the Internet provides an excellent venue for hate-group promotion:

> Whereas extremists once had to stand on street corners spewing their hate and venom—reaching only a few passersby—now they can rant from the safety of their own homes; anyone can easily create a Web site, propelling their message, good or bad, to the entire world. (p. 1)

The ADL further notes that extremist presence in cyberspace is not limited to e-mail and chatrooms, but includes sales of hate-group rock music, merchan- dise, racist video games, special kids' sites, and even the provision of Internet service, because many mainstream Internet service providers (ISPs) and sever- al countries prohibit hate speech or hate sites (see also Back, 2002; Gerstenfeld *et al.*, 2003; Human Rights and Equal Opportunities Commission, 2002).

Extremist groups also effectively promote their agenda by circulating racist and anti-Semitic urban legends online (Back, 2002; Lee & Leets, 2002). Lee and Leets (2002) experimentally tested the effectiveness of online 'persuasive storytelling', specifically of racist urban legends, on adolescents, finding that explicit, low narrative messages (i.e. lacking plots or compelling characters)—perhaps corresponding best to most contemporary urban legends—had the most lasting persuasive effects.

Because of their prevalence and the breadth of ventures, extremist groups are likely increasing prejudice in society, and across societies, by disseminating racist rhetoric and by recruiting members. Several scholars have noted that the qualities of the Internet are especially well suited to hate-group recruitment. The importance of anonymity, for example, in the extensive use of the Internet by extremists and their putative recruiting success, is explained by Levin (2002), who notes that people can access sites and even participate without disclosing their identity. Gerstenfeld et al. (2003) note that the posting of web pages allows for a high degree of image control—something extremist groups might have difficulty with in more traditional forms of mass media. Similarly, Burris et al. (2000) have observed that 'soft core' hate sites (those that are more subtle and misleading, such as sites for children) may serve as effective recruiting tools, and that the borderless nature of the Internet allows supremacists to actively recruit in countries where such activity is illegal (see also Back, 2002).

The promotion and provision of activities typically attractive to young people (e.g. rock music, video games) appears to serve extremist recruitment well (Back, 2002) by appealing to an impressionable audience and making intolerant behavior normative. Simultaneously, it provides an acceptable and safe outlet for those who might otherwise try to avoid the stigma associated with such behavior (McKenna & Bargh, 1998).

Reducing stereotyping and prejudice with the Internet

The preceding discussion has highlighted how the nature of the Internet, especially its anonymity, may contribute to stereotyping and prejudice in society by disinhibiting expressions of bias in the general public and by facilitating recruitment, organization, and information dissemination by racist extremists. Lest we be completely demoralized by this analysis, we should consider that the Internet also affords opportunities to reduce intergroup bias, through the active promotion of tolerance (capitalizing on the ability to reach a broad audience), the facilitation of intergroup contact, the possibility of a long-term reduction in the importance of social categories as Internet-based communication becomes ever more commonplace, and the promise of the Internet for studying and thereby gaining greater understanding of intergroup bias. We consider these possibilities next.

Promoting tolerance

Perhaps the most direct effect on reducing bias on the Internet would be active programs to promote tolerance. This is not a theoretical premise. In addition to groups such as the ADL and the Southern Poverty Law Center (SPLC), with active websites tracking prejudice and discrimination, there are now sites that explicitly promote tolerance. Prominent among these is the SPLC's 'Teaching Tolerance' program (*www.tolerance.org*). The Simon Wiesenthal Center hosts the Museum of Tolerance (*http://www.wiesenthal.com/mot/*) which features an online learning center. The 'Understanding Prejudice' site (*http://www.under-standingprejudice.org/links/reducing.htm*) is a clearing-house of school-based activities, diversity training programs, community development programs, and other tolerance enhancing resources. 'Beyond Prejudice' (*http://www.beyondprejudice.com/reduce_org.html*) is a website dedicated to helping reduce bias within organizations. Other organizations, not primarily devoted to promoting the reduction of prejudice and discrimination, such as the National Association of School Psychologists (see *http://www.nasponline.org/NEAT/tolerance.htm*), offer prejudice-reducing materials on the web. Additionally, numerous organizations, from individual schools and libraries to statewide education departments (e.g. *http://www.cde.ca.gov/spbranch/safety/hmb/hmb.asp*) to national organizations (e.g. *http://www.peacecorps gov/wws/guides/looking/lesson33.html*) to international organizations (e.g. *http://www.unesco.or.id/prog/culture/cl-promo.htm*), incorporate intergroup tolerance-promoting sections in their websites.

One information technological approach to decreasing prejudice that takes into account the potential of the Internet itself for promoting prejudice is to restrict a user's access to bigoted sites. Several software companies offer filtering software, particularly for sheltering children from interfaces their parents prefer they do not access, that can include hate-group or racist sites. The ADL has produced and offers 'Hatefilter'—a filtering program that is tailored for hate sites. According to the ADL:

> Hatefilter is a free software product designed to act as a gatekeeper. It protects children by blocking access to World Wide Web sites of individuals or groups that, in the judgment of the Anti-Defamation League, advocate hatred, bigotry or even violence towards Jews or other groups on the basis of their religion, race, ethnicity, sexual orientation or other immutable characteristics (*http://www.adl.org/hatefilter/*).

The combination of tolerance-promoting and bias-filtering Internet resources may serve to mitigate intergroup bias, especially among young people who use the Internet most and are targeted by racist groups online. However, that such a mitigating effect is really occurring is an empirical question that remains to be answered.

Does Internet-mediated 'contact' reduce bias?

The most prominent and well-tested psychological paradigm for reducing intergroup bias is the contact hypothesis—the idea that bringing people from different groups into direct contact and interaction will reduce stereotyping and prejudice (see Pettigrew & Tropp, 2000, for a thorough review and meta-analysis). It is possible that the Internet, with its ability to promote communication across physical and perhaps cultural boundaries, has the potential to reduce profoundly intergroup bias.

Allport (1954) delineated specific conditions for contact to be effective, including equal status, sanction by authority, common goals, and a non-competitive relationship. With regard to determining if Internet-based intergroup contact can effectively reduce bias, we need to consider first that such interactions are qualitatively different from the types of face-to-face contact that have typically been involved in studies on this topic. One might question whether computer-mediated communication (CMC) is 'contact' at all.

As far as Allport's (1954) conditions are concerned, it is possible that CMC would have mixed effects. Status parity, for example, would likely be enhanced because status cues, such as gender, age, and attractiveness, are less likely to be evident. Authority sanction, on the other hand, may lack palpability in CMC, but it is certainly attainable. Interdependent pursuit of common goals can also be achieved online. Perhaps this, too, would be less tangible, and therefore less effective, than with face-to-face contact, but with increasing work and commerce occurring online, it seems feasible to attain meaningful degrees of these conditions.

Importantly, Pettigrew and Tropp (2004), in their meta-analysis of contact studies, have found that while Allport's (1954) conditions enhance the bias-reducing effects of contact, it is not necessary that they be present simultaneously for bias to be reduced. Mere contact appears to be a sufficient condition for bias reduction, and this reduction appears to be lasting and to generalize beyond the individuals with whom one has contact and even beyond the groups to which they belong (Pettigrew & Tropp, 2004). However, what may pose a more profound limit on most Internet-based intergroup contact is the lack of information about one's interaction partner's group membership, compounded by the lack of salience (the absence of continuing and tangible cues) of that membership even if it is made known. Consequently, there is an irony here in that the very quality of the Internet that enhances equal status—the removal of group identification—may undermine the effects of contact.

Even if group identity can be made salient, online intergroup contact may not have the desired effect. Postmes et al.'s (1998) laboratory-based research on the effects of inter- and intragroup contact in computer-mediated communication indicates that, despite the potential of the Internet to remove demographic and status barriers, identification with one's ingroup and biases toward outgroups can in fact be enhanced through CMC. Postmes *et al.* (2002), in two Internet-based experiments, found that intergroup (in fact, international) communication led to greater polarization when the groups were 'depersonalized' (i.e. when the interaction partners' group membership was relatively salient) as opposed to 'individuated'. They also found that stereotypes were more salient when the outgroup was depersonalized. Similarly, Douglas and McGarty (2001) found that when online communicators were identifiable to an ingroup audience, they exhibited greater stereotyping in descriptions of outgroup members.

These results confirm the complexities of Internet-based intergroup contact. Specifically, the necessary condition, for contact to reduce prejudice, of recognizing the outgroup to which the interaction partners belong, may undermine the prejudice-reducing effects of contact when it occurs on the Internet, perhaps because of the absence of face-to-face, personal interaction and the individuation and empathy that engenders.

In summary, there may be short-term, or even immediate reductions in the expression of prejudice on the Internet, purely as a function of the removal of many group-identity cues. The potential for long-term prejudice reduction from greater intergroup contact via the Internet because of its relative lack of boundaries, however, poses a less propitious scenario. To the extent that Internet-based communication inhibits the transmission of group membership cues and even appears to exacerbate group preferences in some circumstances, significant and widespread reductions in prejudice are not likely. As the medium shifts away from text-based communication to more multimedia (i.e. audiovisual) transmission, this state of affairs may change.

Studying prejudice with the Internet to gain greater understanding

In addition to gaining knowledge of how prejudice operates online (something of increasing importance as more social interaction occurs there), social psychologists have begun using the Internet to investigate more general principles of intergroup bias. The Internet allows for rapid access to many individuals at relatively low cost, through e-mail recruitment and web-based survey and experiment media. With a growing number of social psychological experiments being conducted with computer interface anyway, this development was inevitable.

In addition to making data collection relatively cheap, as discussed above, the Internet opens up access to groups that may otherwise be difficult to recruit, such as members of marginal or stigmatized groups (e.g. Glaser *et al.*,

2002; McKenna & Bargh, 1998, 2000). This allows for surreptitious observation of 'natural' behavior in the tradition of the lost-letter technique (Milgram *et al.*, 1965) that was developed to study helping behavior and later adapted to the study of attitudes, including prejudice (e.g. Montanye *et al.*, 1971). In fact, the lost-letter technique has been adapted directly for the Internet by Stern and Faber (1997) who investigated the extent to which people would return misdirected e-mail messages to the sender as a function of the political views expressed in the message. Although they found no effect of political content, the potential of such a technique is clear.

Shohat and Musch (2003) similarly capitalized on the nature of Internet-based interactions to study, unobtrusively, intergroup bias by manipulating the ethnicity of a seller in an online auction. This study will be discussed more thoroughly below with regard to discrimination, but it serves as an excellent example of the opportunities available for research in this area, and therefore the potential for gaining greater understanding of prejudice in the service of reducing it.

Glaser *et al.* (2002) used the Internet to directly assess what they considered the overestimated impact of economic variations on hate crime (Green *et al.*, 1998). To gain a sense of relative effects of factors that might precipitate hate crime, one would want to study populations that are most likely to have some meaningful variance in this low base-rate behavior. Accordingly, Glaser *et al.* (2002) turned to White racist chatrooms to assess the reactions of participants there to references to job competition with Blacks, Black migration into White neighborhoods, and interracial marriage. The research indicated that denizens of racist chatrooms were significantly more likely to advocate engaging in anti-Black hate crime if the posed scenario involved interracial marriage, and, consistent with archival research results, there was virtually no effect of job competition (an economic factor) on such advocacy of violence. Obtaining meaningful (i.e. potentially predictive) data on advocacy of interracial violence as a function of experimentally controlled variables would be extremely difficult, if at all possible, without the access and anonymity enabled by the Internet. In this case, as with the similar work by McKenna and Bargh (1998) and others, the Internet has allowed for an understanding of social psychological phenomena that might otherwise be beyond our reach.

Lee and Leets (2002), as described above, have also made use of Internet-based access to racist groups, obtaining real content from racist sites and testing the persuasiveness of different types of messages. Using a general population sample, and therefore being able to employ a more standard and straightforward survey method than Glaser *et al.* (2002) could, they were able to achieve considerable understanding of the *transmission* of prejudice using real-world messages from groups that might be difficult to access safely without the

Internet. Perhaps the greater understanding of how prejudice operates and is transmitted, made possible by research of this sort, will ultimately lead to meaningful reductions in prejudice and discrimination and their effects.

While the above-described studies take advantage of the unique characteristics of the Internet that allow access to groups and information that might otherwise be difficult to attain, there is also a massive and active undertaking to harness another strength of the Internet to gain a broad understanding of intergroup bias. The Internet allows for highly cost-effective collection of data, with samples of a magnitude previously unknown even to public opinion pollsters. Nosek *et al.* (2002*a*, *b*) have recognized this potential and, since the mid-1990s, have collected data from literally hundreds of thousands of participants with an ever-expanding and evolving collection of web-based implicit association tests (IAT).

Originally developed as a laboratory-based, computerized measure of nonconscious attitudes and beliefs (i.e. those that reside outside of conscious awareness and control), the IAT, which involves measuring the relative ease (speed and accuracy) with which people categorize when exemplars of concepts are paired one way or another (e.g. Black with negative/White with positive vs. vice versa), has been widely used and well validated (e.g. Greenwald *et al.*, 1998; Greenwald & Nosek, 2001; McConnell & Leibold, 2001). By making a very user-friendly portal to multiple IATs available and widely linked on the web, Banaji, Greenwald, Nosek and their collaborators, have been able to obtain tens of thousands of test results for a number of different types of implicit associations. Furthermore, the samples are so large that, even if they are not representative of a larger population, they are probably important.

Based on over 600,000 individual web-based IATs, Nosek *et al.* (2002*a*) reported, among other findings, that respondents on average showed a clear preference for White over Black, and young over old, and tended to link men with science and career and women with liberal arts and family. Furthermore, the ingroup favoritism that tends to be observed in low-status groups when explicit attitude measures are used is less consistent in the IAT data, with preferences being dictated more by prevailing cultural biases. More specifically, while an overwhelming majority of self-described White respondents show a preference for White over Black, self-described Black participants are about evenly split. While there are clear questions about the representativeness of the samples obtained (e.g. are they skewed toward higher education, higher income, etc.?), the researchers have obtained a fair amount of demographic data on respondents, and this at least allows for comparative analyses.

The web-based IAT is now so well linked and utilized that it has become part of American popular culture, being referred to in at least one prime-time television show ('King of the Hill'), as well as numerous news stories. An adaptation of the procedure is available through the Southern Poverty Law Center's website. These developments indicate that, in addition to the knowledge gained through the analysis of web-based IAT data and the indirect effect that has on reducing prejudice through scientific progress, there is an increasingly direct effect on prejudice reduction through the raising of public awareness[1] of the prevalence of prejudice.

Problems with Internet–based research on prejudice

It should be made clear that using the Internet to study social psychology in general, and prejudice more specifically, is not without hazards (see Skitka & Sargis, this volume, for further discussion). Hamilton (1999) noted that online researchers do not consistently utilize the safeguards typically employed to protect research participants' confidentiality and emotional well-being. In particular, informed consent and thorough debriefing seem less reliable. It is not clear that there is a systematic difference between traditional (in person) social science research procedures and those used online in this regard, but it is likely that, given the well-established procedures in place at most research institutions, fundamental deviations in the research paradigm (such as those associated with the Internet) will be accompanied by deviations in related procedures. In some cases, informed consent is no doubt overlooked due to negligence. In others, for example in quasi-observational research on sensitive groups and topics (e.g. Glaser *et al.*, 2002; Shohat & Musch, 2003; Stern & Faber, 1997), foregoing informed consent is necessary and deliberate. In such cases, obtaining informed consent would undermine the purpose of the research—to observe, surreptitiously, naturalistic behavior in groups to which access might otherwise be impossible.

Glaser *et al.* (2002), for example, addressed these concerns by ensuring that interactions with confederates were entirely voluntary and in no way coercive, that interactions did not deviate from the normative behavior in the environment, and that respondents' anonymity was carefully protected through the use of their own pseudonyms and the immediate assignment of random identification codes. Interestingly, Nosek *et al.* (2002*b*) point out the advantage that the physical absence of an experimenter is likely to reduce the otherwise coercive nature of many laboratory experiments (as evidenced in studies on obedience to authority, e.g. Milgram, 1974).

The trade-off between informed consent and valid research that is sometimes necessitated with reactive populations or sensitive subjects, must be

---

[1] Or, what some have begun calling, 'unconsciousness-raising'.

weighed very carefully and seriously. Just as with surreptitious research techniques of the past, such as the lost-letter method (Milgram *et al.*, 1965), informed consent is not always possible. And much traditional laboratory research involving unobtrusive measures of prejudice and discrimination (see Crosby *et al.*, 1980), while involving some official informed consent, cannot include complete prior information about the actual nature of the research, lest it become obtrusive. Such research must be conducted in as innocuous a manner as is conceivable.

Other ethical concerns raised about Internet-based research have to do with ensuring confidentiality of participants' identities and safe storage of their data, as well as avoiding the inclusion of minors without parental consent (Nosek *et al.*, 2002*b*). Nosek *et al.* (2002*b*) offer some constructive advice on these matters, noting that, thanks to encryption technology, web-based data may in fact be more secure than standard paper-and-pencil or videotaped data used in most social psychological experiments. Additionally, they note that there are established systems for restricting Internet transactions to adults (e.g. 'Adult Check') that could be responsibly employed by researchers.

Even for Internet-based research that is not so unobtrusive, there are unique problems that must be addressed. The anonymity inherent in Internet-based communication, and that is so advantageous for assessing sensitive constructs, can also pose a pitfall to the extent that researchers cannot be sure that participants are who or what they say they are (see also Skitka & Sargis, this volume, for a similar discussion). Nosek *et al.* (2002*a, b*), for example, acknowledge the real possibility that many of their hundreds of thousands of respondents are not giving accurate information about themselves, and many may be engaging in the same tests many times under different identities. Because of the uncontrollability of the constructs the IAT is designed to measure, IAT data analysts can, to a considerable degree of effectiveness, screen data to detect 'cheaters' (i.e. people who intentionally try to manipulate the results of their tests, either to present themselves more positively or simply to cause mischief). However, identifying those who misrepresent themselves on the questionnaires that accompany the IAT is not as straightforward. On the other hand, again because of the extra anonymity inherent in online communication, there is good reason to believe that responses to web-based questions are *more* accurate (Evans *et al.*, 2003). It is too early to tell, and systematic analysis of these issues is warranted, but the net effect of these competing factors may be negligible.

Ecological validity of Internet-based research

There are legitimate questions about the generalizability of attitudes and behaviors assessed online and the representativeness of samples drawn, when a clear selection bias exists based on access to a networked computer and the requisite interests and skills for being active online. Nevertheless, with increasing prevalence of Internet access and increasing time online for users, not to mention improving ratios of productive activity online relative to down time (as a result of rapidly improving transmission technology such as DSL and digital cable), online activities are ever more ecologically valid representations of human social life simply because increasing proportions of our lives are spent online. Internet-based research is no longer just a convenient proxy for 'real' research; online behavior *is real* behavior. This is, perhaps, especially important to keep in mind as we turn our attention now to the behavioral aspect of intergroup bias—discrimination on the Internet.

Discrimination and the Internet

Long heralded as a medium through which equality and democracy could be brought to the masses, the Internet has so far met with mixed success in this regard. One promising area, however, is the Internet's apparent ability to weaken discrimination and discriminatory effects. Internet users are bestowed with the unusual capacity to release as much or as little of their true identity as desired, allowing them to safeguard themselves from the negative reactions they may encounter when these identity cues are salient in daily life. Although the anonymous nature of Internet interactions may reduce discrimination, there are other facets of the Internet to consider in an attempt to understand its overall effects on the broad phenomenon of discrimination.

Discriminatory effects of software

A growing body of research exists on general discrimination experienced through text-based communication, including, but not limited to the Internet, and propagated through computers and their related networks. Because Internet use entails computer use, computer-based discrimination most likely also relates to Internet discrimination. The possibility of computers 'behaving' discriminatorily seems oxymoronic. However, some research illustrates how this might occur. In a study performed by Cooper *et al.* (1990), sex-stereotyped (i.e. with elements typically preferred by boys versus girls) educational computer programs were used by middle school students, with their responses examined for discriminatory effects. Results indicated that using a cross-gender specific type of software increases stress amongst users when used in a public setting, such as a classroom. Importantly, similar situational stress effects were not replicated when the students performed the various tasks in a private environment, perhaps suggesting a possible escape or way to lessen the discriminatory impact of computers. Though not specifically involving the Internet, this finding supports the contention that discrimination is reduced primarily because of the anonymity experienced by computer users. While using computers in a public forum, that protection is likely reduced, perhaps allowing the situational stress to occur.

Cooper *et al.* (1990) examined educational computer programs, while numerous similar programs and games are available online. Because schools and students are incorporating the Internet into educational routines, these discriminatory effects may be consequential.

Cyberostracism

One form of discrimination—social exclusion—may occur online. If it does, it could have real effects on its targets. Williams *et al.* (2000), seeking to examine such effects, labeled the phenomenon 'cyberostracism', and created an online experiment involving a virtual tossing game to study it further. Some participants were assigned to the 'ignored' condition, and the subsequent reactions were tracked. The study demonstrated that ostracized participants experienced a loss of control, more negative mood, and were more likely to conform to others on a later task. Williams *et al.* noted that cyberostracism can occur for highly ambiguous reasons, since it often transpires in chatrooms that lack useful cues present in normal interactions. It is this same ambiguity, however, that can serve as a partial buffer against negative effects. Because of the lack of cues, attributions of the reasons for the ostracism may vary. If race or other stigma cues are made salient by a name or style of response, for example, cyberostracism may still occur and supposed anonymity may only provide partial protection. Williams *et al.* (2002) showed that the attributional protection might help protect self-esteem, and prevent depression and helplessness, but may not be as effective in thwarting perceptions of lacking belongingness or meaningful existence. Studying cyberostracism entails examination of numerous facets. At the very least, it illustrates how the negative effects of discrimination are not likely confined to face-to-face interactions.

Gender harassment on the Internet

Discrimination and harassment experienced by women via the Internet has been another area of study. Gender is more frequently identified than race in online conversations, allowing the possibility for gender discrimination to occur more readily. The Internet was touted as a place for women to finally free themselves of the harassment traditionally experienced in classroom, employment, and other settings, but Biber *et al.* (2002) found that harassment experienced online may in fact be worse, or at least perceived as worse, than traditional harassment. Surveying students' perceptions of 'potentially harassing acts' described as occurring online or in a classroom setting, Biber *et al.* discovered that misogynist comments, including unwanted sexual and gender harassment and sexual coercion, were rated as more threatening and harassing when the comments were made online. The online discourse medium may actually intensify perceived harassment, instead of lessening it.

In an effort to reduce the possibility of discrimination and its effects on the Internet, separate electronic forums have been created for stigmatized groups of people. Systers (one such network) was established in 1987 by female computer scientists, and subsequently studied by Winter and Huff (1996). With electronic harassment common in chatrooms and other areas of the Internet, women programmers desired not only an escape, but a supportive area where their opinions and ideas could be shared. Women reported that men dominated most Internet chatroom discussion, causing a masculine style of speech to become the norm, and alienating women in the process. According to Winter and Huff, many women turned to chatrooms dedicated to women's issues to gain equal access and voice on the Internet, yet surprisingly found that the majority of responses and posts were from men.

The importance of anonymity in online discrimination

Despite the variety of human and social influences on it, the Internet's basic format often produces a reduction in discrimination, largely due to anonymity of potential targets. For example, the value of the ability to remain anonymous via the Internet was made apparent during the conflict in Kosovo, where people could communicate with each other and express their feelings without fear of reprisal from the highly repressive government (McKenna & Bargh, 1998). Computer-mediated conversations provide users with the freedom to release or withhold as much of their identity as they desire, creating a comfortable environment. Many people stigmatized by race, gender, disability, or sexual orientation, for example, seek out the Internet as a place of relief and escape from the 'real world' (McKenna & Bargh, 1998; McKenna & Seidman, this volume). It is the flexibility of anonymity—it being the user's prerogative to share information—that may be responsible for any decrease in discrimination.

In addition to having the ability to disclose less of one's own personality, the anonymity of the Internet permits a user to create an altogether fake identity. According to Riva (2002), the use of fake identities on the Internet is highly prevalent and often takes the form of gender switching. As McKenna and Bargh (2000) explain, the Internet's intrinsic ability to effectively shelter one's true identity allows people the opportunity to try out an assortment of new 'selves', which would be impossible in 'real' life. People chronically battling discrimination can break away from, and even take on, the identity of a member of the high-status group. Many women, in an attempt to circumvent discrimination, choose to change their login names, one of the only identifying markers on the Internet, to a gender neutral name (Winter & Huff, 1996). In any permutation, discrimination is diminished online by the mere fact that potential discriminators are less likely to know that they are speaking with a member of a minority or stigmatized group.

Anonymity, however, can have negative effects on behavior, which can lead to discrimination. As argued earlier, anonymity may actually increase prejudicial expressions. It may also more directly affect discriminatory actions. Anonymity has long been linked to the psychological phenomenon of deindividuation, in which a loosening of morals and self-guided standards of behavior occur (Zimbardo, 1969). People may be more likely to perform antisocial acts under anonymous conditions, with no possible way to be linked to the act, than when their true identity remained evident. Members of racist groups, for example, often use anonymous e-mail accounts to harass and threaten minority group members (McKenna & Bargh, 2000). Furthermore, people in general may be more inclined to post offensive messages or 'flames' in chatrooms, knowing that the message will not be traced back to them (McKenna & Bargh, 2000). The role of deindividuation has been more directly addressed by Postmes *et al.* (1998, 1999; see also Douglas & McGarty, 2001) with regard to groups in cyberspace, but this approach (discussed above) has more to do with group cohesion and influence than with the loss of inhibition and outgroup-directed hostility traditionally associated with deindividuation.

Computer institutional discrimination

With the pervasiveness of computer networks in daily life, many important tasks and decisions are being handled completely by computers. This process of automation—in essence, decisions made by computers—eliminates ad hoc human bias from entering the decision-making process. Automation may be a promising way to reduce discrimination, which occurs in interview processes such as mortgage applications, job applications, car sales, and even health examinations.

Race-based mortgage discrimination, for example, has been long documented (e.g. U.S. Department of Housing and Urban Development, 2000). Mortgage discrimination resulting from personal prejudice is prevalent because the decision to grant a loan involves a high degree of discretion on the part of the loan officer (Openshaw, 2000). Though they may attempt to remain neutral, lending agents' personal preferences and stereotypes can contaminate the process. Mortgage applications are now available online, and instead of a loan officer judging an applicant's merits based on physical appearances, a computer compiles all of the necessary data and makes a decision, which can be binding. Approximately 1.5% of homebuyers obtained their mortgage through an online process, totaling over $20 billion, in 1999 (Openshaw, 2000). The color- (and gender-) blind aspect is the main advantage in completing the online process, as complete anonymity of race and gender can be maintained. Still, caution should also be exercised. It is possible for computers to exhibit forms of institutional discrimination, having a disparate impact on various groups of people depending on how the computers are programmed. Human mediation, either during the process or in the programming stages, can bias computer-based decisions as well. If programs are set up to reproduce common 'profiles' of applicants, or if they collect demographic data, there is potential for discrimination to occur despite the illusion of fairness.

The digital divide

The Internet is often touted as a great equalizing force, allowing parity between participants. In any given interaction, there is the potential for greater equality than in face-to-face interactions because many status cues are absent. Status cues include any characteristic that reflects social inequalities in our society, including gender, age, race, ethnicity, size, and income. These cues can be made irrelevant: when it is required that all other group members share a common bond, social status distinctions are lessened. Networks specifically created for certain types of people, such as the Systers computer scientist electronic forum, serve to accomplish this goal (Winter & Huff, 1996). However, even if there is the potential for equality in interactions on the Internet, there remain clear disparities in access to the Internet itself. Racial and ethnic minorities are dramatically lower in their access to and use of the Internet, and there is some evidence that the gap is widening (Jackson *et al.*, 2001; National Telecommunications and Information Administration, 1995). This disparity, dubbed the 'digital divide', in which relatively privileged people obtain benefits while others do not, challenges the notion of the true egalitarianism of the Internet. The digital divide separates the 'haves' from the 'have nots', denying the latter access not only to the information on the Internet but also to a variety of important services (Hoffman & Novak, 1998).

In a survey by Nielsen Media Research in 1997 (as cited in Hoffman & Novak, 1998), European Americans had considerably more access to computers and the Internet than did African Americans. European Americans were twice as likely to have actually logged on to the Internet in the preceding week. In a 1996 study by Graphic Visualization Research (as cited in Beckles, 1997), 88.6% of users were European American and only 1.3% African American in the U.S. Race differentials have even been found in the lowest income bracket, in which European Americans were six times more likely to have used the Internet in the preceding week and have Internet access at home. Factoring out education differences did not eliminate the racial digital divide, with European Americans still more likely to have access and own computers (Hoffman & Novak, 1998).

Not surprisingly, income positively correlates with computer use. A recent study revealed that 85% of households with incomes above $75,000 possessed a computer at home, while only 19% of households with incomes less than $15,000 did (Borgida *et al.*, 2002). Internet access boasts similar discrepancies at 78% versus 13%. Rural Americans are also lagging behind urban and suburban Americans in Internet access, with low-income rural households boasting the lowest rate of 11.3% (Borgida *et al.*, 2002). As Beckles (1997) states, the 'toll charge' is out of reach of many of the poorer individuals, who are disproportionately minorities. Similar trends are also seen globally.

It is not only that many minority group members lack sufficient capital to participate actively in the information age. In addition to access problems, many African Americans must overcome 'techno-phobia' and need training to use the Internet. They may feel some form of stereotype threat, in which they prefer to avoid the medium rather than confirm the stereotype that African Americans are technologically illiterate (Jackson *et al.*, 2001). With a relatively low number of African American technicians, the African American community has a dearth of 'cultural mentors' to provide training and serve as technical resources (Beckles, 1997). Furthermore, the racial and income disparities in actual use of the Internet serve to sustain and perhaps widen the digital information divide. Students of higher income, and European Americans in particular, more often use special software meant to develop more advanced skills.

Racial disparities in Internet use transcend mere income disparities. In the Jackson *et al.* (2001) study, 787 college students' Internet habits were studied, revealing that racial differences appeared only in e-mail use for this college sample, with European Americans using e-mail more than African Americans. One explanation given for this difference is that, due to the overall lower rate of access to computers, African Americans tend to know fewer people with whom to communicate online. As a result, African Americans are less likely to use the Internet for one of its primary purposes—communication. Some investigators (e.g. Wilson & Gutierrez, 1995) have also noted that cultural biases may exist on the Internet, discouraging its use by minority members. Because there exist such disparities in access, most of the content on the Internet has been developed by and for the most common users—namely, European American middle-class individuals. The overrepresented nature of European American issues creates an environment that is less pertinent to the daily needs of minorities, further isolating them from the information age (Wilson & Gutierrez, 1995).

Lack of Internet access does not merely deny individuals the ability to receive e-mails and communicate with friends. It can have much more pernicious effects. Because the groups with less access are often those that face discrimination in daily life due to status or ethnicity, access limitations prevent them from escaping discrimination. For example, as discussed above, the online mortgage application process has shown promising results in limiting discrimination in the loan approval process. Online mortgage applications are most beneficial to those groups that would be negatively stereotyped and rejected based on their appearance. However, if these same groups of people have disproportionately less opportunity to use computers, they will be less likely to feel comfortable enough to carry out a major transaction via the Internet, even though it could create an important opportunity (buying a home), and save them money and the distress of being rejected.

Also, Internet access gaps do not solely reflect Internet and computer possession, but also the type and quality of the computer as well. Higher-income families often obtain the best technology, whereas lower-income families may only be able to afford slower and outdated computers, software, and ISPs. Though they may technically have 'access', they still lag behind in the ever-changing information age.

To close the digital divide, policy makers may consider a number of alternatives for promoting access to the Internet for lower-income individuals and families. In the U.S., the ongoing moratorium on Internet sales taxes is intended to spur commerce, but it may also have the effect of making Internet use more affordable and appealing to those with lower financial means. Furthermore, efforts by the government to subsidize and promote access to high-speed Internet technologies (e.g. broadband), and thereby reduce costs of such resources, could have a redistributive effect. More radically, governments and non-governmental organizations could consider sponsorship (e.g. direct subsidies, tax credits) of Internet access and computer hardware for underrepresented groups.

Discrimination research and the Internet

Precisely because of its ease of access and anonymity features, the Internet provides a valuable tool with which to conduct research on discrimination. Traditional methods of studying discrimination on the Internet involve simply asking Internet users about their experiences. In one such survey by Winter and Huff (1996), 31% of women recounted events where they had experienced harassment in some way while using the Internet, while 19%

reported specifically being subjected to sexual harassment. Although Winter and Huff provide no comparison rates for non-Internet experiences, these rates indicate that cyberspace is, at the very least, not a safe haven from harassment for women. As mentioned previously, online harassment can lead to discrimination and avoidance of the medium in the future and can even be viewed as more harassing than verbal comments (Biber *et al.*, 2002; Winter & Huff, 1996).

In addition to facilitating discrimination survey dissemination, the Internet affords opportunities to study discriminatory *behavior* unobtrusively. In one such field experiment, Shohat and Musch (2003) studied the effect of a seller's implied ethnicity in an online auction. Two sellers' identities were created, one of German background (michael.ottersbach) and one of Turkish ethnicity (mehmet.orgum). The two sellers had identical profiles and sold identical DVDs on the German eBay auction site. The results showed that the ethnic background of the seller did not significantly alter final sale prices or the total number of bidders on the DVDs, lending support to the notion of equality on the Internet. However, differences were evident in the time the winning bids were received. The German seller obtained his highest and winning offer sooner than did the Turkish seller. The authors hypothesized that the delay may be due to lack of initial trust between the seller and the buyer in the auction since the Turkish stereotype contains 'untrustworthy' as a central characteristic.

These mixed results partially illuminate the discrimination occurring on the Internet, and further, how it affects real life. Stronger discrimination may have resulted if financial risk was increased and trust became a more central concern, or the stereotype manipulation was made more robustly. Still, online transactions such as auctions hold a valuable key for unlocking and fully understanding the extent and variety of discrimination transpiring on and off the Internet.

Conclusions

The effects of the Internet on stereotyping, prejudice, and discrimination, as have been described, are admittedly varied. On the surface, the Internet's ability to hide a user's identity can disinhibit the expression of prejudice, but also holds promise to lessen discrimination's negative influences. With the current predominance of text-based communication, power is bestowed upon the Internet user to decide how much of his or her identity to reveal. The Internet potentially promotes the transmission of bigotry, but is also an effective conduit for the promotion of tolerance and offers considerable potential as a venue for studying, and therefore building, greater understanding of prejudice.

Furthermore, it seems clear that the Internet serves to lessen discrimination prevalent in decisions traditionally based in whole or part on personal judgment, such as loan applications. Moving such historically discrimination-riddled practices online may represent a significant step toward true equality of opportunity.

Despite the promise of the Internet, as noted above, caution must still be maintained. The Internet and computers are not as universally benign as may be hoped. Biber *et al.* (2002) showed discrimination experienced online can be viewed as more harmful than in person. Discrimination can be so pervasive that entirely new networks are created as a means of escape (Winter & Huff, 1996). The anonymity of users online may even encourage discriminatory e-mails or chatroom posts (McKenna & Bargh, 2000). The 'digital divide' is also troublesome, as lack of access for members of historically disadvantaged groups can prevent them from enjoying the Internet's positive effects. Nevertheless, the potential to ameliorate bias is impressive. By carefully examining the Internet's promises and pitfalls, society has an opportunity to reduce prejudice, discrimination, and their consequent inequities.

Researchers interested in prejudice and discrimination on the Internet would be well served to consider issues that have great import, but as yet have not been directly investigated. Intergroup contact is an obvious place to start, and Amichai–Hamburger (2004) has identified facets of the Internet (e.g. accessibility, anonymity, and control) that could serve to overcome obstacles associated with achieving significant, positive intergroup contact (e.g. anxiety and low practicality). The potential for the Internet to facilitate prejudice reduction through intergroup contact is clear and is, at this point, an empirical question. Accordingly, the manner and effects of Internet-based intergroup contact should be tested experimentally. This would, of course, most prudently involve the manipulation of the awareness of the group membership (e.g. race) of interaction partners. Such contact research could also vary the presence of factors deemed important for prejudice reduction (equal status, interdependence, authority sanction) to determine whether or not they are necessary, and test for the generality and longevity of such effects.

Another central question that warrants investigation has to do with the Internet's potential to have paradoxical effects on prejudice and discrimination. We hypothesize that prejudice will more likely be expressed online than face to face, while discrimination will be less likely. However, this has, for the most part (except see Shohat & Musch, 2003) not been directly tested. Such research should employ direct indicators of prejudice and discrimination, such as bigoted statements and allocation of resources. As with research on intergroup contact, these investigations should vary the transparency of group membership to assess its role in the manifestation of bias in Internet-based human interaction.

An increasing proportion of human life, even social life, transpires in cyberspace. A greater understanding of social psychology's most important constructs and society's most important problems, as they play out online, will doubtless benefit humankind.

References

Allport, G.W. (1954). *The nature of prejudice*. New York: Addison–Wesley.

Amichai–Hamburger, Y. (2004). *The contact hypothesis reconsidered: interacting via the Internet*. Manuscript submitted for publication, Bar-Ilan University, Israel.

Anti-Defamation League. (2000). *Combating extremism in cyberspace: the legal issues affecting Internet hate speech*. Washington, DC: Author.

Back, L. (2002). Aryans reading Adorno: cyber-culture and twenty-first century racism. *Ethnic and Racial Studies*, 25, 628–51.

Bargh, J.A. (2002). Beyond simple truths: the human-internet interaction. *Journal of Social Issues*, 58, 1–8.

Banaji, M.R. and Greenwald, A.G. (1995). Implicit gender stereotyping in judgments of fame. *Journal of Personality and Social Psychology*, 68, 181–98.

Beckles, C. (1997). Black struggles in cyberspace: cyber-segregation and cyber-Nazis. *The Western Journal of Black Studies*, 21, 12–17.

Biber, J.K., Doverspike, D., Baznik, D., Cober, A., and Ritter, B.A. (2002). Sexual harassment in online communications: effects of gender and discourse medium. *CyberPsychology & Behavior*, 5, 33–42.

Blair, I.V. (2001). Implicit stereotypes and prejudice. In G. B. Moskowitz (ed), *Cognitive social psychology: the Princeton symposium on the legacy and future of social cognition* (pp. 359–74). Mahwah, NJ: Erlbaum.

Borgida, E., Sullivan, J.L., Oxendine, A., Jackson, M.S., and Riedel, E. (2002). Civic culture meets the digital divide: the role of community electronic networks. *Journal of Social Issues*, 58, 125–41.

Burris, V., Smith, E., and Strahm, A. (2000). White supremacist network on the Internet. *Sociological Focus*, 33, 215–34.

Cooper, J., Hall, J., and Huff, C. (1990). Situational stress as a consequence of sex-stereotyped software. *Personality and Social Psychology Bulletin*, 16, 419–29.

Correll, J., Park, B., Judd, C.M., and Wittenbrink, B. (2002). The police officer's dilemma: using ethnicity to disambiguate potentially hostile individuals. *Journal of Personality and Social Psychology*, 83, 1314–29.

Crosby, F., Bromley, S., and Saxe, L. (1980). Recent unobtrusive studies of Black and White discrimination and prejudice: a literature review. *Psychological Bulletin*, 87, 546–63.

Douglas, K.M. and McGarty, C. (2001). Identifiability and self-presentation: computer-mediated communication and intergroup interaction. *British Journal of Social Psychology*, 40, 399–416.

Evans, D.C., Garcia, D.J., Garcia, D.M., and Baron, R.S. (2003). In the privacy of their own homes: using the Internet to assess racial bias. *Personality and Social Psychology Bulletin*, 29, 273–84.

Fazio, R.H., Jackson, J.R., Dunton, B.C., and Williams, C.J. (1995). Variability in automatic activation as an unobtrusive measure of racial attitudes: a bona fide pipeline? *Journal of Personality and Social Psychology*, **69**, 1013–27.

Franklin, R.A. (2003). *The hate directory*. Available on *http://www.bcpl.net/~rfrankli/hatedir.pdf*.

Friedman, E.J. and Resnick, P. (2001). The social cost of cheap pseudonyms. *Journal of Economics & Management Strategy*, **10**, 173–99.

Gaertner, S.L. and Dovidio, J.F. (1986). The aversive form of racism. In J.F. Dovidio and S.L. Gaertner (eds), *Prejudice, discrimination, and racism* (pp. 61–89). Orlando, FL: Academic Press.

Gerstenfeld, P.B., Grant, D.R., and Chiang, C. (2003). Hate online: a content analysis of extremist Internet sites. *Analyses of Social Issues and Public Policy*, **3**, 29–44.

Glaser, J. (1999). *The relation between stereotyping and prejudice: measures of newly formed automatic associations*. Unpublished doctoral dissertation, Yale University, New Haven, CT.

Glaser, J., Dixit, J., and Green, D.P. (2002). Studying hate crime with the Internet: what makes racists advocate racial violence? *Journal of Social Issues*, **58**, 177–93.

Glick, P. and Fiske, S.T. (2001). Ambivalent sexism. In M.P. Zanna (ed), *Advances in experimental social psychology*, (Vol. 33, pp. 115–88). San Diego, CA: Academic Press.

Green, D.P., Glaser, J., and Rich, A.O. (1998). From lynching to gay-bashing: the elusive connection between economic conditions and hate crime. *Journal of Personality and Social Psychology*, **75**, 82–92.

Greenwald, A.G., McGhee, D.E., and Schwartz, J.L.K. (1998). Measuring individual differences in implicit cognition: the implicit association test. *Journal of Personality and Social Psychology*, **74**, 1464–80.

Greenwald, A.G. and Nosek, B. (2001). Health of the implicit association test at age 3. *Zeitschrift fuer Experimentelle Psychologie*, **48**, 85–93.

Greenwald, A.G., Oakes, M.A., and Hoffman, H. (2003). Targets of discrimination: effects of race on responses to weapons holders. *Journal of Experimental Social Psychology*, **39**, 399–405.

Hamilton, J.C. (1999). The ethics of conducting social-science research on the Internet. *The Chronicle of Higher Education*, **46**, 6–8.

Hilgard, E.R. (1980). The trilogy of mind: cognition, affection, and conation. *Journal of the History of the Behavioral Sciences*, **16**, 107–17.

Hoffman, D.L. and Novak, T.P. (1998). Bridging the racial divide on the Internet. *Science*, **280**, 390–1.

Human Rights and Equal Opportunity Commission. (2002). *Examples of racist material on the Internet*. Sydney, Australia: Human Rights and Equal Opportunity Commission.

Jackson, L.A., Ervin, K.S., Gardner, P.D., and Schmitt, N. (2001). The racial digital divide: motivational, affective, and cognitive correlates of Internet use. *Journal of Applied Social Psychology*, **31**, 2019–46.

Kraut, R., Patterson, M., Lundmark, V., Kiesler, S., Mukopadhyay, T., and Scherlis, W. (1998). Internet paradox: a social technology that reduces social involvement and psychological well-being? *American Psychologist*, **9**, 1017–31.

LaPiere, R.T. (1934). Attitudes vs. actions. *Social Forces*, **13**, 230–7.

Lee, E. and Leets, L. (2002). Persuasive storytelling by hate-groups online. *American Behavioral Scientist*, **45**, 927–57.

Levin, B. (2002). Cyberhate: a legal and historical analysis of extremists' use of computer networks in America. *American Behavioral Scientist*, **45**, 958–88.

Linn, L.S. (1965). Verbal attitudes and overt behavior: a study of racial discrimination. *Social Forces*, **43**, 353–64.

McConahay, J.B. (1986). Modern racism, ambivalence, and the modern racism scale. In S.L. Gaertner and J.F. Dovidio (eds), *Prejudice, discrimination, and racism* (pp. 91–125). New York: Academic Press.

McConnell, A.R. and Leibold, J.M. (2001). Relations among the Implicit Association Test, discriminatory behavior, and explicit measures of racial attitudes. *Journal of Experimental Social Psychology*, **37**, 435–42.

McGuire, W.J. (1985). Attitudes and attitude change. In G. Lindzey and E. Aronson (eds), *The handbook of social psychology* (3rd edn) (Vol. 2, pp. 233–346). New York: Random House.

McGuire, W.J. (1989). The structure of individual attitudes and attitude systems. In A.R. Pratkanis, S.J. Breckler, and A.G. Greenwald (eds), *Attitude structure and function* (pp. 37–69). Hillsdale, NJ: Erlbaum.

McKenna, K.Y.A. and Bargh, J.A. (1998). Coming out in the age of the Internet: identity 'demarginalization' though virtual group participation. *Journal of Personality and Social Psychology*, **75**, 681–94.

McKenna, K.Y.A. and Bargh, J.A. (2000). Plan 9 from cyberspace: the implications of the Internet for personality and social psychology. *Personality and Social Psychology Review*, **4**, 57–75.

Milgram, S. (1974). *Obedience to authority*. New York: Harper & Row.

Milgram, S., Mann, L., and Harter, S. (1965). The lost-letter technique. *Public Opinion Quarterly*, **29**, 437–8.

Montanye, T., Mulberry, R.F., and Hardy, K.R. (1971). Assessing prejudice toward Negroes at three universities using the lost-letter technique. *Psychological Reports*, **29**, 531–7.

National Telecommunications and Information Administration (1995). *Falling through the Net: a survey of the 'have nots' in rural and urban America*. Washington, DC: U.S. Department of Commerce.

Nosek, B.A., Banaji, M.R., and Greenwald, A.G. (2002*a*). Harvesting implicit group attitudes and beliefs from a demonstration website. *Group Dynamics. Special Issue: Groups and Internet*, **6**, 101–15.

Nosek, B.A., Banaji, M.R., and Greenwald, A.G. (2002*b*). E-research: ethics, security, design, and control in psychological research on the Internet. *Journal of Social Issues*, **58**, 161–76.

Openshaw, J. (2000). 'How Net reduces mortgage discrimination.' Article posted on *http://www.channel2000.com*. May 9, 2000.

Pettigrew, T.F. and Tropp, L.R. (2000). Does intergroup contact reduce prejudice? Recent meta-analytic findings. In S. Oskamp (ed), *Reducing prejudice and discrimination* (pp. 93–114). Mahwah, NJ: Erlbaum.

Pettigrew, T.F. and Tropp, L.R. (2004). *A meta-analytic test of intergroup contact theory*. Unpublished manuscript, University of California, Santa Cruz.

Plant, E.A. and Devine, P.G. (1998). Internal and external motivation to respond without prejudice. *Journal of Personality and Social Psychology*, **75**, 811–32.

Postmes, T. and Spears, R. (2002). Contextual moderators of gender differences and stereotyping in computer-mediated group discussions. *Personality and Social Psychology Bulletin*, **28**, 1073–83.

Postmes, T., Spears, R., and Lea, M. (1998). Breaching or building social boundaries? SIDE-effects of computer-mediated communication. *Communication Research. Special Issue: (Mis)communicating Across Boundaries*, **25**, 689–715.

Postmes, T., Spears, R., and Lea, M. (1999). Social identity, normative content, and 'deindividuation' in computer-mediated groups. In N. Ellemers, R. Spears, and B. Doosje (eds), *Social identity: context, commitment, content* (pp. 164–83). Oxford: Blackwell.

Postmes, T., Spears, R., and Lea, M. (2002). Inter-group differentiation in computer-mediated communication: effects of depersonalization. *Group Dynamics. Special Issue: Groups and Internet*, **6**, 3–16.

Postmes, T., Spears, R., Sakhel, K., and De Groot, D. (2001). Social influence in computer-mediated communication: the effects of anonymity on group behavior. *Personality and Social Psychology Bulletin*, **27**, 1243–54.

Richman, W.L., Kiesler, S., Weisband, S., and Drasgow, F. (1999). A meta-analytic study of social desirability distortion in computer-administered questionnaires, traditional questionnaires, and interviews. *Journal of Applied Psychology*, **5**, 754–75.

Riva, G. (2002). The sociocognitive psychology of computer-mediated communication: the present and future of technology-based interactions. *CyberPsychology & Behavior*, **5**, 581–98.

Sherif, M., Harvey, O.J., White, B.J., Hood, W.R., and Sherif, C. (1961). *Intergroup conflict and co-operation: the Robbers' Cave experiment*. Norman, OK: University of Oklahoma.

Shohat, M. and Musch, J. (2003). Online auctions as a research tool: a field experiment on ethnic discrimination. *Swiss Journal of Psychology*, **62**, 223–5.

Simon Wiesenthal Center. (2002). *Digital hate 2002*. New York: The Simon Wiesenthal Center.

Spears, R., Postmes, T., Lea, M., and Wolbert, A. (2002). When are net effects gross products? The power of influence and the influence of power in computer-mediated communication. *Journal of Social Issues*, **58**, 91–107.

Stern, S.E. and Faber, J.E. (1997). The lost e-mail method: Milgram's lost-letter technique in the age of the Internet. *Behavior Research Methods, Instruments, & Computers*, **29**, 260–3.

Tajfel, H. and Turner, J.C. (1979). An integrative theory of intergroup conflict. In W.G. Austin and S. Worchel (eds), *The social psychology of intergroup relations* (pp. 33–47). Monterey, CA: Brooks/Cole.

U.S. Department of Housing and Urban Development (2000). *Unequal burden: income and racial disparities in subprime lending in America*. Washington, DC: Task Force on Predatory Lending.

Williams, K.D., Cheung, C.K.T., and Choi, W. (2000). Cyberostracism: effects of being ignored over the Internet. *Journal of Personality and Social Psychology*, **79**, 748–62.

Williams, K.D., Govan, C.L., Croker, V., Tynan, D., Cruickshank, M., and Lam, A. (2002). Investigations into differences between social- and cyberostracism. *Group Dynamics: Theory, Research, and Practice*, **6**, 65–77.

Wilson, C.C. II and Gutierrez, F. (1995). *Race, multiculturalism, and the media.* Thousand Oaks, CA: Sage.

Winter, D. and Huff, C. (1996). Adapting the Internet: comments from a women-only electronic forum. *The American Sociologist,* 31–54.

Zimbardo, P.G. (1969). The human choice: individuation, reason, and order vs. deindividuation, impulse, and chaos. In W.J. Arnold and D. Levine (eds), *Nebraska Symposium on Motivation* (Vol. 17, pp. 237–307). Lincoln, NE: University of Nebraska Press.

Index